PRAISE FOR THE BOOK

'Rigorously researched, elegantly written, subtle and nuanced in its interpretations, this is the finest biography of an Indian prime minister that I have read'
Ramachandra Guha, author of *India After Gandhi: A History*

'A brilliant book, without a doubt *the* authoritative work on Vajpayee. But it is much more than a biography. An indispensable political history of independent India, this meticulously researched book effectively prosecutes a winning case against the prevalent myths that Vajpayee was a "moderate" or a "Nehru-admiring statesman" in the wrong party. If anything, Choudhary's excellent account shows Vajpayee's consistent conviction in and commitment to the RSS that shaped not only the former prime minister but crucially India's democracy. The book also revises many cosy and complacent views on the Emergency, the JP movement and India's unfolding foreign policy from decolonization to the Nehru era and beyond. A page-turner, the writing style is a combination of sharp insights and judicious detail handled deftly with a light touch. A real achievement, an instant classic and a total triumph!'
Shruti Kapila, Professor of History and Politics, University of Cambridge and author of *Violent Fraternity: Indian Political Thought in the Global Age*

'Calmly and diligently, Abhishek Choudhary cuts through accumulated myth and journalistic commonplaces to reveal the private and public lives of Vajpayee. His carefully researched account of a much-adored but little-known leader doubles as a history of Hindu supremacism; it won't be bettered for a long time'
Pankaj Mishra, author of *Age of Anger: A History of the Present*

'A meticulous and thoroughly readable job'
Shashi Tharoor, author of *An Era of Darkness: The British Empire in India*

'An extraordinary book. Clear-eyed, diligently reported, superbly written and unputdownable. This is biography done right'
Sonia Faleiro, author of *The Good Girls: An Ordinary Killing*

'Abhishek Choudhary's remarkable book is not just a very readable and meticulously researched account of Vajpayee's tumultuous career, but also a compelling analysis of the social reach and wider politics of the Hindu Right in the early decades of

Independence. This exceptionally interesting book is a must-read for anyone curious about the history of the Right in modern India'
Zoya Hasan, Professor Emerita, Centre for Political Studies, JNU, and author of *Ideology and Organization in Indian Politics: Polarisation and the Growing Crisis of the Congress Party, 2009–19*

'This very detailed biography of Vajpayee explores the main facets of a man who has shaped both the Jan Sangh and the BJP over the second half of the twentieth century. It shows how Hindu nationalism has changed in the twenty-first century: till then collegiality prevailed, as evident from Vajpayee's style of leadership. And respect for the institutions of the Indian Republic (including Parliament) was cultivated, as Vajpayee's career as a parliamentarian and a prime minister testify. This is a book to read for understanding the trajectory of Hindutva – and therefore of India'
Christophe Jaffrelot, author of *Modi's India: Hindu Nationalism and the Rise of Ethnic Democracy*

'This deeply researched first volume of Atal Behari Vajpayee's biography provides a compelling portrait of India's first major national leader from the Right. Sensitive to the nuances of political and cultural context, Abhishek Choudhary presents Vajpayee in all his complexity, as he negotiated his inner conflicts and the many contradictions of his personal, ideological and political life'
Niraja Gopal Jayal, Avantha Chair and Professor of Politics, King's College London and co-editor of *The Oxford Companion to Politics in India*

'Unlike others who have tried to project Vajpayee as a lost liberal, this book locates him in the centre of Hindu politics'
Swapan Dasgupta, columnist and author of *Awakening Bharat Mata: The Political Beliefs of the Indian Right*

'In this thoroughly researched and attractively written biography, Abhishek Choudhary skilfully deciphers the enigmatic personality of Atal Behari Vajpayee. The first volume delves into the formative influences on the young Vajpayee and the deep roots of the ideological commitments that shaped his journalistic writings, organizational efforts and parliamentary speeches until 1977'
Sugata Bose, Gardiner Professor of History, Harvard University and author of *His Majesty's Opponent: Subhas Chandra Bose and India's Struggle against Empire*

'A thoroughly researched study of Vajpayee, who, far more than other Hindu nationalist figures, legitimized their participation in India's political life. Anyone seeking to understand why Hindu nationalism plays such a key role in current

Indian politics needs to know Vajpayee's role in making it a powerful force by a shrewd balancing of ideology and pragmatism'

Walter K. Andersen, co-author of *The Brotherhood in Saffron: The Rashtriya Swayamsevak Sangh and Hindu Revivalism*

'Do yourself a favour, read Abhishek Choudhary's biography of Vajpayee. This is political biography done right – and the backstory we need to understand our times … one of the best political biographies to come out of India'

Prem Panicker, Consulting Editor, *IndiaSpend*

'Punctures some of the best known anecdotes about Vajpayee ... reveals aspects of the man we neither knew of nor could have guessed'

Karan Thapar, *Hindustan Times*

'An exhaustive biography of one of India's most popular politicians … Abhishek Choudhary does an extraordinary job of eight years of digging out primary sources unseen by others and talking to dozens who knew Vajpayee intimately to weave a political classic'

M. R. Narayan Swamy, *Federal*

'The early years of [the] late Prime Minister captured in *Vajpayee* are not just instructive on the manner in which Vajpayee dealt with questions of politics and ideology, but also the fluid lines between conservative and liberal politics in the years pre- and post-independence'

Nistula Hebbar, *Hindu*

'[Vajpayee's] life has been reduced to stereotypical notions and snippets … To separate the wheat from the chaff of such representations, we turn to biographers who undertake the painstaking work of sifting through the tiniest details of a person's life, rely on primary sources to sort fact from fiction, and critically assess popular views, while steering clear of unfounded speculations. On all these counts, Abhishek Choudhary's spectacular biography of Vajpayee is a resounding success ... Like all good biographers, Choudhary informs us not just about an individual but about the world they've inhabited and how they've contributed to shaping it. In this regard, this exemplary biography may become the definitive work on Vajpayee, placed in a different league from other recent hagiographic or more speculative accounts of his life'

Gilles Verniers, *India Today*

'A lesson in how to write a political biography in New India – without fear or favour … The first instalment of Abhishek Choudhary's two-volume biography

is one of the most significant works of non-academic history in recent memory … Like Philip Roth's fiction, Choudhary has provided not just an account of a "great" man's life but a vivid portrait of a worldview that today – more often for the worse – seeks to remake India in its insecure image … [This] is as much a history of twentieth-century India from the RSS–Jana Sangh vantage point as it is a biography of Vajpayee'
Aakash Joshi, *Indian Express*

'Abhishek Choudhary's biography has taken the non-fiction world by storm'
Manisha Pande, *Newslaundry*

'When a public figure is as private as Vajpayee was during his lifetime and when there are more myths than facts surrounding the man himself, this is a tall order. But in *Vajpayee*, Choudhary has succeeded admirably … This is also a narrative of the rise of the Hindu right in India, at a time when politics was too fluid to be binaried into distinct sects of left and right … [A] magisterial understanding of a human and political life'
Narayani Basu, *Scroll.in*

'Choudhary's biography marks a departure from the customary reverential tone used by Indians to chronicle deceased greats'
Radhika Ramaseshan, *Tribune*

'Choudhary's book has already received a lot of well-deserved praise … Vajpayee is best understood as a pragmatic but deeply ideological figure trying to make the most of the political contradictions of his times'
Roshan Kishore, *Hindustan Times*

'If you want to understand the layered relationships at the highest echelons in the Sangh Parivar, you can do no better than read this masterpiece of a biography … For someone who has followed the Sangh Parivar closely, and Vajpayee particularly, some of the facts mentioned even surprised me'
Virendra Kapoor, *Open*

'Vajpayee has undoubtedly moved into the realm of canonisation ... Yet, it is only when one reads the latest, well-crafted biography by Abhishek Choudhary that one realises how little is known about the life and times of this charismatic man ... Victorian biographer Lytton Strachey had said it is as difficult to write a good life as it is to live one. In this, Choudhary passes the test commendably. He may have his ideological tilts but an element of empathy flows through the entire work ... It leaves the reader eagerly awaiting the second volume'
Vikram Sampath, *Mint Lounge*

VAJPAYEE

VAJPAYEE

THE ASCENT OF THE HINDU RIGHT 1924–1977

ABHISHEK CHOUDHARY

PICADOR INDIA | THE New India FOUNDATION

First published 2023 by Picador India
an imprint of Pan Macmillan Publishing India Private Limited
707 Kailash Building
26 K. G. Marg, New Delhi 110001
www.panmacmillan.co.in

Pan Macmillan, The Smithson, 6 Briset Street, Farringdon, London EC1M 5NR
Associated companies throughout the world
www.panmacmillan.com

ISBN 978-93-95624-49-7

The research for this book was supported by the New India Foundation.

1 3 5 7 9 8 6 4 2

Typeset in Adobe Garamond Pro by R. Ajith Kumar, New Delhi
Printed and bound in India by Replika Press Pvt. Ltd.

Contents

Preface

GOING BY THE NUMBER OF THINGS RECENTLY NAMED AFTER VAJPAYEE, his stock soars by the hour. This list includes: the newly developed state capital of Chhattisgarh; a dozen-odd welfare schemes and universities, memorials and libraries, airports and stadiums, roads and bridges; a mountain peak here, a long tunnel there, even a newly crossbred variety of lemongrass.

Much of this naming (and renaming) began after his death, on 16 August 2018, and is not entirely surprising. The Bharatiya Janata Party, which he co-founded in 1980 after the Janata coalition's split, now runs the country with an iron fist. They enjoy a bona fide majority at the centre and in ten states, a luxury Atal Behari Vajpayee never enjoyed in his lifetime. For the BJP – a party glaringly devoid of icons – Vajpayee was the first authentic homegrown hero who was loved and respected by the masses. The BJP's rivals often pit his moderation and sagacity in office against the Modi regime's brusqueness.

Despite looming large on the political scene, Vajpayee remains the most enigmatic Indian politician of recent times. Early in my research, I found a key to his enigma: beyond the traditional clichés and the occasional snippets, we know little of value about the first half of his six-decade-long career. Upon understanding his early life, his dilemmas and doublespeak begin to fall into a pattern. This book, first of a two-volume study, attempts to fill that void.

My first task here is to establish that the early Vajpayee was far more critical to the Sangh Parivar's project of Hinduizing India than is universally believed. As the founding editor of the mouthpieces *Rashtradharma* and *Panchjanya* during 1947–48, he was exactly the kind of RSS worker the government held responsible for creating the environment in which Gandhi was murdered. As early as December 1949, *Panchjanya*'s loyalty test for India's Muslims was whether or not they supported returning Hindu structures desecrated centuries ago at Ayodhya, Banaras, Mathura.

The popular narrative about the BJP tends to solely credit the Ayodhya movement of 1989–92 led by L. K. Advani for catapulting the party into power. This is an ideologically lazy, self-deceptive analysis that wholly bypasses an earlier trend. The BJP's forerunner, the Jan Sangh, galloped from four Lok Sabha seats in 1957 to thirty-five in 1967 and ninety in 1977. Vajpayee had been the party's face since 1957, and one of its key strategists and decision-makers. I locate Vajpayee in the larger pantheon of Hindu nationalism by establishing the timeline and causes of his ascent in the first three decades since independence.

My second aim is to fix some basic facts from the first half of Vajpayee's life, which have been lost to myth and misinformation. To quote just one instance, many hagiographies would have you believe that Vajpayee was an academic prodigy. I was shocked and amused to chance upon, in the Gwalior durbar gazetteer of 1938, his eighth-standard board exam results. The school headmaster's son had scored a lowly third division. Sometime later, I was lucky to track down his tenth-standard certificate. 'With distinction in Nil' subjects, it read, 'and was placed in the Second Division'.

Recent books have willy-nilly perpetuated old factual errors, at times even contributing a few new ones. One such popular myth concerns Vajpayee's relationship with Nehru. Like many others before her, a celebrity journalist who recently published a biography, based largely on secondary sources, insists that Vajpayee 'hero-worshipped' Nehru.[1] Multiple accounts also have Nehru announce that the bright new Jan Sangh MP would someday become India's prime minister. Another fable has Vajpayee calling Indira Gandhi an incarnation of Durga after the Indian army captured Dhaka on 16 December 1971. In a clumsy attempt to unveil new information on his private life, another recent book by an academic makes the stunningly misleading claim that Vajpayee's relationship with Rajkumari Kaul – his partner and the mother of their love child – was primarily 'intellectual'.[2]

Dozens of these myths enjoy such wide circulation that they have become entrenched in public memory. Vajpayee's family may have also played their part here by refusing to release his private papers. Rectifying some of these errors took me more unglamorous slogging in the primary and secondary archives than it would have otherwise. Wherever possible, I also borrowed from private collections: a photograph in Mumbai, a letter in Trivandrum, a souvenir in Washington DC.

This volume ends in early 1977, which saw the Sangh Parivar's first tryst with power at the centre, with Vajpayee as the foreign minister; and generally a moment of great idealism after eighteen ghastly months of the Emergency. I leave with enough hints of the strains that would unravel the Janata coalition in July 1979. The second volume captures this, and the rest of Vajpayee's life: his fall from grace in the Sangh Parivar of the mid-1980s; Advani losing his magic touch after the Babri demolition, and Vajpayee conniving to have the party hand over the leadership to him again; the giddying years at 7 RCR; the stroke in 2007 that impaired his speech, eventually rendering him vegetative.

Let me end here with a caveat. My book is an assessment of Vajpayee's life, not a tribute. As such one should read it as a detached, unsentimental (not to say insensitive) take on his career and moral character. Like many quarter-decent biographers, I tackled the beast of accumulated archival material and was surprised to find myself acting by turns mercilessly and tenderly. A biographer, I have learnt, ought not to be awestruck at the beauty of the tapestry: I have tried my best here to examine the underside.[3]

Abhishek Choudhary
New Delhi
March 2023

Part One

A Hindu Soul Ripens
1924–53

1

Bateshwar: The Second Banaras

EARLY REFERENCES TO BATESHWAR, SIXTY-SIX KILOMETRES SOUTHEAST of Agra, are many and varied. Folklore has it that a sadhu lived here under an enormous bat tree (from vat, Sanskrit for banyan). He erected a shrine to Shiva that came to be known as Bateshwar – lord of the banyan.[1] In his travelogue *Indica* (c. 300 BC), the Greek historian Megasthenes named Mathura and Krishnpura as two big cities of the region. Following recent excavations, some archaeologists have concluded Krishnpura to be the site of present-day Bateshwar.[2] Owing to many such associations ancient Bateshwar has been described, though with serious exaggeration, as the second Banaras.

The Ganga–Yamuna doab, at the centre of north India, was vulnerable to attacks from all sides. In the first millennium, the region was ruled by a motley sequence of tiny neighbourhood kingdoms sparring among themselves – Maukharis, then Vardhanas, finally Bhadaurias. Around the turn of the second millennium began the assault from the far-off northwest. The sixteenth century marked a decisive turn. In 1526, the Mughals set up their base northwest of Bateshwar at a new city that was increasingly gaining prominence: Agra.*

In 1580, Akbar's army annexed the region. As part of their strategy learnt from the experiences of the sultanates that preceded them, the Mughals by and large did not interfere with the social structure or the

* The present district of Agra in western Uttar Pradesh uniquely shares its border with two other states – Madhya Pradesh and Rajasthan.

religious practices of the citizenry, and placated the local kings once they surrendered. While the Bhadaurias were subservient to the Mughals, they had the freedom to take up public works in their region. In 1644, the Bhadauria king commissioned the present Bateshwarnath temple on the right bank of the Yamuna. He also launched an annual cattle fair nearby. By the mid-eighteenth century, Bateshwar had a cluster of 170 temples large and small, most of them dedicated to Shiva. Since then the prime attraction of the place has been its white temples on the meandering Yamuna's bank. Providing a rare sight, the Yamuna forms a semi-circle at Bateshwar such that standing anywhere on the opposite bank, one views a magnificent landscape of its white-painted temples.

In 1784, the Maratha kingdom of the Scindias captured the region. Barely two decades later, in December 1803, the Scindias lost the region to the British in the second Anglo–Maratha War. Henceforth, the area was directly governed by the British as a part of what would eventually be known as the United Provinces.

In the grand march of history, new cities rise as often as old ones fall into ruin. The area around Bateshwar had never been optimal for agriculture. Its ancient prosperity was due to its location at the crossroads of several trade routes along the Yamuna, which connected Mathura to nearby cities. But with frequent political turmoil and conquests, the decline of trade along the Yamuna, and a stagnant caste society's failure to respond to the changing world, Bateshwar lost its economic and intellectual lustre.

With one exception. The annual cattle fair that commenced on the night of the full moon of Kartik, around October–November, and lasted a month, continued to be the largest economic event in all of Agra district. Animals were brought for sale from far-flung areas: elephants from Burma, camels from Peshawar, horses from Afghanistan. Every regiment required camels and horses, and on one occasion, in November 1890, the mela was graced by the viceroy himself.*

---

* Less high-profile visitors to the mela have written amusing accounts of their experience. Such as this British official in Gwalior who tried his 'first ride on a camel' at the 1884 fair: 'The owner, to display its speed, broke into a gallop, and we found ourselves unwillingly scouring the plain; the animal eventually pulled up near a dyke, and I was thankful to find myself alive.'

It acquired such a cult status that for a while there was 'no surer index of the general conditions of the masses than these fairs', proclaimed a report from 1880. 'In good years they flourish: in times of scarcity and sickness they fall off ... The larger number present this year is therefore gratifying, as a proof that the surrounding districts are recovering from the disastrous seasons they have lately experienced.'[3]

By the end of the nineteenth century, even this last glory would fade away. Some of this had to do with new markets: 'Many vendors know they can get prizes or sell their animals at Aligarh or Etawah, which are nearer their houses, and do not care to take them to Batesar.' A bigger reason was the exploitative nature of the colonial machinery that wanted high-quality animals at the lowest prices. As a result, the breeders and sellers at Bateshwar began to sell horses outside the fair.[4] Other corruption-ridden fairs in north India began to be referred to as the 'Batesar of the province'.[5] To cut down the administrative costs, even the police station at Bateshwar was abolished in 1902. From time to time, prominent natives of the area wrote applications to the government to connect Bah-Bateshwar by rail. The idea was shot down as 'it is not likely that there would be any considerable traffic except during the period of Batesar fair'.[6]

In the first decade of the twentieth century, Bateshwar was at best mentioned in passing while discussing Agra district. Not only did the town find no mention in a map of the United Provinces, even in the maps of Agra district prepared by the British it came to be assigned only a tiny dot. Around this time a rumour began to spread: that Agra's glory had come at Bateshwar's expense, that Islamic invasions had ruined this abode of the gods. It was in this milieu of economic and intellectual poverty and claims of past glory that Shyamlal Vajpayee spent much of his life.

The Vajpayees of Bateshwar owned some land, but were not adept at farming. Born in 1860, Shyamlal Vajpayee had spent his adolescence studying Hindu scriptures in Banaras – like many of his ancestors. He came home hoping to make a career as a priest and astrologer, and was married off to Sukhdevi of nearby Bhind. The wife lost her first few children in infancy. Having studied his own horoscope carefully, Shyamlal claimed precise knowledge of whether or not his newborn son or daughter would survive. On one such occasion he asked Sukhdevi to not worry, this one time the baby was going to survive: 'Kuchh mat karo, bachcha jeevit rahega.' And soon after, his only son Krishn Behari was born. Almost a century later, his grandchildren continued to recall with pride and awe their grandfather's 'deep understanding of astrology' and his supernatural abilities.[7]

Despite his expertise, Shyamlal struggled to make a living. He was not the only priest in Bateshwar; he was wise but irritable, and too much of a stickler. Once at a high-profile janeu – sacred thread ceremony – at a nearby village, he lashed out at a fellow priest for reciting a mantra loudly when it was supposed to be quietly whispered in the ear of the young boys. A bigger problem was his unavailability. Every once in a while, he would disappear for weeks on end to Banaras or Gaya or Allahabad.

In the end, his only stable source of income was the occasional recital of the Bhagavad Gita in and around Bateshwar. Krishn Behari was brought up in a state of poverty that Brahmins in the late nineteenth century thought of as a given way of life. However, the son broke the age-old cycle. After passing his middle-school exams, he decided that instead of going to Banaras to study Sanskrit, he would go to Agra for high school and teach himself English. Shyamlal did not stop him. 'He was aware that he was living at a time of great transition,' a later-day profile explained. 'Modernity was inevitable.'[8]

Despite occasional travels, Shyamlal had no means of interpreting the wider world. His primal loyalties did not extend beyond fellow Brahmins and a bunch of ancient scriptures. Helped by modern education and the recent spread of Arya Samaj in the region, his son developed early ideas of wider association: historical self-analysis (the accumulated humiliation of Islamic and British rules), pride for the motherland, and the need for sangathan – Hindu unity – to unshackle the much-conquered India. Even if only in an abstract sense, Krishn Behari grew politically conscious in a manner his ancestors had never been; and also better equipped to navigate his way in the world.

After matriculation, he did some odd jobs in Agra and Etawah. He might have liked to study further. But given his family's precarious finances, Krishn Behari took up the position of a Hindi teacher at Victoria Collegiate High School, in Scindia-ruled Gwalior state. As the Hindu monarchy that had defeated the Mughals (and their local collaborators, the Bhadaurias) to briefly control the area around Bateshwar, the Scindias were a fond public memory in Bateshwar. In the early twentieth century, Gwalior was one of only five premier princely states that were accorded a twenty-one-gun salute for their loyalty to the British crown. Maharaja Madho Rao Scindia of Gwalior had a great deal of freedom in running his internal affairs in coordination with a Resident, a representative of the British crown. Gwalior had good schools and hospitals, and was barely 160 kilometres away from Bateshwar. Krishn Behari had lived in small towns of the United Provinces, under administrations tightly run by a handful of British bureaucrats. He must have been thrilled to find himself in Gwalior in the first decade of the twentieth century.

That said, the primary purpose of schools in Gwalior state was not to instill knowledge or critical thinking in the minds of pupils. 'Education can have but one aim, and that is to promote the prosperity and welfare of the country and to afford assistance to the ruler in the task of administration,' stated a key document of the education department. 'It certainly is not expected to degenerate into a prolific source of mischief.'[9]

With time Krishn Behari, who was hard-working and enterprising, found himself a niche. Gwalior was a Maratha monarchy where the elites spoke a mix of English, Marathi and Urdu. But it was geographically located at the heart of the Hindi-speaking belt, where the Khari Boli dialect was now aggressively staking its claim as the national language. Gwalior too felt the ripples of this wave. Krishn Behari had a command over most of Hindi's dialects, as well as a working knowledge of Urdu and English. When the state decided to have an official song of its own written in Hindi, Krishn Behari volunteered for the task. More significantly, he became a frequent contributor to the newly launched state mouthpiece *Jayaji Pratap* – the Glory of Jayaji – a weekly published in both Hindi and English.* Such performances raised his social profile in the cliquish Gwalior durbar.

Soon after he took up the teaching job in Gwalior, Krishn Behari's marriage was arranged to Suma Devi, who came from a Brahmin family of nearby Etawah. It seems the wife stayed behind in Bateshwar, and the husband would come home as often as he could. Around 1909, their first son Awadh Behari was born. The family's enthusiasm dampened when Shyamlal examined the horoscope and declared to his son rather bluntly that the child was going to be a troublemaker: 'Dushman paida hua hai ghar mein; iss se tumhari pategi nahi.' Soon came two more sons, Sada Behari and Prem Behari, and a daughter, Vimla.

The birth of Krishn Behari's fifth child on 25 December 1924 in Bateshwar was routine. Except that, for the first time, Shyamlal was relieved to see the planets and stars perfectly aligned. Gratified, he thought up a short, crisp, unique name for the grandson: Atal – meaning firm, unafraid. The couple would have two more daughters, Kamla and Urmila, in quick succession.

* In the 13 November 1923 issue, which celebrated the forty-seventh birthday of Maharaja Madho Rao Scindia, Krishn Behari wrote sonnets in praise of the king 'on behalf of his 32 lakh subjects', which appeared on the first page of the magazine's Hindi section.

2

Coming of Age: Gwalior, Kanpur

KRISHN BEHARI, BABUJI TO HIS CHILDREN, LIVED IN A RENTED HOUSE in Gwalior. Suma, Ma to the children, moved between Gwalior and Bateshwar, where she looked after her in-laws. For the same reason, Atal spent his earliest years in Bateshwar, making only occasional trips to Gwalior. With great fondness, he would later recall his childhood:

The Yamuna's bank, mounds of sand
On stilts a home of grass and thatch
A courtyard swept with cow-dung
Sounds of bell, the Tulsi patch
On mother's tongue the nectar of the Ramayana's lines.[1]*

Most of Atal's early literacy took place at home. Baba's routine included narrating to his grandchildren chunks from the Hindu epics in Sanskrit and Awadhi. Once in a while he would ask Atal to recite a stanza from one of the epics, hearing which he would correct the grammar and punctuation; the child had to repeat it until he got it right.[2] Atal grew especially fond of *Ramcharitmanas* – the medieval poet Tulsidas's

---

* यमुना तट, टीले रेतीले,
घास-फूस का घर डाँडे पर,
गोबर से लीपे आँगन में,
तुलसी का बिरवा, घण्टी स्वर,
माँ के मुँह से रामायण के दोहे – चौपाई रस घोलें!

rendition of Ram's life – and would later declare it a major inspiration. 'The way Tulsi has summed up the human condition remains unparalleled in world literature.'[3]

Baba was stern but also often affectionate. In lighter moments, he would keep the kids hooked with stories from his youth in Banaras, and the places he had travelled to. Atal would later write a comic description of Shyamlal's daily routine:

> In Baba's sitting room, on the floor
> A straw mat, wooden sandals outside the door
> Those who wish to meet him, unsure:
> Should they wait outside, or step indoors?
> Tilak on the forehead, glasses on the nose,
> an open book, he talks to himself.[4]*

Away from Baba's sight, though, life in Bateshwar was not all that strict. There was enough time for Atala and his siblings to play and generally fool around, doing nothing in particular.† A neighbour-cousin remembered Atala as naughty and restless: 'He would catch hold of goats, and try sucking milk out of their udders.'[5] The floors inside the houses were smoothened with cow dung. Probably because Shyamlal didn't keep enough animals of his own, Atala would 'tip-toe to a neighbour's house and quietly pick up and run away with the dung'. On one occasion, he and some cousins decided to enter into a dilapidated temple by night to see whether the story of ghosts living there was true. They went to the temple with a lantern but, in an anti-climax, didn't find any *bhoot* and had to go back home disappointed.

By the time he turned ten, Atala was not as agile as many other kids:

---

* बाबा की बैठक में बिछी
चटाई, बाहर रखे खड़ाऊँ,
मिलने वाले के मन में
असमंजस, जाऊँ या ना जाऊँ?
माथे तिलक, नाक पर ऐनक, पोथी खुली, स्वयं से बोलें।

† Adding a suffix to names – often 'a' (आ) or 'wa' (वा) or 'ya' (या) – is a common practice in the rural Hindi belt. It is considered a good-natured slang, especially used for friends or someone younger.

'He would play kabbadi with the neighborhood cousins and, from there head to the Yamuna ghat for a bath. Even though he bathed in the Yamuna every day, like everyone else, he couldn't swim well. Out of excitement once, he reached the middle of the river, where Yamuna is deep, and began to drown. An elderly man saw him gasping, and quickly reached out and brought him to the banks.'[6] He never swam again.

In mid-1934, a major change in Atal's life came about. Babuji was promoted and sent off to be headmaster of the Anglo Vernacular Middle School in Barnagar near Ujjain. The parents took the youngest son along, and enrolled him into the AVM School: he was christened 'Atal Behari Lal Vajpayee'. At the time of admission, Babuji entered Atal's date of birth late by sixteen months, so he would later have an additional year to apply for government jobs. He may have similarly thought that a Gwalior state domicile might also be useful. And thus, whereas Atal was born in Bateshwar in 1924, the school certificate proclaimed he was born in Gwalior on 1 May 1926.

Atal would remember this period for another reason. The school, on its annual day fest, organized a debate on the 'Development of railway line laid down in India by the British'. He prepared a speech, and mugged it up. But when his turn came to walk up to the podium, he got cold feet. On the stage he began to stammer, then forgot the speech midway. Hundreds of students and teachers, Babuji among them, were watching him, only making Atal more nervous. Finally, when he couldn't resume, he was asked to leave the podium. It was a humiliating experience for the headmaster's son. All his life Atal remembered the shame of being booed by his schoolmates. It was also an epiphany: 'I learned a lesson that changed my life. I took a pledge that I would never rote-learn a speech.'[7]

The family spent a year at Barnagar before Babuji was transferred back to Gwalior – as headmaster of the Gorkhi Boys' Middle School. Babuji may have fancied sending one of his sons to the most elite school in town: the Sardars' School, a boarding school located in the Gwalior fortress. 'Designed for the education of the upper classes of the Gwalior state', its objective was, 'to turn out gentlemen likely to prove of service to the state'. (It would later be renamed the Scindia School.) Sadly, the school headmaster with a large family had neither the money nor the social capital for that. Atal himself did not radiate academic excellence. Once again he was admitted to Babuji's school. Gorkhi was middlebrow but, with an enrolment of more than 1,000 boys, it was the largest school in all of Scindia state. Most students were upper-caste Hindus, many of them children of the tier-two and tier-three employees of the state. The best among them would join the lower bureaucracy, or take up a teaching position in a school or college as Babuji had done.

Around this time, others in the family discovered Atal's preferences and aversion to things that would last a lifetime. Kamla, two years younger, would recall her brother's fondness for good food, especially sweets. When Ma once sent Atal and Kamla to a neighbour's house with a tray of sweets offered in the puja,

> On the way he got greedy: he quietly took out two pieces of rasgulla and gulped them. When I caught him, he bribed me saying I could also have two pieces, but shouldn't tell Ma about it. By the time we reached the neighbour's house, the box had only two rasgullas left. The next day the neighbourhood aunt came home and taunted my mother for miserliness. Ma must have guessed, for she called me to ask where all the rasgullas had disappeared. I told her Bhaiya ate them all up. Then Atal was called and asked, he said Kamla ate up all the rasgullas. Soon ensued a big fight between us.[8]

Many of Babuji's fellow villagers had followed him to Gwalior, so when the family moved to the locality of Shinde Ki Chhawni, it did not feel particularly displaced. Most kids Atal played with in the evenings were his cousins from Bateshwar, close and distant. One of them, R. P. Shukla, who was a few years younger, later reminisced about Atal's sense of humour. In those times the British soldiers of Scindia, who were allotted larger quarters nearby, celebrated Christmas with enthusiasm. When the clock struck midnight, they would fire canons from the church nearby. Of course 25 December was special to Atal as his own birthday. He would brag that the soldiers were firing canons in his honour: 'Dekho, hamaare janmdin par topein chal rahi hain.'[9] The more gullible of the Bateshwar boys believed him.

He had a talent for wordplay. Early years in the company of Baba and Babuji meant that every child in the Vajpayee household was fluent in Hindi with a smattering of Sanskrit. Now Atal was being formally taught English, Urdu and Marathi at school. Every now and then he would put the new words he was learning to practical application. There lived one Chheda Lal, an employee of the Accountant General's office of Scindia state, nearby. Atal found the name Chheda Lal terribly funny. (The verb 'chhedna' in Hindi means to drill a hole; 'lal' is a noun meaning somebody's son.) He popularized an existing joke around Lal's name among his cousins. Atal taught his cousins that in English, it would be 'Mr Holeson', in Urdu 'Suraakh Ali', and in Marathi 'Bhok Rao'. Every time Chheda Lal walked down their narrow alley, the Bateshwar boys would tease, 'Mr Holeson, aye Bhok Rao!'[10]

Living in a small house in the town meant being always surrounded by elder brothers at home. The unruly Atal would once in a while be rebuked by Babuji.[11] But he was the only son whom Babuji would take along to Arya Samaj gatherings in the city. 'I liked the bhajans and was influenced by the lectures. You would also hear things on the freedom movement.' When the Arya Samaj opened a youth wing – Aryakumar Sabha – in Lashkar, Atal offered himself as 'secretary'. In later life he wondered if such things played a role in his becoming a politician: 'Was this a mere coincidence? Or was it pre-destined?'

In the winter of 1907, the United Provinces government was shocked to learn from an intelligence report that 'Arya Samajists were much in evidence at the Batesar fair and their speeches expressed a good deal of antagonism to the Christian and Mahomedan religion.'[12] Established in 1875 in Bombay, the Arya Samaj had its origins as a movement against superstition and idol worship in Hinduism, and as a response to conversion by Christian missionaries. It soon turned out that one of the Arya Samaj's unstated missions was to rouse political consciousness, even though they were forced to couch their day-to-day work entirely in the domain of social reforms and spiritualism.

The founder Dayananda Saraswati occasionally visited Agra. During his stay in the winter of 1880–81, he gave thirty-two lectures and set up the first branch in the town.[13] Partly due to the Arya Samaj's efforts, by 1902 the phrase 'Hindu nationality' had 'in the Punjab and elsewhere [in north India] already assumed the character of a distinct watchword.' In fact, 'within the last 15 years, there has been no more prominent feature of public life in India than the growth in the strength and vigour of the Hindu revivalist tendencies'.[14]

Gwalior was also one of the Arya Samaj's earliest bastions. Babuji had acquired a master's degree in Hindi on the sidelines, and was influenced by what he read in Hindi literature – which was becoming a potent site for manufacturing the Arya Samaji version of history.* Around the time Atal was born in December 1924, many parts of north India descended into a series of riots. In and around Agra, the government held the Arya Samaj responsible for much of the trouble. Muslims were offended by Hindu processions playing loud music in front of mosques; Hindus were offended by Muslims slaughtering cows. The cause was disproportionate to the violence produced: at the bottom, the struggle was for political power.

Gwalior was free of communal tensions, but the Maratha monarchy was beginning to flaunt its Hindu ethos. As the Urdu vs Hindi battle sharpened, the state promoted Hindi. Its newly launched mouthpiece in Hindi and English, *Jayaji Pratap*, devoted a lot of space to analyzing the horoscopes of all consequential political figures of the world. Many in the Scindia durbar were fond of hunting, but killing a peacock, considered sacred in Hinduism, was a criminal offence. Most of all, popular Hindu

* In *The Hindi Public Sphere 1920–1940,* the historian Francesca Orsini showcases Hindi intellectuals as relying heavily on history as documented in colonial and orientalist sources. But while they studied and absorbed the rationalist conception of history, their own enterprise was radically different. In their interpretation, history was a secular play of power, where conquest did not necessarily bestow moral superiority on the conquerors. Ancient India was a Hindu nation – a loose confederation of Hindu regional kingdoms. Centuries of Indo-Muslim history, with its many dimensions and necessity for pragmatic and ideological compromises, could be brushed aside as if they never existed. Attacks by Afghans, Turks and Iranians were all lumped together as 'Muslim invasions', and their reigns became a narrative break, usually the result of a series of betrayals, with only some attention being given to internal weaknesses and conflicts.

festivals such as Dussehra, Ganesh Chaturthi and Krishna Janmashtami began to be celebrated with great pomp. Poetry recital sessions would be organized, and Babuji didn't miss a chance to speak or recite a poem at these state-sponsored events. By the end of the 1930s, the Arya Samaj permeated politics in Gwalior as it had in the areas surrounding Bateshwar three decades before.

By the mid-1930s, Babuji earned well enough to feed his large family, and had surprisingly also managed to save some money. He had married off two sons, Awadh Behari and Sada Behari, as well as Vimla, the eldest daughter. He had also purchased some land in the narrow alley of Shinde Ki Chhawni – a middle-class locality so named because it housed a large army cantonment whose task had been to defend the Scindias in times of aggression – and built a house there.

After Baba passed away in 1936, Ma, with all her children, moved to Gwalior for good. For a while the family lived together.[15] In the only surviving photo from this time, the patriarchal hierarchy is on ample display: the male members, including Atal, sit on chairs, with Ma next to Babuji in the centre. The sisters Kamla and Vimla and the wives of Awadh Behari and Sada Behari stand at the back, while Urmila squats with the children on the carpet in front. The photo also shows a teenaged Atal as someone fond of dressing well; while the other male members wear white blazers (over dhoti or pants), Atal is wearing a dark blazer. Unlike his siblings, he also wears a white cap. He smiles, exuding the quiet confidence of a Brahmin boy who is looking forward to bigger things in life. The photo gives an impression of a well-knit family that likes to be together.

Atal read everything he could lay his hands on. He devoured every page of *Veer Arjun*, a Hindi weekly founded by Swami Shraddhanand, a popular reformist of the Arya Samaj; and the monthly *Vikram* – to inquire about its arrival, he would make multiple trips to the Gwalior railway station. The Vajpayee siblings competed to grab the magazines. He also occasionally sampled *Kesari*, at a friend's house, and would later credit the Marathi newspaper for improving his proficiency.[16] Historical fiction was a particular favourite: for instance, *Pratap Pratigya*, a play by Jagannath Prasad 'Milind' based on the bravery and valour of the medieval Rajput king of Mewar, Maharana Pratap, who died fighting Akbar's army. Atal also watched the book's adaptation on screen, and would practise the dialogues at home. He loved Vrindavanlal Verma's *Jhansi Ki Rani Lakshmibai*. Even though the novel recounted a painful defeat, it focused on Lakshmibai's heroism and sacrifice in defending her kingdom from the British. 'The actual reasons for the Rani's defeat belong to history, and there is no tampering with them,' writes the historian Francesca Orsini on Verma's novel. 'But the novelist can write against their grain a narrative of collective heroism, a future envisaged in prophecies and a personal thread of "ifs" which hint that another history could have happened and could have been told.'[17]

It pointed towards a deep-rooted inferiority. Whereas the past ought to be faced squarely, the response of the Hindi elite was the response of a defeated people, for whom lying to themselves was the only recourse. These novels interpreted the history of Hindus over the past 1,000 years as not one of abject surrender to Islamic and British rule, rather one of constant struggle and occasional victory. Pre-nineteenth-century sources have Rajputs sharing their worldview with the Muslim warriors, but now they began to be seen in terms of either treason or heroic resistance: 'Rajput rulers who had cooperated and served as Mughal commanders were now seen as traitors, while those who kept fighting, like Maharana Pratap, became national heroes.'[18] And thus Atal had come to have a sharp sense of his past – the *Hindu* past. This past was rooted in the stories woven around what certain Hindi intellectuals would have liked their history to be.

Atal's performance inside the classroom remained less than average. He especially didn't like maths or science. Once he flunked a test and was scolded by his eldest brother Awadh Behari: 'If you are failing now, what will you do with life later?' He sobbed and swallowed his pride. In spring 1938, at the end of eighth grade, Atal sat the Gwalior State Middle School Exams; he was awarded a third division.[19] Even by Gorkhi standards, the headmaster's son had fared below average. (Only one student at Babuji's school had a first division, but twenty-one boys had scored a second division.) Atal had cleared all subjects but didn't have a single distinction – not even in Hindi, in which he had by now a strong vocabulary and a sharp sense of meter and rhyme which he occasionally employed in poems he only read out to friends.

Babuji's own performance as headmaster of Gorkhi was much better. Apart from managing a large family and a large school, and publishing poems, Babuji had found time to co-author books such as *Ground-work of English Translation, Grammar and Composition, Part IV*, which was recommended for middle school teachers in the state. The hard work was rewarded: he was promoted and sent off as the inspector of schools for Bhind district. At long last, after serving the maharaja for more than two decades, Babuji had broken into the lower rung of the elite Scindia bureaucracy.*

Despite faring poorly, Atal managed to get admission to the popular Victoria Collegiate High School, where Babuji had earlier taught. The change was of the kind he desired. With Babuji away in Bhind, there was more freedom. He no longer had to trudge through science textbooks (though maths continued to be compulsory). He got better at debating and, representing the Hindi section, even won some prizes. Atal also became familiar with a new group that had arrived in the town in late 1938: the All India Students' Federation, the first student's body in the country. As a popular school in the heart of the capital, Victoria Collegiate was a good catchment area for the AISF. At its inception in Gwalior, the AISF had Gandhians dominating the body, followed by Marxists and Socialists. His acquaintance with such diverse ideologies broadened Atal's worldview. It also confused him.

Inspired by the Russian revolution, there was in the Hindi sphere talk of social and economic justice, and inclusion of the neglected

* Babuji continued to be a higher performer than all his children: a gazette from 21 February 1941 mentions him being awarded fifteen rupees for his uniform as well as a 'grade promotion of Rs. 25'.

sections – the lower castes, women. But the puzzle never got resolved. Social justice in India meant tackling caste differences and centuries of discrimination; the participants in the debate were often upper-caste males of privilege. Marxists craved social equality without talking about caste, adding another layer of confusion and self-deception. Atal would later be embarrassed about his 'half-formed mind' in high school: 'Along with the Arya Samaj scholars, I was beginning to get influenced by the communist ideas, a proletariat revolution.'[20]

The defective framework is evident in Atal's earliest surviving poem, 'Taj Mahal', written around this time. It mourns the apparent exploitation of Hindu workers by the Mughals during the construction of the grand edifice not far away from his village.

> This Taj Mahal, this Taj Mahal
> As it flows, the stream of Yamuna sobs inconsolably
> This Taj Mahal, built over the tears of every Hindu.*

The wisdom behind the poem were borrowed from the revisionist Arya Samaji version of history he was reading in the novels. Taj Mahal's construction may have been a terribly wasteful expenditure, but it didn't explain why the Hindu dynasty of the Bhadaurias, the ruins of whose fort still dominated the landscape of Bateshwar, had collaborated with the Mughals and fought against the Scindias. Or why the dozens of temples in Bateshwar, built around the same time as the Taj Mahal, survived, despite being in the periphery of the Mughal capital of Agra. But Agra's complex history did not shape Atal's worldview: that was not the point of history. History was meant to remind all Hindus that they belonged to a common, even if imprecisely defined, ancient nation.

Another confused blend of Arya Samaj and Marxism was a poem Atal published in the annual magazine of Victoria Collegiate in 1939.

---

* यह ताजमहल, यह ताजमहल
यमुना की रोती धार विकल
कल-कल, चल-चल
जब रोया हिंदुस्तान सकल
तब बन पाया ताजमहल
यह ताजमहल, यह ताजमहल।

'Kavi aaj suna ek gaan re' exhorts the poet to reactivate the collective responsibility to restore the ancient nation to life. It begins with the fundamental injustice of a 'human enchained by another human'. The colonial exploiters 'erected their palaces over our bones': 'Even as our young sons died scrambling for crumbs, they, drunk on power, plundered us and filled their coffers.' 'They violated our honour, looted our pride.' 'Crying, starving, stumbling – is this our only fate?' Then the poet asserts: 'Hum ub chuke iss jeevan se, ab toh visphot macha denge; hum dhu-dhu jalte angaare, ab toh kuch kar dikhla denge' – We are fed up of this life [of hunger and cries], we must explode; will show our worth, we who are capable of subsuming ourselves.[21]

The 'we' here implied the homogeneous, casteless community of Hindus united against the aggressors. But despite his pledge to jump into a fire, Atal is careful to not make explicit the object of his attack: the reader wouldn't know whether the colonial exploiters repeatedly referred to as 'they' are British or Muslims.

Yet these poems reveal something extraordinary. They speak of the intense rage and victimhood Atal felt; that he had come to have a sharp, if also narrow and confused, sense of India's history and geography, and the need for its revival; and a sense of his own place in the wider world. That these poems were written by an adolescent who had barely hit puberty made them exceptional.

Around the time Atal was born, the two major pro-Hindu outfits – the Hindu Mahasabha and the Arya Samaj – grew obsessed with the idea of sangathan, Hindu unity. It became a more urgent need than the social reform they had occasionally advocated. To put this vague ideal into practice, some key Mahasabha men in Nagpur came together in October 1925, on the eve of the Dussehra festival, to launch the Rashtriya Swayamsevak Sangh.

The founders included K. B. Hedgewar who would, during 1926–31, serve simultaneously as the secretary of the Mahasabha; and B. S. Moonje, who would serve as the president of the Mahasabha during 1927–37.

The Mahasabha itself was born when Bal Gangadhar Tilak's Marathi supporters in the Congress became disenchanted with Gandhi for his apparent appeasement of Muslims. In 1921, soon after Tilak's death, they joined hands with pro-sangathan Congressmen in other provinces to form the All India Hindu Mahasabha. For a while they existed 'both within and outside the Congress' before choosing to split in 1933.[22]

Historians have frequently portrayed the Mahasabha–RSS as Tilak's natural successors. Following the death of the guru, the chelas in fact made a subtle but radical break. For all his extremism, Tilak's chief ambition had been swaraj – self-rule – for which he had conceded, even if reluctantly, separate electorates to the Muslims (in the Lucknow Pact of 1916). In the wake of the Khilafat movement, however, his protégés replaced the British with Muslims as the chief enemy. The Mahasabha–RSS would never openly confront the colonial rule.

Moonje, who attended the Round Table Conference in London in March 1931 as a Mahasabha representative, also found time to travel to Italy to visit places such as the Fascist Academy of Physical Education and even managed to personally meet Mussolini. He was impressed by the fascist system of indoctrination of young boys and girls, and passed on his practical insights to Hedgewar.

While the RSS was for all practical purposes the volunteer offshoot of the Hindu Mahasabha, the founders wanted the two to be seen as separate entities. Unlike the Mahasabha, which became by the 1930s a full-fledged political party claiming to speak on behalf of Hindus, the former had a longer-term aim. The RSS calculated that 'only when a large number of Hindu youths in the country' – three percent at the lower count – 'were sufficiently trained in military tactics to bring about a revolution in India could it afford to challenge the government'. A sensational inside account from 1940 claimed that the purpose of training young men for three years – by making them attend Officer's Training Camps (OTCs) – was to introduce the smartest among them 'into various departments of Government, such as the army, navy, postal, telegraph, railway and administrative services in order that there may be no difficulty in capturing control over the administrative departments in India when the time comes'.[23]

Beginning an association with the RSS marked the highlight of Atal's Victoria Collegiate years. It began with a casual suggestion. At an Arya Samaj function on a Sunday morning, his group was asked by a priest what they did in the evenings. Not much, everyone replied. 'Why don't you try going to the Sangh shakha then?' he proposed. The RSS had recently opened its first branch nearby. 'It had only Maharashtrian boys,' Atal later recalled, 'and naturally all the swayamsevaks spoke in Marathi.'[24] For the Bateshwar boys, the shakha meant a much larger group to play with. Soon, they made attending the evening shakha a part of their daily routine. Together they learnt to march like soldiers did in a drill, attack and defend with a lathi, play khokho and kabaddi, act in imaginary war dramas in which Hindus thrashed Muslims. Atal participated in all the activities, and excelled in not many.

Given the nature and scale of its ambition, the organization did not maintain any records 'so that no documentary proof is available if the RSS ever comes into troubles'. The elders would never speak even 'to any of their own junior members regarding the internal activities or principles of their organization'. In turn ordinary members, swayamsevaks like Atal, 'would have complete faith in the Sanghchalak and would not disclose anything about the RSS to outsiders'. All through the 1930s, the RSS dispatched pracharaks – full-time members – to different parts of the country. A young Maratha by the name of Narayanrao Tarte was sent to Gwalior in 1939.

Shortly before Hedgewar passed away in June 1940, he had appointed a young lecturer of botany at the BHU – Banaras Hindu University – the chain-smoking M. S. Golwalkar, to succeed him. Addressing a meeting in the Bombay Province in November 1940, Golwalkar, with his flowing hair and piercing eyes, 'propounded the pan Hindu theory of the undivided India under the Hindu rule of the Mahasabha'.[25]

Moonje's acquaintance with the Gwalior durbar preceded the RSS' arrival in the town. While Moonje continued to privately advise Hedgewar on the RSS, he divided his time between the Mahasabha and his dream project of opening a school to impart military training to Hindu youths. In 1935, Moonje had managed to convince Jivajirao Scindia to contribute one lakh rupees for the Bhonsala Military School.

The same year Moonje founded the Gwalior branch of the Hindu Mahasabha. In a revealing gesture in March 1938, the twenty-one-year-old maharaja, the chubby-cheeked Jivajirao Scindia, landed up in Nashik to inaugurate the school.

In the 1937 provincial elections, the Hindu Mahasabha was routed: it won merely seventeen out of a total of more than 1,500 seats across British India. Even though the Mahasabha desperately needed funds and like-minded patrons, the party realized it had no chances of securing Hindu votes in the near future. But how did Jivajirao Scindia stand to benefit from the Mahasabha–RSS? Historian Ian Copland, an authority on princely states, cites two factors: one was the princes' 'wish to insure against an uncertain future'. Building bridges with the provincial political parties was a means of insuring that when the transfer of power came, they would not be without friends in New Delhi to protect their interests.[26] Scindia also wished 'to do something grand and memorable on the larger Indian political stage'.* The young maharaja relied on the advice of courtiers, some of whom were admirers of V. D. Savarkar – the chief theorist of Hindutva, and a popular Mahasabha figure. The RSS and the Mahasabha seized the opportunity to expand their activities to Gwalior.

The colonial government had reasons to be less kind to the RSS than the maharaja of Gwalior. Soon after World War II broke out, the government's attention was drawn to the dozens of volunteer organizations which had sprouted in every nook and corner of the country, each of them with a separate uniform and flag, and armed with lathis. Their worst fear was that, in case of an external attack, private militias like the RSS would side with the aggressor. In July 1940, the government imposed a ban on the quasi-military activities of all volunteer organizations: the wearing of khaki uniforms, the performance of drills, lathi-fighting. 'This ban struck

* Copland writes: 'Saddled with the forename George (a sycophantic gesture to the King-Emperor by his anglophile father) Jivaji Rao Scindia of Gwalior had to contend in early life with a possessive mother, the junior maharani, an ignorant woman steeped in fanciful superstition, who ensured that his every move was watched and recorded by spies, with the ministrations of callous court doctors who pumped him full of libido-suppressing drugs in an effort to stop him developing the sexual lusts that "in the end proved fatal to his father", and with the accident of an extremely short stature, which accentuated his sense of himself as emasculated and physically unworthy of his Maratha warrior heritage.'

at the very core of the Sangh's existence,' an intelligence report noted, 'by seeking to suppress those features of the organization which were its chief attractions in the eyes of its youthful recruits, viz., its uniform and its parade-ground activities.'[27] Now they would only do physical exercises, play games and salute the saffron flag.

The partial ban on the RSS came soon after Atal had begun to attend the evening shakha in 1939 at the neighborhood locality of Laxmi Ganj. But the ban was followed far more strictly in the British Indian provinces than princely states like Gwalior, where a friendly maharaja winked. Atal liked being at the shakha so much that he went along with his elder brother Prem Behari to Nagpur in 1940 'just to attend the valedictory function of the camp'. He also managed to get a glimpse of Hedgewar, who had fallen seriously ill.[28] When Golwalkar alighted in Gwalior after taking over as the RSS chief, Atal was part of the group waiting at the station to welcome the 'Guruji'. The leader had a mystical influence on Atal: they were meeting for the first time, but Guruji 'looked at me as if he already recognized me'.[29]

This didn't mean Atal was immediately recognized. A batchmate at his high school who attended the shakha with Atal recalled a scene of him playing kabaddi:

> Wearing his khaki shorts, Atal would go to the other side mumbling kabaddi-kabaddi-kabaddi. He appeared lean and thin, weak. Every time he crossed to the other side whispering kabaddi-kabaddi, the opponents would be happy: they had finally found an easy prey. Then Atal would put his foot forward, and then someone would pull him down. He would fall down – *dharaam*! The opponents would cry with joy. His shirt-pant would get muddied; I guess he would be scolded at home by his mother.[30]

Still, Atal liked to play kabaddi. But he was 'just not interested' in learning to spin the lathi. In the RSS shakha, to excel at the physical events was to get noticed; Atal clearly was less than average. His talents lay elsewhere. Atal was fond of watching *Pratap Pratigya* every time it was enacted on stage, and would practise its dialogues in front of friends. It would prove handy in the mock battle sessions organized by the RSS: Atal brought an actor's dedication, dramatic technique and stage presence to an otherwise dull event. His cousin Manikchand remembered sessions of 'Aakraman aur Pratiraksha' – Attack and Defence – at camps when Atal 'roared as if he were fighting a real battle'.[31]

Atal was also drawn to Babasaheb Apte, the RSS bauddhik pramukh – all-India in charge of intellectual sessions. On Saturdays and Sundays, the local branches of Gwalior would come together for a closed-door intellectual session. It was here that Atal's skills as a debater and writer of verses proved handy. On one occasion Moonje came to Victoria Collegiate High School to impress on the young pupils the need for Hindus to join the imperial army during World War II in as large numbers as possible. Atal was asked to deliver a five-minute speech welcoming the visitors – Moonje; Dattatreya Parchure, who headed the Gwalior branch of the Mahasabha; and the retired chief of the Scindia army, Vishnupant Phadke. Atal would have impressed the elders at Mahasabha–RSS. For, soon after he attended his first-year OTC in Nagpur in the summer of 1941, he was appointed the bauddhik karyawaah for Gwalior.

Atal sat his high school exams in March 1941. English and maths were compulsory; as optional subjects he chose Hindi, history and Sanskrit. He had been insatiably reading all three optional subjects outside of class, and it reflected in his poems. But, as earlier, he had not studied the curriculum well enough from the point of view of the exam. The results came out three months later: Atal had passed the board exam but, as his certificate read, underlining his scores, 'With distinction in Nil and was placed in the Second Division'.[32]

Even so, in the summer of 1941 he secured admission to Victoria College, the most prestigious centre of higher education in Gwalior state, for a four-year integrated intermediate and bachelor's degree in arts. Soon after Atal joined, F. G. Pearce was appointed as the principal of the college. An Indophile educationist, Pearce was a critic of the western education system, and frequently spoke and wrote articles about the ashram system of ancient India – the only way 'we can make a clean break with the graduate factory': 'Here is a fine system of ancient Indian education which served our forefathers well, would enable us to avoid pitfalls of mass-production methods.'[33] The college had other prominent faculty members: Guru Prasad Tandon, son of the veteran Congress leader P. D. Tandon, taught Hindi; a young lecturer of Urdu, Jan Nisar Akhtar, would later renown himself as an Urdu poet and lyricist in Bombay cinema. Atal liked the place. He would at last only be studying subjects he wanted to; and, for the first time, there was a place that offered him the prospect of female company, though women were hugely outnumbered by boys.

At home too there was more freedom. Earlier bullied by elder brothers, now he quietly began to assert himself over his younger, unmarried sisters. Kamla 'liked to sit in the doorway for long hours'. Atal didn't like that; darvaaja-dalaan was a male preserve – women were not to step outside the courtyard. As soon as he would see Kamla near the door, 'he would rebuke me to go inside. We would fight about this often, then the matter would reach Ma. On one occasion he dragged me by my feet. I wept for a long time.'[34]

As the bauddhik karyawaah for his hometown, Atal's association with the RSS deepened. The job entailed giving weekly lectures, which was exhausting but helped Atal sharpen his craft of public speaking.[35] The responsibility shaped his behaviour at college: 'He would speak less,' a batchmate said. 'On every issue, big or small, he would measure his words carefully.'[36]At the same time, it stiffened his Arya Samaji worldview, and this came out in what would become his most celebrated poem.

'Those days Harivansh Rai Bachchan's poems were very popular,' Atal would recall later. He thought deeply over one of Bachchan's poems, 'Pyaala', from the collection *Madhubala*. Bachchan uses the pyaala – an earthen bowl used to drink alcohol – as a metaphor for the transience of human life, and the need to train oneself to relish the ongoing moment: 'Mitti ka tan, masti ka mann, chhan bhar jeevan – mera parichay.' For Atal, a romantic poet like Bachchan was an odd inspiration. In 'Hindu Tan Mann', Atal transmuted Bachchan's poem into a history of untarnished Hindu sophistication since ancient times:

When did I ever desire to conquer the world?
I have only taught myself to conquer the mind, look within.

When did I torture someone in the name of my gods Krishna and Ram?
Did I ever massacre in hordes to inflict Hinduism upon the world?
Could anyone claim that I broke a mosque in Kabul?
Not another slice of earth, only determined to win hearts everywhere.
My body and mind, every ounce of my existence, is Hindu –
That's my only identity.[37]*

'Hindu Tan Mann' is intensely Arya Samaji, unencumbered by any confused notions of caste-class inequality. It is confident of tone and at the same time argumentative. Atal first recited it at his second-year OTC in Lucknow, during May–June 1942, to strong clapping.[38]

By this time the authorities had found out that the RSS was violating the ban, even though 'the official attitude of the Sangh is one of compliance'. Its leadership was warned by the Home Department that 'breaches of the ban on uniforms and drill will not in future be permitted'.[39] The warnings went unheeded. But neither this nor the RSS' 'occasional precipitation of communal trouble' was the government's main problem with the Sangh. 'It has been suggested in some quarters that the Sangh has pro-Japanese tendencies. Evidence of this is scanty, and by no means convincing. The most that can be said at present is that the Sangh might be drawn into pro-Japanese activities through its connection with the All-India Hindu Mahasabha, if the latter itself initiates or develops such activities.' In March 1943, the government noted that a ban on the training camps 'would hit the Sangh without having to single it out as an object of attack'.[40] In the end they did nothing. The government was broke due to war expenses, and had higher priorities.

---

* होकर स्वतंत्र मैंने कब चाहा है कर लूं जग को गुलाम?
मैंने तो सदा सिखाया करना अपने मन को गुलाम।
गोपाल-राम के नामों पर कब मैंने अत्याचार किए?
कब दुनिया को हिन्दू करने घर-घर में नरसंहार किए?
कोई बतलाए काबुल में जा कर कितनी तोड़ीं मस्जिद?
भूभाग नहीं, शत-शत मानव के हृदय जीतने का निश्चय।
हिन्दू तन-मन, हिन्दू जीवन, रग-रग हिन्दू मेरा परिचय!

Victoria College also introduced Atal to broader nationalist politics through the AISF. Founded in 1936 in Lucknow, by P. C. Joshi of the Communist Party of India and Jayaprakash Narayan of the Congress Socialist Party, the AISF had spread across the country. In September 1938, the Gwalior branch of AISF was founded in Victoria College. Officially the AISF was not linked to a political party. Behind the scenes, however, every party was trying to infiltrate its cadre base.

The AISF in Gwalior embodied the confusion at the national level. Supporters of Congress and CPI constituted the two largest groups, but there were also others: the socialists, the Forward Bloc, the Mahasabha–RSS sympathizers.[41] Even so, they must have made enough impact for the news to reach the Secretary of State in London. In the summer of 1941, the Secretary of State was pissed off with Jivajirao Scindia for his failure to check 'a good deal of subversive activity in Gwalior, including anti-war demonstrations by the Gwalior Students' Federation in the capital of the state'.[42]

All through 1942, Gwalior state was preoccupied with two major concerns. One was war emergency, such as a Japanese air strike: the administration had checkposts all across the state for stationing civil guard volunteers and emergency first-aid posts, including one near Atal's house in Shinde Ki Chhawni. The second cause for alarm was the increasing popularity of the Congress. Tensions heightened after Gandhi's Quit India call on 8 August. The local unit of the Congress passed a resolution asking the maharaja to sever relations with the British and demanding a participatory form of government. On 17 August, 'to suppress the agitation' in the wake of Gandhi's arrest, the Gwalior administration shut down schools and colleges for a fortnight.[43]

This didn't stop the Congress and their sympathizers in the Gwalior AISF from taking part in protests, circulating underground literature, hosting runaway leaders from British India; and in some rare cases, helping saboteurs in cities by supplying arms and ammunition. The RSS and the Mahasabha were ambivalent about Quit India. Mahasabha president Savarkar was determinedly opposed apparently because it would hurt the militarization of Hindus. The RSS too, having already annoyed the government, didn't want to risk being banned altogether. On the ground, though, at least some RSS supporters at Victoria College tugged in the opposite direction: they didn't want to remain mere spectators when others were boycotting and sabotaging all things British.[44]

Atal, now a popular second-year intermediate student at Victoria College, joined the protestors. Standing in the centre of the capital, the campus was kept under constant surveillance by the government. The administration came up with a 'list of students who took part in the strike'. The sixty-eight names included the brothers Atal and Prem Behari.[45] Atal would later claim that his arrest then was 'imminent'. He may have been right, for the administration began rounding up the offenders.

A senior minister who kept track of student activities informed Babuji that his sons were indulging in anti-government propaganda. Krishn Behari was in his mid-fifties, and would soon retire after serving the state for thirty years. With a large family to feed and two daughters to marry off, Babuji would most certainly have liked an extension. But the war-time expenses had drained the state exchequer, and some of the employment extensions were cancelled. With his sons openly defying the government, whatever little chance Babuji had for one was lost. He may even have feared that the government might refuse him pension, as had happened with some employees whose family members had defied the durbar. In a panic, Babuji admonished his sons, and sent them to the least unsafe place he knew: Bateshwar.

Like most first-generation city dwellers, the Vajpayees were deeply attached to their native place. After Baba's death in 1936, the thatch house upon the hillock had needed occasional upkeep. But the village was not as trouble-free as Babuji thought. Soon after they reached Bateshwar, Atal and Prem Behari casually participated in an incident that got them arrested. Atal described it in his confessional statement:

> On August 27, 1942, Ala was being recited in Bateshwar bazaar. At about 2 p.m. Kakua alias Liladhar and Mahuan came to the Ala and delivered a speech and persuaded the people to break the forest laws. Two hundred people went to the Forest Office and I along with my brother followed

> the crowd and reached Bateshwar Forest Office. I and my brother stayed below and all other people went up. I do not know the name of any other person, except Kakua and Mahuan, who was there... I could not know who was razing the wall to the ground but the bricks were certainly falling ... I along with my brother started to go to Maipura and the crowd was behind us. The above-mentioned persons forcibly turned out the goats from the cattle-pound and the crowd proceeded towards Bichkoli. Ten or twelve persons were in the Forest Office. I was at a distance of 100 yards. I did not render any assistance in demolishing the government building. Thereafter, we went to our respective homes.[46]

Two days later the police arrived to arrest Atal (Accused No. 29), Prem Behari and nine others named in the FIR. They were locked up at the Agra jail. When the brothers were brought to the court, they gave identical confessional statements. Atal gave his father's name simply as Gauri Shankar, Babuji's nickname in the village. (One wonders if Atal chose not to mention Babuji's official name out of fear that it could land his father in trouble in Gwalior.) Three weeks later, on 23 September 1942, Atal and Prem Behari were released as there 'is not sufficient evidence or reasonable ground of suspicion to justify the forwarding of the accused to a magistrate'.[47]

All this while Krishn Behari was desperately trying to use his contacts to secure the release of his sons. Prem Behari later said that his father had managed to get in touch with one of his caste brethren, Girija Shankar Vajpayee, a senior member in the Viceroy's Council: 'At his intervention both of us brothers were released.'[48] By another account, Babuji went to the Agra jail wearing his inspector's uniform, and effectively pleaded the innocence of his sons. The government was soft on the families of its employees arrested after August 1942, simply because lower bureaucracy was the administration's backbone, to be used in successfully crushing the movement. The court of the special judge at Agra finally sentenced three of the arrested. This included the main ringleader of the Bateshwar sabotage case, Liladhar Vajpayee, whom both Atal and Prem Behari had named in their confessional statement: he was awarded three years' rigorous imprisonment. (Though Atal's statement was not used as evidence in court, it may have been one of the minor factors in Liladhar being sentenced.) Significantly, for the damages to government property, the villagers of Bateshwar were collectively made to pay a fine of ₹2,500.[49]

Neither Atal's arrest nor the attack on Bateshwar Forest Office was significant by Quit India standards. Atal never talked in detail about his ordeal, partly because thousands of people across north India – including some from Bateshwar – underwent rigorous imprisonment of anywhere between three years to a lifetime. On the contrary, Atal's accidental arrest served him exceedingly well. The twenty-four-day stint at Agra jail lent him the aura of a man who was willing to jump into the fire. Here was someone who, unlike the Brahmin Marxists of Victoria College, lived his poetry. At poetry gatherings he began to be introduced as an 'udaymaan kavi' – a fiery young poet.[50]

Making use of his newfound popularity, Atal contested the 1943 students' union elections for the post of general secretary. His group of friends had made a calculation: the RSS–Mahasabha had a strong base at Victoria College, and Atal was friends with many sympathizers of the Congress and CPI in the AISF, to whom he could appeal to vote for him. Atal was so confident of his win that in the heat of the campaign he issued a challenge: 'If my opponent wins even half as many votes as I do, I will concede defeat and won't contest another election.'[51] He won.

Atal continued to do well at college. The gazette of December 1943 mentions 'A.B. Vajpai' winning the second prize in the Hindi essay-writing competition held during the Madhav Jayanti celebrations.[52] He was part of the college 'literature committee'; for their annual festival in winter 1943, the committee managed to get Rahul Sankrityayan, who had travelled around the world and established himself as the first writer of travelogues in Hindi. A group photo after the event has Sankrityayan sitting with the faculty coordinators, with Atal and his gang – Deshraj Singh, Ramkumar Chaturvedi 'Chanchal' – standing at the back.

With close friends there were also light moments. Chanchal, friend and fellow poet, never forgot a prank Atal played on him when they were part of the group selected to represent Victoria College at an intra-university poetry competition at Agra University, to which the college was affiliated:

> As soon as we boarded the Punjab Mail that would take us to Agra, Atal guru asked me, 'Would you like to taste the offering I made to Lord Hanuman?' Now who would refuse Hanumanji ka prasad! He opened a box and gave me some sweets. It was not until the train reached Morena that I grasped what it really was: my eyes turned red, head began to spin; with great difficultly I reached Agra ... He had an old habit of having maajum [a sweet confection made of bhang]. Atal really needed his daily dose. Till the time maajum reached his belly, he would not look conscious enough.[53]

The bhang-loving poet was aware that Agra University was a hostile venue – partly because someone from Victoria College routinely won the first prize, which the others resented. The campus had a girls' hostel, whose anglicized students took the first row, and hooted every time a participant from Gwalior climbed up the stage. On his turn, Atal began to recite a semi-autobiographical poem on Quit India, the 'golden morning that was 9 August 1942' – 'Nau august san bayalis ka lohit swarna prabhat.' The girls began to hoot: 'prabhat, prabhat, prabhat'. For a few moments Atal felt nervous and annoyed, and took a pause. But by 1943 he had been on the podium too many times to be intimidated by an expectedly hostile audience. The artist inside him had come to like the high: Atal finished his long poem in which he extolled Gandhi (who 'roared like a cloud') and Jawahar (the 'lion'), and pledged to gear up for the 'third war of independence' which would finally bring freedom to India. He won the second prize.[54]

Close friends like Chanchal began to understand Atal's approach to making a speech that would last a lifetime: 'He would first research the topic deeply; then he would make a list of bullet points on a sheet; only after that would he decide the introduction and conclusion.' The seemingly natural presentation on stage was in fact a result of careful planning. 'Even if he planned to crack jokes, he would rehearse these in advance.'[55]

One of the side effects of being arrested was that Babuji didn't let Atal attend the third-year OTC in 1943. By the summer of 1944, Atal had rehabilitated himself enough in his father's eyes to be allowed to go to the Nagpur OTC for forty days. As with earlier Sangh training camps, friends would remember Atal for his artistry and his poems.

In his last year at Victoria College, 1944–45, Atal fought and won the students' union election for vice president. The college principal doubled up as the president of the students' union, and Atal cherished his occasional conversations with F. G. Pearce on administrative issues: waiving the fees for poor students, making scholarships and books available to the needy, and so on. 'Due to the Second World War, it was difficult to get kerosene oil,' remembered a contemporary. Few houses in Gwalior had electricity. In the absence of kerosene, most college students struggled to study during the exams. 'On behalf of the students' union, Atal led a delegation to a senior official and managed to convince him to allot a special quota of kerosene for the students.'[56]

While Atal was friends with many communists at the AISF, he viewed them with suspicion – especially after their opposition to Quit India, arguing that India should prefer to support Britain in its fight against fascism in World War II. The most revealing example is his relationship with Suman, a young lecturer of Hindi. Shivmangal Singh 'Suman' had once been taught by Babuji at school, and was later influenced by Marx. Suman had published a poetry collection, *Jeevan Ke Gaan* – Anthems of Life. Many of the poems were about farmers and poverty and class differences. In the college magazine, Atal published a scathing review in verse.[57] He mocked Suman's privilege and hypocrisy in writing about the poor. Suman had a 'pretty house, prettier wife' and yet he 'cries of deprivation': such a huge contrast between 'the verses he publishes' and 'the life he leads'. Suman's poems were not born of experience; 'this can't be the anthem of life'.*

In the only surviving group photo of the college students' union, taken maybe in early 1945, Atal is the only student sitting on a chair

---

* सुन्दर गृह, गृहणी सुंदरतर
फिर अभाव का यह कैसा स्वर
कविता कहाँ, कहाँ जीवन है
दिल से निकली तान नहीं है
यह जीवन का गान नहीं है।

with other faculty members – indicating that he had acquired a certain respectability in college. His stint as Vice President during 1944–45 would become memorable for one particular incident when the college organized a joint kavi samellan and mushaira. Suman, along with other progressive poets, was also to participate. To warm up for the show, the young lecturer had held a party where he had invited some close friends like Jan Nisar Akhtar and guest poets for drinks. The session began at 8 p.m. and it seems Suman didn't keep track of the time. As the other poets recited, Atal sent a trusted emissary to Suman's house to call the guest poets to the venue. The emissary returned to report that Suman and his friends were drunk; it was 10 p.m. by then. Exasperated, Atal consulted Pearce and Professor Bagchi, the faculty advisor of the union, and they decided to cancel the event. Atal went to the podium and declared that the session was over. Because the inebriated included college faculty members, the audience was not explained the reasons. The story travelled wide. Even though it had been a collective decision, it bolstered his image.[58] Until his last days, Atal would relate this incident to illustrate that he really was, like his name, *atal* – a firm, no-nonsense leader.

Towards the end of his bachelor's at Victoria College, Atal had made up his mind to study further, 'but resources were scarce.' Babuji had retired, and the two younger sisters were yet to be married. Atal had become popular enough for the state durbar to have vaguely heard of him. Gwalior state used to give scholarships to meritorious students to pursue higher studies: 'When they began to shortlist students whose higher education would be funded, my name was there.' Jivajirao Scindia sanctioned him a handsome scholarship of ₹75 per month. Gwalior didn't have a college that offered a post-graduate degree, but Atal had applied and managed to get admission at Dayanand Anglo Vedic College in Kanpur. DAV College 'had a huge, impressive campus. It was easy to get accommodation in the hostel.'[59] Partly because Atal wasn't certain of what he wanted for a career, and may have wished to hedge for wider choices, he took admission for a master's degree in political science as well as an LLB. Prem Behari was already a second-year LLB student at DAV.

As Atal geared himself up to live away from family for the first time, Babuji sprung a major surprise: he wanted to come along and enroll himself for an LLB too. Babuji was conscious that some of the topmost bureaucrats in the education department wrote 'MA (Cambridge)' with their name, and he had often wondered if a proper university degree would have helped him rise further in his career. The pension from the Scindias was puny. A new law degree would perhaps enhance his post-retirement career options. Since two of his younger sons were studying at DAV College, he would be able to sustain himself there at little extra cost.

Thus the father-son duo landed up in Kanpur. The news of a retired man studying with his youngest son became amusing enough to be published in local newspapers. Atal was allotted a room to share with his father. Rather than eating in the mess, the duo would cook their meals in the hostel. Atal didn't mind having home-made food, and 'we would always have a glass of milk before we went to sleep.' Before long, though, Atal realized that his father's constant presence curtailed his freedom. It was also frequently embarrassing. If for some reason Babuji skipped a class, the son would be asked to explain his absence. Partly to avoid the awkwardness, Atal stopped going to the law classes and focused more on his MA.[60]

For the first few months, Kanpur once again brought into play the old, unresolved intellectual confusion in Atal's mind. 'The world war was ongoing, and this topic would often be discussed,' a contemporary recalled. 'After the war got over, would the British really agree to make India independent – as they were promising?'[61] In the last year of college, everyone in Atal's group had avidly read and debated *One World*, the American politician-author Wendell Willkie's dispassionate account of his travels during the World War to countries in the East which were supporting the Axis powers. Among other recommendations, Willkie made a compelling pitch for India's freedom after the war. In his conclusions, Willkie had castigated the 'military despotism of Hitler and the autocracy of Japan, and the fading dictatorship of the fascist Italy'.[62]*

As a student of political science, Atal keenly observed the final outcome of World War II. Willkie's prophecy was proved accurate. Italy and Germany, whose leaders Atal had been taught to idolize at the OTCs, had suffered a grim fate. In the last week of April 1945, Mussolini, whose ideas on race and military tactics the Mahasabha–RSS felt inspired by, was shot dead by his fellow countrymen and hung upside down at a petrol pump in Milan. Two days later Hitler, keen to avoid a similar fate, shot himself in the head. Russia winning the war had given the communists – and their Indian counterparts – a temporary moral boost, even though their opposition to Quit India had made the Indian communists less popular in the eyes of the youth.

Kanpur was a major hub of trade-union activity. But unlike its textile and leather workers, most communist activists in Kanpur were high-caste Hindus, some of whom came from an Arya Samaj background. The RSS ecosystem was much weaker in Kanpur than it was in Gwalior. Atal was no longer the bauddhik karyawaah, nor was he attending the shakha. Atal's behaviour in Kanpur confused many fellow Sangh adherents. One of them often saw him hanging out with the popular trade-union leader of the city, Sant Singh 'Yusuf'. Another contemporary of Atal at DAV College would recall Atal's friendship with Ganesh Prasad, a communist known for his debating skills. Seeing Atal in Prasad's company, his old friends wondered whether Atal had become a communist.

Soon, big events would declare their urgency and Atal would put aside the intellectual quibbles of his mind. In February 1946, Atal's old poem on Quit India was belatedly published in the Hindi weekly *Abhyudaya.* It grandiosely exhorted the reader to believe that the 'winds of 1949 would bring about a cataclysm' – 'the third war of independence' – vaguely hinting at achieving independence three years later, but not a faint hint

* Willkie was especially scathing about Germany's treatment of Jews: A 'peace-professing dictator lured the people first to minority persecution, then to war. This intolerance gave the German nation the momentary strength of complete regimentation. Actually, it has undermined and weakened the social structure so that when the tide of war turns, collapse is likely to be sudden and complete.'

of anything like the partition that was to come.[63] Around the same time, the results of elections in the British provinces were announced. The Muslim League had outperformed the Congress in Bengal, Sind and Punjab. In the first two it formed a government. The League improved its tally from 108 out of a total of 1,585 seats in 1937 to 430 in 1946. By contrast the Mahasabha was annihilated: it won only three seats across all the provinces, down from seventeen. The League's Mohammad Ali Jinnah made a more vociferous pitch for partition.

The Mahasabha–RSS were stunned. It was in this atmosphere of anxiety and desperation that Atal decided to try his hand as a pracharak, full-timer of the RSS. During the summer break, May–June 1946, he was sent by the regional coordinator Bhaurao Deoras to Sandila, a sleepy Muslim-majority hamlet ninety kilometres north of Kanpur.

Soon after he reached Sandila, Atal realized that while it had been easy to convince parents in Gwalior, many of them Marathi speakers and Arya Samajis, to allow their children to attend the shakha, the villagers in Sandila were less excited about the RSS taking up the mantle on behalf of all Hindus. 'We would walk, sometimes up to 6–7 miles, to the nearby villages,' said the RSS worker who made arrangements for Atal's stay. 'We were once returning from the village when he caught fever. I arranged for an ox-cart, and by the time we got back it was late at night.' It turned out that the fever was typhoid. Atal became bed-ridden. He looked 'emaciated, bones on his face clearly marked'. In that tiny house with no furniture and only a thin mattress, Atal wrote poems to pass the time. On one occasion his host mistook the bed-ridden Atal's hand-wringing and mumbling in the throes of composition for an epileptic seizure: 'I wondered whether he was hallucinating, and whether fever had anything to do with it. When I came and knocked, he tried to hide a paper he had in his hand below the sheet on the floor.'[64]

It was one thing to write 'Amar aag hai' – extolling Hinduism as the fountain from which emerged all the knowledge that the world benefited from, and chide the West for being 'obsessed with individualism'. Or to claim that every Hindu was 'desperate to die' for the motherland.[65] The real task of Hindutva was anti-Islamic sangathan, and that would require decades of brute, unglamorous labour. Typhoid was a bad omen: Atal was physically too frail and temperamentally too unsuited to become a pracharak.

The communal situation after Atal returned to Kanpur went further downhill. The city was an important centre of the Muslim League. In mid-August 1946, it launched Direct Action. 'At a time like this, I found the Sangh's work to awaken and unite the Hindus essential,' Atal would later recall. 'We would go to the dangerous areas in and around Kanpur city, teach the Hindus how to prepare themselves to resist a possible attack. At night, swayamsevaks would be called to the shakha, and sent to patrol the sensitive areas.'[66]

In other ways life went on as usual. Bhaiya Prem Behari had found a job in Kanpur, and he brought along his wife, Rajeshwari. Atal would visit them every Saturday. He would go to the Ganga for a bath, make thandhai there – doubtless mixed with bhang – and come back and ask Bhabhi to make dishes he liked.[67] But he was terribly nervous about what he would do post his master's: 'I could [take another year to] finish my law degree and then start a practice.' He would have found a lecturer's job somewhere in Gwalior state, but 'I would have to repay the scholarship amount that the state had spent on my education'. A scholarship from the Scindia durbar required every winner to sign a bond, under which they were to serve the Scindia state for three years after finishing their degrees. Often people requested to be exempted, even if it meant paying the penalty.

In the first week of 1947, the durbar issued an order under which any winner who didn't want to come back to serve the state must pay 'an interest at the rate of 3% from the date from which the scholarship has been granted'.[68] Babuji didn't have the money for this, so under normal circumstances Atal couldn't think of defaulting. And yet, he was too idealistic to accept a lecturer's job: to do so would be to concede to mediocrity at an early age, and at a most tumultuous moment in the nation's history. Atal decided to bide his time, secretly pinning his hopes on his dream 'third route – to become a journalist'.[69]

Sometime in mid-1947, Guruji Golwalkar, on his way to inspect an OTC in Banaras, stopped over in Kanpur. At the function held to honour Guruji at a shakha near DAV College, Atal recited a poem especially prepared for the occasion.* Guruji had met Atal on some occasions, and even vaguely recalled the face of the 'baal swayamsevak' who sang 'Hindu Tan Mann' with great feeling. But Atal had never had a chance to talk to Guruji at length. Guruji asked Atal to accompany him to Banaras. It is possible that on this journey he dropped Atal a hint that would rejuvenate him: the RSS was considering launching a Hindi press at Lucknow.

It remains a mystery how Atal managed to convince the Gwalior durbar to waive the penalty for defaulting on his scholarship. Perhaps someone higher up in the Mahasabha–RSS circles put in a word. It is more likely that by this time the maharaja himself stopped caring. With paramountcy due to lapse in August 1947, the durbar had infinitely bigger things to worry about. The terms of independence were such that Gwalior had no other option than to merge with the Indian Union. All Jivajirao Scindia could do was to bargain as shrewdly as possible with the Patel–Nehru duo before signing the instrument of accession.

In July 1947, Atal was preparing to leave Kanpur for Lucknow. He had wrapped up his MA on an indifferent note: he scored a third division, whereas Babuji passed his LLB with a second division.[70] Adding to the gloom was the prospect of partition hanging over the DAV College hostel. Atal spent a large chunk of his days working on an ambitious polemic on the millennium-long history of Islam in India that was to be published in the inaugural issue of the RSS mouthpiece *Rashtradharma*. At night he accompanied hostel friends, lathi in hand, on patrols to guard Hindu localities.

Around mid-July, the Mahasabha in the United Provinces had placed before the Congress government a dozen-odd demands, failing which the party threatened the government in Lucknow with a satyagraha.† The

* The poem could be summarized thus: 'Just as king Bhagirath brought Ganga on earth, which rejuvenated India in the ancient times, Guruji has given the nation a new consciousness which will keep India energized for ages.'

† The RSS–Mahasabha were strategically appropriating the word 'satyagraha' – a Gandhian innovation – to thwart much of what Gandhi held dear in the summer of 1947.

regional unit of the Mahasabha, led by its president Mahant Digvijaynath and vice president Tej Narain (who doubled up as the RSS Lucknow sanghchalak), demanded that Hindus alone should be recruited in the armed police and the proposed home guard organization; the post of Home Minister of UP be given to a Hindu; Hindi should be made the official language in the courts, the police and other government departments; cow slaughter should be banned. And one other demand that Atal may have been following more closely: that the ban on government servants becoming members of the RSS should be lifted.[71]

Two factors had given the Mahasabha the confidence to raise its fist at the Congress government. Several prominent Congressmen in UP – such as P. D. Tandon, the speaker of the Legislative Assembly – sympathized with the Mahasabha's demands. The major section of the local Hindi press too supported the Mahasabha, quietly or blatantly. After vacillating for a while, the UP premier G. B. Pant responded to the demands on 21 July in a long letter, and in a tone that was polite but final. Pant thought that most of the demands were of an all-India nature, and therefore could be decided only by the central cabinet. On others he disagreed. For example, on the Mahasabha's demand to replace the well-regarded home minister Rafi Ahmed Kidwai by a Hindu, Pant said: 'Given loyalty, efficiency and impartiality, Government can't make any distinction between its officers on communal grounds.'[72] As for government servants not being allowed to join the RSS, Pant pointed out that they were 'required to keep aloof from all party and communal organizations', and not allowed to join the Congress's volunteer wing Seva Dal either. 'Any other course is bound to give rise to serious complications. This is the general principle followed in all democratic countries. There was never any desire to make any invidious distinction between the RSS and other similar bodies…' Pant suggested that the RSS men might consider joining home guards and other defence services.[73]

The Mahasabha was not satisfied. Senior Congressman Dr Sampurnanand was assigned to the Nath–Narain duo: Sampurnanand told them that 'for the first time since the time of Prithviraj [Chauhan]', India had received the 'opportunity to develop the country according to what might be called Hindu ideals'.[74] Of course partition was a curse and 'must be undone'.

But in the meantime they should 'conserve what they had received'. Sampurnanand was amenable to the idea that cow slaughter should be banned, but promulgating legislation would take some time. The pep talk did not work, and the Mahasabha went ahead with its agitation on 27 July. By midnight of 1 August, the police had arrested seventy people, including Mahant Digvijaynath, who was taken into custody while he was attempting to hoist the Hindu Mahasabha flag in Aminudaullah Park.[75] The satyagraha collapsed.

On the evening of 3 August, Pant addressed a gathering of 50,000 at Kanpur's Phoolbagh. The UP premier dropped his conciliatory tone: 'Where were these Mahasabha leaders at the time when British imperialists were trying to crush Hindu culture and the freedom movement of the country?' Pant informed the audience that the Mahasabha had never raised its voice against the slaughter of cows to feed the British Army in India. Now that the British were quitting, their sense of devotion towards the cow had been suddenly aroused, which was 'nothing but hypocrisy'. 'Though our pleasure is not unmixed with the pain of partition, yet it is a great event in history… Anyone who demonstrates against rejoicing and displays black flags on that historic day [of 15 August] is a traitor.'[76]

Atal was not a traitor, though he was uninterested in celebrating 15 August. He had spent the previous night patrolling: 'Many of us had gathered in the hostel. A group of people from a nearby Hindu locality came to see us. They said there were strong rumours that at night miscreants from the nearby Muslim locality would attack us. We had among us some well-built students, and we reassured them: "You will sleep peacefully. We will guard your locality."'[77] They did. India's constituent assembly met at midnight, because of some astrological injunctions against taking over power during daytime. Being out on patrol, Atal could not tune into the radio to hear Nehru's much-revised speech on India's apparent 'tryst with destiny'. Some parts of Kanpur saw killings and arson over the next few weeks. By and large, the city didn't present an occasion significant enough to test Atal's martial skills and agility in spinning a lathi or charging an adversary, which were suspect among his peers.

All his life Atal recalled the celebration on 15 August 1947 at his college for its 'most strange combination of joy and gloom. Joy over gaining freedom after a thousand years of bondage, and gloom over the vivisection of the motherland.' He wrote that day: 'Freedom has come to India walking over dead bodies ... [Ask the Hindu refugees of East Bengal] who bear the vagaries of rains and storms on the pavements of Calcutta: are they excited about 15 August? If you are ashamed of hearing their grief merely because they are Hindus, come along with me across the border to see how civilizations are crushed.' Pakistan is where the 'hungry are given bullets to eat ... and where dry throats chant slogans of Jihad ... Over Lahore, Karachi, Dhaka hovers the dark shadow of death.' India's freedom was incomplete: 'How can I celebrate just now? Just a matter of some more time. The day isn't far we will enjoin the trifurcated India into a united nation again: all of our mountains, from Gilgit in the west to Garo in the east, will together celebrate the freedom.' But that 'golden day demands sacrifices: do not lose yourself in what you have found, focus on what you have lost.'[78]

The college had invited a former vice-chancellor of Agra University to preside over the Independence Day celebrations. Atal's forceful polemic moved the chief guest. 'He took out a ten rupee note from the inner pocket of his long coat, and placed it in my hand,' Atal would reminisce. 'I have received many awards in life ... But I hold those 10 rupees given by Prof. Diwanchand as the most priceless.'[79]

Babuji, who had finished his law degree, went back to Gwalior. No one in Atal's family was personally harmed in the partition. Atal's younger sister Kamla, since getting married, was living in a small town on the outskirts of Lahore. Her wedding was the only occasion when Atal had crossed what was now the Radcliffe Line separating India from West Pakistan, and even made a trip to Anarkali Bazaar in old Lahore. Kamla and her in-laws relocated safely to Agra. The next few weeks saw the worst religious violence in India's history. Even in a relatively unaffected place like Gwalior, in retaliation against the murder of Hindus in railway trains coming from West Punjab, 'hundreds of Muslims were stripped naked, identified, killed and thrown out of the trains that traversed Gwalior state. There were days when 20 or 30 Muslim bodies were collected by the state police alongside the railway line.'[80] It was no coincidence that among the princely states Gwalior was, as a secret IB – Intelligence Bureau – report pointed out, 'the greatest stronghold of RSS and H.M. Sabha, the RSS following numbering nearly 65,000'.[81]

But Babuji, who wrote an account of partition violence, did not mention his town at all. He was concerned about the plight of the Hindus and Sikhs of West Punjab, now in Pakistan: 'The Punjabis of the past suffered massive assaults. Even so, in the history of the mankind, the present-day carnage will rarely find a parallel.'[82] Babuji's account also revealed that no one in the Vajpayee household was excited by independence: 'At the heart of the divided motherland, lamps were lit and sweets distributed to mark the independence. Some cities were lit up so brightly they gave Diwali a competition. And yet, there was darkness inside every heart; the sweets tasted bland.' Babuji announced he would 'sacrifice all joy that brings bloodshed, rape, robbery and wholesome destruction of life and property'. The Vajpayees may also have been apprehensive – like everyone in the RSS–Mahasabha – of Gwalior's accession to the Indian Union. Many Hindus in Gwalior had come to idealize the state as a miniature Hindu Rashtra. Accession meant the domination of life and polity by an apparently pro-Muslim Congress, and destruction of the state's distinctively Hindu ethos.

Atal was by late August in Lucknow to help the RSS launch the monthly *Rashtradharma*. The Nagpur-based outfit had in the past avoided public promotion for fear of being banned. With no such fear now, they were desperate to expand in the Hindi heartland. Setting up a press in Lucknow was part of the outreach. *Rashtradharma* would be the RSS's entry into the fast-growing world of Hindi publishing. They needed young, raw adherents who could devote themselves without demanding too much in return. Atal and others had little experience of journalism. He was made a co-editor, though it was more of an apprenticeship; there was no salary.

August 1947 was not the happiest time to start a professional career. The master's-degree holder had simply made the best of a terrible situation. He was flirting with the idea of enrolling for a PhD in Lucknow, and may have calculated that with food and lodging expenses covered by the Sangh, he would manage to sustain himself, and divide his time between working and studying.

He didn't have much idea of the larger picture. Atal had no idea that the RSS's activities – its role in partition riots, vigilantism, publication of anti-government propaganda (*Rashtradharma* and other mouthpieces across the country) – would lead to a serious discord between Jawaharlal Nehru and Sardar Vallabhbhai Patel, who were to together decide the fate of the newly independent country. For now, the twenty-two-year-old co-editor believed in the pious mission of saving India from the Islamists and the pro-Muslim Congress government in Delhi.

3

Fear and Loathing in Lucknow

AFTER REACHING LUCKNOW, ATAL MOVED INTO THE LOCAL RSS OFFICE at 6 A. P. Sen Road near the Charbagh railway station. A volunteer provided a room in his house at Aminabad, which was within walking distance, to serve as the temporary *Rashtradharma* office.[1] The main brain behind the mouthpiece was the provincial organizer of the RSS in UP, Bhaurao Deoras.

A Brahmin from Nagpur, Bhaurao Deoras was among the earliest batches of children to have attended an RSS shakha, in late 1927, under the direct tutelage of Hedgewar. In 1937, twenty-year-old Bhaurao was sent to Lucknow to expand the Sangh in UP. Since Hedgewar had no money to spare, Bhaurao did everything from selling balloons on pavements to giving private tuitions to schoolchildren to make ends meet.[2] He persisted and, with time, managed to set up self-sustaining shakhas in Lucknow, Kanpur and Banaras. Bhaurao developed a knack for winning over people who had been trained to be hostile to the RSS – especially low-rank police and intelligence officials – which partly explains how the RSS grew during the World War II years despite bans on its activities.[3]

By the mid-1940s, the Sangh had raised enough from its volunteers and sympathizers in UP to sustain its activities. Bhaurao's biggest achievement was to recruit young men who were willing to submit themselves wholeheartedly to Sangh work. The most promising of his finds was the self-effacing Deendayal Upadhyaya, who had joined as a pracharak in 1942 in Lakhimpur, in Oudh, and was content with the Sangh organizing his meals and lodging. He rose swiftly to become Bhaurao's trusted deputy. Deendayal was to oversee the publication of *Rashtradharma*; Atal would informally report to him on a day-to-day basis.

Atal would share editorial responsibilities with Rajiv Lochan Agnihotri, an RSS pracharak from Rewa state. The monthly issues were to follow the Hindu calendar: the first one was slated to come out on 31 August 1947, coinciding with the Rakhi festival. It was decided to print 3,000 copies.[4] Given that the average circulation of a popular Hindi journal around the time was no more than 500, this was an ambitious number – hinting at the magazine's ample financial backing. A local volunteer called Radheshyam Kapoor was made the publisher. The money came from the Sangh networks, some of it siphoned off from the funds the RSS had collected for the welfare of displaced refugees. To avoid legal traps, however, *Rashtradharma* was not registered in the name of Bhaurao or Deendayal. The mouthpiece would not mention any association with the RSS at all.

The first issue had Atal's imprint all over it. The magazine opened with his celebrated 'Hindu Tan Mann'. Atal was not keen 'to put [his] poem on the first page. But Bhauraoji kept insisting, so I agreed.'[5] Contributions were either made in-house – Atal, Deendayal and Rajiv contributed an essay each – or gathered from the massive pool of the RSS's prominent workers and sympathizers.* The striking feature of the first issue was its romanticization of cultural revival and lack of concern with the specific problems of the day. Most articles either highlighted the glory of ancient India or presented historical fiction based on Hindu scriptures. Atal's essay, which he had been working on since Kanpur, was published as 'Muslim Rajya: Beej, Vikas aur Fal' – Muslim State: Seed,

* The back cover of *Rashtradharma*'s first issue carried an ad for 'Krishnayan', a mahakavya (epic in verse), based on the life of Lord Krishna, which attempted to do for Krishna what Tulsidas had done for Ram. Its author was Dwarka Prasad Mishra, a Congressman, now a 'Minister, Central Provinces and Berar'. The book had an effusive blurb by another celebrated Congressman, Rajendra Prasad, who called it 'epoch-making and, like *Ramcharitmanas*, deserves to find a place in every house'.

Growth and Fruit. At nineteen pages and more than 8,000 words, it was an angry, passionate, elliptical, rambling piece of polemic attempting an overarching summary of the long history of Islam in India.

'The seeds of this poisonous tree [partition] were sown not in 1940' when the League first passed a resolution demanding a separate homeland for Indian Muslims, 'not even 150–200 years ago' when the British ensconced themselves in India through trade, deceit and support from local elites, 'rather many, many centuries ago, with meticulous planning and a definite objective that had now at last come to fruition'.[6] Islam's mission had never been 'to trade and exploit the society economically. Nor did they intend to settle their rapidly increasing population here. They had only one motto: kill the infidels, spread Islam.'[7]

Just as 'we' in his poems implied a homogeneous community of Hindus, 'they' referred to a global network of Islam at the turn of the first millennium. While historical accounts lean towards the economic rather than the religious motives for the frequent attacks from the north-west, nearly all agree that the Afghans, Turks and Persians were also frequently at each other's throats. At a time when Hindus–Sikhs were killing and, in turn, getting killed by Muslims, this narrative brought a certain urgency. Centuries-old events were inspiring many – some of them from the RSS, not unlike Atal – to kill and, if need be, die to save India for the Hindus.

The essay moved swiftly to the seventeenth century, when the British arrived, with Atal arguing that the 'Muslim Sultanate' was gasping for its last breath as the Marathas had wrested power back from the Mughals. After the soldiers' mutiny in 1857, the British began to realize that to rule India the best strategy was to have an Anglo-Muslim axis that could be used to counter the Hindus. As the Muslims 'shed tears at Bahadur Shah's grave, they pledged to awaken political consciousness ... to once again establish the rule of Muslims in Hindustan'. Atal charged Muslim politicians and intellectuals with steering the Muslim masses towards separatism: 'Only two years after the Congress was founded, on 20 December 1887, Syed Ahmed Khan made a historic speech in Lucknow supporting a policy of separatism and exhorting Muslims to boycott Congress.' Similarly, the essay marshalled poems from Allama Iqbal's popular 1909 collection of Urdu verses, *Shikwa* (Lament), extolling the glories of the past, lamenting to Allah the downgraded fortunes of Muslims, stoking a desire for an exclusive new homeland.

In the early twentieth century, the British 'asked the Hindus and Muslims to first unite before they would give us any reforms'. But it was only the Hindus who 'kept chasing the mirage of Hindu-Muslim unity, and always lost in our quest. The British kept the Muslims in good humour by giving them a large chunk of benefits. We the Hindus kept looking to them with expectant eyes, and whenever we got a piece or a half, satisfied ourselves and made shrieks of sacrifice ... In the beginning Congress at least nominally opposed the separate electorates in the name of unity and nationalism, but accepted it in 1916.' This sentence had a clever evasion. Atal did not name Tilak, but he was tangentially blaming the mentor of the Mahasabha–RSS founders for having facilitated the partition. The Congress was cowardly and devoid of political instincts, a party supposedly representing Hindus, but one that failed to understand the designs of the Anglo-Muslim axis. A tiny group of cruel and shrewd British men running India were keen to use all available tools – suppression, constitutional reforms, diplomacy – to prolong their empire.

Atal now came to the man whom everyone in the RSS and the Mahasabha detested: Mahatma Gandhi. They thought Gandhi useful as a moralist and spiritualist, but essentially devoid of political instincts. World War I (1914–18) had, Atal wrote, 'fuelled the Pan-Islamist ambitions of Indian Muslims. Around this time, Gandhiji, along with the Ali brothers, frequently invited the Afghans to invade India. But fortunately the Gandhi-Muslim conspiracy got noticed, and thus 30 years ago that disgusting attempt to convert India into Pakistan was thwarted.'[8]

This was in fact the oldest RSS–Mahasabha charge against Gandhi, made famous by elders such as B. S. Moonje repeating it ad nauseam over the decades. Some background here is necessary: During May–June 1919, the Afghans and the British had fought a bloody war ending in 2,000 casualties, both Afghan and British-Indian, before a peace treaty was signed. Towards the end of 1919, Gandhi had also begun mobilizing support from Hindus and Muslims for the joint Khilafat and Non-Cooperation movements. In a *Young India* article on 4 May 1921, Gandhi wrote he would 'in a sense, certainly assist the Amir of Afghanistan, if he waged war against the British Government. That is to say, I would openly tell my countrymen that it would be a crime to help a Government which had lost the confidence of a nation to remain in power.' In the same article Gandhi clarified what he meant: that the British government often used geopolitics and 'the Afghan bogey' to deny independence to India, and thus 'kept us under the perpetual fear of our neighbours and the whole world, and drained India of her splendid resources, so that she has lost faith in herself either for defence or for dealing with the simple problem of the growing poverty'.[9]

Perhaps because the article created some confusion, Gandhi clarified two weeks later that 'not only do I not want the Afghans or anybody to come to our assistance' by invading India, but that he would in fact 'strain every nerve to keep the Afghans out of the Indian border'.[10] Still, there was nothing more brutal and immoral than for Indians to be ruled by the British, and he could 'contemplate an Afghan invasion with perfect equanimity so far as India's safety is concerned' even though 'it is a superstition to suppose that they will overrun India if the British post at the frontier was withdrawn'. Atal's claim that Gandhi was 'inviting' the *Muslim* Afghans to attack *Hindu* India was a serious leap of interpretation.

Interestingly, Atal also came to see the Quit India movement of 1942 in a new light. Exactly five years before, he had been locked up in the Agra jail for sabotaging government property. Now he declared Quit India to be a waste of time and resources. 'Whereas the second world war was a time to strengthen ourselves militarily, the opportunity was wasted on individual satyagraha which ended, as always, with sitting purposelessly in the jail. During this period the League, on the other hand, made strides: they used the opportunity to form governments in many provinces, and to send Muslims in hordes in the imperial army.' Muslims had successfully used terror and diplomacy by turns, and a fearful and confused Congress surrendered: 'For the greed of the colonial office, they agreed to the nation being chopped into pieces. Iron-man Patel, who had announced that "even if earth and skies come together, we will not give them Pakistan", supported the partition. Even after saying "Kill me before you divide the country", Gandhiji agreed to the proposal for creation of Pakistan by the Congress Working Committee.' The creation of Pakistan was 'a political abortion unparalleled in the world history' with three butchers – the British, the Muslim League and the Gandhi-led Congress.

The dangers from Islam did not end with the 'fruit' – the creation of Pakistan. The Muslims in Pakistan 'aim to first make themselves stable there, and then trample on the rest [of India].' Quoting a recent editorial from the Muslim League mouthpiece, *Dawn*, which suggested that 'the five crore Muslims, who are forced to live in the Hindu-India, will have to fight another battle for their freedom', Atal argued that the Muslims who had opted to live in India were to be seen as traitors:

> After Pakistan came into existence, Indian Muslims have changed colours like lizards. They keep pledging their loyalty to the Indian Union, and have agreed to bow down before the tricolour flag. Some people are overexcited to see this sudden change in their mentality. In reality this is no reason to be happy. The Muslims have only one motive, and that is to strengthen Pakistan. And to fulfil this overarching goal, they are desperate to do everything ... Thinking of Hindus as disunited, the League will do everything to weaken India's strength, and in that struggle the Indian Muslims will act as fifth columnists.[11]

In the summer of 1947, what Atal was writing was popular belief among Hindus – including many senior Congressmen. It was forgotten that many Muslims had in fact voted Congress, not Muslim League, in the 1945–46 elections. Hardly a Muslim who chose to live in India was part of the global Islamic jihad network, as Atal believed.

'Despite losing Dunkirk, the British did not lose the second world war.' This prompted Atal to return, almost abruptly, from fearing a total takeover of India by Islam to a 'pious image of undivided Hindu Rashtra that throbs in our hearts': 'From the glacial peaks of Hindukush to the blue waters that wash Kanyakumari's feet, from the shores of the great Indus to the torrents of Brahmaputra, Hindustan is one – undivided, indivisible ... This so-called Land of the Pure is only a dwarfish Muslim state. We have brought the ruin of many Muslim empires in past; so many times we have merged back Pakistan into Hindustan.'

The partition was only an embarrassing interlude that had to be undone at a favourable moment. But the co-editor did not explain how exactly this was going to be achieved. By the end of August 1947, the causes of partition were irrelevant. Only the effect mattered: an ongoing genocide. Any attempt to undo partition by force would lead to an infinitely bigger loss of lives and property. And if by some wild chance the reunification became a possibility, would it guarantee protection of life and property for all Hindus and Muslims for all time to come?

In retrospect, Atal's confused essay is the most succinct summary of Hindutva's neurosis and lack of intellectual coherence or organizational strategy in 1947. If the RSS–Mahasabha dreamt of Akhand Bharat – a reunified India – why were they so keen to write off all Muslims who had chosen to live in India as traitors? Why were they plotting across provinces (as the government would soon find out) to force these Muslims to vacate India?

The first issue of *Rashtradharma* did well, partly because the RSS sympathizers everywhere purchased it. Atal was ecstatic: 'We in fact had to print an extra 500 copies.'[12] The next issue stood out for its articles by two people Atal revered. One was by V. D. Savarkar, the chief theorist of Hindutva; his piece was a summary in Hindi of his popular 1923 essay 'Essentials of Hindutva' written while in prison in Ratnagiri. The second one was on *Rashtra-raksha* – Guarding the Nation – by a certain 'Krishn Behari Lal Vajpayee BA, LLB'.

Babuji, who may have been one of the oldest people in the country to earn a law degree, clearly liked to flaunt it. Like other contributors, Babuji too fired into Gandhi: 'For the man who preaches "die if you must but never kill", the most lethal weapon is suicide. Bhagwan Krishna has called such men impotent ... Had political leadership been in stronger hands, we wouldn't have had to make such sheepish, disgusting compromise [of partition], nor would we have had to see such massacre and demonic acts.'[13] Mellowing a little afterwards, he lamented that Gandhi's steadfast idealism in politics was the 'height of unfamiliarity with human behaviour'. Babuji ended by recommending that Gandhi, who claimed to have offered a vision of Ram Rajya, ought to reread Tulsidas. After all, on the way to Lanka to bring back Sita, even Ram had to threaten the tempestuous sea to calm down to allow his makeshift army of monkeys to cross: 'Bole Ram sakopi tab, bhay bin hoye na preeti' – Ram was forced to concede that without fear there could be no love or friendship. In case anyone forgot, for 'Ram Rajya to flourish Ravan's destruction was necessary'.

All 6,000 copies of the second issue were sold out. Vaulting on the success of the first two issues, the RSS purchased a printing press of its own in the Sadar Bazaar area of Lucknow. The entire team moved into the premises of the newly designated 'Bharat Press'. Since the office was short-staffed, everyone taught themselves the nuts and bolts of publishing: composing (every single letter had to be set by hand), proofreading, working the machine, binding and, on occasion, carrying copies on their bicycles to deliver to subscribers.

With time the mouthpiece began to occasionally threaten the government. The joint October–November 1947 issue saber-rattled: 'Brave Hindu sangathanists can't be scared away by Nehru and his coterie. To guard the honour and pride of Hindus, they would not hesitate in meeting fate. But imagine what would happen if they succeeded in establishing the Hindu state? What fate should then befall Nehru and other betrayers of Hindu Rashtra?'[14] An article in December mourned Gandhi's habit of juxtaposing verses from the Quran and the Gita in his prayer meetings: 'It only means that non-Hindus have come to heavily influence his psyche.' Gandhi was an egotist whose achievements were 'personal, his failures social: in his victory Hindus have only lost.'[15]

The work never ended. Atal translated contributions from Marathi into an effortfully Sanskritized Hindi. He also desperately asked everyone he knew – family and friends in Gwalior, batchmates from Kanpur, the Sangh brotherhood in different cities – to write for free. The young co-editor was overworked but hardly unfulfilled. The November issue carried a 'happy announcement' of the launch of its 'weekly edition'. Atal and Rajiv Lochan Agnihotri would jointly edit the new mouthpiece too.

Atal also occasionally donned a city reporter's hat. One such occasion was 6 January 1948, when he went to hear Deputy Prime Minister Patel, who had come to Lucknow to address a crowd of Muslims. Lucknow had in the recent past been a popular centre for the Muslim League, many of whose supporters were still undecided on whether or not to stay in India. Atal heard a prominent Congressman from Bihar, Syed Mahmud, making a 'provocative and threatening speech' on behalf of Muslims, 'hearing which Sardar Patel's face turned red with anger. "Those of you who feel even a little bit of affection for Pakistan must leave India at the earliest," thundered Patel.'[16] What Pakistan was doing in Kashmir was wrong, and Indian Muslims 'should boldly come forward to denounce Pakistan'. If they did not, 'their professions of loyalty would be suspect'.[17] Patel was being harsh, for many Muslims who had chosen to live in India had repeatedly pledged their loyalty.[18]*

This rebuke to Muslims from the toughest Congressmen was music to Atal's ears: 'after hearing Sardar Patel's frank speech, the faces of fundamentalist Muslim politicians there drooped, while the patriotic citizens in the crowd clapped fervently'. He was also thrilled to hear what Patel had to say about the Sangh: 'In the Congress those who are in power feel that by virtue of authority they will be able to crush the RSS. By force you cannot suppress an organization, danda is meant for thieves and dacoits ... RSS men are not thieves and dacoits. They are patriots ... Only their trend of thought is diverted. They are to be won over by Congressmen with love.'[19] Patel also mildly chided the RSS and the Mahasabha: 'No good will be served by remaining aloof. If you think that you are the only custodians of Hinduism, you are mistaken ... There is much more tolerance in Hinduism than is interpreted for it in certain quarters.' Patel invited both the RSS and the Mahasabha 'to join the Congress' and appealed to the RSS 'not to weaken the administration by creating unrest in the country'.[20]

Atal may have noticed that some of Patel's sting was directed at Nehru. But he did not know that, far from winning over the RSS, Nehru had

* For example Amir Ali Khan, the prince of Mahmudabad, had resigned on 21 October from the Muslim League, saying it had 'outlived its utility and it should be wound up': 'Faithful Indian Muslims are determined to die fighting for the Indian Union, even if this fight be against the Dominion of Pakistan.'

been for several months desperate to ban it. No one in the RSS knew that only the previous week, on 29 December, Nehru had reprimanded UP premier Pant: 'You told me that you were going to take action against the RSS. When is this going to happen?'[21] More generally, the prime minister was worried that many of his fellow 'Congressmen, without thinking, are attracted to this development of fascist and Nazi modes of thought and practice ... we will ignore it at our peril.'[22] The confrontation between Nehru and Patel had reached a crescendo in January 1948. It called for a climax.

Nehru and Patel had both been part of Gandhi's innermost circle, each staking his youth and family life to the freedom struggle. But after they joined office in the interim government, in mid-1946, their differences of upbringing and temperament gradually began to hamper the administrative work that demanded a great degree of collaboration.* Aware of Gandhi's preference for Nehru to lead India after independence, Patel had grabbed three fat ministries: Information and Broadcasting; Home, which gave him command over the mammoth police and intelligence apparatus; and the newly created States ministry, whose task was to beseech or beat the 560-odd maharajas and nawabs into merging with the yet-to-be-born Indian Union. With three ministries and an iron grip on the Congress organization, Deputy Prime Minister Patel was in many ways as powerful as Prime Minister Nehru.

Soon after Patel took over as Home Minister, the outgoing intelligence chief N. P. A. Smith strongly recommended that he ban private armies like the RSS: 'This may, perhaps, not be a practicable proposition in the immediate present of communal sensitiveness, but it should clearly be a target for the future.'[23] Smith's concern was genuine, for the same month

* As someone who had as an adolescent ploughed the fields in his village in Gujarat, Patel scorned Nehru's socialist, anti-capitalist vision as too text-bookish. By the end of 1946, Viceroy Archie Wavell noticed that Patel 'with [the industrialist G. D.] Birla's backing was trying to break Nehru'. Quietly at first, Patel had also begun to regard Gandhi's advice 'with some contemptuous tolerance'.

(November 1946) the RSS was found engineering a riot in Meerut.[24] Patel disregarded the advice. With the League's success, he had become bitter about Muslims. He felt he could rely on a Hindu volunteer organization like the RSS far more than communists or Muslim volunteer outfits.

During the partition violence in Punjab and Delhi, Patel availed the RSS's services. He nominated the Punjab RSS chief, Dewan Badri Das, as the acting governor, and gave the Sangh the 'whole work of organizing refugees coming from Pakistan'.* The relief work they carried out among the incoming refugees in Delhi was an insignificant fraction of what the tragedy required.† But with a high-pitched campaign, the RSS volunteers managed to grab a lion's share of the credit.

Not until the partition violence was Nehru alerted to the mischief by the RSS and the Akalis.‡ Thereafter, he called them 'terrorists' and

---

* As per D. R. Goyal, a young pracharak in Punjab, who later became a bitter critic of the Sangh, 'for their work in evacuating refugees from West Punjab, Congress leaders of Punjab almost entirely gave themselves up to the RSS'. Just as often, they also indulged in killing and arson and forcing Muslims to vacate India. The RSS's modus operandi was such that while many of its members were arrested for manufacturing bombs and grenades, the organization itself was careful that none of its office bearers were linked to such activities.

Ved Mehta's memoir *The Ledge Between the Streams* has revealing insights from an articulate RSS full-timer of Lahore, who hated Gandhi and Buddha for having made the Hindus effeminate and cowardly: 'We Hindus have to change if we are to survive and rule India – the only language a Muslim understands is that of a knife and a grenade.' One side effect was that the half-trained RSS volunteers made grenades that sometimes exploded prematurely and blew them up.

† In *Secularism, Decolonisation, and the Cold War in South and Southeast Asia*, the historian Clemens Six documents the Sangh's significant growth in the national capital, from merely six branches in 1937 to around 100 at the time of partition. On 26 August, the RSS men put up posters in Old Delhi announcing that on 30 August 'all remaining Muslims in Delhi would be slaughtered'. Many local leaders of the RSS were arrested. But they were released after half an hour 'by order of the Congress high command' – meaning Patel's office. In the charged atmosphere of violence in Delhi, the RSS became increasingly popular among the Congressmen and bureaucrats. Many of the seniormost police officials in Delhi had family in West Pakistan and their suffering at the hands of Muslims across the haphazardly drawn Radcliffe Line made them keen for revenge: they 'secretly encouraged RSS people and Hindu Sabhites'. It would have taken tremendous effort for the home minister to completely purge the administration of the RSS influence, and Patel had neither the time nor the inclination for it. The RSS was also keen to enlist many of the incoming Sikh and Hindu refugees.

‡ Until August 1947, Nehru had neither occasion nor the means to seriously ponder the question of the RSS – or of Hindu communalism in general. One of the fallouts of turf

'fascists', who were 'no different than Jinnah's thugs'.[25] The prime minister indirectly blamed his deputy: 'Had the intelligence system been effective, the movement might have been nipped in the bud.'[26] He tried convincing Patel, unsuccessfully, to throw out the RSS's sympathizers in the police and administration.* Speaking to Viceroy Mountbatten, who was dispatched by London to oversee the partition, Patel ridiculed Nehru: 'I regret our leader has followed his lofty ideas into the skies and has no contact left with the earth or reality.'[27] On the communal question, the trust gap between the two soon widened beyond repair.†

Two events in September–October 1947 drove Nehru's ire. One was in the United Provinces, which fell under the supervision of Atal's boss Bhaurao Deoras. The UP Police led by B. B. L. Jaitley raided the RSS premises in Kandhla village of Muzaffarnagar and came back with 'incontrovertible evidence of a dastardly conspiracy to create a communal holocaust throughout the western districts of the province'.[28] They seized

---

wars between Nehru and Patel was that at the peak of communal violence, the prime minister had no access to real-time intelligence. For many weeks, Nehru did not know that the RSS in Punjab had collaborated with the Akalis and the ex-INA soldiers.

* On 30 September Nehru complained to Patel that 'while the connection of the RSS with disturbances [in Delhi and Punjab] is fairly well known, still noted members of the RSS were appointed as special magistrates and special police officers. This seemed very odd to me.' Patel replied that most of these appointees were Congressmen, and he could not help it if some of them had begun to sympathize with the RSS.

† Nehru quietly encouraged his close associate, the fiery and wealthy Mridula Sarabhai, to set up an 'independent intelligence organisation manned by many workers' which issued, exactly like the IB, cyclostyled bulletins which she sent to everyone who mattered – including Patel, who by now disliked her more than mildly. Sarabhai put up tented camps near all police stations in Delhi to be run by volunteers. She believed that the 'administration was partial to [the incoming Hindu] refugees and hostile to [resident] Muslims and that in general, the police could not be trusted.'

Rightists in the cabinet had different plans: Defence Minister Baldev Singh, a Sikh known to be close to Tara Singh and the Akalis, was flirting with the idea of training the RSS and Akalis in East Punjab to be sent across to West Punjab as spies to gather intelligence. On 6 October 1947, Baldev Singh wrote to Patel suggesting that 'to organize a secret service' across the border was 'the only way we can get reliable information and I feel we should not hesitate to take the help of such people': 'Rashtrya Sawam Sewak Singh [sic] will supply trained men for "Field Work" and Shree Golwalkarjee, the head of Sang[h] might be consulted. Other such organisations in the Punjab, still secretly working, can also be asked to give help.' A copy of this letter was marked to the Minister for Industry and Supply, Dr Syama Prasad Mookerji, the only Mahasabha leader in the central Cabinet.

two large steel trunks containing accurate maps of 'every town and village in the vast area, prominently marking out the Muslim localities and habitations'.*

In Jammu & Kashmir, where Maharaja Hari Singh had rejected the option of joining India and instead chosen independence, the RSS had offered to help counteract the influence of the pro-Congress National Conference, which had a huge following among the Muslims in the valley of Kashmir.† Towards the end of September, the RSS joined the Jathas from Patiala state, whose maharaja was a close friend of Hari Singh, and together they 'crossed the border and were massacring Muslims' in Kashmir's villages.[29] They were joined in this by Hari Singh's own Dogra soldiers. The maharaja claimed, with some justification, that his troops were merely securing Kashmir against armed raiders from Pakistan who had entered the state in the first week of September. But there was no justification for driving out Muslims from the maharaja's stronghold of Jammu. Muslims had been a thin majority in Jammu, and were now being forced by the RSS as well as Hindu–Sikh refugees from West Punjab to vacate, or get killed.

Hagiographies by RSS insiders claim that Golwalkar's services were employed by Patel to impress upon the maharaja, who held the RSS chief in great esteem, to join the Indian Union. Golwalkar's letters from September 1947 in Marathi to the RSS's regional organizer of Punjab

---

* Pant simply said he would place the matter 'for consideration by Cabinet at its next meeting'. The officials were aghast at the premier's pusillanimity, but Jaitley also realized that Pant, who had dealt strictly with the Mahasabha agitation only two months before, had his limits: 'RSS sympathisers, both covert and overt, were to be found in the Congress party itself and even in the Cabinet'. RSS roots had gone so deep into the body politic that even when police came up with robust evidence against it, the provincial Congress high command hesitated to act.

† The National Conference leader Sheikh Abdullah enjoyed Nehru's friendship and trust, and was asked to take over the governance of the state from the maharaja. Obviously His Highness resisted this encroachment. With the government funds at their disposal in Punjab, the RSS had also quickly set up an organizational network in the neighbouring J&K. The RSS 'got active support from the Maharaja who wanted to use them against Sheikh Abdullah. The RSS responded to the friendship on purely communal considerations and in spite of the fact that he was reluctant to accede to India.'

and J&K, Madhavrao Muley, do mention his plans to make a 'trip to Srinagar on a chartered flight' in mid-October 'to meet the Maharaja of Kashmir'.[30]

Golwalkar, with his long, flowing hair and intense eyes, vermilion on forehead, clad in a silk kurta and moving about in chartered planes, conjures the image of a dubious godman rather than a pious soul involved in cultural renaissance. He met the maharaja on the morning of 18 October. But the claim that 'Guruji made an important contribution' in J&K's accession to India is doubtful because the maharaja continued to vacillate.[31] On 22 October, His Highness's life turned upside down when Pathan tribals from the north pounced on Kashmir, determined to capture Srinagar. Five days later he was forced, out of desperation, to sign the instrument of accession.

Nehru was worried the RSS's involvement in killing innocent Muslims in Kashmir could be used by Pakistan to corner India diplomatically: 'If by any chance the UNO intervenes, it is Sheikh Abdullah and his following that will impress them and show them that the people of Kashmir are fighting for their freedom against the raiders. The RSS will merely support Liaquat Ali Khan's case against us.'*[32] The assessment was accurate. On 8 December, Mountbatten called a meeting in Lahore to discuss Kashmir. The two prime ministers traded charges as to which side had begun the attack first. Liaquat asserted that the tribesmen attacked only after the 'Akali Sikhs and RSS bands' began to murder the Muslims in Jammu. Nehru refuted the allegation, but the damage was done.

By this time Nehru was suspicious that the RSS was in J&K 'with Patel's connivance.'[33] He sought help from Gandhi, who still exerted

---

* In J&K too, the prime minister found out about the RSS's deadly excursions a few weeks late. On 30 October, a livid Nehru complained to Patel that 'RSS volunteers have been organised in East Punjab to be sent to Jammu for a campaign against the Muslims.' However, Nehru was confident, as he wrote to a friend two weeks later, that 'the fate of Kashmir is not going to be decided by the RSS, not even of Jammu, and the sooner this is appreciated the better. The only person in the state who, as an individual, will have the biggest say in the matter will be Sheikh Abdullah. If anyone can save Kashmir, it is Sheikh Abdullah and not the RSS or anyone else.'

great moral authority over the government.* On 16 November, a secret session of the AICC in Delhi reviewed the question of the communal organizations and private armies. Gandhi's unequivocal opinion was that their rise was 'fraught with tremendous dangers'. [34] Private armies like the RSS 'must be regarded as a menace to the hard-won freedom of the country' and ought to be banned.[35] Patel was not convinced, for a meeting of provincial premiers and home ministers a few days later 'unanimously agreed that the stage when the Sangh should be dealt with as an association had not arrived and that individuals should be continued to [be] dealt with sternly as hitherto.'[36] This was serious evasion.

On the evening of 8 December, Golwalkar bragged at a secret RSS meeting on the outskirts of Delhi that Mahatma Gandhi could easily be killed: 'We have the means whereby such men can be immediately silenced, but it is our tradition not to be inimical to Hindus. If we are compelled, we will have to resort to that course too.'[37] Sounding more like a military commander of the medieval Maratha Confederacy than a celibate sage, Guruji gave the call to prepare 'for guerrilla warfare on the lines and tactics of Shivaji. The Sangh will not rest content until it has finished Pakistan.' They had nothing to fear from the government, which would sooner or later crumble before the sheer force of RSS support: 'If anyone stood in our way we will have to finish them too, Nehru Government or any other Government.'[38]

There remains a key question about the winter of 1947–48: Why was Patel soft on the RSS despite being asked by everyone – from Smith to Jaitley, Nehru to Gandhi – to act against them? Patel confided to Jaitley that it was 'extremely difficult to ban the RSS because he thought that the Muslims were against them [the Congress government] and that he did not want Hindu public also to go against them'.[39] Even though intelligence reports pointed towards vague threats of a right-wing coup,

* The Mahatma had himself met Golwalkar a few times: at the first meeting he was 'partly impressed', but by the third meeting he had come to have a 'very strong opinion against Golwalkar and the RSS and said that it was impossible to rely on their words' – that the RSS felt 'no compunction in acting in exact contradiction to what they said'. This was a shrewd and accurate assessment of an organization that used duality as a conscious strategy.

Patel knew these were largely empty threats.* As Nehru and Patel had shown in Kashmir, a determined Indian state was capable of crushing armed aggression. For now the Sardar had assigned himself higher priorities – such as settling the geography of Kashmir and Hyderabad and tackling the rising communist threat. Even though he was aware of the RSS sabotaging the administration, the deputy PM only chided them mildly.

Speaking in Jaipur on 17 December, he 'appreciated the enthusiasm of young men, but that should be diverted into constructive channels. There is a great deal to be done to make India militarily strong. Very substantial industrial effort must back the army. All that cannot be achieved by the lathis of the Sangh which are being used for breaking the heads of a handful of Muslims.' There was no point in hoping to subsume Pakistan back into the Indian Union; it would come 'of its own accord' if it must.[40] The year 1947 closed with Nehru grumbling to Patel about the RSS sabotaging 'Abdullah's efforts at creating order' in the Himalayan valley, and the deputy brushing off the reports as unreliable.[41]†

When Atal heard Patel's speech in Lucknow on 6 January, the young editor did not know that the latter's eloquence and bluntness was a result of his rift with Nehru becoming 'dangerously wide'. The buzz in Delhi's diplomatic circles was that the Sardar 'might possibly resign from the

---

* The intelligence reports variously mentioned the RSS stashing arms in Jammu and Alwar; of the Akalis manufacturing weapons at Tarn Taran; and that a number of central Indian rulers had been meeting regularly with communal organizations at Katra in Rajgarh to formulate a plan 'to overthrow the Nehru Govt'.

† To defend J&K state from external aggression, arms and ammunitions were sent to be divided between the maharaja's state army and Abdullah's newly appointed homeguards. It turned out that some arms from the quota were diverted to RSS men, possibly with Patel's knowledge. On 30 December, Nehru complained to Patel 'about the way the arms we have sent for them have been kept back and distributed to RSS people. While Jammu was in imminent danger, a large part of the consignment of arms was just held back and Bakshi's Home Guards were fighting often without rifles and always with too little ammunition and dying in the process … the RSS is being supported and armed at the cost of Bakshi's Home Guards and propaganda is being openly carried on by posters and otherwise against Sheikh Abdullah. In some distant parts of the State, where there are no invaders, the RSS is creating trouble by sending their emissaries.'

Government and go into opposition'.[42] There were also rumours that four other ministers wanted to resign. These included Industries Minister Syama Prasad Mookerji and Defence Minister Baldev Singh, with whom the Deputy PM got along rather well. Patel may have entertained a vague idea of leading sometime in the near future a right-of-centre front comprising Congress conservatives, RSS–Mahasabha, Akalis and others.

The new weekly mouthpiece to be launched on 14 January 1948 was given the name *Panchjanya*, after Krishna's shankh – conch shell – which he blew to energize the Pandavas against the Kauravas in the Mahabharata war at Kurukshetra. The name subtly signalled that the Bharat Press Pandavas were itching for a confrontation with the Nehru-led Kauravas. Published in a fifteen-by-ten-inch format, *Panchjanya* was almost twice the size of *Rashtradharma*. Unlike the monthly, the weekly's focus was current affairs with a sprinkling of op-eds, historical fiction, satire, memoir, letters. It keenly sought advertisements, proclaiming that its copies 'reach all of India', and promising '20 percent commission' to agents who helped to bring in ads, provided they were 'not foreign or vulgar or unaesthetic'.[43] In its second week, *Panchjanya* declared itself India's leading Hindi weekly – 'Hindustan ka pramukh Hindi saptahik'.[44]

On 14 January, the festive day of Makar Sankranti, 600 kilometres away in Delhi the clouds were ominous. The previous day Gandhi had sat on a fast unto death. The stated purpose was to restore communal relations in the wake of the recent riots, though Gandhi was also upset with the Cabinet for withholding the payment of sterling balances that India owed to Pakistan. Another aim was to bring about reconciliation between Nehru and Patel. A British High Commission cable noted that 'any improvement in the communal situation in the Indian Union resulting from Gandhi's fast must certainly strengthen Nehru's policy that India should not become a theocratic state'. There was also speculation of 'some definite understanding' between Nehru and Gandhi 'that at some given moment the fast would be raised'.[45]

Even as a weakened Gandhi lay in pain at Birla House, RSS volunteers marched through central Delhi shouting slogans that the old man should feel free to die: 'Boodhe ko marne do.'[46] For formality's sake, however, by the fifth day of Gandhi's fast even RSS folks were forced to pledge themselves to protect Muslims. An observer wondered: 'Time alone will show whether the RSS's association with other parties in giving these assurances [seven assurances for the protection of Muslim life, property and faith] represents a real change of heart by this organization or whether it is only temporary change brought about by moral pressure from Congress and other leaders.'[47]

There was no change of heart. In the second issue of *Panchjanya*, Atal and friends mocked Gandhi, asking, 'Hridayon Ke Toofaan Band Ho Gaye Kya?' – Have the storms of your heart calmed down now? The weekly presumed that the fast had the calculated aim of hurting Hindu interests. At the beginning of his fast, Gandhi had mentioned to journalists that his fast was 'in the cause of the Muslims of India; as such, it is certainly against Hindus–Sikhs of India and the Muslims of Pakistan. But among his conditions to break his fast, there is not even one proposal on the minorities of Pakistan. On the contrary, many of his conditions would hurt the homeless minorities [of Hindus–Sikhs] from Pakistan who have thronged here.' *Panchjanya* especially took Gandhi to task for his fourth demand: 'Non-Muslims should not object to Delhi Muslims returning to their homes from Pakistan.' The mouthpiece argued that they were 'given military training by Pakistan … They had left India bag and baggage out of their love for Pakistan. Clearly, they are still emotionally tied to Pakistan. Would it be a good thing to trust them?'[48]

Gandhi's otherwise successful fast failed on one major count. The Deputy PM was still adamant on being 'released' from the government. In the early evening of 30 January, Patel had a long and intense but inconclusive conversation on the matter with Gandhi. Immediately after meeting Patel, Gandhi went to his evening prayers. 'He reached to see 500 people waiting for him,' *Panchjanya* reported a few days later.

> The crowd parted into two halves to give him way, and Mahatmaji went towards the platform. When he reached there, a 36-year-old man stepped forward to touch his feet: he told Mahatmaji, 'you are late today'.

> Mahatmaji responded with a yes. By then he had taken out a revolver, and fired on Mahatmaji. One bullet missed, but two of them hit him in the chest, and other two in his belly … The crowd immediately caught hold of the criminal. His name is Nathuram Vinayak Godse.[49]

This article was most likely a joint effort between Atal and Rajiv Lochan Agnihotri. Its detached tone had a special purpose: to inform all concerned that the RSS was a wholly separate entity from the Mahasabha. And, especially, that the RSS had nothing whatsoever to do with Godse killing Gandhi.

> Even though the criminal is a member of the Hindu Mahasabha, a rumour is being spread among people and government officials that the RSS is also involved in it … At many places Sangh workers have also been arrested. But as more evidence presents itself and the public anger subsides, the misconceptions will disappear, and the public will also be able to see the truth clearly.[50]*

Patel became the recipient of anger in high places for the lapse in security: some socialists and communists demanded his resignation. Devastated and numb, Patel was faced with a quandary he had avoided thus far. At first he considered banning both the RSS and the Mahasabha. But there existed 'no law at present' against communal political parties.[51] Also, banning the Mahasabha could look like a case of vendetta against a rival political party. Since the government had already been debating banning the RSS for maintaining a private army, it was convenient to simply do this, and separately nab the suspect members of the Mahasabha.

---

* It seems the relationship between the party and the volunteer organization had begun to get strained around 1945. During World War II, the RSS had grown exponentially and begun drawing the support of many conservative Congressmen in the provinces. Exactly around this time, the Mahasabha became depressed on account of having fared terribly in the 1945–46 elections. With patronage from the Congress conservatives, the RSS became less keen to openly oppose the Congress – the reason the RSS did not formally support the July 1947 satyagraha launched by the UP Mahasabha, even though its vice president doubled up as the RSS sanghchalak of Lucknow. They continued to work as closely as two organizations could. But with the RSS becoming more powerful than the Mahasabha now, the 'tail wags the dog'.

The ban had two components: the old complaint that the RSS functioned as a private army. The more urgent one was not so much the Sangh's direct involvement in Gandhi's murder as it was their inspiring an environment of hatred in which any aggrieved Hindu could have stabbed the Mahatma, or blown him away with a country-made bomb. In a carefully worded press communique on 4 February 1948, the Home Ministry informed everyone that in the recent past the government had given the RSS the benefit of the doubt. It reminded the RSS of the warning given to it only two months ago.

> The objectionable and harmful activities of the Sangh have, however, continued unabated and the cult of violence sponsored and inspired by the activities of the Sangh has claimed many victims. The latest and the most precious to fall was Gandhiji himself. In these circumstances, it is the bounden duty of the government to take affective measures to curb this reappearance of violence in a virulent form and, as a first step to the end, they have decided to declare the Sangh as an unlawful association.[52]

The Home Ministry's approach to enforcing the ban was mystifying. It should have begun with a crackdown on the RSS's central and provincial working committees and then, in top-down order, nabbed all other important workers. Instead, the circular sent to provinces with the guideline that '*all* leaders and active workers of the RSS should be arrested and detained under appropriate provisions' was interpreted literally. Over the next few weeks, 3,500 arrests were made in UP alone.[53] But this included only 250 ideologically driven hard nuts; the rest were casual shakha-goers, many of them minors from villages and small towns who were about to sit their school board exams in a few weeks. This gave the crackdown the nature of a spectacle.

What was Atal's immediate response to the news of Gandhi's murder? Given his temperament, he might not have personally approved of pumping bullets into the seventy-seven-year-old Mahatma's chest. He did not distribute sweets, as RSS–Mahasabha members had across the country, or condone those who 'drank liquor in celebration'.[54] But Atal most certainly did not consider Gandhi's death a serious loss to mankind.

The dozens of articles he had written and edited holding the Mahatma responsible for India's partition and condemning him for pandering to Muslims had most certainly contributed to poisoning the air that ultimately led to his assassination. He was exactly the kind of 'active worker' the government wanted to thrash.

Atal faced a tough time in Lucknow. The RSS's machismo had melted away: Golwalkar, who heard the news of Gandhi's murder on a tour to Madras, sent a telegram to Nehru and Patel expressing shock at the 'cruel and fatal attack on a great personality' – a calculated U-turn. He instructed the organization to observe a thirteen-day mourning at the 'sad death of revered Mahatmaji'.[55] Nehru howled in agony: 'These people have the blood of Mahatma Gandhi on their hands, and pious disclaimers and dissociation now have no meaning.'[56]

On 4 February, the provincial governments were asked to raid and seal 'all places which are used for purposes of the Sangh'. Everyone at Bharat Press knew it was the beginning of something terrible. And yet, they were keen to present their side of the story. Knowing they were running against time, they nervously rushed through the publication of the fourth issue: 'A request to the readers of *Panchjanya*: To explain this most catastrophic of events, we have advanced the publication of the issue, which is only eight pages. Our readers will hopefully forgive the inconvenience.'

Apart from dissociating itself from the Mahasabha and Godse, *Panchjanya* wanted to inform the government that 'in our hearts we revere the Mahatma as much as a Congress worker does. If differences are cited to be the reason [for the Sangh's alleged involvement in his murder], don't Congressmen disagree among themselves too?'[57] It lamented that the 'Sanghchalak of United Provinces, Narendrajeet Singh, and about 500 volunteers have been arrested and sent to the Kanpur Jail', and that 'warrant has been issued against many Sangh workers of Lucknow too.' On 5 February, the district magistrate of Lucknow ordered the police to raid every place associated with the RSS. All movable property was to be seized, the buildings sealed. The seized items included the press and cyclostyling machines, chequebooks, RSS uniforms (leather belts, black caps), photographs of Sangh leaders, a jeep, bicycles.[58] They tried to hide. But one by one, everyone in Atal's immediate circle got captured – Bhaurao in Kanpur, Deendayal in Delhi, Rajiv Lochan Agnihotri in Lucknow – and locked up in jails.

Except Atal. It helped that his name was not on the police's hit list for UP. He had been associated full-time with the RSS for less than six months, and then again only as an editor. Unlike the UP office bearers of the RSS, many of them now in jail, the police or the CID did not yet have a profile or photo of him. Shrewdness or luck – a bit of both perhaps – Atal was one of the few popular workers of the Sangh in UP who remained at large.*

Gandhi's gruesome murder shocked India into sanity. The plot was seen as a major intelligence failure, and the IB went into overdrive issuing false alarms. It suggested that the RSS was preparing for nationwide assassinations: the security of ministers was beefed up everywhere; some communists feared that they were going to be 'the first target now of the RSS, for, having removed Mahatma Gandhi from the scene, the only impediments to their dream of a Hindu Raj are the communist party of India and a few top-ranking leaders of the Congress'.[59] This was a bizarre exaggeration of the RSS's organizational strength as well as the level of coordination among the alt-rightists who, with help from maharajas, were said to be preparing to take over Delhi in a coup.†

In reality, the RSS was hit more severely than ever before. On the ground, some Congressmen helped secure the release of the RSS detainees – partly to buy their allegiance.[60] With varied success, communists and socialists too found in Gandhi's murder an occasion to poach its

* There exists no record of how exactly he evaded arrest in the first few days of the crackdown. It is possible that he hid himself at an unsuspicious place like his sister's house in the Aminabad area of Lucknow.

† By the end of February, Patel informed Nehru that 'the conspiracy of Bapu's assassination was not so wide as is generally assumed, but was restricted' to only ten men; 'it also clearly emerges from these statements that the RSS was not involved in it at all. It was a fanatical wing of the Hindu Mahasabha directly under Savarkar that [hatched] the conspiracy and saw it through.'

cadres. It was in this state of sagging spirits that the Sangh launched an underground movement, steered by mid-level full-timers like Atal who had evaded arrest.

Since the ban prohibited assembly, they began to hunt for safe proxies. In every province sprung up this social club and that sports team. Activities in UP where Atal was one of the underground leaders included: Hanuman Gada Club; Virendra Bhojanalaya; Deshbandhu Industries, a limited business concern; reading clubs named after Gandhi and Nehru; swimming trips to the Ganga and Gomti; volleyball games; marriages, and other private ceremonies.[61] There was no clear boundary between non-political activities – religious, social, educational, recreational – which were legal and political gatherings which were banned. The Punjab premier lamented to Patel that he was 'unable to lay our hands on them because outwardly they do not commit any offence'.[62]

Atal showed up in Allahabad to run the underground movement there. With all of its infrastructure seized and men imprisoned, the RSS had no means to communicate with its cadres or to defend itself against the government's charges. Either he or someone in the RSS got in touch with the celebrated publisher Ram Rakh Sehgal of Allahabad and convinced him to allow them to use his press for movement work.* Given the strict regulation of newsprint by the government, 'our problem was that the Sangh did not have paper,' recounted Devendra Swaroop, a young RSS volunteer who got acquainted with Atal around this time. They were both attached to *Crisis*, an English weekly of Sehgal's: '*Crisis* used to have articles by us, but only using pseudonyms.'[63]

A major drawback of the all-out crackdown was dispersed arrests and the unmanageable logistics of taking care of the mostly boisterous young volunteers, with the result that the police could not focus on nabbing the ringmasters. This resulted in a patchy implementation of the ban in most places. It would have taken sustained political and bureaucratic will

* Sehgal had sealed his reputation in the 1920s by publishing the ultra-progressive Hindi magazine *Chaand*, which advocated the choice of abortion for women (drawing rebuke from Gandhi in *Navjivan*), and carried pieces by young revolutionaries like Bhagat Singh before they became household names. By the mid-1940s, though, Sehgal's publishing concerns were making losses, his stardom had begun to fade, and by some accounts he had begun to sympathize with the Sangh.

to break the RSS – from amending the legal loopholes (to restrict RSS gatherings in the garb of clubs and picnics); to rigorously identifying and throwing out active RSS sympathizers from the government; to closing down publishers like Sehgal who were letting underground ringleaders like Atal use their press to present Sangh viewpoints. Had Nehru held the Home Ministry, some of this may have transpired. Patel lacked the will, especially after he was convinced that the RSS was not directly involved.*

The RSS needed an outsider to champion the cause of its innocence, preferably someone who knew both Nehru and Patel. They found a willing party in Mauli Chandra Sharma, a tier-two Delhi Congressman. Sharma had recently been responsible for the arrangements for Gandhi's cremation – from choosing the priest to ensuring that conches were blown and bells tolled as the crowd sat around the Mahatma's pyre. He was later praised by Congress conservatives for making sure the event looked appropriately Hindu, rather than like some 'Christian-style [minimalist] funeral' that Nehru had initially suggested.[64]

It speaks volumes of the porous boundary between the Congress and RSS–Mahasabha – *and* between secularism and communalism – that the man who made the arrangements for Gandhi's cremation was the son of a prominent Mahasabha leader. Assisted by Sangh volunteers, Sharma floated the 'Council of Civil Liberties' – Janadhikar Samiti – and began to meet every major politician to argue the RSS's innocence.

They managed to impress Patel, who was now unsure of what to do with the RSS. Kashmir and Hyderabad remained tense, and the RSS was desperate to offer its services.† Patel conveyed to Sharma that the government would deal with Hyderabad on its own, without help from

* The grief of Gandhi's murder, and the shock and anger at several parties holding him responsible for the death, imploded on 5 March when Patel suffered a massive heart attack. When he opened his eyes after the attack, Sardar's first words were, 'I had to go with Bapu. He has gone alone.'

† The mediator Sharma was keen to impress Patel with a plan to send a few thousand volunteers trained in guerrilla tactics to enter districts of Hyderabad adjoining Marathwada, and capture some territories and police posts. This would hopefully provoke the nizam into a confrontation, at which point the government could send in the army. The RSS had apparently even raised money for the operation, and it just needed Sardar's blessings and logistical support.

the RSS. But just in case the government needed them in an emergency, Patel added in English, 'Keep your boys ready in necessity.'[65] Here was the classic Patel dilemma on the question of communalism: he had recently written to S. P. Mookerji warning him of the long-term 'dangers inherent in an organisation run in secret on military or semi-military lines' and that he had 'received rather disquieting reports of the revival' of the RSS evidently defying the ban.[66] Yet, if the occasion demanded, he wouldn't shy away from strategically using them.

With the ban loosening in July, Atal came back to Lucknow. His co-editor Agnihotri had been released. The Bharat Press owners had filed petitions in the court. In the case of *Rashtradharma*, the Lucknow district sessions court gave, unbelievably, a favourable judgement saying there was 'no evidence to prove this journal's association with the RSS'.[67] Similarly, all seized material was returned because the volunteers argued successfully that these belonged to 'me and my friends personally'. The court declared itself unable to find that any of the items were used for the propagation of Sangh activities. *Panchjanya* resumed publication.

Atal remained low-key: he spent time publishing in *Panchjanya* old poems he had written in college. He read out his poems at events such as the one marked to celebrate Tulsidas's birth anniversary, presumably also an occasion to brainstorm on strategies to revoke the ban. Though Babuji was worried about the future of his brightest son, Atal did not return home. Gandhi's assassination plot was traced to Gwalior: the investigations revealed that Godse had procured his pistol there.* Most of the Bateshwar boys 'never went back to the Sangh' shakha.[68] The Vajpayees were lucky that the implementation of the ban by the durbar was poor. Babuji and Prem Behari did not get arrested.

Not long ago Viceroy Wavell had deemed Jivajirao Scindia 'a nice lad' who 'means well, but cares more for his horses and racing than anything else'.[69] The trauma of losing power had made His Highness a self-conscious strategist. Privately, he continued to court the RSS–Mahasabha leadership. But advised to cultivate a favourable image in

* There were rumours that Godse had practised shooting a dummy Gandhi at the house of Dr Parchure, who had been the recipient of Atal's rousing welcome speech many years before at school.

Sardar Patel's watchful eyes, he decided to butter up the government by offering a generous donation of ₹10 lakhs for Gandhiji's Memorial Fund. Patel replied to thank him but, aware of the Gwalior durbar's duality, bluntly added: 'By now you must have heard how deeply involved some of the Hindu Mahasabha circles in Gwalior [were in the Mahatma's murder]. Tongues are already wagging about the alleged part which Your Highness and the State have taken in promoting Mahasabha activities in the State ... It is fortunate that you withdrew yourself in time from this embarrassing situation. Otherwise, I am afraid you would have found yourself in deep waters.'[70] In his reply, the maharaja profusely thanked Patel for his 'fatherly interest in my welfare'.

Patel had now mastered the art of kissing his sacrificial lambs before chopping their heads off. In less than six months after the accessions were signed in mid-1947, he had decided that autonomous states were not feasible from the economic or security point of view. In states like Gwalior, he used the tragedy of the Mahatma's murder as a catalyst for full integration with India.[71] By mid-1948, Gwalior and adjoining kingdoms were merged into a new state called Madhya Bharat. As with maharajas elsewhere, His Highness Jivajirao Scindia was gifted the dummy post of governor, *rajpramukh*, in Gwalior.

On 17 July, Patel convened a meeting of the provincial premiers to discuss the future of the RSS. Prompted in large part by the Council of Civil Liberties, thousands of volunteers had filed habeas corpus applications, and the high courts across provinces produced judgements asking the government to release them. It was now decided to detain only the most troublesome ones, and release the rest. But most premiers bitterly complained that the RSS had violated the ban since the very beginning and that it refused to show any signs of remorse. Its members may or may have not killed Gandhi, but the older charge of the organization functioning like a private, secretive militia remained.[72] An undecided Patel was strictly advised to not revoke the ban.

Golwalkar was released in early August 1948 only to find himself under house arrest. He was not allowed to even publish an article without permission. The frustrated chief shot off angry letters to Nehru and Patel. Golwalkar refused to believe that the provincial premiers could have prevailed upon Patel. Writing to the prime minister on 11 August, Golwalkar pleaded the RSS's innocence in Gandhi's murder, and expressed concern about the fast-deteriorating 'mental condition of the authorities in general and yourself in particular' towards the RSS.[73] He ended the letter by asking Nehru to not let 'the ghastly dreams of last few months embitter our mutual love'. Golwalkar's chutzpah was on display again in another letter offering help to the government in fighting the communists: 'With the alarming happenings in Burma, Indochina, Java and other neighbouring states, we can envisage the nature of the menace.'[74] He urged Nehru to 'consider this problem coolly and help to create an atmosphere in which the RSS will be able to help the government' – smug and oblivious that Nehru hated communists less fervidly than he hated the RSS.

To be sure, Golwalkar's lack of tact or courtesy or basic reasoning could only partly be explained as anger. It was as much a result of his personal temperament and years of playing god incarnate to his subordinates, giving orders without having to explain their logic. Nehru was provoked.* But entangling himself would have meant encroaching on his deputy's turf, so he forwarded the correspondence.

Patel was keen to avoid a confrontation. The deputy PM urged 'bhai Shri Golwalkar' to abjure violence and 'revive Sangh by imbuing it with a fresh culture and policies. And that new culture and policies can only be based on the principles and values of the Congress.'[75] Patel was 'wholly convinced that the RSS can serve the country only by joining the Congress; not separately or in opposition.'

In another time Golwalkar may have considered the proposal favourably, but now the RSS chief's sizeable ego would not allow it: 'I believe that cultural work should be entirely free from the political

* Nehru replied to Golwalkar only sporadically. He pointed out the RSS's failed attempts to create a pogrom in Muzaffarnagar, adding that the 'UP government sent you a note on some of the evidence they had collected about such activities of the RSS'. Golwalkar hit back, mocking the prime minister: If the government had 'incriminating evidence against the RSS or certain of its members, is it not right to expect at least a few successful prosecutions against the alleged wrongdoers?'

scramble and should not be tagged on to any political party.'[76] Citing the government's lack of evidence of the RSS's involvement in violence anywhere, he demanded an unconditional revocation of the ban.

Patel was hurt by Golwalkar's curt response. He had invited Golwalkar to Delhi for negotiations; now he asked him to 'make immediate arrangements to return to Nagpur'. In reaction, on 13 December, the RSS chief exhorted his volunteers to launch a satyagraha: 'We have been forced into this only course by the narrow mindedness of the government, their greed for perpetration of party domination and their intolerance of the existence of every other form of thought and action.'[77] The Sardar had had enough. Over the next few hours, Golwalkar was swiftly arrested and carted off to Betul jail, where he was locked up once again.

In August 1948, around the time Golwalkar returned home to find himself confined in every way, Atal was sent to Banaras. The RSS was to launch 'the best Hindi weekly on truth, justice and fairness' that was 'soon to be published' from the holiest of Hindu cities. They named it *Chetna* – True Consciousness – and launching it may have been part of the RSS's older plan of expanding its communication outreach.[78] An issue would cost 30 paisa. The advertisements also offered, rather deviously, annual subscriptions for ₹10, even though a banned RSS knew that a minor confrontation with the government would shut it down.

Atal did not have the money to rent a space in Banaras to live or work. He found refuge in the house of an old friend from the OTC days, Rajaram Dravid, who lived in the Dudh Vinayak locality and had been a contributor to *Rashtradharma*. Dravid came from a Tamil family of Sanskrit scholars who had settled in Banaras. He was enrolled for a PhD in philosophy at the BHU. Atal was given a tiny room on the first floor of Dravid's house. From here he began to coordinate the publication of *Chetna*. Dravid's family, his mother especially, became fond of the amiable young editor. Atal in turn did not mind some affection and home-made food.

The bigger problem of newsprint and a printing press was solved by one Bhagwandas Arora, possibly with some reluctance. A small-time businessman with literary inclinations, Arora had spent the previous few years looking after Mahasabha work in Banaras city, so much so that he 'suffered heavy loss' in his businesses.[79] By December 1947, he had 'decided to keep aloof from the political sphere' and resigned from all his Mahasabha posts. He had a printing press in Ash Bhairo, and was hoping to launch a newspaper and make a livelihood out of it. The RSS seem to have convinced Arora to help: he allowed Atal to use his infrastructure.

A few hiccups notwithstanding, Atal managed to churn out a weekly mimicking *Panchjanya*'s fifteen-by-ten-inch format. It was 'published with Dravid's name on it' as the editor.[80] Atal operated shrewdly enough to not attract much attention. The first issue was strategically published on 2 October, the assassinated Mahatma's birthday. To butter up the government, the 'Sangh naturally wanted to identify itself with Gandhiji.'[81]

But Golwalkar's machismo made a clampdown inescapable. In the meantime, the UP CID also got wind of *Chetna*'s publication.[82] A raid in Banaras on 23 December produced 'about 3,000 cyclostyled bulletins and a cyclostyle machine. 13 persons were arrested in this connection under section 17, C.L.A. Act.'[83] The faux editor and the reluctant printer, Dravid and Arora, became the scapegoats and were taken to jail. The police found out about Atal and raided Dravid's house. But the kotwal was misled by Dravid's neighbours, and the ringleader had a narrow escape.[84] He went underground once again, no one knew where.

The fate of the RSS satyagraha called by Golwalkar in Delhi was no better. The chief had taken a risk grossly disproportionate to his resources. After a year of the ban, the RSS had no more than 3,000 hardcore volunteers. But the clarion call was given after Guruji conferred with his lieutenants in Delhi: the strategy was that after making a large number of arrests, the 'government would be compelled to negotiate'.[85] 'Every day about 30 to 40 volunteers would appear, shout slogans and be arrested,' the top police official of Delhi at the time recalled.[86] The plan was to send the volunteers in small batches so they could prolong the movement over two or three months.

Patel ordered the nuisance to be crushed in a week. It was decided to rob the satyagrahis of a chance at martyrdom: instead of throwing them in jail, the police were asked to 'take them to the borders of Delhi, give them a ducking in the Jamuna canal, and leave them there to shiver on a cold December night'. This time only the key people were to be nailed: the financiers and coordinators, as well as active sympathizers who were providing the satyagrahis food and lodging. With 200 blank warrants issued, most ringleaders were rounded up soon enough.

Seeing the satyagraha fizzle out, Golwalkar needed a face-saver. He opened talks with the government. Patel refused, asking him to first withdraw the satyagraha unconditionally. Some third-party mediators were brought on board to massage Golwalkar's trampled ego, convincing him, against all evidence, that the satyagraha had in fact achieved a 'moral victory'. The RSS chief called off the satyagraha on 20 January. The RSS workers arrested in UP included many minors, and the government's priority was to release them first as it did not want to 'blast off young lives'. When one such detainee emerged from the Lucknow Central Jail, he was surprised to be received at the entrance by the elusive Atalji.[87]

Meeting the provincial premiers again to discuss the unbanning of the RSS, the Home Ministry prepared a list of conditions. The RSS had to write up a detailed constitution. It had to make the source of its finances transparent, by publishing 'annual audited accounts'. So far, in the committees of the RSS, at all levels most people were nominated from above. From now on posts had to be filled only through elections. The RSS chief's power and functioning were not known with any degree of precision; the government wanted all traces of its dictatorial character removed. Golwalkar was reminded that every influential post in the Sangh was held by 'persons belonging to a particular community from a certain area' – Chitpawan Brahmins from and around Nagpur – and was asked to make it demographically diverse.[88] Lastly, the RSS's condition of a 'lifelong obligation' for full-time members had more in common with secret societies than with democratic groups functioning in full public view; this too had to change.[89]

Expectedly, Golwalkar exploded, shooting off sarcastic letters to Patel full of mock apologies and claims of higher morality, calling for an 'impartial tribunal' to judge the charges against the RSS. Patel's office responded that the government was the 'final judge' and it did not need to be lectured to by any tribunal. While Patel did not want to prosecute Golwalkar, he instructed that the noose be further tightened as the RSS chief had been challenging him to prove the allegation. The government had intercepted his correspondence with RSS functionaries, most of whom were released and desperately awaiting his instructions. The usually cautious RSS chief had not much choice in jail to exchange information other than through letters: the government accused him of 'abusing confidence' – that he had been promising the government one thing and instructing his followers otherwise. Patel was happy to have 'succeeded in catching Golwalkar on the wrong foot'.[90] An overpowered RSS leadership sought the backchannel services of the Congressman Mauli Chandra Sharma to inform the government of their rethink on key matters. Golwalkar was forced to agree to the government's demands, especially that of publishing a rigorous constitution. The final draft was shown to Patel in early July 1949. Then, with surprising speed, a communique was issued on 11 July lifting the ban.

Patel had earlier hoped to cure the RSS 'of their madness by making them realise their true responsibilities'.[91] After the ban was revoked, he expected Nagpur to fulfil two of his old demands. One, he wanted its young volunteers and office bearers to join Congress. The entry for 3 August 1949 in the diary of Maniben, Patel's daughter and assistant, reads: 'Glad at release of Golwalkar – ready to welcome in Congress. Bapu's [Patel's] task to make their entry easy.'[92] Second, he wanted to use the 'well disciplined organization' strategically against communists. As per T. G. Sanjevi, the Director of the IB and a close confidant of Patel, the RSS was not 'a danger to Government at this time but it might become so at a later date'. For now, the government found it 'expedient to use the RSS as a buffer against communism'.[93]

To put it simply, Patel was not sure whether he would be able to cure the RSS's madness, but he was keen to take chances. The government had earlier debated if it could extract a promise from the RSS on functioning as a purely cultural organization. But, 'as there is no law at present banning communal political organisations, Government could not properly insist on the RSS confining itself to cultural activities'.[94] While finalizing the constitution, the backchannel negotiators had used linguistic jugglery in a manner that satisfied both the RSS and the government. According to Article 4(a) of its constitution, 'The Sangh is aloof from politics, and is devoted to social and cultural fields only. However, the Swayamsevaks are free, as individuals, to join any party, institution, or front, political or otherwise.'[95]*

Significantly, Patel had lifted the ban after discussing the matter with Nehru, who thought that prolonged repression had a 'bad odour' about it. 'We can always take action, when necessity arises.'[96] On 16 August, the Deputy PM met the Sangh chief at Birla House in Bombay. Patel immediately updated Nehru that he had explained to Golwalkar 'the pitfalls which the RSS should avoid' and particularly 'warned him against the suicidal policy of the Savarkar group ... I found him quite receptive ... he will not give us any trouble and will now adapt himself to the new requirements.'[97]

Aware that conservatives in Congress shared Patel's affection for the RSS, Nehru met Golwalkar a few times to see if there existed a common ground. Part of the reason may have been private. The meetings were arranged by Shraddha Mata, a fiery, attractive sadhvi in her early thirties with whom Nehru was having a quiet affair. She had been introduced to the prime minister through his cabinet colleague S. P. Mookerji and other Congress conservatives, who hoped that the charming sadhvi would manage to persuade Nehru on the need to Hinduize the polity. 'I do not know what success I have had,' Nehru responded to Patel when asked about her, 'but she has had none.'†[98]

But unlike his deputy, Nehru wanted to have nothing to do with the RSS. In early August, when he was asked at a press conference whether, as rumour had it, he would 'seek the cooperation of the RSS for fighting the Communist menace', Nehru responded unequivocally: 'We do not frankly trust the RSS very much.' What about the 'general impression

---

* Cleverly, the communique made no mention of whether or not the RSS could involve itself in politics. It simply said that 'the organization should be given an opportunity to function as a democratic cultural organisation owing loyalty to the Indian Constitution and recognizing the National Flag, eschewing secrecy and abjuring violence'.

† The sadhvi later claimed that she had requested Nehru to meet the RSS chief because it was 'obligatory for two of the most important people in the country' to talk, and that she was 'glad to have succeeded in my efforts'. She had had 'detailed conversations with Panditji on the aims and vision of the RSS; and Panditji said that if they worked only on cultural lines, he would never have an objection'.

among the public' that the 'RSS is in the confidence of the government as against the Communists'? He gave a muted reply in five words: 'The impression is completely wrong.'[99]

On 13 July 1949, only two days after the ban on the Sangh was lifted, Atal addressed a crowd of 600 in the eastern UP district of Gorakhpur. He attacked the government for having 'blundered in banning the RSS', the only organization which really cared for the Hindus.* They 'did not deserve thanks', for 'it had taken them 1½ years to correct the mistake'.[100] Clearly the RSS was wholly unrepentant, arrogant even, about keeping its basic character unchanged.

After his release Golwalkar toured across the country, arriving in Lucknow on 31 August, where he was given a tremendous reception with 15,000 volunteers coming from eighteen districts of UP to greet him. 'In pouring rain, he was taken out in a procession and that evening he addressed a gathering (50,000) in Sanskritised Hindi.'[101] From Lucknow, Guruji proceeded to Banaras where Atal joined him. Wherever he went, Guruji was greeted by mammoth crowds of RSS supporters. Occasionally small processions were carried out to protest his release. Atal wrote an edit criticizing the opponents of Guruji who waved black flags at him in Banaras, pelted stones in Gosainganj and wanted to kill the RSS chief (with a knife) in Muzaffarpur.

The ban on the RSS was the first major expression of independent India's secular vision. But its confused implementation – legal loopholes, wide sympathy for the RSS among conservative Congressmen, most of all Patel's own extended ambivalence – ensured that the actual practice of secularism in India was going to be considerably less than smooth.[102]

---

* Atal was seconded by a new friend, Hanuman Poddar, who made a similar speech. Poddar had once been a protégé of Gandhi, but had later fallen out due to his disagreements over the Mahatma's reformist zeal, and joined the Mahasabha. He was among the thousands of RSS–Mahasabha workers who, after Gandhi's assassination, suffered Patel's wrath and were jailed. For many years Poddar ran Gita Press, an influential Hindi publishing house known for successfully selling popular Hindu religious texts at low prices.

4

The Sangh's Most Loyal Son

ATAL'S DEVOTION TO THE SANGH WHEN ITS CREDIBILITY WAS AT AN all-time low earned him the trust of its higher echelons. Back in Lucknow to edit *Panchjanya,* he began to tour UP to speak at the RSS meetings. The subjects he hectored on included the language debate, the Hindu Code Bill, cow protection – subjects on which the Congress conservatives across north India were on the same page as that of the Hindu nationalists. Much of it stemmed from the anxiety of caste elites against the radical reforms that the new constitution inflicted on the age-old Hindu order.

Encouraged in all likelihood by the UP Congressmen, the RSS also took up the cause of Hindi.* They pursued it under the aegis of the

---

* In early 1949, Atal was introduced to Congressman P. D. Tandon by his son Guru Prasad, who had taught Atal at Victoria College. Tandon had landed himself in a minor controversy when, despite holding a constitutional post of prominence – Speaker of the UP Legislative Assembly – he walked into a jail in Lucknow to meet some of his acquaintances from the RSS. Tandon had also been running the Hindi Sahitya Sammelan, whose main plank was to make Hindi the national language. In mid-April 1949 in Lucknow, as the time for the final decision on the language question neared, Tandon organized the eighth session of the UP Sahitya Sammelan – 'to support the claim of Hindi in Devanagari script to be the lingua franca of India'. It was a high-profile event, because most ministers in the UP government were keen to push Hindi as the national language. The reception committee was chaired by Chandra Bhanu Gupta, the Minister of Civil Supplies, UP. Atal was tasked with assisting Gupta in the reception committee. He also participated in cycle marches, distributing pamphlets to popularize the event. By one account, Atal even made a short welcome speech at the inaugural session on 17 April. Sampurnanand, who held the Education portfolio, argued that by giving Urdu 'the status of a State language … a fraud would be perpetrated on the people'. This view was more similar to that of an editor of

Vidyarthi Parishad, a students' body whose branches had first sprouted in July 1948 across UP towns. They rolled out a literacy campaign in the rural districts. State intelligence soon discovered that the Vidyarthi Parishad was actually 'intended to be a cover for Sangh activities' during the ban.[1] After the ban was lifted, the RSS scaled it up and formally launched it on an all-India level as the Akhil Bharatiya Vidyarthi Parishad. To get a sense of the public mood, the ABVP was found distributing printed pamphlets in many districts in order to secure people's opinion on: whether the name of the newly independent dominion should be India or Bharat Varsh; the national language Hindi or Hindustani; the constitution written in Hindi or English; which of the two songs, 'Jana Gana Mana' and 'Vande Mataram', was more suitable as the national anthem. Given the widespread disquiet on the question of language, the Constituent Assembly passed a resolution on 14 September to keep English as the state language for the next fifteen years. Hindi was declared the official language, not the national language.

On 30 October, the ABVP celebrated Hindi Diwas across the country. Atal was sent to Kanpur, where he presided over a public meeting in Shraddhanand Park in the evening: 'Despite heavy rains, Hindi-lovers gathered in large numbers, and the venue became a canopy of umbrellas.'[2] The next month, on 25 November, the local branch of the ABVP in Shahjahanpur celebrated Hindi Diwas. Chairing the ceremony, Atal claimed that while every Indian language deserves to be called a national language, Hindi is the 'eldest daughter of Sanskrit, and it's also the most popular, and ought to be the natural choice of people' for the national language.[3] 'Shri Atal Behari Bajpai, Editor of *Panch Janya*,' reported the UP CID, 'exhorted the students to compel government to accept Hindi as a national language.'[4]

In early October, while Nehru was on his first trip to the United States,

---

an RSS mouthpiece than one would have expected from the UP Education Minister.

Nehru, who felt 'more and more a stranger' in his home state, rebuked G. B. Pant: 'Urdu belongs more to the UP than to the whole of Pakistan ... we are becoming rather artificial in our passion ... Language is a delicate instrument and I have always loved the play of words and phrases. I see no beauty or grace or exactitude in the new Hindi that is developing in the UP for official purposes. That seems to me rather a tragedy.'

the Congress Working Committee passed a resolution backed by Patel allowing RSS members to join the grand old party. Congressmen were divided. Among those who supported the RSS's entry included powerful tier-two Congressmen like D. P. Mishra, P. D. Tandon and Charan Singh. When Nehru returned in mid-November, the resolution was adjourned *sine die*. The official objection was dual membership: no Congressman could belong to a volunteer organization other than its own Sewa Dal. 'The real thing is more basic about the approach of the RSS to national and other problems,' Nehru divulged at a press conference: 'It does not fit in with the Congress mentality.'[5]

This incensed the editor of *Panchjanya*. Now the grapes were sour: 'Congress is merely an organization to fulfil political needs. But the RSS's mission is to save the soul of the nation – its culture.' In another editorial, Atal declared Nehru's personality 'a contradiction': What could one make of a prime minister who took pride in being called a democrat, even as he blackmailed his colleagues in the party and the cabinet into following his will and sometimes even threatened to fight the masses? 'Individualism and collectivism, democracy and dictatorship, materialism and spiritualism – he spouts them all in the same breath.'[6]

The RSS dubbed the new Constitution of India adopted on 26 November 1949 as 'imported' from the West: 'I would prefer India to drown itself in the sea rather than become a carbon copy of other nations,' Golwalkar told a shakha in Aligarh on 30 December.[7] *Panchjanya* also carried essays by celebrated Hindi writers Rahul Sankrityayan and Mahadevi Verma on this subject. While both wrote angry, sentimental essays criticizing the government for breaking away from past knowledge and tradition that India had to offer, neither had anything concrete to offer by way of an alternative. The RSS was especially opposed to codifying Hindu personal laws – a cornerstone of which was caste equality and gender parity – seeing it as Nehru's attempt to destroy the sanctity of Hindu joint family life. 'Since we would shortly have democratic governments based on adult franchise, we should leave out questions like the Hindu Code Bill for the time being,' Atal unburdened himself in an editorial. 'This misguided enthusiasm to reform will hurt Indian culture and give rise to fissiparous tendencies.'[8]

Once in a while *Panchjanya* picked battles that appeared, on the surface at least, quaint and amusing. Consider Atal rousing his readers to demand that government reintroduce vanaspati in the market 'with a separate colour and smell to distinguish it from ghee'. The government was trying to promote the hydrogenated vegetable oil as an alternative, less expensive medium of cooking following its failure to fulfil the demand for ghee. Atal presented the Congress as a stooge of capitalists who, 'in their greed for money, want to aggressively promote it. By calling it ghee and making it look like ghee, they are destroying the health of the country.'[9] The loud opposition to vegetable oil had less to do with its nutritional disadvantages and more to do with its connection to the cow. The RSS believed that the government's promotion of vanaspati was aimed at undermining the economic importance of the cow – the main plank of cow-protection groups.

Some of the Congress conservatives had been lobbying not just for a centralized ban on cow slaughter, but also, bizarrely, to include it among the nation's roster of fundamental rights (which would have made the life of a cow at par with that of humans).[10] They proposed an economic and nutritional rationale, arguing that the new republic ought to drink the milk rather than eat the meat of a venerated animal.

This was mostly an obfuscation. As Atal later obliquely admitted towards the end of an editorial, the resistance was more out of the fear of losing religious authority – 'the fury that Hindu hearts feel to see Muslims killing cows ... The experts on Islam have told us that Islam does not prescribe killing cows.' Cow-rearing was an integral part of Indian culture, and 'as true Indians the Muslims should have no hesitation in adopting this practice'.

Like Gandhi earlier, Nehru was opposed to enacting such a law mainly because he did not want to constrain Muslims in the new, self-consciously secular, republic. But he also knew that the demand had the private sympathy of many conservatives in his party. Liberals and conservatives of all stripes pitched economic reasoning to argue their case. The central government retorted that a blanket ban on cow slaughter would be 'detrimental to the export trade' and 'the tanning industry in the country'.[11] Atal passionately responded:

> Some people think that if we stop exporting leather, India will not get dollars in return, which will affect our economy. By this logic, in order to earn forex one must kill cows. Rajshree [P. D.] Tandon has a satisfactory response for such people: he says that by exporting leather, we do get dollars in return, but that is used mostly in importing luxury goods. If we stop importing luxury goods, the need for exporting leather gets obviated. The purpose of export is to enhance our country's prosperity. Of what use is an export that hurts the physical health and cultural confidence of a people.[12]

A mid-way solution was effected: Nehru was forced to mention cow protection in the directive principles of state policy.[13] Even so, neither the conservative Congressmen nor the RSS were thrilled. For Atal and his ilk, protecting the cow was a 'national duty', and until a centralized ban was put in place, they would not 'consider our independence as real'.[14] Over the next few years, Congress conservatives in four Hindi-speaking states succeeded in passing laws banning cow slaughter.

By the end of 1949, Gandhi's assassination seemed to belong to a distant past. The RSS–Mahasabha had abandoned the fantasy of Akhand Bharat for the time being, to reach for the more low-hanging fruits. Even in the early 1940s, there had been instances in Atal's hometown of Gwalior of obscure mosques and mazaars being converted into temples, and vice versa in some Muslim princely states. Now the rightists attempted something infinitely grander and dangerous. The UP CID reported on 18 November: 'Babri mosque in Ayodhya stands on the site of a temple which was demolished during the Moghul period. Vairagis [ascetics] of Ayodhya, backed by certain influential individuals, are now agitating the local Hindu public.'[15]

The Mahasabha leader Digvijaynath was spearheading the agitation, aided, among others, by Atal's RSS colleagues. One such person was Nanaji Deshmukh, a Marathi-speaking Brahmin in his early thirties who had started off as a pracharak in Gorakhpur and had recently been moved to Lucknow to support Atal and others in running the mouthpieces. By one account, Nanaji was helping organize 'non-stop bhajans at the Ram Janmbhoomi site'.[16] In its 18 December issue, *Panchjanya* took the controversy ahead in an essay with a long headline: 'The victory symbols of the Mughal state are a blot on the forehead of a completely sovereign democratic state'.

This was 'not simply because they are Hindu structures which were desecrated by the Muslims, but also because they are the symbols of our slavery, our weakness, our cowardice; they are a challenge to our manhood; and till the time they continue to exist, we cannot be free from our ancestral debt nor can we walk with self-esteem and our heads high.' Such places included: 'The mosque in Ayodhya built over the birthplace of Ram; the desecrated and corrupted temple of Vishweshwar at Kashi; the ruins of Somnath, witness to Muslim dogmatism; construction of Syed Salar's tomb at the memorial of Maharaja Suheldev [in Bahraich in UP]; Adhai-Din-Ka-Jhopra in Ajmer; and thousands of such sacred religious and historical monuments'. But it was not just the government's responsibility: 'This is going to be the litmus test. Indian Muslims and their politicians keep pledging their loyalty to India … The real test of loyalty will be on the question of Ayodhya, Kashi, Mathura, Bahraich. If they don't want to restore to sanctity the birth place of Ram, it would not be possible to call them lovers of India.'[17]

The essay was not assigned a byline, but it may well have been written by the editor himself. A week later, on the night of 22 December, the Mahasabha arranged for a sadhu to smuggle an idol into the mosque and declared it Ramlala virajmaan – an infant Ram as the presiding deity. Now that Lord Ram had ensconced himself inside the mosque, he could not be moved. This covert operation created a volcano that would simmer for decades before exploding, outliving many of its perpetrators.

On his twenty-fifth birthday, Atal was overworked and sceptical about the world; his politics had become intensely, irrevocably personal. This

1. The bend in the river: the Yamuna at Bateshwar

2. Atal, natty at eight, with Babuji

3. The Vajpayees were on many days a happy family, patriarchy notwithstanding.
L to R, standing: Kamla, Mrs Awadh Behari, Mrs Sada Behari, Vimla; sitting: Atal, Prem, Awadh, Babuji, Ma, Sada, Vimla's husband; on the ground: nieces Shanta and Kiran, and Urmila

4. K. B. Hedgewar in late middle age, before RSS iconographers immortalized him in his signature black cap

5. B. S. Moonje, whose role in founding the RSS remains insufficiently acknowledged

6. Gorkhi Boys' Middle School, where Babuji served as the headmaster and Atal studied from 1935 to 1938

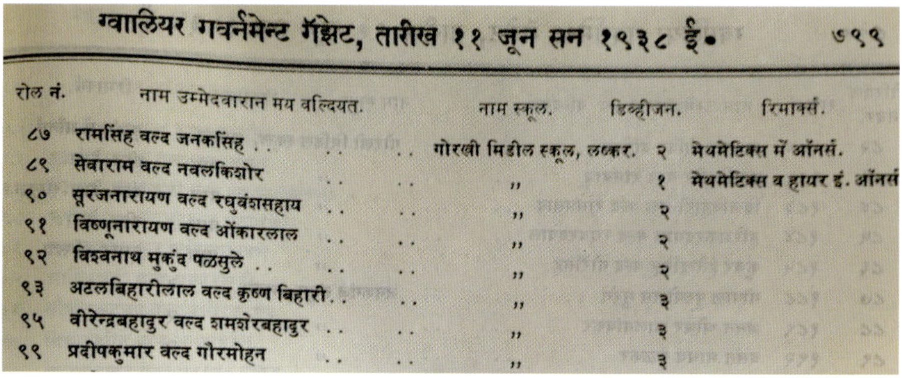

ग्वालियर गव्हर्नमेन्ट गॅझेट, तारीख ११ जून सन १९३८ ई. ७९९

रोल नं.	नाम उम्मेदवारान मय वल्दियत.	नाम स्कूल.	डिव्हीजन.	रिमार्क्स.
८७	रामसिंह वल्द जनकसिंह	गोरखी मिडील स्कूल, लश्कर.	२	मेथमेटिक्स में ऑनर्स.
८९	सेवाराम वल्द नवलकिशोर	"	१	मेथमेटिक्स व हायर इं. ऑनर्स
९०	सूरजनारायण वल्द रघुवंशसहाय	"	२	
९१	विष्णूनारायण वल्द ओंकारलाल	"	२	
९२	विश्वनाथ मुकुंद पळसुले	"	२	
९३	अटलबिहारीलाल वल्द कृष्ण बिहारी	"	३	
९५	वीरेन्द्रबहादुर वल्द शमशेरबहादुर	"	३	
९९	प्रदीपकुमार वल्द गौरमोहन	"	३	

7. Despite his flair for wordplay, the headmaster's son (13) graduated his middle-school exams in the third division.

8. Vijaya Raje and Jivajirao Scindia soon after their wedding in 1941

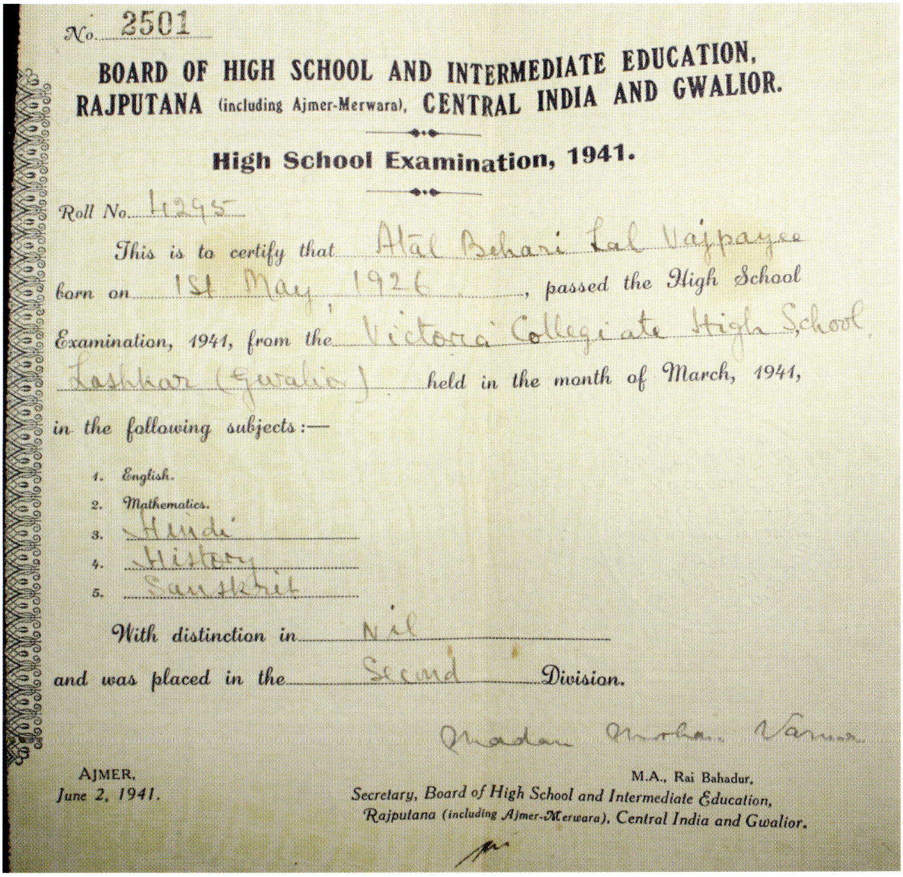

No. 2501

BOARD OF HIGH SCHOOL AND INTERMEDIATE EDUCATION,
RAJPUTANA (including Ajmer-Merwara), CENTRAL INDIA AND GWALIOR.

High School Examination, 1941.

Roll No. 4295

This is to certify that Atal Behari Lal Vajpayee born on 1st May, 1926, passed the High School Examination, 1941, from the Victoria Collegiate High School Lashkar (Gwalior) held in the month of March, 1941, in the following subjects:—

1. English.
2. Mathematics.
3. Hindi
4. History
5. Sanskrit

With distinction in Nil

and was placed in the Second Division.

Madan Mohan Varma

AJMER,
June 2, 1941.

M.A., Rai Bahadur,
Secretary, Board of High School and Intermediate Education,
Rajputana (including Ajmer-Merwara), Central India and Gwalior.

9. *Atal's high-school exam marksheet: 'With distinction in* *__Nil__* *and was placed in the* *__Second__* *Division'*

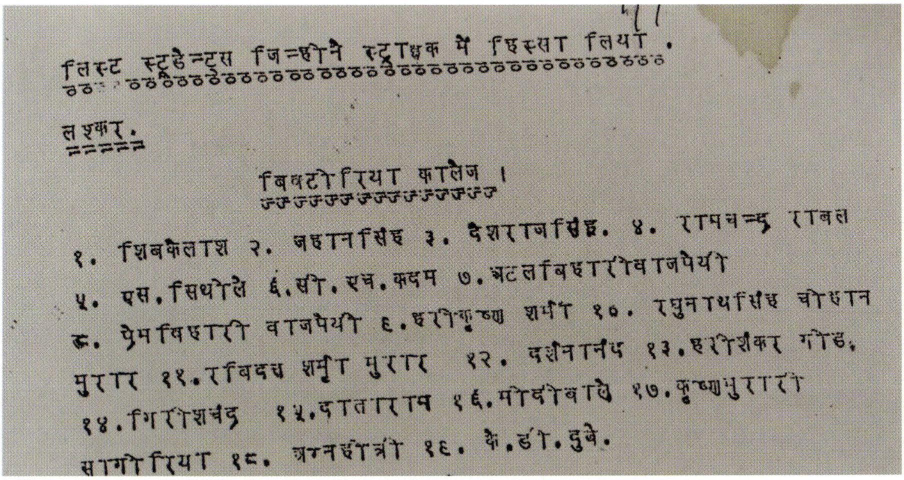

लिस्ट स्टूडेन्ट्स जिन्होंने स्ट्राइक में हिस्सा लिया.

लश्कर.

विक्टोरिया कालेज ।

१. शिवकैलाश २. जहानसिंह ३. देशराजसिंह. ४. रामचन्द्र रावत
५. एस. सिथोले ६. सी. एच. कदम ७. अटलबिहारी वाजपेयी
८. प्रेमबिहारी वाजपेयी ९. हरीकृष्ण शर्मा १०. रघुनाथसिंह चौहान
मुरार ११. रविदत्त शर्मा मुरार १२. दर्शनानंद १३. हरीशंकर गौड़,
१४. गिरीशचंद्र १५. दाताराम १६. मोदीवाले १७. कृष्णमुरारी
सागोरिया १८. अग्निहोत्री १९. के. डी. दुबे.

10. *A Gwalior durbar admonition for the Vajpayee brothers, Atal (7) and Prem (8), 'who took part in the [Quit India] strike' in August 1942*

11. The Victoria College Students' Union, 1943. L to R, standing: Atal (third from left), Deshraj (fifth); sitting: Professors S. K. Bagchi (first from left), F. G. Pearce (centre), Guru Prasad Tandon (sixth)

12. *Atal at the DAV College Kanpur (front row, centre)*

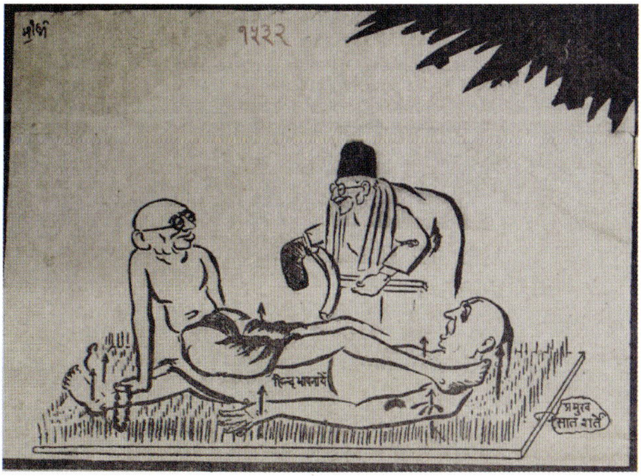

13. *The second issue of* Panchjanya, *in late January 1948, mocks Gandhi's last fast.*

14. *Beginning in 1950, Atal's bylines were accompanied, in what was the first hint of fame, by a close-up picture.*

15. a) L to R: Atal (in his black RSS cap), L. K. Advani and B. S. Shekhawat at a Jan Sangh meeting in Kota in the winter of 1952–53

15. b) L to R: Eknath Ranade, Deendayal Upadhyaya, K. R. Malkani and Atal in Kota in the winter of 1952–53

reflected in his op-eds, such as the one he wrote for the year-end issue – an introspective, wistful, impassioned wrap-up simply titled '1949': 'Another year of our small lives has passed. Assessing the year gone by is a useful way to draw up a plan for the upcoming one. But today we feel no such desire, because the year gone by was our year of defeats and hopelessness; in the upcoming year too, we see no hope.'[18]

The chief worry was the uncertain future of the organization whose sacrifice had saved the nation's soul. Atal was certain that the 'Sangh is the only ray of hope for a country jeopardized by divisions of party, province, language; and darkness born out of the ego of men opposed to each other'. All eyes in 1950 were going to be turned towards this only 'fiery organization capable of converting idealism into concrete pragmatism, and build a society and nation over it ... You can blind us, like Prithviraj [Chauhan] had once been, but you can't snatch the dream in our hearts. And to fulfil that dream we shall devote every day and every night of 1950.'[19]

Indeed, he devoted every day and night. Everyone at the Bharat Press lodged at a building which had houses resembling '10 x 15 [feet] Bombay chawls, a mile away from the office'. Around August 1950, Atal was shifted to *Swadesh*, a daily newspaper launched the previous year. Being assigned the responsibility to run a daily was a promotion for him. But being constantly moved was an ominous sign that the RSS were flexing its muscles with little resources. The logistics of gathering and printing news with shoddy infrastructure (broken chairs, no telephone) and limited staff meant longer hours spent slogging – in Atal's case, not least because he wrote an op-ed every day. A colleague would later describe his life in Lucknow thus:

> There were days when he was in the office working continuously from 9 AM till 9 PM. After that, we would start winding up to go to dinner. Atalji would be sitting quiet, awfully quiet. I would ask, 'Atalji, what happened, you look so low?' He would hold out his arm to me and ask: 'touch and see if I am running a fever'... He would quietly leave the office for the lodge. He had high fever so he would go to bed without eating anything. No medicine, no treatment. The next morning he would still

> have a fever, but he would come to work anyway. *Swadesh* was so short-staffed that we couldn't afford taking a break for even a day or two... It went on like that for years.[20]

Atal was living amid pracharaks, most of whom had had a less fulfilling childhood than him: Deendayal had been orphaned at seven; Nanaji had not told anyone that his mother had killed herself by jumping into a well when he was barely a toddler. These young Brahmins were small-town men born into caste privilege but lacking the means to make something of their lives. The Sangh had offered them at once a pious mission (to save Hinduism from the twin evils of Muslims and a pro-Muslim Congress) and a potentially rewarding, if somewhat risky, career. Living with men in their late twenties and early thirties who had taken a vow of life-long celibacy, Atal too led a life of emotional and sexual repression.

Sometimes this struggle showed in the pages of *Panchjanya*, with the young editor playing moral policeman. He implored the UP government to prohibit children of sixteen years and below from watching films: 'Cinema is one of the reasons for the decline in the moral character of India's youth; and since government controls the cinema industry, it bears the responsibility entirely. For an annual income of merely 60–70 lakhs, no civilized nation would like to see its future citizens degraded.'[21] The immediate reason for the outburst was the megahit *Barsaat*, a film of passion and melancholy, which twenty-four-year-old Raj Kapoor had directed and acted in. Following another controversy, the screening of *Barsaat* had been stopped six months after its release. But, Atal protested, its 'dirty, vulgar songs' could still be heard everywhere. He feigned shock at a song extolling the heroine's 'patli kamar, tirchhi nazar' – slender waist and occasionally flirtatious glance – 'a vulgar song echoing from the lips of every Lucknow child'. The All India Radio's policy in this regard was also 'pernicious' and they needed to exercise caution in the selection of songs which were aired.[22]

Intellectually, he was growing. In his post-ban avatar as the editor, Atal developed a niche: India's relations with the rest of the world. His writings on foreign policy displayed an ingenuity that was missing elsewhere. Not long ago, hardly anyone in the RSS had the inclination or the academic grounding required to analyze the pros and cons of India's diplomatic relations. After the communist revolution in China in October 1949, they could no longer ignore the new enemy across the northern border. The communists were not merely competitors for political power, their conception of society wrote off all of India's past heritage as feudal.

Atal was certain India must at all times treat both China and Russia as part of one team with the medium-term communist agenda of reddening up all of South Asia. Nehru had argued the opposite: that China had a personality of its own, and no one should treat it as a mere camp follower of the USSR. Atal did not trust the communists, but he also looked down upon the US as 'a country drunk on dollars and atom bombs' whose primary interest was to flood Indian markets with its goods. Even so, unlike Nehru, he felt that the communist camp was less trustworthy than the capitalist camp: 'Communist China is a reality, just as their anti-India stand is a reality too: to accept one and ignore another can hurt India.' [23]

Foreign policy had to be realist, unsentimental, transactional. He fired into the Mahasabha president N. B. Khare for criticizing the government's policy of offering help to South Korea. On 25 June 1950, North Korea, under the auspices of the Soviet Union and China, had invaded its southern neighbour. The United Nations, backed mainly by American forces, sought assistance from all countries. While India did not want to get involved militarily, it was keen to contribute in other ways. Innocent in matters of foreign policy, Khare lamented that India had eschewed its non-alignment principles to become a lackey of the British-American front. Atal was livid:

> By proposing to help South Korea, India has simply opposed the [Chinese] aggression, it has not collaborated with anyone ... Can the Hindu Sabha refute the truth that if efforts are not made today to stop the Communist juggernaut, tomorrow India may also get enslaved by them? In which case, Dr Khare should enlighten us whether the India of his dreams should side with the USSR or the USA ... To become popular, a political party needs a clear ideology and solid, creative organizational work. Mere pompous jibes won't achieve much.[24]

Atal's takedown of Khare was symbolic. Everyone from Golwalkar down to the RSS volunteers noticed that a twenty-five-year-old editor was berating the sixty-five-year-old president of the party that had birthed the RSS. The young editor was beginning to find an independent voice, and he was using it to demonstrate that the RSS could be flexible while holding its core beliefs intact.

On 8 April 1950, Industries Minister S. P. Mookerji resigned from the central cabinet over his opposition to the Liaquat–Nehru Pact. While the suffering of East Bengal Hindus indeed reigned supreme in his heart, Mookerji's resignation also had an element of strategy that he downplayed. He was a minister without a party. He had resigned from the Mahasabha in December 1948, after it vetoed his proposals that the party should allow non-Hindus to become its members or quit politics altogether and restrict itself to cultural work. Elections were to be announced the following year. The Congress was expected to win enough seats to achieve a majority. Mookerji, who had reservations against Nehru's flagship programmes like the Hindu Code Bill, calculated that he would lose his cabinet berth.

Mookerji was also among the first to notice the terminal decline in Patel's health. By early 1950, the deputy PM was spitting blood and missing cabinet meetings, which strengthened the Nehru–Maulana Azad leftist faction; Mookerji, as the most popular Bengali in the cabinet, felt suffocated in his limited domain as the industries minister. If the forty-nine-year-old bhadralok had to chart out for himself a separate path, now was the time to go out with a bang.

After his resignation, Mookerji met Golwalkar at least thrice to seek his support for launching a party. He had known well the RSS's founders, the fellow Mahasabhaites Hedgewar and Moonje. After Hedgewar's death in 1940, he had written to Golwalkar, shocked that 'doctor saheb's' illness had taken 'a fatal turn', calling the death 'an irreparable loss to India' and hoping that 'the great work which he started will continue without break'.[25] On at least one occasion in the past, a faction of the AISF sympathizing with the RSS–Mahasabha had also presented him a purse.[26]

In the summer of 1950, however, Golwalkar was counting on Patel for political patronage.* The RSS chief was not personally interested in day-to-day party politics, even if by now many of his brightest young men were thus inclined; he was not particularly excited about risking his organization for a political start-up. The RSS praised Mookerji's sacrifice, but stopped short of promises of partnership. They were keenly awaiting the result of the Congress presidential election.

All through the summer, Hindus were fleeing East Pakistan – which had been relatively quiet during 1947 – towards West Bengal, alleging persecution. Since they vastly outnumbered Muslims going to East Pakistan, conservatives pointed fingers at Nehru's Pakistan policy. Patel and others had in the past suggested an exchange of population, an option Nehru had strongly ruled out. While acknowledging the gravity of the problem, the proposed solution, Nehru insisted, would mean 'establish[ing] a Hindu State'. It was also impractical, and would hurt India diplomatically.[27]† Significantly, the prime minister also expected his colleagues to act calmly and plan for the likelihood of 'East Bengal joining West Bengal at some future date.'[28]‡

---

* In fact, the week after Mookerji resigned, Golwalkar came to Delhi to talk to Patel about the RSS's programmes to raise money, clothes, medicines, etc. for the Hindu refugees who were fleeing East Pakistan. Keen to impress Patel, the RSS had by early June raised ₹5.6 lakhs.

† The prime minister thought such a step would 'completely put an end to a stand we have taken as a secular State and it would create communal trouble ... Every Moslem in India would feel an alien and in effect we would have established a Hindu State. Our world position, which is high at present, would suffer irretrievably ... Then again how would one pick out Moslems, who are undoubtedly citizens of India, to be sent to East Bengal. None of them will want to go voluntarily and we would have to employ force. Neither the international nor domestic law could justify this pushing out of our own citizens to a foreign country which does not want them. If there is no other alternative, it will be better to stop receiving refugees from East Bengal, i.e. just put up a barrier against all of them unless there is some special reasons that permit could be granted.'

‡ Nehru would often repeat the gist of his letter, first written to the West Bengal chief minister Bidhan Chandra Roy on 22 March 1948: 'It seems to me that the only clear policy that we can have is to think in terms of East Bengal joining West Bengal ... Obviously this can

Soon, the torrent of refugees choking the West Bengal economy became a more urgent malady than the prime minister's fanciful vision of East Pakistan's voluntary reunification. It brought new friction between him and his ailing deputy. This reflected in the presidential election, in which Patel was supporting P. D. Tandon knowing that Nehru, who thought of Tandon as a reactionary, was opposed to working with him.

Atal was thrilled when Tandon, whom he knew well by now, won the election on 27 August.[29]* Some RSS full-timers assured local workers that the new Congress president would help 'purify and promote Hindu culture and civilization and that the Sangh had now every chance of making progress'.[30] Next, the RSS was secretly hoping for a split in the Congress. *Panchjanya* prodded Patel to take over as prime minister and save the country from 'empty idealism': 'If he covets the highest post, he should fearlessly press his demand.' Nehru could look after foreign affairs: 'Working under Patel, and tasked with implementing Patel's foreign policy, his airy idealism would find realistic checks.'[31] But despite Tandon's win and the Chinese annexation of Tibet, Patel showed no desire to attempt a cabinet coup. In fact Sardar did not have enough life in him for a fight: he died on 15 December 1950.

Unlike in his *Rashtradharma* essay three years ago, Atal now contrasted

---

only happen if the people of East Bengal so desire. There can be no compulsion in the matter. Both geography and a common language and culture seem to make it inevitable for East and West Bengal to hang together. East Bengal will continue to feel neglected and by-passed so long the centre of gravity of Pakistan is in western Pakistan. That centre of gravity is bound to continue to remain the West, this will lead Eastern Pakistan drifting further and further away ... If the ultimate aim is for Eastern Pakistan to join West Bengal and the Indian Union, we should not encourage any tendencies or activities which come in the way of this development. Natural forces are working in favour of this change and the only real obstruction to it can come through our own mistakes or over-zealousness. It is for this reason, among others, that it is wrong to encourage any large scale migration from East Bengal to the west. Indeed if such a migration takes place, West Bengal and to some extent the Indian Union would be overwhelmed. The problem, therefore, before us is how to keep up the spirits of Hindus in East Bengal and how to help them in so far as we can. If they come over to West Bengal, we must look after them. But it is no service to them to ask them or to encourage them to join the vast mass of refugees who can at best be poorly cared for.'

* 'For the first time after 1920,' Atal wrote in *Swadesh*, 'when Lokmanya Tilak passed away, Congress has decided to take the cultural nationalist route.'

Patel's legacy with Nehru's. The deputy PM could 'tell a friend from a foe; he knew that a foe had to be crushed and a friend given his due position'.[32] The obvious hint was at Patel's affection for the RSS, and Nehru's apparent fondness for communists and Muslims. The death of the man they were beginning to think of as their chief patron made the RSS apprehensive.

Reluctantly at first, the Sangh began a programme of collaboration with Mookerji, who had relocated to Calcutta. A month later, in mid-January 1951, Mookerji came to Delhi to attend a meeting with senior-most RSS workers and sympathizers like Mauli Chandra Sharma, to draw up tentative plans to form an all-India party.[33] They only agreed on the decision to launch a new party named Bharatiya Jan Sangh: the RSS would float units in Delhi and the nearby regions of Punjab and PEPSU.* Mookerji was to do the same in West Bengal. If the response was good, they would consider coalescing into an all-India party.

Over the next few months, Mookerji busied himself with grooming the unit in West Bengal, even as he awaited action from the RSS. He had been in touch with regional parties, some of which, such as the Ganatantra Parishad of Orissa, were considering the possibility of merging under an all-India Bharatiya Jan Sangh. Feeling anxious, Mookerji frequently wrote to the RSS and Jan Sangh men, but 'I have not received any reply'.[34] In early July, Mookerji lost his patience when he saw press reports from the RSS saying it was still open to 'cooperation with Congress'. At Mauli Chandra Sharma, who was in Delhi, he flung a final warning:

> A report has been circulated here that both you and Balrajji [Madhok] have declared that Bharatiya Jan Sangh, Punjab, has nothing to do with Bengal Jan Sangh. This has created great confusion here. Have you all dropped the idea of an all India organisation? If that is so, I can settle my plan accordingly. This will be a wrong step from every point of view but of course the decision will not be mine. I have not received any report from Nagpur either.[35]

---

* Patiala and the East Punjab States Union had been formed in 1948 by merging eight princely states, in many of which the RSS had had a strong presence since the early 1940s.

Why had Golwalkar not yet given Mookerji a reply despite being aware that elections were due in less than six months? The RSS was closely watching the bitter ideological struggle between Nehru and the Congress conservatives. In early September 1951, Tandon was forced to resign as president; the prime minister took over the position. In a closely related incident, D. P. Mishra, the home minister of Madhya Pradesh (and a prominent RSS sympathizer) resigned from the Congress altogether. With its chances destroyed, the RSS got back to Mookerji.

On 21 October, the All India Bharatiya Jan Sangh was hurriedly launched at a convention held in the premises of an Arya Samaj school in Delhi. A pandal was erected, and Mookerji sat with other leaders on a rostrum. In the background hung paintings of Shivaji, Rana Pratap, and Lord Krishna persuading the guilt-ridden Arjuna to take up arms to fight the Kauravas. The backdrop also had a deepak – an earthern lamp – the party symbol given them by the Election Commission, painted in saffron. From the pandal also hung banners inscribed with 'Sangh shakth kali yuge' – in the age of Kali there is force only in the Sangh.[36]

The proceedings opened with everyone gathered singing 'Vande Mataram', which the Congress conservatives and the RSS had unsuccessfully campaigned to make India's national anthem. In his presidential address, Mookerji stoutly denied Nehru's charge that the new party was communal. After all, unlike the Mahasabha, the new party was open to all Indians, and it 'would strive to ensure full protection and equal rights of citizenship to all minorities'. Also, in a break from the RSS's approach to history, Mookerji explained that the 'BJS staunchly believes that India's culture and civilization is a result of struggles between and influences from ideologies both native and foreign'.[37] Partition had to be annulled 'through peaceful means'.[38] This was in contrast to what some of the overexcited RSS exports to the new-born party were already shouting at the venue: 'Ek dhakka aur do, Pakistan tod do'. One more push, and we will shatter Pakistan.[39] For now the nuances could be put aside. Elections were round the corner, and a party-less leader had found a match in a leaderless party.

Despite what his resume would later claim, Atal had no direct role in the formation of the Jan Sangh; he attended the launch in Delhi as a journalist.[40] He was having a hard time keeping *Swadesh*, which was showing no signs of breaking even, afloat in Lucknow. When the party began to distribute tickets for the upcoming assembly and parliamentary elections, Atal may have felt a glimmer of hope.

The Jan Sangh candidates in UP were mostly conservative small-town elites, who had nursed a grievance against Nehru for abolishing zamindari or for pushing the Hindu Code Bill. Such candidates were expected to fund their own campaigns. Additionally, Atal and others at Bharat Press hoped that these candidates would place ads in *Panchjanya* and *Swadesh*. Starved of funds, Bharat Press accepted ads from the most dubious of candidates. In turn, Atal was occasionally sent to address rallies to help the candidates. He had no prior acquaintance with most of them but he didn't have much choice.[41]

The delay in the RSS's collaboration with Mookerji meant that the newborn party's only star campaigner did not have enough time to travel across the country. A plan was drawn up to use the two months he had in order of priority: West Bengal came first because, as a letter from the Delhi office enlightened its volunteers, 'much of the organisation work there depends on his individual attention. He has his own constituency also to work in where he is being opposed by the Congress with all its resources and pressure.'[42] During his campaigns in Bengal, Nehru stung his former cabinet colleague by calling the Jan Sangh an 'illegitimate child of the RSS and the Hindu Mahasabha'.[43] Next came Punjab, where the Jan Sangh hoped to still cash in on the goodwill created among Sikhs and Hindus during the partition. Followed by Madhya Pradesh, which included areas where the RSS had been born and reared – Nagpur and its surroundings. Mookerji's itinerary for December looked like this: '4 days to UP, 3 to Rajasthan, 3 to Bihar, 2 to Madhya Bharat, 1 to PEPSU, and 1 to Delhi', after which he wanted to revisit Bengal for the last leg of the campaign.[44*]

---

* When the Karnataka office requested Mookerji to at least show his face once in Bangalore and Mysore, it was refused: 'Very unwillingly … it had to be decided to postpone the Karnataka visit just for the present … We are dropping Gujarat, Saurashtra, Assam and

It was on this four-day election tour to UP that Atal first met Mookerji. Like many of his RSS fraternity, he travelled with the troops but only 'as a journalist'. Nanaji Deshmukh, who roomed with Atal in Lucknow, recalled: 'Once Dr Mookerji got delayed in reaching the venue, so Atalji was asked to take the stage and speak for a while so the audience wouldn't run away.'[45] For the first time, everyone in the Jan Sangh noticed Atal's talent for speaking on vexed issues to a mostly illiterate electorate, using lingo that was colloquial and jargon-free, funny and sarcastic. Travelling in the Hindi belt, Mookerji also became self-conscious of a major handicap. He was a fiery orator in Bengali and English, but his Hindi was considerably less than charming. Every now and then in the middle of a speech, the Jan Sangh president fumbled. Mookerji was familiar with the Sangh's Hindi mouthpieces, and may have seen Atal as someone who could assist him in some way. But for now, Atal did not accompany Syama babu outside UP.

The party was contesting 93 Lok Sabha and 742 assembly seats across the country. For all his enthusiasm, Mookerji had neither his chief opponent Nehru's physical agility nor the deep pockets to hire planes and military Dakotas to reduce the pain of travel. Given these limitations, the party despatched plucky young orators like Atal to campaign in constituencies that Mookerji missed out on his way.* In Madhya Pradesh Mookerji covered 1,000 miles by rail and road, visiting Bilaspur, Raipur, Amravati, Akola, Jabalpur and Nagpur. In a press conference at Nagpur, Mookerji said the Jan Sangh was 'only three months old and they could not expect spectacular results'. He saw the Jan Sangh's future as a 'nucleus of a well-knit opposition party within and without the legislature'.[46]

One of the places Mookerji missed in Madhya Pradesh was Wardha, an old bastion of the RSS. An adolescent RSS volunteer in Wardha who was asked to spread the word about the *Swadesh* editor's public meeting recalled: 'Some of us sat on a cycle rickshaw and cried into the mike "Atalji ka bhaashan hai Cotton Market mein, aap jaroor aaiye"' – please

---

for the time being Vindhya Pradesh also because it is physically not possible to take all the provinces.'

* Though the minimum age required to contest the 1952 Lok Sabha elections was twenty-five, no one in the party considered fielding the *Swadesh* editor.

come to hear Atalji speak at Cotton Market.[47] The volunteer had 'heard his name, and read his poems, but didn't know how he looked. Even at that time he was famous in the Sangh circles'. But Atal was too obscure for most people in Wardha to have heard of him, let alone vote for a Jan Sangh candidate based on his speech.

Mookerji desperately wanted to win at least ten Lok Sabha seats so that he could 'set this man [Nehru] right'.[48] The results in February 1952 were depressing: the party won only three seats in the Lok Sabha including, mercifully, Mookerji's own; and thirty-three in the state legislatures. In some provinces like East Punjab, where the Jan Sangh looked strong, they got nothing.[49] Privately, Mookerji may have blamed the debacle on Golwalkar's vacillation and opportunism: had the RSS sealed the agreement in mid-1950 or even January 1951 (when the talks began), Mookerji would have had the time to erect at least a semblance of organization everywhere, as well as a chance to bring regional parties like the Ganatantra Parishad of Orissa, which had won six Lok Sabha seats, into the Jan Sangh. He would also have had more time to plan the campaigning.

The elections brought only one piece of luck. Since the Jan Sangh had bagged more than three per cent of votes, the Election Commission recognized it as a national party. Mookerji tried hard to bring together a working coalition of about thirty-five MPs from right-wing parties – the Hindu Mahasabha, Jan Sangh, Akali Dal, Ram Rajya Parishad, Gantantra Parishad, independents.[50] They would work like a team in the lower house, and would be free to carry on the programmes of their respective parties outside the legislature.*

Mookerji found himself hampered by original new ideas on which to corner the government and, especially, a massive financial crunch that hampered the running of his own party. Many of the party's supporters

* At one such meeting on 28 March, a suggestion was made to include the socialists, with whom the Jan Sangh had on some occasions during the election cooperated. Mookerji opposed this, because 'the socialists and the KMPP' – Kisan Mazdoor Praja Party – 'believed in the revolutionary methods of changing the present order in the country like the communists, though to a lesser degree, hence the right-wing parties could not align with them'.

who had pinned their hopes on the election – businessmen, wealthy refugees – were disappointed by the results; they did not see a future for the Jan Sangh. The enthusiasm of the RSS, which had been reluctant to partner with Mookerji to begin with, also began to wane. The Delhi Sangh in-charge, Hansraj Gupta, who had funded the party during the election, politely declined to help with more money. Soon, the Jan Sangh didn't have enough to pay the rent for its central office in Delhi, or even the office peon's salary. At the end of May, its central office had a bank balance of 'Rs. 26/- only'.[51]

Things went further downhill when Jan Sangh members from outside the RSS fold discovered that Nagpur was quietly scheming to control the newborn party. At a party meeting in mid-May, Mauli Sharma 'disclosed with heavy heart that RSS on the strength of which they had counted much had not only deceived them but that the RSS people were acting as fifth columnists in the party'. The Jan Sangh was used by RSS workers as 'a stage for vilification of the govt. but they do not owe allegiance to the Jan Sangh and always give priority to their RSS work.' Mookerji interrupted Sharma's vitriol to state calmly that 'the Jan Sangh had no connection with the RSS organisation but that individual RSS workers were members of the Jan Sangh' and that any 'worker found doing mischief should be kicked out of the party'.[52]

Easier said than done. It had been an unfeasible model to begin with: Mookerji relied on manpower and, embarrassingly for the proud bhadralok, funding from the RSS. At the same time, his stature and temperament were wholly averse to being remote-controlled by Nagpur. Privately, he worried that 'our entire strength comes from the RSS ... but the two sides are still unable to mentally adjust themselves to each other. This arrangement may not last forever ... we should get more people from outside [the RSS] who would give us their whole-hearted support.'[53] Mookerji envisaged the Jan Sangh to be a traditional conservative party, something of a cross between the Congress and the Mahasabha. His best hope lay for the medium run when, with some electoral success, the party would be able to raise its own cadres and manage its finances without help from Golwalkar. At the moment, though, Mookerji desperately needed an emotive idea with which to corner Nehru; an idea that would enliven all – the RSS, his party, and the tenuous right-wing coalition in Lok Sabha he wanted to collaborate with.

The electoral debacle had a swift, if indirect, impact on Atal's journalistic career. Right before the elections, one Amarnath Bajaj, with backing and funds from the RSS in Delhi, had acquired Arjun Press which published *Veer Arjun*, an old Arya Samaj weekly that Atal had grown up reading in Gwalior.* The purpose may have been to use it for both RSS and Jan Sangh work. But faced with a financial crunch, the RSS decided to shut down some of its mouthpieces: *Swadesh* was one of them. Atal had tried hard to save the newspaper. In a depressed state he churned out one last editorial 'Alvida' – Goodbye – mourning the end of his stint in Lucknow.

He was asked by the Sangh to relocate to Delhi to take charge at *Veer Arjun*. The press was near the New Delhi railway station in central Delhi, three kilometres from the local RSS office in Jhandewalan, where lived most of the Sangh elders. The office was on the ground floor; Atal was given a room on the first floor that he was to share with another staffer. As always there would be no pay, but his expenses would be taken care of.

Earlier, each time the RSS had a major disagreement with the government, he had threatened to start a mass agitation. Now it was clear that the masses had thrown in their lot with the Nehru-led Congress. Atal's own campaigns during the elections had produced nought. Journalism seemed less romantic to him now, not least because *Veer Arjun* was the fourth publication he was heading in less than five years. As per the Jan Sangh accounts of early February 1952, Arjun Press owed the party 'Rs. 195', indicating that the press was running at a loss.[54]

At the same time, for a village-born Brahmin who had only lived in small towns, moving to the national capital also meant new possibilities – proximity to great events and consequential people. The Jan Sangh's

* Bajaj had previously been an employee of the Railway Cleaning Accounts Office. He had been caught helping the RSS in the December 1948 satyagraha in Delhi by using the cyclostyle machines in his office to print posters for the RSS, which cost him his job. He was now trying to resurrect himself in another avatar.

immediate challenge was to overcome the post-election depression and erect an organizational structure to attract the masses. Apart from being an editor, Atal was now also one of the RSS's popular young faces who enjoyed the trust of the top brass. 'Atalji began to be invited to speak at public meetings in Delhi and nearby UP districts,' an associate at *Veer Arjun* recalled. He 'began to get occupied on most weekends with the party work'.[55]

As earlier, Atal appealed to the Sangh network and old friends to send contributions. He teased Devendra Verma, an old friend in Gwalior and now a popular poet: 'It is pointless to ask you for your poems. I suppose you don't write unless paid for.'[56] The effect was as desired, with Verma dispatching some of his verses. Atal also wanted friends to spread the word so he could hoard 'contributions for the *Veer Arjun* weekly from emerging poets and writers'. Friends may have helped, for one Balkrishna Bhardwaj of Gwalior sent a poem on 'Pyaar Ke Prasphutit Maadak Raag' – the eruptive melody of love – and the chaos and pleasure it brought to an adolescent heart. The prudish editor was not amused. Unusually for someone who had no money to pay his contributors, Atal erupted: he refused to publish the poem, chastising Bhardwaj to 'rise above the narrow individualistic visions of life'. The amateur contributor heeded the advice and sent a poem on the necessity of Kashmir's integration with India. This time the editor was pleased. 'We have already received lots of poems on Kashmir,' Atal responded, 'but will soon publish yours: please wait.'[57]

Mookerji's first impulse was to agitate on traditional social and economic issues of the day – beginning with food inflation, especially the increase in the prices of rationed wheat. But by the time the Jan Sangh recovered from the shock of defeat, the issue had been hijacked by the communists and socialists, who had fared better at the polls. Low on morale, the party had, its president lamented in mid-May, kept itself 'aloof as a mere spectator'.[58] The RSS launched a massive signature campaign with the intention to force the government to bring a central legislation to ban the killing of cows. Mookerji sympathized with it from a distance, but did not think it a strong enough plank to start a countrywide agitation. Unable to come up with any new ideas, the party fell back on an old obsession: Kashmir.

Jammu & Kashmir was the only Muslim-majority state of India that was also, under Sheikh Abdullah's leadership, determined to remain autonomous. Given their hostile relationship in the past, Abdullah, the new prime minister of J&K, was keen to pay the former ruling class of Dogras back in their own coin. Soon after taking over he had, in July 1950, carried out radical land reforms without paying any compensation, which had hurt many of the Dogra jagirdars. In theory the Jan Sangh supported land reforms, with Mookerji mentioning in his presidential speech of October 1951 that the 'abolition of zamindari along with other integrated measures will usher in agricultural reforms necessary for the country. But compensation should be paid.'[59] Since the party drew much of its support from the landed class and some lapsed maharajas, its private stand was more ambiguous.

The Dogras resented the decline in their economic and political influence. It did not help that officials sent by Abdullah to run the administration in Jammu 'did not conduct themselves well' either.[60] Unfortunately, for someone who had spent years in the prison, Abdullah acquired a reputation for becoming 'notoriously intolerant of dissent', frequently locking up opposition workers without trial, sometimes for years.[61]

Matters worsened during the 1951 assembly elections. The nominations for forty-five out of forty-nine Praja Parishad candidates were declared invalid on flimsy grounds.[62] The Parishad boycotted the election; the National Conference had a walkover on all of its seventy-five seats. With no space for manoeuvre, the Praja Parishad began to agitate for removing the special status granted to J&K and to fully merge the state, same as the other 600-plus monarchies, with India. The Parishad's most popular slogan was 'Ek Vidhan, Ek Nishan, Ek Pradhan' – one constitution, one flag, one premier – for all of India. If a full merger was not possible, the Praja Parishad demanded that Jammu should be separated from Kashmir and merged with Punjab or Himachal Pradesh.

The Jan Sangh saw the Parishad's campaign as a natural cause to attach itself to: the party in Delhi decided to celebrate the last week of June 1952 as 'Kashmir Week'. On 26 June, addressing a crowd of 1,500 people at Gandhi Grounds, 'Attal Behari Bajpai emphasized that they would not hesitate to lay down their lives, if need be, for the integration of Kashmir with India.' He also argued that 'if hereditary rulership was to be terminated in Kashmir, it should also be terminated in Hyderabad'.[63]

The crisis simmered for a while, with the Jan Sangh's attention shifting to the refugee crisis in East Pakistan. The Praja Parishad was irked that under the special status granted to J&K by Article 370, Abdullah had the freedom to make his own laws (on most matters except defence and foreign affairs) and fly a separate flag (which was the National Conference flag with minor alterations). When the J&K government flew it over Jammu secretariat on 17 November, the Praja Parishad gave a call for a do-or-die agitation. The J&K government cracked down on the protestors, arresting the elderly president Prem Nath Dogra and others. Being a sister organization, the Jan Sangh was asked to help make the agitation popular across country. As the Jan Sangh geared up for its annual session to be held in Kanpur during 29–31 December, the party also finalized the logistics of the 'mass movement in which leaders and volunteers would proceed to Kashmir to help the Praja Parishad agitation'.[64]

Meanwhile, failing to take off, *Veer Arjun* was shut down by December 1952. All through December, the unemployed Atal and his Sangh colleagues convened public gatherings across Delhi where they delivered 'usual type speeches explaining the background of the movement and denouncing the policy of the government of India in regard to Kashmir.' They refuted Nehru's 'statement in the Parliament describing the Praja Parishad movement as communal' or that it 'possessed fire arms or aimed at the restoration of Jagirs.'[65] They also appealed for funds in aid of the satyagraha. Atal was too embroiled in such events to realize this his life as a journalist had screeched to an 'abrupt full-stop'.[66]

At Kanpur, the party formally passed a resolution supporting the Jammu satyagraha for the integration of J&K with the rest of India.

The overexcited younger delegates of the party, the majority of them from the RSS, egged Mookerji on to challenge Nehru to 'face the Jan Sangh Satyagraha in the rest of India as well'.[67] The president counselled patience, saying he would first discuss the matter with the prime ministers. Back in Delhi, Mookerji began a protracted correspondence with Nehru and Abdullah, urging the latter to open dialogue with the Praja Parishad leadership and come up with a compromise.

This did not go anywhere. Nehru knew that the Praja Parishad derived all its energy from the RSS and the maharaja, and he detested both. Therefore he did not ask Abdullah to hear out the Dogras, even though by early 1953 it was no longer only jagirdars venting their frustration at Abdullah's socialist government: the movement was becoming popular among the Hindus of Jammu region, and some of their grievances were genuine. The prime minister was livid with the Parishad and the Jan Sangh because the agitation had weakened India's position in the UN, and would further complicate any compromise with Pakistan. Worse, it was making the Muslims of J&K suspicious of a shared future with India. In his replies to Mookerji in February 1953, Nehru emphasized that for any talks to take place the Praja Parishad had to first 'stop the agitation completely and then deal with any grievances'.[68] A confrontation was unavoidable.

The Jan Sangh's decision to plunge itself wholeheartedly into the Jammu satyagraha gave Atal's life another swift, unexpected turn. Sometime in January–February 1953, he was appointed Mookerji's private secretary. This was partly because other bright young men in the RSS–Jan Sangh had already been assigned important tasks: Deendayal, the general secretary of the UP Jan Sangh was promoted at Kanpur to the post of National General Secretary of the party. The UP charge was handed over to Nanaji who had, among other things, successfully organized the Kanpur annual session. Atal was not yet a member of the Jan Sangh's working committee. Being referred to as Mookerji's private secretary would lend his presence at public meetings a certain weight. But he would not take up the role as it was commonly understood – assisting the master behind the scenes with day-to-day official work.

Atal's first assignment was to travel alone in the Hindi heartland to popularize the Jammu satyagraha among the masses. In the past year, he had come to have more than just an acquaintance with the Jan Sangh president. Atal had travelled with Mookerji in early August 1952 to Jammu and 'discovered his simplicity and ease of manners':

> Soon after we boarded the train in the evening, I looked for his hold-all so I could make his bed. I was quite surprised to see that he was only carrying a suitcase. It had a bedsheet, a tiny pillow, and a thin blanket. I was quite embarrassed to then open my own, heavy hold-all, which had a rather fat quilt and mattress. When I opened my eyes the next morning, he was already up and shaving. I looked at his shaving kit, and noticed that he didn't have a mirror. I said, 'You don't have a mirror?' Dr Mookerji replied with a chuckle, 'I have been shaving for so long, should I not be expert enough to manage without a mirror?'[69]

Mookerji was quite unlike the other powerful men he had revered – Jivajirao Scindia, Guruji Golwalkar – who exuded the aura of a deity commanding its followers. Atal was conscious that Mookerji belonged to an elite Calcutta family; that he had studied law at Lincoln's Inn and come back to become the youngest vice chancellor of Calcutta University, after which he turned to politics, getting appointed before long as a minister in the central cabinet. Yet Mookerji was perfectly comfortable travelling third class with the young editor of *Veer Arjun*, cracking jokes and sharing anecdotes of his meetings with powerful people, frequently soliciting the opinions of young Jan Sangh workers.

Atal observed that unlike the top-down hierarchy inside the RSS, Mookerji 'respected the viewpoint of even the pettiest of workers; and because they hesitated to speak up in front of him, he would prod them repeatedly'. His sense of democracy was evident on 'occasions when Jan Sangh workers did not agree with him, and he failed to convince them. On such occasions he gladly accepted the viewpoint of his younger colleagues'. Syama babu's simplicity, warmth and large-heartedness lent him a charisma that Atal had never before perceived in anyone: 'He patted your back once with love, and you would be ready to die for him.'[70] He became for Atal a model of how a man in public life ought to conduct himself. Even though the job was largely symbolic, he felt blessed to be attached to the former cabinet minister.

Atal travelled widely in UP: 'On 26 March, Sri Vajpayee, the private secretary of Dr Syama Prasad Mookerji … began his tour of eastern Uttar Pradesh to popularize the movement,' reported *Panchjanya*.[71] Constantly on the move, over the next two weeks he covered more than a dozen districts. Everywhere he informed and incited his audience: 'Isn't it surprising that even the well educated people in eastern UP are unaware that Sheikh Abdullah has stitched a separate flag for himself?'

> It doesn't take much time to reach Jammu – via train till Pathankot, and from there by road. And if you have just about enough money for the fare, you can board a train in Delhi at night and by next afternoon you will reach Jammu soaking in the beautiful views of snow-capped mountains. But far more important than train or bus or the money to reach there is something else – a permit … If you don't possess this permit, those great inventions like railways and cars, and the currency in your pocket minted dutifully by the government, have no worth.[72]

After addressing a crowd in Ballia, he overheard some khadi-wearing Congressmen whispering among themselves that the talk of 'two constitutions, two prime ministers, two symbols' in J&K was untrue, and that the Jan Sangh was in the business of 'spreading canards'. Everywhere Atal insisted that it was a democratic movement: 'Leaders of the Parishad and Jan Sangh understand rather well that the rajas and maharajas are a thing of the past. This is *janyug* – the age of masses, which has no place for monarchy and dynasties.'[73] This was an insincere, if not entirely false, claim.

His trip went more or less smoothly. It seems the UP government quietly sympathized with the agitation. Unlike in Punjab, where most Jan Sangh leaders were detained, Atal was not arrested. The only exception was Ajamgarh where, on 1 April, the district administration imposed Article

144, and cancelled the meeting 'just two hours before Atalji was to make his speech'.[74] By the end of the first month of the Jammu satyagraha, UP had sent off more than 500 of the 1,200 agitators gather in Delhi from across country. Atal deserved some of the credit.

Panchjanya carried, for the first time, a photo of Atal giving a speech at the Lucknow station while seeing off satyagrahis led by Radheshyam Kapoor – a former colleague who was still running Bharat Press. It is a revealing image, the first visible sign of Atal having plunged into public life. Surrounded by satyagrahis, he stands erect in his lean five-foot-six frame sporting a white dhoti-kurta, having shunned Western clothing, his right hand waving towards the sky, his lips slightly contorted with the force of an intense speech.[75] Towards the end of his trip, he informed a reporter that UP was 'in full preparation for supplying Satyagrahis to Delhi continuously'.[76]

Atal was soon called back to Delhi to accompany Mookerji on a trip to Madhya Bharat on 10 April – beginning with his hometown, Gwalior. To welcome the Jan Sangh boss to Gwalior, many provincial leaders of his own party and the Mahasabha descended from all across central India. (Gwalior was one of the only four constituencies where the Mahasabha had redeemed itself by winning the Lok Sabha election.) Mookerji held a press conference, attended among others by Atal's childhood hero Jagannath Milind, editor of the durbar mouthpiece now suitably renamed *Madhya Bharat Sandesh*. At a public meeting in the evening, the native son played to the gallery, claiming that Gwalior had 'never been behind in the battle for independence' – a blatant falsehood – but the audience was stirred. They were especially moved when Atal pledged that to keep Mookerji's word, every child of his hometown would happily embrace prison: 'Gwalior ka bachcha-bachcha jail jaane ko taiyaar hoga.'[77]

On a trip to Kota with Mookerji, Atal ran into a tall, wiry Sindhi refugee in his mid-twenties. Like most youngsters in the Sangh, the Kota pracharak Lal Krishna Advani had read Atal's 'powerful editorials and some of his poems'. Advani found him 'intense': 'I could easily tell that he was imbued with youthful idealism and carried around him the aura of a poet who had drifted into politics. Something was smouldering within him, and the fire in his belly produced an unmistakable glow on his face.' The private secretary did not make much of the Sindhi pracharak just then, but Advani was mesmerized by the 'extraordinary young man' whom 'I must get to know'.[78] But the number of satyagrahis from UP was slackening, and Atal was asked to make another trip. The Allahabad Jan Sangh was sent an express telegram: 'Atalji reaching 29th Janata' [Express].[79]

The prime minister was furious with the news of the RSS–Jan Sangh satyagrahis thronging Delhi's roads. He asked the new home minister Kailash Nath Katju to ban the Jan Sangh, but Katju was reluctant to take this extreme step.[80] Nehru then summoned his top cops and ordered them to crush the satyagraha, or 'he would call the army out'.[81]

This was an overreaction.* The satyagraha was more dust than heat: the Delhi police noticed that every day a few dozen 'volunteers dressed like ordinary citizens, would appear suddenly in a park, fish out their distinctive caps from their pockets, put them on and shout slogans. The police could not anticipate their appearance in advance and naturally there was a time lag before these people were rounded up.'[82] The agitation was well organized, but hardly the mass movement that would force Nehru's hand.

Mookerji decided to collide with Abdullah head on by entering Jammu without a permit. The J&K government had earlier made a public announcement that Mookerji would be arrested if he crossed the border.[83] Pre-decided as the last resort, on the morning of 8 May, the Jan Sangh president boarded a passenger train in Delhi that would take him through Punjab into Jammu. He was accompanied on the trip by Atal and a few other young party activists. They had not applied for a permit to enter J&K, knowing well that they would not be granted one. But on reaching Ambala, Mookerji sent a telegram to Abdullah about his plan to proceed to Jammu, hoping 'to see you also if possible'.[84] Over the next three days, the Jan Sangh chief addressed public and closed-door meetings

* Nehru was probably triggered by the joint Jan Sangh–Mahasabha candidates winning three out of four assembly by-polls in Delhi with Kashmir as their main plank.

in Punjab – Ambala, Karnal, Phagwara, Jullundur, Amritsar, Pathankot.

At Pathankot, he was informed that he would be allowed to enter J&K without a permit. The Jan Sangh supporters and young men like Atal travelling with him took it as a moral victory – a sign that the government was being forced on the backfoot by the satyagraha. They shouted slogans saying Nehru had been compelled to bow down: 'Permit system toot gayi, Nehru sarkar jhuk gayi.' Atal noticed that Mookerji was 'overcome by a deep sense of responsibility. "By allowing me to proceed to Jammu without a permit," he said, "the government has burdened me with considerable responsibility"; for a moment I saw him immersed in deep thoughts [about how he should react to this kind gesture].'[85]

On the early evening of 11 May, the entourage was to cross the bridge over the Ravi river to enter J&K's Kathua district, and travel further by jeep 100 kilometres northwest to Jammu city. 'As our jeep proceeded towards the Madhopur bridge,' Atal wrote, 'some of our activists who were standing there came and informed Doctor saab: "there appears something suspicious". These activists were standing near the bridge and, from the conversation of policemen they had overheard, they guessed that Doctor saab would be arrested as soon as he entered Jammu.'[86]

Mookerji did not pay attention, probably because he was prepared in advance for such an encounter. The entourage crossed the bridge to find the road blocked by a posse of Kashmir policemen. Perhaps the government had changed its mind, for the police officer took out an order of arrest under the Public Safety Act of the state. It mentioned that the Jan Sangh president 'has acted, is acting and is about to act in a manner prejudicial to public safety and peace'. Mookerji got down from the jeep and, as planned, instructed two of his Jan Sangh colleagues to accompany him. Atal and others were asked to return to Delhi. A bit dramatically, Mookerji said to them: 'Go back and tell everyone that I have entered Jammu and Kashmir – if only as a prisoner.' Syama babu and both his colleagues were kept in captivity in Srinagar.

There was nothing particularly surprising about it. Later that night, Jan Sangh workers met at the RSS office in Jhandewalan in Delhi to discuss the future course of action. The consensus at the meeting was that the Punjab unit should be asked to intensify their movement in Pathankot, and that the Delhi Jan Sangh should simply assist the Punjab team 'by sending a few jathas'. The final decision on this point was postponed till 'the return of Shri Atal Behari Bajpai' from Punjab.[87] But by the time Atal returned a few days later, the Delhi police had jailed most of the RSS–Jan Sangh's key workers. The presidents of the Hindu Mahasabha and Ram Rajya Parishad, N. C. Chatterjee and Karpatri Maharaj, were also locked up. The satyagraha collapsed.

Atal now lived in the newly erected RSS office in Jhandewalan, behind one of the oldest temples in Delhi.[88]* The place was being 'used as a Boarding House for the Satyagrahis from outside & the RSS kitchen in the same building is being run for feeding the outsider Satyagrahis'. Unsurprisingly, the place was frequently raided. Atal did not hide himself, but he was not arrested. This may have been because his name was not included in the 'List of active workers of Bhartiya Jan Sangh, Hindu Maha Sabha, & Ram Rajya Parishad'. Instead, the intelligence reports showed him 'out in Uttar Pradesh'.[89] At the same time, he had no clear brief for the near future. He busied himself by writing an article here and addressing an assembly by-election meeting there. The private secretary was awaiting the release of his boss.

Atal was unaware that Syama babu's health was fast deteriorating in jail. Mookerji suffered from a heart disease and high blood pressure. Having travelled together, Atal knew about the strict instructions the Jan Sangh office issued regarding Syama babu's diet – 'not cooked but boiled, without any Ghee or spices … some curd and fruits can supplement' – and his rest hours, during which he was not to be disturbed, except in an emergency.[90] Mookerji had been advised in the past to avoid staying in places too far above sea level. Given his medical condition, the Jan Sangh president should have been imprisoned in or around Jammu – not Srinagar. On the morning of 22 June, Mookerji suffered a severe heart attack, passing away in the early hours of the 23rd.[91]

The news stunned RSS–Jan Sangh. Overcome by anger and disbelief, they declared that Sheikh Abdullah had conspired to kill Mookerji. To be

* The government was annoyed that the Jhandewalan trust which owned the land had given it to the RSS: the land was 'registered on the name of Guru Golwalkar, on 99 years lease'.

sure, there were many first-hand rumours suggesting a lapse in Mookerji's treatment. But his death had less to do with conspiracy, more with the authorities' failure to provide the extra care that an ailing VIP prisoner should have received. The news sank Atal into a depression. Three weeks later, he attempted a stream-of-consciousness obituary:

> Every evening, as the sun begins to set, my eyes visualize a fast jeep, speeding across Pathankot towards Jammu. Slogans ring in my ears: *Permit system toot gayi, Nehru sarkar jhuk gayi*. The glowing faces celebrating victory come alive in my consciousness. Large crowds everywhere, their hands joined in greeting him – both sides of the road, at shops, from windows and balconies and roof-tops. For a moment I forget myself, his greatness overshadows my ineptitude. But the very next moment, I enter the harsh world of reality, and find the sun has disappeared; I only see a lonely sky, with blood splattered all over it.[92]

Since the party had expected only the worst from Abdullah, now everyone clamoured for Nehru's head. Atal smelt conspiracy in Mookerji's arrest across the border in J&K, rather than on the Indian side in Pathankot. When the matter was discussed in parliament, Nehru evaded the demand for an enquiry, claiming that the government had never promised Mookerji an entry without permit. Atal was horrified:

> Even though he swears by 'Satyamev Jayate', Pt. Nehru lied in the Parliament to salvage his fake prestige. But no one other than his khaddar-wearing sycophants believe him. Frightened by the popularity of an old colleague, overpowered by his tenacity and vigour, the Prime Minister violated Doctor saab's personal freedom by taking him outside the protection of the Supreme Court, and putting him under house-arrest indefinitely, which in the end killed him ... Dr. Mookerji often referred to Pt. Nehru as 'one of the world's great men'. Despite differences, he had great reverence for Nehruji. But what did he get back in return? Only a mysterious death far away from near and dear ones and millions of his followers.[93]

In Mookerji's death, the Jan Sangh lost its only leader who had considerable charisma, respect and influence. The party was 'rendered orphan', the central working committee that met in Delhi on 3 July admitted. A majority of the attendees were 'in favour of the withdrawal of the Praja Parishad movement', and soon enough this transpired.[94]

The party approached its sympathizers one by one – Congressmen P. D. Tandon and Hriday Nath Kunzru, and D. P. Mishra, who had resigned from the Congress in September 1951 – inviting them to take over as president. But the Jan Sangh was a sinking ship no one wished to captain. Mauli Chandra Sharma, one of the two general secretaries, was appointed president for the time being. Sharma lacked Mookerji's stature and his ability to manage the contradictions of a political start-up heavily dependent for money and manpower on the RSS. This, along with Sharma's law practice, meant that for all purposes it was Deendayal, the other general secretary, who began to run the party on a daily basis.

Atal did not yet have a formal role in the party. The list of 225 delegates who assembled at Allahabad on 15–16 August 1953 to discuss the party's future doesn't mention his name. But a booklet he had written in July after Mookerji's death, *Mrityu ya Hatya* (Death or Assassination), was being sold at the venue for 'four paise per copy'.[95]

Deendayal had bigger plans for his protégé. Over the next two months, Atal toured all across Bombay State and UP to establish the party's district-level branches and, especially, to campaign for municipal elections in the two states.[96] His focus everywhere was more on macro issues, less on the local ones that were crucial for winning elections for a demoralized party. He never spent more than a day in one place; his brief was to give the young Jan Sangh cadre in small towns, who fought elections almost entirely on instincts, a basic lesson in ideology. The responsibility for bringing local issues to limelight lay with the party's organizing secretaries – Dattopant Thengadi for Madhya Pradesh (which included the Marathi-speaking Vidarbha); Nana Deshmukh for UP – who moved only within their assigned states.

In Kolhapur, Bombay State, Atal lambasted Nehru: 'If the Prime Minister is sure Dr. Mookerji died a natural death he has no reason to avoid the national demand for an impartial enquiry'.[97] Events in

Kashmir, including Mookerji's untimely demise, had precipitated an unforeseen slump in Nehru's relationship with Abdullah. In early August, Abdullah was dismissed as J&K's prime minister on charges of conspiring against India by espousing the cause of an independent Kashmir. He was jailed and replaced by his deputy, the more pliant Bakshi Ghulam Mohammad. Abdullah's arrest was solid proof that 'the Jan Sangh stand had triumphed'. On most other matters, he painted in broad strokes: It was 'foolish to boast of an independent policy when foreign aid was sought at every stage. The Five Year Plan had been borrowed from Russia and the Community projects from America.' Only 'the Jan Sangh had an independent economic policy which could solve all problems of the country'.[98]

On his first trip to Bombay, Atal did not cut a great first impression on his host. One Bakshiji, who received him at Bombay Central station, was not aware of Atal's talent as a crowd-puller. As he saw Atal observing with amazement the double-decker buses on the road, Bakshi mistook him for being naive and introverted. As per an exaggerated account, Atal was so keen to save party funds that he had not eaten anything throughout his Delhi–Bombay train journey.[99] Bakshi took Atal home and fed him, but he was nonplussed as to why Deendayal had sent a young small-town man to address a crowd in the big city. That the orator did not have a suitable outfit for the occasion did not help either.

> Atal took out a pair of dhoti-kurta from his bag. When Bakshiji saw that his kurta was torn from the sleeve, he said, 'Arey, you will speak from Jan Sangh's platform wearing a torn kurta.' Embarrassed, Atal said, 'I have another one.' But when he pulled out the other kurta, it was torn near the neck. Atal said innocently, "I will wear my jacket over it." Bakshiji chided him, 'Jacket in this heat? People will laugh at you.'[100]

He put on his jacket nonetheless and together they left for the venue at Vile Parle. Once on stage, Atal was a different person altogether – an actor confidently playing his role. After he had floored the crowd with his wisdom and wit, Bakshi embraced Atal.

When the party scored its maiden victory in Bombay State, in the

Jalgaon Municipal by-election, Atal's 'whirl-wind tours' received some of the credit. In UP municipal elections, the Jan Sangh more than saved face.* But Atal was sceptical: 'Even though the Jan Sangh has fared better than the Praja Socialist Party, we should not conclude that people have reposed complete faith in us. The pace at which people are turning against Congress, it must be replaced by a strong, effective party.' Even so, for now the three parties ought to join hands to improve the sanitation and health facilities in the UP towns. The failure to work together would 'shatter the already low morale of the people' who would then be easily entrapped by the communists.[101]

As things stood, it was not the communists but the Sangh's friends-turned-foes, the Akali Dal of Punjab, whose demands were beginning to grate the Jan Sangh. The Akalis had been agitating over the demand for a Punjabi suba – a Punjabi-speaking state. The government was wary because it seemed to be another way of asking for a Sikh-majority state. Punjab's strategic geography demanded that the state be kept strong enough to tackle any challenges from across the western border. Since its inception, the Jan Sangh had been staunchly opposed to the creation of linguistic states because they feared it would fuel separatist tendencies that could break India further.

On 26 November, 'Atalji Bharat Press Sadar Bazar Lucknow' received a telegram from the Delhi office: 'you due PEPSU come immediately'.[102] To prepare for the Jan Sangh's annual session in Bombay in January 1954, conferences were to be held in the party's provincial branches. Perhaps because Atal had travelled across Punjab in connection with the Praja Parishad movement, Deendayalji wanted him to go to PEPSU to 'supervise the provincial elections' in order to appoint the new working committee there.

This was different from Atal's previous assignments: he was formally declared a 'Central Adhikari' – a member of the Jan Sangh's central working committee – and was to go to Barnala two weeks in advance to oversee preparations for the conference to be held there on 12–13

---

* In Bulandshahr, the Jan Sangh candidate defeated a Congress MLA to win the president's election; in Vrindavan, the Jan Sangh secured sixteen out of twenty seats and also won the election for chairmanship.

December. He boarded the train in Lucknow the same evening so as to reach Delhi the next morning. On 28 November, the PEPSU team cabled the Delhi office: 'Send Atalji Barnala today Punjab Mail via Bhatinda.'[103]

For the last six years, Atal had embodied the RSS's studied ambiguity – a political activist among journalists and a journalist among politicians. He now became, a few weeks short of turning twenty-nine, a full-time politician.

Part Two

Between the Alleged Assassinations 1953–68

5

An Implosive Sorrow

ALL THROUGH THE WINTER OF 1953–54, THE SUCCESSION CRISIS IN the post-Mookerji Jan Sangh simmered. It was mostly a result of the RSS's attempt to control its newborn child. One faction supported an increased role for Nagpur in the party's day-to-day affairs. Arrayed against it were non-RSS men like the acting president Mauli Chandra Sharma but also, significantly, many of the Sangh's brightest activists who had been dispatched to work for the party. This included Guru Dutt Vaidya and Kunwar Lal Gupta, respectively the Delhi unit's president and secretary. At the heart of the dispute was a man operating mostly behind the scenes.

Vasantrao Oak had been the chief organizer of the RSS in Delhi, and later the sharirik pramukh – the all-India in-charge for physical instruction – before he became one of the founding members of the Jan Sangh in 1951. Flamboyant and well connected across parties in the capital, Oak had once unofficially been the most powerful man in the RSS after Golwalkar. He played a crucial role in getting the organization unbanned in 1949 by recruiting outsiders like Sharma to mediate with the government. At the time of the Jan Sangh's inception, Oak had created around himself a coterie of RSS supporters in Delhi and started acting independently. When confronted, he recommended that the RSS disband on the grounds that 'the Jan Sangh could carry out the task of national rejuvenation more effectively than a non-political association'.[1] For Nagpur, such talk was blasphemy. Presently Oak was Sharma's chief backer.

The confrontation began with petty disputes over financial matters immediately after Mookerji's death. The Jan Sangh's bank accounts were controlled by the RSS. With Mookerji gone, the cashier of the party, an RSS full-timer, now refused to sign cheques for party work. Each side began to accuse the other of misappropriating party funds.[2] Tensions exploded on the eve of the annual session in Bombay in January 1954. The party constitution gave the president the right to select its thirty-member working committee. Among his other plans, Sharma was keen to promote Oak as one of the two general secretaries. At the last moment, Deendayal handed over to him a complete list of thirty names: it did not feature Oak. After more wrangling a compromise was achieved, which was nevertheless tilted in the RSS's favour: most of the would-be members were RSS pracharaks.[3] Oak was not made a general secretary, but retained on the working committee.

As Deendayal's trusted lieutenant, Atal turned out to be one of the prime beneficiaries of the coup even though he was not an active participant. He was inducted as one of four members from UP – the youngest working committee member in the party. Over the past few weeks, there had been in Delhi a furore over Pakistan's proposed military alliance with the US. When the topic was discussed at the annual session in Bombay, Atal seconded the resolution 'to take immediate steps to provide universal military training to the youth of the country to meet any emergency that might arise'.[4] He even composed a prose poem for the occasion, challenging Pakistan: no one should have been surprised to see a people 'who weren't even ashamed to divide their mother' in 1947 now selling their sovereignty for American dollars. 'Not one, not two, you can sign 20 alliances. But India will never succumb.' This melodramatic performance in the midst of dull speeches was 'clapped over more than any other speech at the session'.[5] Making use of his availability, the local units of the Jan Sangh persuaded Atal to speak at other venues in Bombay and Pune. In Pune, 'though the meeting was to be held at 6:30 pm, the venue was jam-packed half-an-hour in advance'.[6]

Based in Delhi now, Atal ate and slept at the RSS's Jhandewalan office, from where he commuted to the Jan Sangh office at the nearby Ajmeri Gate. He travelled frequently across north India, where he gave hour-long speeches explaining the Jan Sangh's philosophy and working techniques. To the mostly ill-informed Jan Sangh worker, driven more by instinct than ideology, such speeches provided a bit of theoretical grounding on the party's approach to the issues of the day. Atal travelled to Punjab to address meetings to draw support against the Akali demand for a Sikh-majority state. He travelled to UP, where the RSS–Jan Sangh was extending support to the Ram Rajya Parishad to force the government to ban cow slaughter. 'The use of cow fat to make cartridges had led to the rebellion of 1857,' he would tell his audience: 'There will soon be another revolution on the question of cow.'[7]

Of late Atal had been spending time trying to understand economics, or at least understand it enough to articulate his party's exposition of the government's failures. This was partly because the government's new planning agenda ignored the party's core base. Couching the disillusionment in populist terms, its chief criticism of the Congress-led planning was that it 'relied too heavily on the ideas and resources of the West.' On the other hand Deendayal, the party's chief economic theorist, put forth 'labor-intensive, small-scale, self-reliant industrialization with the village or town as its unit as the key to retaining Indian ways of life while reaching a state of moderate economic well-being.'[8]

Borrowing in part from Deendayal, Atal wrote that a rise in unemployment during a period when a five-year plan was in operation indicated some basic defect in economic planning. The country must answer the question of 'man or machine'. In the name of cottage industries, the government had done nothing more than throw a few crumbs now and then to assuage political discontentment: 'The Jan Sangh stands for a complete metamorphosis of this situation so that heavy industry has to adjust itself according to the position of cottage industry.'

Elsewhere, Atal chided students for their 'contempt for manual labour which the university student of today has developed'.[9] At the annual session in Jodhpur in December 1954, he moved a resolution calling upon the Jan Sangh branches 'all over the country to take up the question of growing unemployment as the most important economic programme before it', threatening to launch an agitation to have 'work for all' included as a fundamental right.[10]

Meanwhile, the succession drama within the party was heading towards a climax. Atal's allegiance to Deendayal had initially created confusion, partly because his ex-boss at *Veer Arjun*, Amarnath Bajaj, was now firmly in the Sharma–Oak camp. Frustrated with the RSS-dominated working committee, Sharma resigned as president in early November. Atal's allegiance became clear only when, on 7 November, he volunteered to head a three-member subcommittee to prepare a report on the Delhi unit's chaotic affairs.[11] A few weeks later, the subcommittee ordered the Delhi working committee to be dissolved 'to root out indiscipline in the organisation'.[12] Eventually, the rebels were all expelled from the party. The Jan Sangh was now securely the RSS's adjunct, and would continue to be so for all time.

Less competition at the top meant a swift ascent. The annual session at Jodhpur, held during the last week of December 1954, brought Atal a major promotion. The RSS had managed to convince Prem Nath Dogra, the septuagenarian leader of the Praja Parishad, to become the Jan Sangh president. Dogra had reluctantly agreed, though the hierarchy was now clear: Deendayal would remain the de facto boss. Thus began a tradition of ornamental presidents, in central as well as state units, even as the real power was vested in the general secretary at the centre and in the organizing secretaries appointed by him in the states. The party constitution was amended to allow only one general secretary as opposed to the earlier two. Instead, two additional secretarial posts were created in the central team to assist Deendayal Upadhyaya – Atal for north India, and a Kannadiga named Jagganath Rao Joshi for south India.[13]

More importantly, Atal was appointed one of the four members of the Jan Sangh parliamentary board. By this time the party had made up its mind to field him in an election. Soon enough an occasion presented itself. In 1954 Nehru had decided to send his younger sister Vijaya Lakshmi Pandit, who represented Lucknow in the parliament, as the high commissioner to the United Kingdom. The election for the vacant seat was scheduled for 27 February 1955. The party filed Atal's nomination. He was to compete with Triloki Singh, a popular Praja Socialist Party leader, and Sheorajvati Nehru, a distant relative of the prime minister, from the ruling party. The debutant Jan Sanghi knew he had 'little chance of winning'.[14] But he was determined to lose as bravely as possible.

The campaign was launched in Lucknow on 23 January, 'the auspicious day of Subhas Chandra Bose's birthday'. The UP Jan Sangh president made an appeal for donations on Atal's behalf: 'I can say with complete confidence that Vajpayee will compensate the great loss of the Lok Sabha due to the death of Dr. Mookerji.'[15] Possibly because his competitors were much elder and of a higher stature, Atal's resume was given a makeover. He was to be presented as a prodigy, a self-made man who had chosen to give up an assured career and the fulfilment of conjugal life to save India's soul.

For this myth to appear sufficiently smooth, fictions were introduced (almost certainly aided by the candidate himself): that Atal was born in Gwalior, not Bateshwar, possibly because Gwalior sounded more cosmopolitan and evoked nostalgia for a city that flaunted – unlike Lucknow – its Hindu ethos. Or that he had an 'M.A., L.L.B.' – another falsehood, as Atal had abandoned his law degree. His participation in the Quit India movement was exaggerated: 'At the time he was a student in Gwalior. When the police began to chase him, he set up his base at Bateshwar to speed up the movement. There he encouraged the villagers too, and together they broke the forest laws ... he remained locked up inside the Agra Jail for a long time.'[16]

At the peak of campaigning, on 10 February, the state government announced the acceptance of the Dr Sitaram Committee report that recommended a ban on the killing of cows in UP. Even as the governor K. M. Munshi announced the news in the assembly, a crowd of Ram Rajya Parishad and Jan Sangh workers led by Atal agitated outside. The UP Congress may have timed the announcement to rob the opponents of one of its core issues. But the Jan Sangh appropriated the decision as an outcome of their sustained agitation: Atal and Prabhudatt Brahmachari – the leader of the cow-protection movement

– led a procession in Lucknow 'to celebrate UP government's decision to ban cow slaughter completely'.[17] It was a major consolation for Brahmachari, who had independently jumped into the electoral ring in 1952, standing up against the reforms unleashed by the Hindu Code Bill (through inheritance and marriage laws). He had challenged the loftiest of all, Nehru, in the Phulpur constituency, and was devastated at being trounced.

Apart from making public addresses, the candidate personally visited the houses of as many voters as possible. As polling neared, the entire Jan Sangh leadership alighted in Lucknow; Deendayal and Nanaji had been camped there for weeks. On 23 February, a large procession of Jan Sangh supporters, most of them on bicycles, followed an open jeep, atop which sat Atal and President Dogra. They waved to and greeted the crowds on the road.

But the candidate felt distracted: his thoughts often wandered to his ailing father. Suffering from stomach troubles in Gwalior, Babuji had moved to Bateshwar for a few months, hoping to recuperate by way of its clean air and water. Atal may not have approved of a sick Babuji living on his own in the village. Babuji repeatedly assured him that he was managing just about fine on his own, that in fact he was happy to be briefly away from Gwalior. He wrote to 'Chiranjeevi Atal':

> I wanted to come to Lucknow so that I could take part in your election campaign. But on the 4th and 5th [February] I came down with such severe acidity that I felt that God did not want me to go there just yet. Nothing to be discouraged about; the faulty stars should realign soon … There might come an opportunity in future when you and I will both fight elections together – just as we studied together at DAV College. My body is here, but my mind and heart and soul and wishes are all with you. Keep working hard, without fretting about the outcome. Krishn.[18]

The youngest son had been doing exactly that. But everyone outside the RSS–Jan Sangh circles was confident that Atal would not be able to make a dent. On the eve of the poll, the *Times of India* postulated that Atal's candidature was 'significant only for his potentialities to cut into the Congress vote'.[19]

Not many people came out to vote, 'an anti-climax to last week's bitter electioneering' in the city.[20] Only thirty-four per cent of the 337,000 voters exercised their franchise. Atal lost, but the defeat was graceful.* Even though he finished third, the fact that he had polled twenty-eight per cent of the vote, thereby converting the two-party contest into a triangular one, surprised his detractors.[21] The young Jan Sanghi received almost no Muslim votes, but the party was gratified that more Hindus had voted for him than for the prime minister's relative, and that in the rural areas the Jan Sangh had fetched more votes than both its rivals. Atal's strong performance would enhance his clout inside the party.

Back home in Gwalior, the family was struggling financially. Atal's eldest brother Awadh Behari, who did not get along with Babuji – proving Baba's prophecy right – landed a job with the revenue department of the Madhya Pradesh government in Bhopal and moved with his family, breaking off contact with Ma–Babuji. Prem Behari had taken a teaching job in Morena, where he moved with his wife and kids. Only Sada Behari continued to live in Gwalior with Ma–Babuji. He ran a ragtag printing press, and was bogged down by another karmic curse: in pursuit of a son, they had six daughters. The girls would grow up yearning for but never receiving their Dadi's affection.

Atal did not earn a monthly salary from which he could send money back home. When he went home for festivals, especially for the annual mela in Gwalior that began on the night of the Kartik full moon sometime in October–November, Ma would try to cajole Atal into taking up a regular job and getting married. On one occasion he reproached Ma for harbouring false expectations: 'How much happiness and comfort have the other daughters-in-law brought you?'[22] He also rebuked a distant uncle who had looked at Atal's palm and predicted that not only was he to get married, he would in fact father 'six girls'. The bachelor retorted, 'Well, I won't get married, so there is no question of any girls being born.'[23]

* Mrs Nehru got 49,324 votes, Triloki Singh 34,578, Atal Behari Vajpayee 33,986.

Babuji had fulfilled all his major responsibilities. He had married off his three daughters and divided his property among the three sons, including the house he had built at Shinde Ki Chhavni. (Estranged from his eldest son, Babuji had disinherited Awadh Behari.) He was the president of the Gwalior district Jan Sangh, and fancied fighting an election in the near future. Putting his law degree to use, he had begun to practise, though he never attained enough distinction to be able to earn anything. He maintained a regular column in *Panchjanya*, 'Durangi Duniya' – a collection of funny, sarcastic nuggets from the past week. He also churned out a few books of prose as well as verse. But while Babuji enjoyed writing, none of his literary pursuits brought him any money. Even though Babuji and Ma were not particularly old – Babuji was now sixty-five, Ma a few years younger – neither was in good health. That, along with the burden of a household of ten on a meagre pension, meant Babuji would frequently lose his temper.

Soon, Babuji was suffering a gastric attack 'once or twice every week' and had difficulty digesting his meals. This was when, wishing to recuperate, he decided to spend some time in Bateshwar. Gwalior was 'the land of my karma, and to be active on the field one needs a fit body. When the body becomes weak, one should take a break from karma-bhoomi'. For a while the village did uplift Babuji's health and spirits. He wrote to Atal that he felt 'happier here than I am generally at Lashkar' [in Gwalior]; that his gastric attacks had ceased; the 'only complaint is that my stool is not clean. By the grace of God, that will also get better gradually.' Unlike in Gwalior, 'where every day brought an opportunity to ignite new tensions', there was no one in Bateshwar to quarrel with.

One of the daughters came to tend to Babuji. He wrote to Atal, 'Perhaps you are not aware that a daughter feels in her heart more affection for her father than a son does. This virtue is God-given.' Babuji spent much of his time reciting the Ramayana and the Gita in temples, and reading the bundle of newspapers and journals Atal would send him. Any leftover time he spent writing essays for *Madhya Bharat Sandesh* 'so people in Gwalior don't forget me'. Babuji assured Atal that he had 'enough vitality inside me to withstand the disease'. He sought inspiration from Arjun in the Mahabharata who, confronted with moral dilemmas on the battlefield, had taken two vows: 'na dainyam na palaynam' – to never feel helpless, and to never run away.[24]

Babuji had a 'strong desire to come to Lucknow' to help Atal with his campaigning. Unfortunately, by the end of February, his health had begun to steadily deteriorate. After he was brought to Lucknow around the first week of March, Atal used his contacts to get Babuji admitted to the Lucknow Medical College's hospital. The diagnosis was alarming: Babuji had late-stage gastric cancer. The tumour had grown slowly over time, and was spotted a bit too late. This did not seem to dampen Babuji's zest for life. He decided to write a new column for *Panchjanaya* called 'Naya Lucknauwa' – the New Lucknowite. A few days before he was operated upon, on 27 March, the New Lucknowite sent from his hospital bed included some tacky, sarcastic verses chiding the government for imposing through its budget new taxes on an aggrieved middle class.[25]

By this time Ma, along with Prem Behari and Sada Behari, had arrived in Lucknow. A week after the operation, Babuji developed ascites; the abdominal swelling proved fatal. He breathed his last on the evening of 8 April. Ideally the cremation should have taken place in Gwalior or Bateshwar, but for logistical reasons it was performed in Lucknow. Even though Awadh Behari, the eldest son, was to light the pyre as per tradition, he did not reach in time: the youngest, Atal, performed the duty. Some of Atal's colleagues from the RSS–Jan Sangh attended the cremation. A 'deeply saddened' *Panchjanya* family extended 'our sympathy and condolences to dear brother Atalji' for Babuji's untimely death. The Vindhya Pradesh unit of Jan Sangh passed a condolence resolution for the 'well-known Shri Krishn Behari Vajpayee, who was devoted to the service of literature'.[26] Five decades later, Atal would still recall Babuji's death as the 'saddest moment in my life'.[27]

The family had barely recovered when another tragedy came to light. For a while Ma had suffered from sores in her cheeks that refused to heal. As with most patriarchal families, Babuji's illness had been prioritized over Ma's. It turned out that decades of tobacco-chewing had made her right cheek tumorous: she was diagnosed with mouth cancer. Either the family could not afford her treatment, or the disease was (as with Babuji) detected quite late: Ma was not admitted to a hospital. Before long she was unable to swallow food and grew weaker by the day, surviving mainly on pineapple and pomegranate juice. Sada Behari's wife became the target of her invalid mother-in-law's jibes, even though she was the only woman around to tend to Ma full-time. Every time the doctor came to clean her mouth and change the dressing, Ma would scream in pain. Sometimes she had to be given anaesthesia.

The end was near. With his new party responsibilities in Delhi, Atal could come home only intermittently. One of Sada Behari's daughters, the then ten-year-old Kanti, vividly remembered one such occasion: 'Chachaji sitting beside Dadi, reading to her from the Gita in Sanskrit as she lay on the bed. Tears trickled down his cheeks as he flipped the pages. I would wonder why Chachaji was crying.'[28]

Jostling for political geographies dominated the latter half of 1955. Only one of them obsessed the Jan Sangh: the movement to liberate Goa. A Portuguese colony since the early sixteenth century, Goa was one of the few places in the country still under foreign rule. The occasional attempts by the natives to demand autonomy, both peaceful and violent, had so far been crushed by the Portuguese. After the French government was forced to grant Pondicherry autonomy in 1954, the socialists revived the struggle. That year, the All-Party Goa Liberation Committee was formed with the aim of aiding the civil disobedience campaign.

While inaugurating Atal's campaign in Lucknow on 23 January, Deendayal had first hinted at the party's plans to mobilize volunteers to be sent to Goa. He urged the government to either take military action in Goa or, alternatively, allow satyagrahis to enter Goa to protest there by peaceful means.[29] With participation of this kind, the Jan Sangh could fend off the everyday charges levelled against them by Congressmen of having played no part in the freedom movement. Now was the time to go the whole hog!

Goa's liberation was inevitable, but there were diplomatic tangles. One of the founding member of the NATO, Portugal had presented India as an aggressor on its territory. Hoping to watch the evolving situation before exercising the last resort – sending the army – the Nehru government had been dissuading the satyagrahis. On Independence Day, 15 August 1955, the Portuguese government in Goa opened fire on the satyagrahis. In a group led by Jagannath Rao Joshi, Atal's counterpart in south India, three Jan Sangh workers were shot dead. Joshi himself was thrashed and locked up in a Goa jail.

Atal had addressed some of these men who had congregated in Delhi from across north India before they left for Goa. The news of the attack found him in Deogarh in Rajasthan, where he had come to address the party's provincial annual session. He fumed, 'Our prime minister had said that he would not tolerate any nonsense in Goa. Now, could anything be more impudent than shooting peaceful and unarmed satyagrahis dead? How long will the Indian government watch even as the Portuguese inflict barbaric atrocities on us?'[30] From Deogarh he rushed to Bombay to collect the ashes of the dead men and bring them back to Delhi, where they were handed over to satyagrahis from Haridwar returning home so they may be immersed in the Ganga.[31]

The Jan Sangh decided to capitalize on the fervid emotions generated by the deaths. In the latter half of September, Atal travelled across Bombay State with the prime purpose of overseeing the preparation of satyagrahis to be dispatched to Goa on 2 October – Gandhi's birth anniversary – as decided by the socialists-led opposition. Everywhere, he held press conferences and public meetings, interacted with and encouraged the local party cadres. On 23 September, the Jalgaon municipality, which included four Jan Sangh members, threw a reception to present Atal a 'certificate of honour'. From Jalgaon Atal left for Dhulia, the hometown of Uttamrao Patil, the Bombay State Jan Sangh President and MLC in Bombay. From Dhulia Atal went to Nashik and Aurangabad, finally reaching Pune on 2 October. Speaking at a gathering that day to send off the satyagrahis, he chided the Bombay State chief minister Morarji Desai for alleging that opposition parties were participating in the Goa struggle only 'to discredit the Congress and to derive electoral benefits'. With his penchant for hyperbole, Atal rued:

> I do not know whether we should laugh or cry at Morarjibhai – at his narrow, polluted, deformed mindset ... Whatever Congress does, whatever policy the government adopts, the duty of the Indian masses

> is rather clear ... To fight the battle to liberate Goa is our birthright. We have every right to die for the freedom of our [Goan] brothers, and no one can snatch it away. The ashes from the martyrs' pyre still have heat in them. The Indian blood shed on 15 August in Goa is still fresh. We will not rest until Goa is liberated.[32]

In reality, the police arrested the satyagrahis – mostly socialists, but also Mahasabha and Jan Sangh workers like Patil – in Sawantwadi, a few kilometres ahead of Goa. Atal plodded on, his two-week-long trip in Bombay State concluding on 5 October.[33]

Around the same time as Atal, Indira Gandhi – Nehru's daughter who had recently been made a Congress Working Committee member – was also touring Bombay State. Expectedly, government officials used the state machinery to make her visit comfortable and successful. Like her father, she often laid into the RSS–Jan Sangh. In Nashik she said that the people who demanded a ban on cow slaughter were the same people who once 'lick[ed] the shoes of the British'. Atal bitterly resented Indira's entitlement: in Dhulia, a government school playground was sanctioned for her speech, but denied to him. 'The power-intoxicated Congress may deny the Jan Sangh a place for meeting,' he later announced in Bombay, 'but it cannot deny [us] a place in the hearts of the people.'[34]

The second aspect of his tour, infinitely more consequential, was the release, on 30 September, of the report of the SRC – States Reorganization Commission. Atal arrived in Bombay a week later to notice that the demand for linguistic states had supplanted Goa as everybody's chief concern. The idea of linguistic states catered to the 'new pride, the new sense of self' that the independence had fostered.[35] More urgently, though, the SRC had been set up in response to the movements in states opposed to Hindi alone being adopted as the official language.

The Jan Sangh had at its inception championed the cause of Hindi. It had also been a votary of the unitary state, and was opposed to any movement for the demand of a separate state, linguistic or otherwise.*

---

* Andhra Pradesh was, in October 1953, the first state Nehru was forced to carve out of the Madras State after the Telegu speakers-led agitation precipitated Potti Sreeramulu's death by fasting. Conceding Andhra escalated the clamour for linguistic states in other parts of the country, forcing the government to appoint an SRC to study each of these demands in details.

The commission also leaned towards the assumption that the creation of states based solely on linguistic lines might impede national unity. While it recommended carving out three states in the south, the SRC deemed the linguistic demands in Punjab and Bombay State as more tangled.

Travelling from one small town in Bombay State to another, Atal had met the Samyukta Maharashtra (United Maharashtra) fanatics everywhere, chanting 'they would not rest till their demand was conceded'.[36] Obsessed with the Goa liberation agitation, the Sangh Parivar – a phrase now used to collectively refer to the RSS and its affiliates such as the Jan Sangh and ABVP – was caught wholly off guard by this sub-nationalist surge in many parts of the country. As a Brahmin from the Hindi heartland, where the elites moved effortlessly between their regional tongues on one hand and canonized Hindi on the other, Atal struggled to appreciate the anxiety of Marathi speakers desiring a separate state. It was an odd occasion where the Sangh Parivar's views temporarily aligned with Nehru's. Atal realized that the local cadres of Jan Sangh too – as indeed the Congress cadres – were tempted.

The Jan Sangh secretary for north India didn't budge. At Baroda in the last week of January 1956, Atal exhorted the Marathi and Gujarati speakers to accept, as recommended by the SRC, 'the formation of a bilingual Bombay State'. This was suicidal, considering the Gujarati nationalists would soon launch a Mahagujarat movement demanding a separate state as well as the city of Bombay. On his flights of fancy, the heartland Brahmin could not fathom the sub-national anxieties: 'To ensure the unity of the nation, it is essential to dissolve state assemblies and establish a unitary administration' at the centre.[37] In Patna a few weeks later, he mourned 'Marathis refusing to live with Gujaratis, Sikhs refusing to live with the Hindus. This disease can hollow up the body of the nation.' Also, 'What is the urgency in spending billions of rupees over erecting new states and assemblies for them?'[38]

The Sangh Parivar was wary because the linguistic movements unveiled another fault line, risking the birth of separatism in multiple corners. More than anywhere else, they feared this in Sikh-majority Punjab. After the SRC's rejection of the demand for Punjabi Suba, the central government had been parleying with the Akalis for a settlement. They arrived at a compromise. As per the 'Regional Formula', only PEPSU was to be merged with Punjab, not Himachal Pradesh. The newly coalesced Punjab was to be divided into two zones – one Punjabi-speaking and the other Hindi-speaking – recognizing both Gurmukhi and Devanagari scripts. It would continue to have one chief minister and council of ministers, one legislature, one governor and only one high court. In early March 1956, the Akali Dal officially accepted this formula.

Convinced that the Formula was a precursor to the Punjabi Suba, the aggrieved supporters of United Punjab – the local units of the Jan Sangh, the Arya Samaj and others – launched an agitation to have it revoked. Around 20 May, Atal left for Haryana, the Hindu-majority territory of Punjab adjacent to Delhi. Over the next week, he visited twenty-five places to satisfy himself that Haryana had rejected the Regional Formula: 'If at all there are to be regional committees, the two regions should be equal in population, having fixed equal representatives in the cabinet. They want larger financial allocations in view of their area's backwardness.'[39] After Haryana, he left for Jullundur to attend the all-party Maha Punjab Samiti Sammelan held on 26–27 May. Speaking at half-past midnight, Atal 'electrified the audience with his magical eloquence'. The conference threatened the government to come up with a 'satisfactory response' by June 17, failing which they would launch a satyagraha.[40]

That day, an unruly procession of Maha Punjab supporters, the majority among them Jan Sangh sympathizers, were brutally lathi-charged by the police in Hoshiarpur. Sent by the party to fact-find, Atal was irate that the police had 'not spared even women and children'.[41] Another protest was organized in Karnal a week later. Amid high security, 15,000 protestors shouted slogans against the Regional Formula and calling for United Punjab, as had been recommended by the SRC. The people marching in the crowd included Atal, Karpatri Maharaj of the Ram Rajya Parishad and the Mahasabha president V. G. Deshpande.[42] But the die had been cast: the new Punjab state came into being on 1 November 1956, signalling an ill omen for the Jan Sangh on the eve of general elections.

The seventy-one-year-old Jan Sangh president Premnath Dogra, who had neither the energy nor the intellectual curiosity to think about the world beyond his hometown Jammu, was occasionally persuaded to travel to the Hindi heartland. On his twenty-day UP tour during November–December 1955, he was accompanied first by Deendayal and then, on the second leg, which commenced in Banaras, by Atal.

It was there, on the road with Dogra, that Atal received the tragic, though hardly unexpected, news from home: he rushed to Gwalior. Once again the eldest son failed to turn up on time: Atal lit Ma's funeral pyre. 'The successive death of both his parents broke something inside him,' Prem Behari's wife Rajeshwari later remarked.[43] In his weak moments, the youngest son felt that he had let his parents down in some fundamental ways: Atal was now thirty-one, and without a salaried job. Had he taken up the lecturer's job in 1947, he could have provided better treatment for his parents, which might have at least delayed their deaths. Nor had he fulfilled one of Ma's last desires, to bless her youngest son's bride. Finding no outlet for grief, he plunged himself back into work.

The Jan Sangh had been, for a while, negotiating a merger with the Hindu Mahasabha and the Ram Rajya Parishad. In his speeches, Atal vaguely hoped that the merger would 'fill the vacuum of an opposition' after the 1957 general elections. But there had been no progress on this front. Some of the blame lay with Atal himself. He had earlier ranted that the Mahasabha in Bombay State was 'as good as dead'.[44] He believed the Mahasabha's dwindling base had fuelled the ascent of socialists and communists, whom he held responsible for trumpeting the cause of an exclusive Marathi-speaking state.* He lashed out at the Mahasabha for squandering the legacy of Shivaji and Tilak. 'The old guard of its leadership have either renounced politics or are too old for active participation. In Poona the activities of the Hindu Sabha are limited to the columns of the *Kesari* – including its membership drive ... the system of a commission of "one anna per member" for the worker who enrolled the members also failed to bring results.' Atal had discovered that the Mahasabha workers on the ground 'would like the Sabha to merge its

* The communists had been demanding linguistic states even before independence.

political entity in the Jan Sangh, limiting its independent activities only to the social sphere'.[45]

The Mahasabha leadership continued to vacillate. The inertia may have had to do with a hurt ego (from playing subservient to a party that had once been their offshoot) as well as with some practical difficulties (many in the Mahasabha still disagreed with Jan Sangh's policy of allowing Muslims to become members). When Atal continued to shoot his mouth off, the ruffled Mahasabha president V. G. Deshpande hit back saying the merger was a complicated decision that needed patience: 'I may suggest [to] my friends in Jana Sangh that there is much time left for apportioning blame on each other if unfortunately we do not succeed in our objective.'[46]

Collaborating with the Ram Rajya Parishad proved to be a bigger race to the bottom of human association. Its leader Karpatri Maharaj was opposed to even the most rudimentary social reforms. At a meeting to discuss the merger, he likened the RSS–Jan Sangh tradition of people from across the castes eating together (such as at the annual sessions and OTCs) to a feast of dogs: 'Sab mil kar kutton ki tarah khaate hain.' He also insisted that non-upper-castes ought not to touch the sacred ancient texts: 'Ved mantra toh shudra padh hi nahi sakte.' Even by RSS–Jan Sangh's narrow interpretation of the past – with its unresolved inferiority complex, and only inchoate signs of moral awakening – lack of the Hindu unity had been India's chief crisis. Karpatri Maharaj's views were repugnant to Atal and his colleagues.[47]

The merger remained doomed. The party gathered in mid-April 1956 for its annual session in Jaipur. The second general elections were only six months away. Keen to secure enough votes to retain its status as a national party, the Jan Sangh's young nine-member parliamentary board decided to fight at least 100 Lok Sabha and 570 legislative assembly seats. Among the immediate strategies to corner the government was an agitation against the newly launched sales tax.

As the government saw it, sales tax had to be imposed to compensate for the loss of revenue due to alcohol prohibition, and to meet the increased expenses for development projects. The Jan Sangh had always ridiculed Nehru's emphasis on heavy industries – high dams, steel plants – as wasteful expenditure. 'We know that economic activities must go on, and everyone must bear some taxes,' said Atal at an all-party public meeting in Lucknow on the evening of 25 April. 'But it's wholly inappropriate to impose taxes in this manner, even as the government is indulging in an extravaganza of 10 crore rupees in projects like the Bhakra Nangal [dam]. Till the time government stops such misuse, what is the rationale behind imposing sales tax?'[48]

Early in the morning of 25 April, he led a Jan Sangh procession through the streets of Lucknow shouting 'bikri kar hatwa kar rahenge' – we will not rest till the sales tax is rolled back – to the Assembly House at 10 a.m. There he denounced the government for levying tax 'even on daily necessities of life' such as salt, food grains, clothes and books.[49] The next few weeks Atal travelled through the rural districts of UP and Bihar, where the potential for outrage on sales tax was highest. But the enterprise lacked conviction: a party that had once opposed land reforms was now acting holier-than-thou over relatively peripheral issues. In any case, the legislation was not going to come into force till the next year; the opposition strike was mostly aimed at making themselves visible during the campaign.

The year 1956 saw one more event that went to the heart of the Jan Sangh's existential neurosis. Atal tracked the communal Muslim press with a moth-like attraction, a habit he had developed in his earlier avatar as the editor of RSS mouthpieces. During August–September 1956, a Kanpur Urdu daily, *Siyasat Jadid*, reproduced portions from an American book, with inflammatory headlines such as 'PROPHET INSULTED IN GOVERNOR MUNSHI'S PUBLICATION'.* Possibly unfamiliar with the Western approach to life writing, the Urdu daily was offended by the suggestions of promiscuity and violence in the life of Prophet Muhammad, even though this was not the first time a Western biography of the Prophet had levelled these charges. A bigger cause of hurt was the Hindi translation being carried out by Bharatiya Vidya Bhavan, whose founder was the UP governor K. M. Munshi.[50] Protests began with

* In 1942 two American writers had profiled major personalities down the ages – Moses, Buddha, Prophet Muhammad, Gandhi – for a book, *Living Biographies of Religious Leaders*. Sometime in 1955, a translated version of the book was printed in India as part of a collaboration between the book's American publisher and the Bombay-based Bharatiya Vidya Bhavan.

agitations led by Muslims across north India. There were rumours that some students at the Aligarh Muslim University had burnt copies of the Gita and shouted slogans of 'Pakistan Zindabad'.* The agitation escalated into communal riots – especially in Aligarh and Jabalpur – with more than a dozen people getting killed and curfew being imposed over many cities.

Seizing the moment, the Jan Sangh gave a call for protest meetings all across the country. On 16 September, Lucknow city remained shut owing to the strike. At a public meeting that evening, Atal had barely grabbed the mike when it began to rain heavily. But his large Hindu audience stayed in place. He began by congratulating the UP government for refusing to ban the book 'despite heavy pressure' from the centre. The Bihar and Bengal governments had banned it because they had no qualms encouraging Muslim communalism in exchange for votes: the 'decision was taken on political rather than legal grounds'. Atal argued for Islam to adapt itself to changing times:

> Muslims need to understand that ... we are in 1956; we can't adopt the ways of 1500 or 1600 AD. We have no issues if Muslims want to keep their heads locked forever, but they cannot force us to do the same.[51]

Referring to the desecration of the Gita at AMU, he said, 'Everyone calls our beloved deity Krishna a thief', and yet a Hindu welcomes that description of him as a 'chit chor' – heart-stealer. The AMU was 'a factory for manufacturing anti-nationals' that ought to be shut down. He also criticized the leftists for condoning the Muslim agitation: 'The communists must remember that even though they had supported the creation of Pakistan, it was the communists who were the first to be banned in Pakistan.'[52]

To be sure it was a vexed issue. The *Living Biographies* controversy was the first major expression of Muslim communalism since partition, and the demand for an all-out ban on the book meant an assault on the

---

* Founded in 1875 by Syed Ahmed Khan, the Aligarh Muslim University aimed to impart modern education to Indian Muslims, thereby contributing to a socio-political renaissance. The Sangh Parivar has often viewed the AMU with suspicion, partly due to the university's staunch support for the Muslim League in the 1940s.

freedom of the press. The prime minister himself felt that some of the slogans shouted at AMU were 'not only anti-national but also treasonable'. The AMU vice chancellor Zakir Husain rebuked his students for causing 'pain to the soul of the Prophet'.[53]

In some ways, Atal's views on citizenship and secularism were beginning to broaden. He no longer thought of all Indian Muslims as active collaborators in the Pakistan project who had stayed back only to sabotage the truncated land of the Hindus. But he still doubted their loyalty. On the one hand, Muslims were a homogeneous herd who had chosen to 'keep their heads locked up' in the medieval age. On the other, there was no need for Hinduism to reform itself; it only had to assert its antiquity.

When the Jan Sangh's central working committee met in Delhi on 30 December to finalize the election manifesto, Atal moved a resolution on 'Indian culture', arguing that territorial unity alone could not be the basis of nationalism: 'The realisation of being the nationals of one nation requires the unifying bonds of culture.'[54] The Sangh Parivar operated with the sentimental conviction that by cajoling Muslims to worship Hindu warriors (Shivaji, Rana Pratap) and deities (Ram, Krishna) and celebrate festivals like Holi and Diwali, India would restore its apparent ancient glory.

The speech Atal made after his resolution was also revelatory of his party's desperation to reach for ideas accessible to their needs. His exposition of cultural nationalism meant a simultaneous appropriation and othering of Congress icons: he was still certain that 'it was Congress's adulation of Muslims that first gave them ideas on the two-nation theory'. A few minutes later, he evoked the same Congress stalwarts Lokmanya Tilak and Mahatma Gandhi as 'supreme devotees of Indian culture'. The present-day Congress had forgotten those values: 'Now it's up to the Jan Sangh to carry that flag and fully accomplish the task begun by those departed souls.' With the Nehru-led Congress's leftist turn, it was easier for the saffron brotherhood to appropriate Congress icons whose politics contained shades of conservatism – Tilak, Madan Mohan Malaviya, Lala Lajpat Rai, even Gandhi.

The intellectual vacuum of the Sangh Parivar was on ample display in a long interview Atal gave that week to *Panchjanya* 'to dispel the confusion among Muslims and Christians'. The Jan Sangh was beginning to self-consciously present itself as a moderate party. Asked if the party's agenda was to convert all Muslims and Christians to Hinduism, Atal replied that all minorities would have 'complete freedom to pursue their own faith, and would not be discriminated against in any manner'. He was keen to distance himself and his party from both the Mahasabha and the Congress:

> Nehruji thinks of Jan Sangh and Mahasabha as the same thing, while Savarkarji calls us 'Doosri Congress'. Both these assumptions are incorrect. The Jan Sangh does not oppose Muslims, even though it does not advocate a compromise with their anti-national attitude … The Jan Sangh wants to refine their sensibilities. The policy of discrimination [against Muslims, as pursued by the Mahasabha] is neither practical nor advisable. Muslims in India haven't, most of them, come from outside. They are India's children. Now they cannot be dragged out of the country. The need is to cultivate inside them affection for India. But for that a conversation is necessary. By shutting the door you cannot keep a conversation going.[55]

Would it be possible 'to instil into Indian Muslims a sense of unflinching loyalty towards India'? The 'task has become difficult now', he said, but 'not impossible'.

> Indian Muslims should think about it with a calm mind. Now that they are going to live in India, why not give it their full-fledged allegiance? The constitution grants them equal rights. But with rights also come responsibilities. They must perform the duties expected out of citizens. And the fundamental basis of those duties is a complete loyalty towards India.[56]

Did he have a criterion for loyalty? With the bland entitlement of a Hindi-belt Brahmin, he furrowed his brow before answering:

> They should search their hearts, and ask: Should Kashmir remain a part of India, or should it go to Pakistan? If their answer is in India's favour, and

> if they are also willing to take up arms against Pakistan to keep Kashmir in India, then no one can doubt their loyalty. For all such patriots, Jan Sangh's gates are wide open.[57]

Since October 1956, Atal had been constantly on the road, travelling from one state to another to finalize the seats the Jan Sangh wanted to contest. Incessant travel had begun to affect his health. Like Babuji, he too was beginning to have abdominal disorders.[58] Upon returning, he filed the nomination from Lucknow, inaugurating his campaign on Makar Sankranti in mid-January. Everywhere, he chided the Congress for its failures: to generate jobs, to universalize primary health and education, to check the prices of necessary goods. As earlier, he had little to offer on how his party would do things differently. It was easier to indulge in silky rhetoric.

> Jan Sangh's aim is to create a political, social and economic democracy, in which all men and women will have equal opportunities and freedoms. Apart from making India strong and prosperous, Jan Sangh also wants to make India a progressive and self-aware nation; one which can successfully tackle an external aggression, and make an impact in the comity of nations by contributing to world peace.[59]

Occasionally his criticisms were pointed and sharp. Speaking to a Lucknow crowd in mid-February 1957, he rued the government's desire to nationalize all industries: 'Today the government wants to control everything – insurance, cement industry, manufacture of textbooks, hotels, motor cars. All of this is being done in the name of inefficiency in the private sector … But who is going to be held responsible if the government-led industries don't function efficiently?' The government should 'only run industries which are necessary for national security, leaving the rest to the private sector'.[60]

The public bluster was in stark contrast to his private assessment. The party had neither a popular leader nor a mass base; they also had no money. Decades later, he would reminisce about the comic tragedy that was the Jan Sangh election machinery in the winter of 1956–57: 'It was hard to find candidates to fight the elections. The few who agreed after great persuasion wanted to fight for the Legislative Assembly. It involved less expenditure. Even if one lost, there was hope of garnering enough votes to save one's security deposit. Out of sheer fluke, there was also a chance of winning.'[61]

Atal was one of the rare Jan Sangh candidates who stood a reasonable chance of winning a Lok Sabha seat; he was certainly more popular now than he had been two years ago. His party men further expanded the list of fictions in his resume: 'The biggest proof of his talent,' *Panchjanya* now asserted, 'is that all through his student life he never stood second.'[62] In order to hedge their chances, the party fielded him from both Lucknow and another place whose 'geography or history I had no clue of' despite having travelled widely across UP.

Standing on the banks of the Ghaghara river, Balrampur was a minor princely state that had been merged with Uttar Pradesh in 1947. The decision to fight from here was prompted by the RSS–Jan Sangh's having cultivated here, partly thanks to patronage in the past by its Hindu maharaja, a strong organizational network. The Congress gave its ticket to Haidar Hussain, the sitting MP from Gonda, which was now delimited to carve out a separate constituency in Balrampur. An alumnus of Oxford and Lincoln's Inn, Hussain was a reputed lawyer from Lucknow, and had been a member of the constituent assembly. With his full-time legal practice and other involvements in Lucknow and Delhi, he had not paid adequate attention to his rural constituency in eastern UP. The socialists and communists had no great base there, and did not contest. Briefly, Karpatri Maharaj had flirted with the idea of fielding an RRP candidate, but was convinced to back down so as to not hurt the cause of Hindu consolidation. It was now going to be a straight contest between Atal and Sir Haidar.

At the last moment, Atal was fielded from one more constituency: Mathura. This was the only area in UP where the Jan Sangh had swept the 1953 municipal elections. When no suitable candidates for the Lok Sabha presented themselves, 'everyone looked at me'. It was a dubious distinction to be the only candidate in the country to juggle three seats.

The party issued appeals for his election funds for Balrampur:

'Everyone knows that an election today cannot be fought without finances. But where would Shri Vajpayee, who has submitted his entire life to the service of the nation, bring money from?' Every party worker was goaded to 'send at least one rupee towards this fund'.[63] The candidate later painted a hilarious picture of his overnight metre-gauge train trip to Balrampur to file his nomination:

> I spread my sheet on the narrow berth and slept. When I woke up, I found the train halted at a station. I raised the shutter to find hundreds of crows, perched on the trees nearby, making a humongous kaawn-kaawn call. The entire sky echoed with their cawing. I asked – what station is this? Came the answer – Kauwapur.[64]

It was a hint of the chaos to come. Balrampur, still a station away, had a curious demography. The twenty per cent Muslim population included most of the rich landlords in the region, whom the less landed upper castes, Thakurs and Brahmins, who were also the chief local supporters of the Jan Sangh, now resented. Atal found the Hindus in Balrampur living 'under the perpetual terror of [its Muslim] landlords' who, 'apart from exploiting the peasantry economically, also discriminated on religious grounds. I toured places where striking gongs and blowing conch shells' – rituals sacred to Hindus – 'was prohibited'.[65] The largest chunk of the constituency, however, comprised low-caste subsistent farmers – Khatiks, Kahaars and Ahirs – and Tharu tribals, who lived along its border with Nepal in the north. It was this bunch of floating voters upon whom hinged Atal's fate.

The Lucknow team dispatched a jeep to Balrampur for his campaign. The party workers in the constituency too arranged a rickety jeep, whose engine broke down every few kilometres; they also collected funds so that both jeeps could run. Metalled roads often came to an abrupt end, leading the vehicles onto a mud path where they would invariably get stuck. Everyone including the candidate would get down and push the jeep until the engine came back to life. A bullock cart was also arranged as an alternative. But parts of Balrampur constituency didn't even have wide footpaths. To traverse them bicycles were arranged. Helped by a 'team of 50 cyclists, Atalji would go from village to village, house to house, asking for votes'. Sometimes it became too dark to return to the town, and the team would halt in one of the villages. During one such halt, it rained so heavily that the next morning any travel on wheels was declared impossible. The party workers arranged for a palanquin, but an embarrassed Atal refused. After a mare was arranged as an alternative, the candidate set off, sitting awkwardly on its back.[66]

With the polls over in early March, Atal had, for the first time in many years, no hectic itinerary; he went home. The early election news was discouraging. In Lucknow, he improved his tally but lost narrowly to the Congress candidate. (Had it been a tri-cornered contest like the 1955 by-election, he might have pulled off a narrow win.) In Mathura, he was savagely thrashed: the constituency returned the popular Jat leader Mahendra Pratap, a maharaja turned Gandhian who had been nominated for the Nobel Peace Prize in 1932. Fighting independently, he had 'succeeded in fully exploiting the anti-Congress sentiment'.[67] Even though Atal had 10 per cent of the votes, he came in fourth and lost his security deposit. The shame rankled throughout his life.[68]*

All through 23 March, the day of counting in Balrampur, phones in the Lucknow Jan Sangh office rang incessantly to enquire about Atal's fate. Only at 9 p.m. did it become clear that he had defeated his Congress adversary by around 10,000 votes.† Atal was more relieved than elated: had the Congress fielded a Hindu candidate, he might not have pulled this one off either. In faraway Nagpur, a few adolescent RSS volunteers pedalled away fast on their rickety cycles to announce the joyful news to their friends: 'Atalji jeet gaye'.[69]

Not unexpectedly, opposing the creation of linguistic states had wrecked the fortunes of rightist parties at the ballot. All this while, Atal had continued to refer to the need for a unitary state as 'the most important political task' in the country. While both Congress and CPI had improved their seat tally in the Lok Sabha, the Mahasabha and the RRP secured one and zero respectively; the presidents of both parties,

---

* He was still bitter four decades later: 'Either the local unit should not have coaxed me to fight, or else, since they had thrown me into the ring, they should have ensured that people voted for me. There could be no justification for even the most ardent supporters of Jan Sangh deserting it.'

† Atal gathered 118,380 (52.2 per cent) votes against Hussain's 108,568 (47.8 per cent).

Deshpande and Karpatri Maharaj, lost. With a total of six per cent votes in the Lok Sabha elections, the Jan Sangh succeeded in retaining its all-India recognition, improving its performance marginally: four seats in the Lok Sabha and fifty-one in the assemblies.

Atal arrived in Lucknow on the evening of 31 March to a grand welcome at the railway station. As soon as he deboarded, party workers showered petals over him even as a troupe of elderly women performed aarti. The crowd shouted 'Atal Behari Vajpayee ki – jai' and 'Syama Prasad Mookerji ki – jai'. He climbed into an open jeep that would lead the victory procession to Aminudaullah Park. On the way, Atal was garlanded with currency notes and flowers several times.[70] Over the next few days, he was invited to a plethora of functions in Lucknow. The most surreal among them was to be felicitated in a formal ceremony by his own '*Panchjanya* family'. Journalism had been his first love, but 'time and circumstances flung me into the political arena; now that I am here, I must shoulder its responsibilities'. Humble in victory, he paid special tribute to his mentor: 'All great men have the quality of pushing ahead their protégés even as they choose to recede into the background … the credit for whatever I am goes to Deendayalji who, as the brain behind *Rashtradharma*, gave a direction to our lives.'[71]

In quieter moments Atal would have sorely missed three people who had shaped him, but whose lives had in quick succession been abruptly cut off: certainly Mookerji, but also Ma and, especially, Babuji. To some extent, his success was a consolation for the grief their deaths had inflicted on him. At age thirty-two, Atala of Bateshwar became the first RSS swayamsevak to rise up the ranks and claim a seat in the Indian parliament.

6

Beloved Nemesis: The Nehru Years

HIS PARLIAMENTARY CAREER GOT OFF TO A JERKY START. IN THE LATE afternoon of 10 May 1957, Vajpayee joined the queue inside the Lok Sabha as members trooped, one state after the other, to the podium to take oath alongside stalwarts and imposters of politics. Watching them with interest was the second-term prime minister Jawaharlal Nehru, presently at the zenith of his popularity across the world. Atal Behari Vajpayee had spent the larger part of the decade opposing Nehru. Now he was going to be face to face with the chief dynamo of Indian politics. Speaking for the first time on 15 May, he wasted no time in sniping: Nehru's foreign policy was confused; on Kashmir and Goa he was 'feeble and indecisive'; his answer to all questions was 'neti, neti' – not this, not that – the Vedic theory of finding god by negating all that god was not:

> Would we liberate one-third of Kashmir by sending the army? No no. Would we gift it away to Pakistan? No no ... Would we take police action in Goa? No no. Would we then permit a satyagraha there by our people? No no. Would we leave Goa to Portugal's mercies? No no.[1]

He may have been a bit nervous, but he was hardly unprepared. The finance minister had spent a greater part of that morning delivering the budget speech for the year 1957–58: Vajpayee's speech in response revealed that it was politics, not economics, that was the Jan Sangh's topmost concern. Nehru – more than twice his age at sixty-eight, and infinitely higher in stature – listened quietly. He was stung. In his reply the next day, he referred to Vajpayee as 'a new netaji from our opposition party' who was good only at churning out platitudes: 'Unke hathiyaar mujhe zara baazaru maalum hue'. Nehru wrote Vajpayee off in a few sentences before moving on to more substantial criticism: 'Election still bears heavy on his mind, it seemed he thinks of the Lok Sabha too as an election meeting.'[2]

Unlike freshmen MPs of the Congress, there was considerable onus on Vajpayee – also the leader of the Jan Sangh parliamentary party – to perform. Critiquing Nehru to his face required weeks of planning. The Kota pracharak L. K. Advani – one of the few RSS full-timers who spoke and wrote decent English and displayed intellectual curiosity – was brought to Delhi to assist Vajpayee with research. Vajpayee and Premjibhai Assar – the Jan Sangh MP from Ratnagiri in Bombay State – were allocated the 30 Rajendra Prasad Marg bungalow. Advani too moved in with them. After that, there was a constant stream of visitors from the Sangh Parivar. Some days the three residents divided the chores among themselves, Vajpayee making khichdi or kheer, a skill he had picked up from Babuji during their Kanpur days.[3]

In his early months as parliamentarian, Vajpayee hardly ever skipped a session. He bombarded the government with queries during Question Hour (and insisted that all his queries, posed in Hindi, must always be responded to in Hindi).[4] He tabled adjournment motions that were often ruled out.[5] Once when he was not given a chance to speak despite repeated requests to the Chair, he walked out of the house in protest.[6]

Sometimes he obsessed over issues no one else cared about. At session after session, he tabled non-official resolutions urging the inclusion of Sindhi in the Eighth Schedule of the Constitution. Seeing him repeatedly raise the issue of the Hindu refugees who had migrated from West Pakistan and were forced to live at Purana Qila, the rehabilitation minister Mehr Chand Khanna groused: 'I fail to understand what interest Shri Vajpayee has in the refugees of Delhi.' Everyone noticed the hyperactive Jan Sanghi filing ninety-six amendments to the Delhi Municipal Corporation Act – nearly an amendment for every clause in the bill – before it was passed in December 1957. Vajpayee thought the government was reluctant to give the DMC requisite power. The Jan Sangh was gaining strength in the capital, and a sturdy DMC boded well for its future.

After a decade in office, Nehru's authority and stature had reached an inflection point: from here he could only fall. Ironically, the first major blow came from inside his family. In mid-December 1957 Feroze Gandhi, Indira's estranged husband, shot to fame for exposing in parliament dubious investments made by the recently nationalized Life Insurance Corporation to assist a corrupt Kanpur businessman named Haridas Mundhra. In doing so, the second-term Congress parliamentarian from Raebareli locked horns with his father-in-law's close colleagues. Over the next few months the Mundhra scandal kept the government on a hook, forcing the finance minister T. T. Krishnamachari to resign. The new Jan Sangh MP relished the spectacles unfolding inside the house.

When the house was in recess, Vajpayee travelled as before for party work. Most of his speeches were devoted to national issues. Everywhere he regaled his audiences, many of whose faces were familiar to him, with gossip from Lutyens' Delhi: 'If Krishnamachari's tenure were audited properly, it would reveal more sensational things than the Mundhra scandal,' he said in Satna at the annual session of the MP Jan Sangh.[7] His melodramatic rendering, moving swiftly from roar to whisper, kept his audience spellbound. For a crowd that barely understood economics, his presence was at once entertaining and educative and inspiring.

In September 1958, Vajpayee was invited to Nagpur to address a railway labour union. Earlier that year, the Lok Sabha had burst into laughter when he punned on the Railway Minister's name during a discussion on the railway budget. Complaining of insecurity of life due to increasing number of accidents on the railways, Vajpayee said that 'things were so bad that when one bought a railway ticket, there was every chance that one would have to bid farewell to "jag" (world) and "jivan" (life). Under such conditions one ultimately travelled with "Ram" on his lips. The Railway Minister Mr. Jagjivan Ram smiled.'[8]

The Sangh Parivar had floated its labour wing in 1955 – the Bharatiya Mazdoor Sangh. The main man behind the BMS was Dattopant Thengadi, a Marathi pracharak who had in the past been deputed as the Jan Sangh's organizing secretary in central India, and with whom

Vajpayee had travelled in Vidarbha in 1953. The BMS and Jan Sangh were beginning to interact: Vajpayee was nominated as the president of the All India Railway Station Masters' Union, which was struggling to get itself registered. The union had taken its grievances to the Railway Ministry, but instead of giving them a hearing, they were threatened with sacking. Addressing the union on 7 September, Vajpayee galvanized them to 'bargain [with the government] as hard as possible by protesting ... You will have our full support inside and outside parliament, and we promise to assist you in your struggle.'[9]

While parliament was in session, he often drew upon his travels, hoping to imbue his arguments with a touch of ground reality. In mid-February 1958, he voiced his worries of food scarcity across the Hindi heartland: that he had 'seen with my own eyes hundreds of people leaving their homes for other states in search of work. It was like a wholesale migration of population.'[10] He was right; food-grain production had fallen by almost 10 per cent in the last year, and prices of grain had shot up. Among the worst affected was the MP's own constituency: Balrampur often got either too much rain or too little of it; its population density was among the highest in the country; ration shops were few; and most of the dealers sold their stock in the black market. During his travels to Balrampur and elsewhere, Vajpayee had seen 'people come from as far as 2–3 miles, and wait in queue for long periods, forgoing the day's wages.' He argued for the number of ration shops to be increased.[11]

As the food situation worsened, the Jan Sangh decided, in late July 1958, to start an agitation combining the dual issues of food distress and the plethora of new taxes. It teamed up with socialists and communists to gherao government offices and enforce hartaal in eastern UP districts. In early September, Vajpayee chose to take part in the Vasooli-Roko Aandolan – anti-tax movement – and court arrest. A crowd of Jan Sanghis gathered at Lucknow station to see their young MP off to Balrampur to conduct satyagraha. While boarding the train, he insisted: 'I don't want to be outside [the jail] only to see people dying of hunger.'[12] The agitation had spread, and by this time hundreds of Jan Sangh workers had been arrested across UP. Vajpayee was accompanied in this satyagraha by a Dalit MLA of his party from Gonda, Dasrath Lal, and thirty-three others. It was a symbolic protest; they achieved nothing more than gheraoing the district headquarters. They were arrested and ordered by the magistrate to pay a collective fine of ₹200 or spend a month in jail. The satyagrahis made a virtue of spending a few days in the district jail at Gonda.[13]

For a while, Nehru mostly ignored the young Jan Sanghi as a minor nuisance. But some things were unpardonable. Vajpayee occasionally travelled to Jammu and nearby areas in the valley, and returned to make passionate pleas in parliament to revoke Article 370. In mid-February 1958 Pir Maqbool Gilani, a key aide of Sheikh Abdullah, met and complained to the prime minister that he and other Kashmiris were not being given a permit to enter their home state by the Bakshi government, even as trigger-happy Jan Sanghis like Vajpayee 'are allowed to go to Jammu and deliver objectionable speeches'. Nehru immediately shot off a letter to the J&K chief minister Bakhshi Ghulam Mohammad: Vajpayee was 'a highly objectionable person' who was capable of creating 'much mischief in Jammu, and upset thereby the policy that you are following'.[14] That day he also separately wrote to the cabinet secretary Vishnu Sahay, asking him to ensure that the Jan Sanghi was in future denied permission to visit the Himalayan state: 'I do not like men like Vajpayee being allowed free entry.'[15]

The animosity between the two began to melt, at first inconspicuously, in the second year. This became apparent during a discussion on the international situation in mid-August 1958. While Vajpayee praised Nehru's overall steering of the country's foreign policy, he also mildly chided the prime minister for entangling himself unnecessarily in international events which had no direct repercussions for India.

> We may like to keep ourselves isolated but events would take us in the grip. However, the question is whether we can discuss in some details the policy of keeping ourselves actually aloof from the disputes of other countries. One requires a voice to speak, but to keep quiet one requires both voice and wisdom. In the international sphere we have developed a

tendency of speaking a little more than necessary, and it is my submission that we should practice the art of keeping quiet.[16]

Vajpayee was referring to the recent coup in Iraq, which had overthrown the country's US-backed monarchy. Suspecting a Soviet conspiracy, the western powers dispatched marines and troops to the area. Nehru felt annoyed to see the US and Britain 'misread the situation'. By thinking of developments 'solely in terms of communism and anti-communism', the Western powers had ignored the feelings of the Iraqi masses.[17] Nehru warned them against intervening in Iraq, even as he agreed to the Russian premier Nikita Khrushchev's suggestion of an immediate meeting between the premiers of the United States, the Soviet Union, Britain, France and India, along with the secretary-general of the United Nations. The reaction of the Western countries was less than favourable; the meeting was shelved, and the issue was referred to the General Assembly. Vajpayee felt that Nehru's haste to intervene created an impression that the Russians liked India, while the Americans did not: 'In short, Russia, in her Cold War, made us a pawn in her publicity fight and we allowed ourselves to be used.'[18]

To his credit, the prime minister did not take offence at being lectured on international relations by a first-term MP who did not yet hold a passport. Of late Nehru had himself been wondering whether being 'a crusader on the world stage' was taking too much of his time and attention away from the dire economic situation at home.[19] He thanked Vajpayee for acknowledging that India's foreign policy was on the right track, adding that he was in 'complete agreement' on the need to keep quiet unless India's interests were involved. At the same time, Nehru clarified that he was forced to intervene immediately as both sides were psyched for a confrontation in Iraq: 'All the strategic plans were already there and the armies knew that they had to move from here to there to destroy a particular city and drop atom bombs at such and such place.'[20]

With personal acquaintance, Vajpayee's respect for the prime minister had grown. He noticed that despite the occasional fits of temper Nehru displayed in parliament, he was amazingly tolerant and unjudgmental towards opposition members. For his part, Nehru did not mind receiving occasional praise and constructive advice from an adversary who was otherwise always gunning for him; the prime minister could also use the acquaintanceship to build bridges with this insignificant but most vocal of opposition parties. Nehru was beginning to think of Vajpayee as a likeable, bright young man in an otherwise regressive party.* While they continued to bicker inside and outside parliament over matters big and small, personally they continued to be warm.†

By the end of his second year in parliament, Vajpayee had stretched his limits as the leader of the four-member Jan Sangh. With time he had realized that the speech-making that impressed the crowd at party gatherings was less effective in the business of law-making. He had improved himself: his speeches now had a rhythm that parliament demanded – more pointed and coercive, desperate for immediate attention. But days of research on a subject, followed by patiently sitting all day – in the fourth or fifth row, with three other colleagues – awaiting his turn, depressed him. Sometimes, within the allotted time limit for a debate, his turn just didn't come. On others, when he got a chance to speak, his words would not influence the government's decision. Some mornings he woke up and scanned the newspapers only to find that there

---

* That said, Nehru never prophesied a prime ministership for Vajpayee.

† Nehru was upset with MPs like Vajpayee courting arrest in September 1958, only a few days after he had suggested that MPs of distress-affected areas go to their constituencies to help spread order. A month later, Vajpayee mocked Nehru's proposal to exchange enclaves on the eastern border with Pakistan as 'bhudaan' – a gift of land. 'The Constitution of India does not empower anybody to give away Indian land to others,' he railed against the Nehru-Noon Agreement in parliament on 8 December: 'We can annex territory belonging to others, but we cannot give away our land to others. Nobody, not even the Prime Minister, has the right to deprive any citizen of his nationality and citizenship.' He threatened a country-wide agitation. Despite opposition from Jan Sangh and socialists, Nehru went ahead with the transfer hoping to win Pakistan's trust to solve the larger tangle in Kashmir. Speaking at a public meeting in Baroda on 2 November, Nehru noticed a small crowd of RSS–Jan Sangh activists waving placards opposing the Nehru-Noon Agreement. While Nehru wrote them off as the 'only ones who can be trusted upon to be wrong on every issue', he pointed out that even the Sangh Parivar had 'some decent people', wishing they had more such people. It was a qualifier meant for Vajpayee.

was no mention at all of his speech that had been heard with attention in parliament the previous day. Was he slogging away in a vacuum?

In early 1959, India found itself pulled into a major crisis on its northern borders. The Chinese had brutally crushed an uprising in Tibet. On 23 March, Vajpayee tabled an adjournment motion for a discussion on the situation. Nehru only made a cautious statement saying India had 'no intention of interfering in the internal affairs of China with whom we have friendly relations'.[21]* At the same time, he hoped that the Dalai Lama 'who is held in veneration by our people ... is safe'.[22]

On the morning of 30 March, Vajpayee and Balraj Madhok – secretary of the Jan Sangh's north zone – led party men and citizens in front of the Chinese embassy in protest against the 'ruthless suppression of the Tibetan people by China'. Two days earlier, the Chinese government had through its official press agency accused the Indian government of fomenting the uprising in Tibet; it went to the extent of alleging that the Indian town of Kalimpong was the base of the revolt by reactionaries. Vajpayee found this to be an outrageous accusation, especially when Nehru had consciously refrained from saying anything against China. He urged Nehru to now side with the Tibetans. The demonstrators carried placards and shouted slogans: 'Down with Chinese imperialism', 'Dalai Lama zindabad'.† They wanted to present a memorandum to a representative of the embassy. When no one came out to receive it, they threw copies of it into the compound.[23]

To be sure, India had so far played no role in fomenting the uprising in Tibet. But things were getting complicated even as the Jan Sanghis

* It is not entirely clear how much Nehru knew about the ongoing CIA-backed resistance in Tibet, but he always maintained that American involvement there 'would do more harm than good'.

† This was only the second time that a demonstration was organized in front of the Chinese embassy since its establishment in 1949. The first demonstration took place in 1950 at the time of China's invasion of Tibet.

protested outside the Chinese embassy: the Dalai Lama, the spiritual leader of the Tibetans, fled Lhasa for his life. Granted asylum by New Delhi, he entered the country on 31 March.[24] The Chinese interpreted this as further proof of Indian culpability.

Over the next few months, the opposition crossed swords with the prime minister on the Tibet–China conundrum. Outside the parliament, his own close friend Jayaprakash Narayan spearheaded the attack; inside, the PSP's Acharya Kripalani and Vajpayee did. Speaking on 8 May, the Jan Sanghi pilloried Nehru for signing the Sino-Indian agreement in 1954 and committing 'a great blunder by accepting Chinese suzerainty over Tibet'. Now that China had rendered the pact meaningless by violating its promises to respect Tibet's autonomy, India too ought to 'review our position'. Nehru shot back, saying there had been 'no choice left to India' in 1954; that the British government earlier had recognized Chinese suzerainty over Tibet; and that his acceptance was not charity, rather the only practical solution:

> For us to refuse to acknowledge Chinese suzerainty would not have helped Tibet in the slightest. It would have meant not only a complete break with China, but also a much harsher occupation of Tibet right up to our frontiers, and India would then have been considered a hostile country with designs on Tibet.[25]

But it was Vajpayee's provocative proposal to the government to give the Dalai Lama full freedom to 'organise a fight for the freedom of his country from Indian soil', with the hint that Indian volunteers might also help him in the task, that got Nehru's goat.[26] The prime minister fired back, insisting that Vajpayee's proposal 'challenged all the basic assumptions' of India's policy on Tibet–China which had been accepted by the country with remarkable unanimity:

> For the hon. Member to suggest that we should allow him [the Dalai Lama] to do something which he has not himself suggested, that is, making India the headquarters of some kind of a campaign and that we should allow the hon. Member and his party to join in this campaign

> is something that seems to be so odd, so remarkable of utterance, that I cannot imagine how even he could have made it if he had thought about it ... What exactly he expects us to do is not clear except maybe perhaps to hold public meeting in Ramlila Maidan and deliver speeches. That is not the way foreign policy of a country is conducted.

Nehru was being slightly evasive. During his meeting with the Dalai Lama two weeks ago, the monk had in fact sought help with achieving 'independence in the long run'. Nehru had outright refused to give it: to do so would mean going to war with China, for which India had neither the desire nor the means. Even if the Dalai Lama requested help from the US or Britain, they would merely 'exploit Tibet in their Cold War with the Soviet Union'.[27] Nehru repeated some of these arguments:

> If we accept the hon. Member Shri Vajpayee's statement, we should, more or less, prepare for an armed conflict on this issue. We cannot pat somebody on the back and tell him to fight and say, we will cheer you from the background ... I take it that we aim at, whatever problems may arise first of all, a peaceful solution of those problems. Peaceful solutions are not brought about by warlike speeches and warlike approaches ...[28]

China may have violated some parts of the 1954 agreement, but it was not reason enough to interfere in Tibet. Nehru suggested that Vajpayee read up on the matter to understand its present-day complexities.

At the peak of the summer of 1959, Delhi's attention briefly shifted to Kerala. In the assembly elections held two years ago, the CPI had outperformed the Congress there. For the first time ever, a communist government came to power by ballot in 1957. The government put itself to work by initiating radical reforms in land tenure and education. The Education Bill, which sought to regulate private educational institutions in Kerala, became controversial. Powerful interest groups in the state, such as the Nairs and the Catholics, who managed many of these private institutions, launched agitations to oppose the takeover.[29] On 13 June, the police opened fire at a protest led by a group of Catholics, killing seven. Soon the southern state was rocked by mass agitations demanding the resignation of E. M. S. Namboodiripad's government. The RSS–Jan Sangh barely had a presence in Kerala. In the past, they had held Muslims and Christians – who together made up around 45 per cent of the population – responsible for the communists' success. Even so, their local cadres allied with the anti-communist elites of both communities to make the agitation successful.[30]

Vajpayee, who had never been to Kerala, issued a press statement in Delhi on 15 June, warning of 'a situation bordering on civil war'.[31] A few weeks later he took a plane to Kerala. He was taken along by RSS–Jan Sangh workers to see what he wanted to see: he met factory workers who had been given death threats for not joining the communist labour union; he met parents who were told to marry off their daughters to communists; the communists had set up their own cell courts which issued summons, and anyone who disobeyed the cell court was stabbed. In Kottayam and Trivandrum, Vajpayee addressed crowds participating in their 'freedom struggle against communists'.[32] Back in Delhi, he offered his expert opinion: 'Twenty-six months of Communist rule in Kerala has sufficiently proved that Communism and democracy were incompatible'.[33] In his later narration, there was an element of exaggeration. But Vajpayee was correct in that that there was in Kerala, especially among Congress supporters, an atmosphere of fear. The Congressmen from the state had managed to convince Indira Gandhi, who had been appointed the party president in January 1959, of the need to enforce President's rule in the state. Nehru was reluctant, but the mounting pressure from party members made him dismiss the Namboodiripad government on 31 July.

When the matter came up in parliament on 20 August, Vajpayee defended the central government's decision more convincingly than did most Congressmen. 'There can be no greater friend of the communist party than the Prime Minister,' he argued. That the CPI had got an opportunity to entrench itself in India had partly to do with Nehru's generosity. At the same time, the CPI 'forgets that prime minister is a great democrat'. Vajpayee reminded the house that he was not a great admirer of the Congress. And yet, the communist misadministration in Kerala was worse than Congress rule in thirteen other states.[34] This may have been partly true: when elections were held in Kerala in early 1960, the Congress won a handsome majority. The Jan Sangh fielded three seats, and lost its deposits in each of them. But given the border tensions with China, the Congress was by some distance a lesser evil than the CPI.

As the annual convention of the UN General Assembly neared, Vajpayee moved a private member's resolution to recommend to the government to raise the Tibetan issue at the UN.[35] Anticipating a discussion in the Indian parliament, the American ambassador confabulated with Nehru, informing him of Americans' support for such a proposal. Nehru was reluctant because, apart from the deteriorating friendship with China which he would have liked to mend, there were also technical issues: communist China was not a UN member yet, nor could it be said that there had been an *invasion* of Tibet by the Chinese, as Tibet was a part of China.[36]

Vajpayee believed these were lame excuses. Arguing his case in parliament on 21 August, the first-term MP countered the government's logic: was it not true that India joined other nations in condemning North Korea even though the latter was not a UN member? Nor did he agree that discussing Tibet might intensify the Cold War: had not the world joined in denouncing the Anglo-French invasion of Egypt in July 1956? India had a 'moral responsibility' towards Tibet. After all, Nehru had advised the Dalai Lama to come to an agreement with communist China in 1950: 'India wanted that China and Tibet should settle the issue by peaceful negotiations and our prime minister advised the Dalai Lama to come to an agreement with Communist China in view of the assurances given by the Prime Minister of China ... As a result of those assurances the Dalai Lama came to an agreement, the 17-point agreement with China.'[37]

Nehru responded that the young MP had 'got these things rather mixed up'. While it had indeed been his desire to see Tibet and China negotiate an agreement, India was never a party to any agreement between the two: 'So, it is not correct to say that they [China] had given us an assurance which they broke later.'[38] Vajpayee persisted. But his resolution had so little support that the Speaker did not feel it necessary to formally count the numbers for and against the motion; it was 'negatived'.[39]

It was in such a dejected state that, a week later, he requested Nehru to issue a White Paper detailing 'our border dispute with the Chinese and this cartographic aggression'.[40] (The idea had come from Vajpayee's assistant, Advani, who had 'learnt from my study of the functioning of the House of Commons in Britain that a member could demand from the government White Paper containing specific information on an important topical issue. Atalji and I did a fair amount of research on the subject.'[41]) The prime minister agreed, but wanted 'a little time'. However, given the incessant border skirmishes in the NEFA – North-East Frontier Agency – and everyday pestering on the subject by opposition MPs, on 7 September he submitted to the parliament a copy containing 'Notes, Memoranda and Letter exchanged and Agreements signed between the Governments of India and China: 1954–1959'.[42]

On 12 September, the White Paper was discussed for five hours. It was the last day of the session, and five hours proved too short a duration for so explosive a debate. Ideally, the Speaker should have dispensed with a couple of speakers from the Congress benches. But he did not, with the result that Vajpayee got crowded out. The Jan Sanghi felt humiliated. Without waiting to hear Nehru's conclusion, a fuming Vajpayee stormed out of the house: 'I represent an important viewpoint in this country ... It is not fair [to deny me a chance to speak].'[43]

It was not difficult to guess what he would have wanted to say. In Jullundur two days later, he gave a press conference demanding that 'China be served with an ultimatum to vacate within a fixed period the areas occupied by her in Indian territory. China should be categorically told that negotiations with it would be held only after it had vacated aggression and only on the basis of China's acceptance of the McMahon Line.'[44] India had to get its land back, 'even if that necessitated a war'.[45]

The demand for the White Paper was just Vajpayee having another crack at influencing government policy on Tibet. This time he had lit a tinderbox: 'The exchanges ranged from those concerning trifling disputes, occasioned by the straying by armed patrols into territory claimed by the other side, to larger questions about the status of the border in the west and the east and disagreements about the meaning of the rebellion in Tibet.' Sadly for the prime minister, the circulation of the White Paper was immediately succeeded by defence minister Krishna Menon's public fallout with his Chief of Army Staff, General K. S. Thimayya. Vajpayee thought of Menon as a man with 'pronounced communist leanings' who was 'singularly unsuited to implement the Prime Minister's policy of non-alignment'. As such Vajpayee's sympathies naturally gravitated towards the general who had threatened to resign.[46] The White Paper further fed anger against Krishna Menon.

During the winter session, Vajpayee floated some wild conspiracy theories. Demanding that Menon be immediately sacked, he held that there were rumours about the defence minister attempting a coup at some future date; he was known to be assiduously building up a personal following in the armed forces; there were apprehensions about Menon 'scheming to capture power with the help of his trusted army lieutenants' after Nehru's death. Not to mention Menon would be readily supported in these designs by the CPI, with its loyalties beyond the borders. He hoped Nehru 'will not allow personal friendship to stand in the way of the needs of national security'.[47]

He also mocked Nehru's previous blind trust in the northern neighbour. 'If we had relied a little more on military preparedness and a little less on Chinese friendship, we would not be in our present parlous state.' That said, he had little by way of a solution. In classic RSS tradition, Vajpayee wanted Nehru 'to give a call to drive the Chinese from the land and the nation will respond unitedly.'[48] The threat of throwing out the enemy by force was the manifestation of a curious Sangh psychology: that if enough Indians (preferably Hindus, especially RSS-trained) together stood up at the border with lathis, the enemy would run away scared; and that as a last resort, it could even substitute military strategy or peaceful negotiations.

Vajpayee often assured the prime minister that he did not wish to exploit the border crisis for the advantage of his party. Yet, in most ways he was doing exactly that.* He had at last winded up the year on a satisfactory note. The Sangh Parivar was pleased about the Jan Sangh group 'shoot[ing] into the limelight' in parliament, and exerting a weight disproportionate to the party's puny strength.[49] Vajpayee himself spoke in the tone of an underdog who had cut through the odds to succeed. At the annual session of the provincial Jan Sangh in Nagpur in January 1960, he recalled the words of a Congress leader who, after Mookerji's death, had predicted the party's death: 'Jan Sangh's head is gone, it cannot survive.' Those words were 'a stab in [my] heart', but the Jan Sangh was 'like the son of Shiva and Parvati'. Even if someone beheads it, it will find another head to keep itself alive: 'And it shall grow to be revered by the world. So it has come to be.'[50]

Releasing the White Paper limited Nehru's options of a back channel as a diplomatic compromise. The ongoing correspondence between Nehru and the Chinese premier Chou En-lai was now a matter of public scrutiny in India.[51] Vajpayee took great personal interest in every exchange. Nehru had refused in December Chou's proposal for a meeting in Rangoon. But owing to the continuing stalemate, he changed his mind on 5 February and invited him to Delhi for talks.[52]

The news hit Vajpayee 'like a bomb – sudden, unrequired, humiliating'. As long as Chinese aggression continued on Indian territory, he apprised a crowd of Jan Sangh supporters on 17 February, there should be no

---

* In Sikar for the annual session of the Rajasthan Jan Sangh on 29 December, he focused on Nehru's 'failure to share information with the Lok Sabha when he came to know in 1957 about the construction of the Aksai Chin road by the Chinese'. He wondered whether this vital information was given even to the president – the head of the state and the commander-in-chief of the armed forces – and the central cabinet: 'I am afraid that this information was kept confined to the files of the External Affairs Ministry only; there cannot be a more serious lapse than this.' Vajpayee's charge was not without merit. At the same time, it must be pointed out that Nehru had kept the relevant cabinet ministers and chief ministers in the know about the incursions since 1958.

further negotiation with China.[53] Later that day Vajpayee attacked Nehru in parliament for bothering 'more about world opinion than the adverse psychological toll it would take on 40 crore Indians'. The 'government should have exploited the winter season to drive the Chinese aggressors out of the Indian territory'. On the contrary, Nehru was preparing himself for talks to give away Aksai Chin. (But how could India have thrashed the Chinese, who had an army five times larger, and were equipped with the latest Soviet weapons?) Perhaps Vajpayee thought the Americans would readily help India. Famously, that day he accused the prime minister of speaking with a forked tongue:

> One is a man who talked about a nation in arms. In the Rajya Sabha, he had repeated Churchill's words – 'blood, toil, and tears'. That was the face of a national hero who wants to tackle aggression with self-esteem and confidence. Another is the face of an abject weakling unable to guard the nation's honour. One face reflects Churchill, who brought victory to Britain; the other reflects Chamberlain, who encouraged Hitler with his appeasement. I am sorry to say, but we have standing before us a man who exhibits a peculiar divided personality.[54]

Nehru had been absent from the house all day, and coincidentally entered exactly as Vajpayee launched his frontal attack on him. The prime minister may have been a bit hurt, but he was also amused and chose not to take the criticism to heart. In the evening, Vajpayee bumped into the prime minister at a banquet. Nehru complimented him saying 'it was a solid speech' and walked away smiling.[55]

The Jan Sangh national executive met in Delhi to think up an emergency plan to force Nehru to cancel the proposed meeting with the Chinese premier. In the first phase, the party's 350-odd district units were to apply themselves to mobilize the masses 'against the invitation and any sort of possible let-down by the government'.[56] On 20 March, Golwalkar roared from Delhi's Ramlila Maidan: 'We can resist ten Chinas, if need be, if only we are united and strong.' As often, the hallucinating Guruji was far from an objective view of the problem: 'This Panchsheel is not worth even the paper it is written on.' It was 1960, and India and the world had accepted the partition as a fait accompli. Guruji thought otherwise: 'How can partition be a settled fact when the entire world itself is unsettled?'[57]

Expectedly, Nehru did not cancel. By mid-March, the Jan Sangh was warning the government against arranging a public reception for the Chinese premier, which they threatened to boycott. At the same time, they decided to not stage, as earlier planned, black flag demonstrations on 19 April, the day of Chou's arrival. Instead, to mobilize public opinion and inject courage into Nehru, 10–17 April was to be observed by Jan Sangh branches across the country variously as 'Stand Firm Week' and 'No Surrender Week'. To this effect, the central office issued a circular to its district units.[58]

On the afternoon of 17 April, a fleet of motorcycles and scooters heading a mile-long colourful procession of 15,000 left the Jan Sangh office at Ajmeri Gate to reach Teen Murti Bhawan, the prime minister's residence. The banners and placards displayed a wide variety of mottos and slogans. One showed Nehru warmly hugging a smiling Chou: it bore the caption 'Beware of the Chou smile'. Among the slogans shouted were 'Panditji ko kah dete hain, hum Ladakh na jaane denge' – We are warning Panditji, we won't let him give away [Aksai Chin in] Ladakh; and 'Nehruji, mat samjho bhai, dhokebaaz hai Chou En-lai' – Chou En-lai is no brother of ours, he is a cheat.

The journalists covering this spectacle included representatives of the Chinese embassy: they were 'eagerly lapping up with their tape recorders and cameras all that they could get, not omitting even the slogans and speeches'. Such methods of protest were normal, banal even, in India, but not so much in the communist republic. On the eve of his visit, Chou was aware that at least some Indians considered him a 'cheat'. Vajpayee emerged after handing over to the prime minister a four-page memo, and informed the crowd that Nehru had 'told us categorically' that he would act firm in his negotations with the Chinese premier. The demonstration ended with slogans hailing Mother India: 'Bharat Mata ki jai'.[59]

Theatrics from the opposition ensured that the meeting was damned before it even began. To quote Nehru's biographer, Chou had a 'clearer idea than Nehru of where power and interest lay, and by now they had become paired antagonists locked together. As a result, in the talks between the two prime ministers, there was not even a distant approach to a solution.'[60]

On the morning of 25 September 1960, Vajpayee boarded a plane for Washington DC. He was off to the US on his first foreign trip, a 'two-month study tour'. The invitation from the American government was for him to be present as an observer during the ongoing presidential election campaign. As reported in the *Organiser*, he was also invited for his 'special interest in the welfare of the Railway labour'.[61] The mouthpiece did not mention another, perhaps the more important, reason for Vajpayee's visit: Nehru had included him in the list of delegates for the UN General Assembly session.

The Cold War was raging, and the General Assembly session was where heads of influential states with dinosaur-sized egos were expected to descend in order to bully and abuse the rival side. Russia had in May shot down an American U-2 spy plane after spotting it over its territory (the plane had taken off from an American base in Pakistan). An irate Nikita Khrushchev was further offended when the US refused to apologize for its espionage mission.[62] Khrushchev cancelled his invitation to the President Eisenhower, who was to visit Moscow in July. Instead, he sent warm letters to other heads of governments such as Nehru to join him at the UN in New York in September for a collective review of the crisis. Vajpayee knew there would be fireworks to be witnessed.

This was the first major occasion of someone from the Sangh Parivar formally travelling as a guest of the American government, whose impression of the RSS had been less than flattering. (In the recent past, they had questioned the Indian government on its treatment of Muslims.) Their present interest in the Jan Sangh had to do with the party's opposition to communism, and its emergence as a possible counterweight to the Congress in the distant future. The pupil carried from his Guruji an affectionate but dull and patronising message for the Americans, 'the youngest and the most virile' people who had 'by force of world events' found themselves to be the most powerful nation after the end of World War II. Golwalkar lectured the Americans on how to tackle communism with help from the ancient Indian philosophy of Advaita: 'May the people of the U.S.A. remember the clarion call of Swami Vivekananda, join with Bharat in bonds of inviolable friendship, and victory to the forces of Dharma is assured.' The Delhi Jan Sangh arranged a function to wish Vajpayee bon voyage.[63]

In Washington DC, he found company in N. M. (Appa) Ghatate, who was studying for a doctorate in International Relations at American University.* Appa had befriended him in Delhi as a law student in 1957 and, even though he was younger than Vajpayee by more than a decade, the Jan Sangh MP treated him as an equal. Appa recalled his friend going to the Indian embassy in Washington DC a few times 'wearing a dhoti and a band-gala jacket' and returning from the formal occasions terribly bored. For Vajpayee the idea of a 'study tour' was to travel as widely as possible – as he had done back home before becoming an MP.

He began his study by watching a TV debate in a Chinese restaurant (in what would be the beginning of a lifelong gluttony for the cuisine of a country he considered India's arch-enemy). On 26 September, for the first time in the history of US elections, the two rival candidates for the presidency, Democrat John F. Kennedy and Republican Richard Nixon, locked horns on television, to help some 100 million Americans make up their minds about which of the two to send to the White House. This was the first in a series of four TV debates. 'A sort of running commentary on the debate continued all through', partly owing 'to the unending rounds of drinks which accompanied them. I happened to ask for water and several of those present rushed to offer me drinks asking me to drink to the success of their respective favourites! They appeared disappointed to know that I did not even smoke.'

This was a careful evasion. He did not smoke – the death of his parents from cancer was still fresh in his mind – but by now he drank in moderate

* Ghatate's father had been one of the RSS's founders, and it was at his house in Nagpur, under his parents' care, that Hedgewar had breathed his last.

quantities. He noticed that both the candidates exuded generosity: 'Ready to strike, both appeared reluctant to wound.' And he remarked that the audience, in their assessment of the two candidates, ruthlessly dissected their merits and demerits: 'There is no hero-worshipping about them.' On finding out who he was, some people prodded Vajpayee about his preference. After he returned to his hotel, the state officials too wanted to know: 'My answer would be invariably vague. As an Indian, I did not consider it proper to indicate preferences.'[64]

On 2 October, he read in the papers that Nehru and Khrushchev could be addressing the UN the next day. The same afternoon, he caught a train to New York, leaving one of his two suitcases in Washington DC: 'You get no coolies at the station and carrying two suitcases isn't much fun.' At the last moment, 'thanks to Krishna Menon's and Dinesh Singh's assistance, I was able to secure an admittance-pass for the first row'. The next morning he went past the security checks and the 'flags of 99 nations [that] fluttered over the entrance' to the Assembly Hall. For the first time, he saw important heads of states about whom he had only read in the media.[65]

Presently Khrushchev arrived. 'Ignoring ex-President Truman's advice, US newsmen and cameramen have been flocking around K,' Vajpayee noticed. 'The master-propagandist that he is, Khrushchev knows how to keep all attention focused upon himself.' At some point Khrushchev rose and launched an attack on the UN secretary general Dag Hammarskjöld, accusing him of being biased towards the Western countries. 'Hammarskjoeld's reply was tit for Khrushchev's tat.' Soon the two sides were thumping desks and jeering at each other – a sight Vajpayee was familiar with back home.[66]

Then came Nehru's turn to speak: 'There was a flutter in the assembly and all delegates moving here and there rushed to their respective seats. Pandit Nehru was in his white Gandhi cap, coca-cola coloured *sherwani*, the invariable red rose, and *churidar pajamas*.' Vajpayee noticed 'his confident manner of address, his clear and perfect accents, his well-formed turns of expression', and suddenly felt proud of his prime minister. But pride soon turned to annoyance:

> The Prime Minister would have done well to use a word more suited to describe China's aggressive occupation of 12,500 square miles of Indian territory than 'a controversy' ... the Prime Minister thereby missed an invaluable opportunity for canvassing international opinion in India's favour over this issue ... It is likely that Russia too – if all the reports of Sino-Russian differences are not entirely fictitious – might have relished it ... So far as the question of China's admission to the UN went, the UN was already seized of the matter, and India's opinion could have been expressed when that issue came up for consideration ... But like the Ten Commandments, India's foreign policy has come to comprise of a bundle of Thou shalt nots and Thou Shalts and advocacy of China's case is one of the Thou Shalts.[67]

Holding forth again two days later, Nehru, Vajpayee wrote, 'forgot that he was speaking not in the Indian parliament but in the UN General Assembly'. In order to ease the prevailing Cold War tensions, Nehru, along with the premiers of four other major non-aligned countries – Egypt, Ghana, Indonesia and Yugoslavia – moved a resolution recommending the renewal of contact between the US and USSR premiers. When the debate on the five-nation resolution began on 5 October, the Australian prime minister Robert Menzies moved an amendment, calling for a meeting of the Big Four (including France and Britain) instead of the Big Two. Menzies accused the five non-aligned nations of siding with the USSR to carve the world into two sections, and demanded to know why the UK and France had been excluded by the resolution. A bitter Nehru responded that Menzies was doing an 'injustice to his own intelligence and that of the United Nations!' After all, it was the USSR's deteriorated relations with the US, rather than the UK or France, which were the root cause of much of the tension. Nehru saw the amendment as an inane attempt to sabotage the resolution. Watching the spectacle, Vajpayee wrote:

> His face ruddy with anger, and his voice quivering with excitement he lashed out at the Australian Prime Minister just as he does when attacking opposition members in the Indian Parliament. The various delegations

> present were stunned to behold this mood of the Indian Prime Minister. When after the speech I met him to congratulate him, he himself accepted that he became somewhat unmindful as to where he was ... But then, it would not be a Pandit Nehru if he were not to indulge in occasional fits of temper![68]

Even though the five-nation resolution was not carried, he was proud to see that the Indian prime minister enjoyed, as the natural spokesman of the Afro-Asian force (now forty-four out of ninety-nine), massive clout. At the same time, Vajpayee was upset to be told that India was not going to support Malaya's UN resolution on Tibet. When the debate finally took place on 10 October, followed by voting, India chose to abstain. Sitting in the audience, he marked the cruel irony that among the companions India had in its neutrality on Tibet was the imperialist Portugal: 'Edifying company this indeed!'[69]

For most of his stay in New York, he was in the company of Maharajakrishna Rasgotra, a young IFS officer who had been posted two years ago in the permanent mission of India to the UN. When not at the UN headquarters, Vajpayee divided his time writing (dutifully dispatching all his experiences for the RSS mouthpieces) and exploring the city with Rasgotra. An expert on decolonization, Rasgotra deepened the Jan Sanghi's understanding of the UN. In return, the MP shared nuggets from his parliament life. In contrast to the public image of a rabble rouser always sniping at Nehru, Rasgotra felt Vajpayee had 'very high regard for Panditji', and that there was 'quietly a relationship, sort of, building up between the two'.[70]

Vajpayee was not impressed by the speeches at the UN: 'He thought the speeches in the assembly plenary were argumentative without being persuasive, and read from texts in dull monotones, they bored the listener. In some cases there were flashes of bitterness, even anger and fire, but there was no humour.'[71] After a while a sleepy Vajpayee would urge Rasgotra to go out for chai and conversation: 'Chaliye, chai peete hain, aur logon se milte hain.' Rasgotra had been instructed by Nehru's office to introduce the first-time visitor to leaders from all continents, so that he 'gets a sense of how the real world works'. 'Which I did, taking him around here and there, inviting people for lunch to meet him, delegates from different countries.' One evening he threw for Vajpayee 'a big party at my flat in New York', an occasion Vajpayee always remembered and thanked him for.

They were both eligible bachelors in their early thirties, and also had some light camaraderie. Rasgotra took him to museums and art galleries, but these did not evoke any great interest in the young Jan Sanghi. A few times Rasgotra also took him to nightclubs. It was not clear to Vajpayee what a nightclub was exactly. Rasgotra assured him that it was not a strip club: 'Nagn nritya nahin hota hai. You would get to see what shape modern music is taking – there is jazz, instrumental, local music.' Vajpayee got excited: 'Chaliye, yeh bhi ek nayi duniya hai.' On such informal outings he drank a peg or two. But there were real limits to how informal Vajpayee could get with his companion. He did not confide in Rasgotra about the ongoing tumult in his private life.

Over the next few weeks Vajpayee travelled across the US. Even though his gaze was often intensely inward, there were frequent surprises too. He realized that his impression that Americans had no place for spiritual or moral life values was ill-founded. In Worthington, Ohio, he visited a church. In his sermon, the minister 'appealed to the audience not to consider material prosperity [as the] be-all and end-all of life and to take to the path of God ... The weekly receipts of churches come to handsome amounts. At several places I found that construction of churches was being undertaken on an entirely voluntary basis, and prominent citizens of the place personally lent a hand in the actual building work.' In the family with which he had been lodged at Worthington, 'not only was everyone a teetotaller, none of them even smoked'. And, 'among the smaller contestants for US presidency were candidates of the Vegetarian League and Prohibition Party as well'. He was especially gratified to see young Americans practising at several yoga centres.[72]

He also felt that the dignity of manual labour was 'too natural and deeply rooted a facet of American life to need any sermonizing and speechifying'. Given the minimum-wage rule, most Americans couldn't afford domestic servants or chauffeurs. 'Everyone does his own chores – right up to washing his dishes.' And if a guest chose to wash his dishes after the meals, 'he is in no way dissuaded from doing so. The cleaning of dishes and after-dinner chat continue simultaneously.'[73]

Most crucially, though, for the first time the poet of Hindu-Tan-Mann saw for himself proof of a multi-ethnic nation. On a trip to Hibbing in Minnesota, possibly to study its labour union system (Hibbing being the largest iron ore centre in the world), he noticed that even though the city was barely sixty-five years old, 'people belonging to 37 different nationalities live here'. Education and a common language – English – had 'completely united the entire populace'. This came to his attention again a few days later in Cleveland. When his university professor host took him out for sightseeing, Vajpayee saw that the city – situated on the sea coast, with Canada just beyond – was 'girdled by a string of beautiful gardens each named after someone [from] the other group of settlers (Italians, Germans, Poles) from Europe'. He asked his host how, with such diverse ethnic origins, the US existed as one national entity. The host replied that a 'powerful common urge to start a new life' and 'the desire to maintain it everlastingly is the tie that welds them'.[74]

Vajpayee was frequently asked about the Indo-US relationship. His usual reply was in terms of 'a common faith in democratic ideals'. Occasionally he also tore into American foreign policy, as he did while speaking to reporters in Honolulu, Hawaii:

> I think the time has come when the American people should carefully ponder over the merits of rendering military, financial and moral assistance to fascist regimes, which in the ultimate analysis are as destructive, if not more, as Communist governments. In order to combat Communism effectively, and to win the minds, hearts and souls of world's peoples, there is need to establish nobler and higher life-values in every sphere of life – political, economic and social – and then throughout the world and not only in the US.[75]

He primarily had in mind Pakistan, whose military alliance with the US six years ago he had mocked as selling sovereignty for dollars. But he also mentioned the examples of Chiang Kai-shek (in Taiwan) and Syngman Rhee (in South Korea). Their fate 'is a warning for all those who in their anxiety to rescue the world from Communist onslaughts commit the folly of thrusting corrupt, inefficient and unpopular regimes on the people'.[76]

While he was happy to meet religious-minded Americans, he also on some occasions politely urged them to discard the view that 'the only way to save the uncommitted nations from the "godless creed of Communism" is to bring them under the "protective canopy of Christianity"'. By converting the natives, missionaries were not doing India a favour. It might be a great creed, 'but Christians ought not to forget that the eastern countries are proud of their own heritage of ancient religions. To exploit their destitution for this end will naturally lead to bitterness and conflict. If Communism is to be countered not only on economic and political planes but on the religious plane as well, it is imperative that the Christian world should strive to understand other religions like Hinduism and also be ready to co-exist with them.'[77]

In between his travels, Vajpayee had been keenly following the presidential campaign. The Kennedy–Nixon TV debates had turned bitter. 'There was no more of the common objectives talk and none of the earlier exchange of I-respect-you platitudes either,' he wrote. Now they pounced at each other for distorting facts and lying about events.[78] He also had a chance to briefly meet the two candidates. Vajpayee felt Nixon – who was also currently the vice president and suffering from incumbency fatigue – to be anti-India. If by any chance the Republican won, 'Islamabad would feel very happy'.[79] But Kennedy stood a higher chance. The forty-three-year-old Democrat, with his 'cheerful countenance, impressive oratory, charming wife' had performed better in the four TV debates which 'served not only to counter Republican attacks that he lacked "experience" and "maturity" but also showed him comparatively higher in stature than Nixon'.

The officials arranged for Vajpayee to join Kennedy's team during the last leg of his campaign, from 5 to 7 November, in Connecticut. The Indian visitor was introduced to everyone in Kennedy's campaign team – including his three sisters, and Chester Bowles, the former governor of Connecticut (and later ambassador in Delhi), who 'expressed delight that I had come'. It was hectic: travelling with Kennedy's team, Vajpayee remained awake on the night of 5–6 November. The team reached Hartford airport at 1 a.m.

> When Mr. Kennedy left the airport in an open car, the wind had a cold sting in it, and all the newsmen had muffled themselves up in woollens from top to toe. But the Democratic candidate was in his usual grey suit, white shirt and blue tie, and without any headwear. And to reply to the cheering throng that lined both sides of the entire route even at that odd hour, he had to remain standing all along. On either side of the road from the airport to Waterbury, was a sea of faces. Innocent faces, young faces, and kindly old faces – all would beam on seeing Mr. Kennedy. Many would break through the cordons to get a 'touch' of the hero.[80]

While the team looked tired, 'Kennedy was bubbling with life and cheer'. By this time both the candidates had 'developed the art of drawing freshness and vigour from the seething crowds. Prime Minister Nehru is considered a master at this art.'[81]

Like election campaigns everywhere, both sides employed stratagems. Vajpayee saw a juvenile girl carrying a banner: 'Republicans for Kennedy'. But when he visited the local Democratic Party office, he saw a person making such placards. Another one read: 'Mexico for Kennedy'. The local mayor, who was showing him around, smiled and said, 'We ought to have one reading – "India for Kennedy"'. Vajpayee was tired, though not as much as one of the journalists covering Kennedy's campaign for weeks. The journalist confided: 'I care a hang about who becomes the president of United States; what I need at the moment is a bed to stretch myself on.'[82]

The elections were held on 7 November: Kennedy narrowly won. The next week, after a forty-five-day tour across eastern and central US states, Vajpayee returned to Delhi. It had been an enjoyable trip, and he was clearly in awe of his host country. Summing up his impressions, he issued a statement on 'America's Just Fears' of India's tilt towards the USSR. Vouchsafing the American desire for peace, he pointed out two recent developments – Khrushchev's attempt to wreck the UN conference and the emergence of Fidel Castro barely ninety miles from American shores – had 'strengthened this distrust and suspicion'. If India chose its spokesperson there with 'more discernment and care, I am sure misunderstanding in the US about India's foreign policy would be removed easily'.[83] The young MP would soon travel to other countries. Often, he would return home rejuvenated and intellectually enriched.

In February 1961, the first major communal riots after the partition flared up in and around Jabalpur. The prime minister was convinced that the RSS–Jan Sangh cadres had a hand in it. For a while, he toyed with the idea of banning the communal organizations and political parties.[84] But parties like the Jan Sangh did not accept that they were communal. Nehru was also aware that the roots of this trouble lay deep: sections of his own party were as rabid as the Sanghis.

For Vajpayee, this was the beginning of a lifelong duality. While he was keen to project a liberal image for his party, the RSS–Jan Sangh footsoldiers continued to pursue instrumentalist tactics (such as igniting or fuelling a riot) to maintain their domination and sometimes to benefit from polarization in an election. The Jan Sangh elders did not have a firm enough grip on their party cadres, the majority of whom came from the RSS (and reported to the parent organization). Moreover, given the Jan Sangh's symbiotic relationship with the RSS, the party leadership was complicit in using the communal divide for electoral advantages. This then was the dilemma of the top leadership vis-à-vis the actual situation on the ground.

The birth of the Swatantra party in 1959 – chiefly against centralization in Nehru's economic policies, collective farming in particular – brought the Jan Sangh an opportunity to lay out its priorities more clearly. Vajpayee welcomed the new party led by C. Rajagopalachari, hoping 'it will aid in the crystallisation of public opinion on economic issues'. At the same time, the Jan Sangh had failed to shed its image of an urban Brahmin–Bania party. Vajpayee was keen to expand his party elsewhere, and avoid being seen as pro-rich or a party of maharajas – which is what Swatantra seemed to be. He believed that with the Congress, the socialist as well as the communist parties on the extreme left, and 'the new party on the extreme right', it would be easier for the Jan Sangh 'to fulfil its role of a middle-of-the-road party'.[85] The Jan Sangh, as he saw it, was proudly Hindu but at the same time moderate, evolving with the changing times.

His urge to be seen as progressive became evident on the Dowry Prohibition Bill in early May 1961. The two houses differed over some clauses, with the Rajya Sabha demanding a more stringent law than the Lok Sabha, leading to, for the first time, a joint meeting of the two houses. Not long before, Vajpayee had vociferously opposed the Hindu Code Bill. Now he supported the bill to ban dowry, an extension of the former, now aborted, bill. Speaking on 6 May, he treaded a tightrope when he argued that legislation was only the first step towards doing away with the dowry system: 'The evils which have crept into our society ought to be eradicated. But can a society be reformed only by law? [I think] everyone would agree that laws should come as a stamp of approval from the public, a law cannot replace the popular opinion ... The need is to make our country economically better-off, spread education, break the barriers of caste, so men and women could marry freely by mutual consent. Only then can we end dowry.'[86] In some ways, this was the standard fallback for caste elites: reform must come, but let us first achieve the ideal conditions for it.

The government had moved an amendment, excluding from the definition of dowry voluntary gifts (in cash and jewellery) to the bride by her family. Many Rajya Sabha members protested, arguing that this would defeat the very purpose of enacting a law. Vajpayee suggested a middle path by way of an amendment: the total cost of the gifts to be given at the time of marriage be limited to 2,000 rupees.[87] His proposal was rejected.

As a remedy to the country's many fissures – communal, linguistic, sub-national – the prime minister set up an all-party National Integration

Committee in early 1961. It was followed by a meeting of chief ministers, leading up to a National Integration Conference. Nehru nominated Vajpayee as the only member from the Jan Sangh to be on the committee. Vajpayee attended the conference on 29 September, though he protested the non-inclusion of his party president and general secretary. He also disagreed with Nehru on the prime minister's wish for an 'adequate representation for the minorities' in police, civil and defence services. In his speech, Vajpayee castigated the NIC for trying to introduce the communal factor into appointments.

Simultaneously, on some other issues his tone was one of compromise. While he continued to be riled by what he had always thought was an anti-Hindu bias in school and college history textbooks, Vajpayee now argued for the inclusion of freedom fighters and historical personalities from all religions, provinces and ideologies; and against the colonial historiography of dividing Indian history into Hindu, Muslim and British periods. For history should be of the people, not the rulers.

> It is this classification of historical periods on a communal basis which has made a section take pride even in the vandalism of Mahmud Ghazni, Mohammad Ghori and Aurangzeb. No doubt the vandals were Muslims but they should not be considered representatives of Islam. Their doings were motivated primarily by the instinct of rapacity and domination. Just as it is essential for Muslims not to blunder into considering these aggressors and tyrants as their ancestors, so also it is necessary for the rest of society not to hold the entire Muslim community as answerable for the sins of these marauders. The Indian Muslim indeed deserves sympathy and consideration from his other compatriots for having become a victim of history while the rest of society looked on helplessly.[88]

Not many in his saffron brotherhood would have agreed with the above assessment. In the second week of November 1961, the Jan Sangh's General Council met in Banaras: the chief purpose was to finalize the manifesto for the upcoming elections. With the backdrop of the threat on the northern border, an MLA from Madhya Pradesh moved an amendment demanding the party to state specifically that the Jan Sangh would manufacture atomic weapons. His view was widely endorsed. Deendayal asked Vajpayee to explain.

He focused on two aspects of the proposed amendment: moral and practical. While the party did not rule out the use of any weapon, 'we must be fully conscious of the tremendous havoc wrought by nuclear weapons not only on the present generation but for future progeny as well'. India had two options: 'to join the nuclear race ourselves, or to strive to restrain others from joining it ... We can, if we like decide that as the race is on, and as our immediate neighbour [China] who has hostile designs against us, is trying to join this race, we too should embark on the same. But then our efforts for disarmament against nuclear tests would lose their moral basis.' For now, India ought to focus on manufacturing conventional weapons. Then again, the 'manufacture of atomic weapons would entail huge finances. Would it be proper in the present circumstances to fritter away our limited resources on such an undertaking?'[89] Vajpayee's arguments prevailed: the amendment was rejected by a majority vote.

Around this time, a newly released exchange of letters between two premiers saw Nehru complaining about having 'recently lost some more territory'. For the first time it became apparent that not only had China captured Indian territory in Ladakh in the past, it was in fact continuing to expand. On 4 December – the last week of the second Lok Sabha session – Vajpayee launched a verbal assault on Nehru for minimizing the fact of aggression: the government had withheld the news that China had built three new military posts in the western sector because it feared an adverse impact on the elections. The solutions the Jan Sangh MP offered included breaking diplomatic ties with China, and expanding the road network and modes of communication in Ladakh on a war footing.[90]

The government may have been equivocal and inept on the question of Chinese aggression. But in mid-December 1961, almost out of nowhere, it decided to finally liberate Goa by marching troops and conducting air raids. It came ridiculously easy: the Portuguese surrendered in two days. Even though the timing had to do with the elections, Vajpayee deemed the armed action to liberate Goa, lasting all of twenty-six hours, 'a Christmas gift'.[91]

The Jan Sangh was now far more confident of entering the battle of ballots than it had been on the previous two occasions. The party's stand on the border issue had stuck a popular chord, for which a good chunk of the credit went to Vajpayee himself. He had spoken in parliament for a total of twenty-three hours and fifty-two minutes, the second longest among all opposition members.[92] In addition, despite being threatened with a ban after the Jabalpur riots, the party had won some crucial by-elections in the summer – including Balraj Madhok from the New Delhi Lok Sabha constituency. The party was keen to fight the upcoming general election as aggressively as possible.

A 'Private Circulation Only' pamphlet urged party workers to make door-to-door contact and indulge in whisper campaigning.[93] At its worst, it meant trotting out fake news on Nehru, such as the prime minister eating 'the calf's tongue for his breakfast'.[94] Vajpayee may not have been personally involved with these campaigns, but it is impossible that he was ignorant of misinformation being strategically spread in constituencies including his own.

The party decided to field its star from Balrampur and Lucknow, the two constituencies Vajpayee was by now familiar with. Apparently because none of the UP Congressmen were keen to face him in Balrampur, the party set up an unusual candidate from outside: Subhadra Joshi, the Lok Sabha MP from Kaithal in Punjab. Fiery and well connected with Delhi's left-liberal circles, Joshi simultaneously ran the Sampradayikata Virodhi Samiti – the Committee to Oppose Communalism. Married to the Delhi communist leader B. D. Joshi, the Congress MP dived into Balrampur out of an activist zeal to fight the Sangh Parivar's blue-eyed boy.

On reaching Balrampur, Joshi wasted no time in launching a vituperative attack on the Jan Sangh in general and the RSS in particular, hoping to scare off the middle and lower castes from voting for Vajpayee. In contrast to the conservative UP Congressmen, the imported leftist from Punjab also demanded that Urdu, the 'expression of a unified Hindu-

Muslim culture', be used for official purposes in the area; and 'children whose mother tongue is Urdu should have the right to receive education in their mother tongue'.[95] Not surprisingly, Muslims, who constituted 23 per cent of the population, flocked to her meetings. Joshi managed to get the popular Bombay actor Balraj Sahni to campaign for her – one of the earliest instances of a Hindi film star campaigning for a politician.[96] The prime minister, who had not bothered to campaign in Balrampur in 1957, also turned up. As always, Nehru assaulted the RSS–Jan Sangh, and 'turned the tide' in Joshi's favour.[97] But he also mentioned in passing that the otherwise reactionary Jan Sangh also had some bright members. Vajpayee felt that Nehru's caveat 'actually helped me'.[98]

As the day of polling approached, there were clashes, verbal and bloody, between Jan Sangh and Congress volunteers. Wherever she went, Joshi repeated that if she won, she would serve her constituency all thirty days of each month. In a rare lapse, Vajpayee made a crude sexist comment: 'Subhadraji says she will be here all thirty days of the month. How is she going to do that? Some days a month, women are hardly in a position to serve!'[99] On 1 February, the driver of Jan Sangh's publicity van was stabbed. On the day of polling, 21 February, two Congress workers were killed and many on both sides injured; curfew was imposed in parts of the constituency.[100]

The results were announced on 8 March 1962: Subhadra Joshi had pulled off a narrow but stylish victory; Vajpayee lost by a meagre 2,052 votes.[101] He managed to convince the Election Commission to recount the votes, but this did not help matters. He knew the reason for his narrow defeat: the Mahasabha had put up a candidate, aware that this was only going to eat into the Jan Sangh's share of votes: it secured a total of 5,046. One of the first congratulatory messages Joshi received was a telegram from Indira Gandhi: 'Khoob ladi mardaani woh toh Jhansi waali rani thi' – Like a man she fought, the Queen of Jhansi. The lines were from an iconic poem by Joshi's namesake Subhadra Chauhan.[102] As on two previous occasions, Vajpayee had no luck in Lucknow either. While he polled 37.5 per cent of the votes, he was outmanoeuvred by the Congress.

Shocked by his unexpected defeat in Balrampur, Vajpayee floated conspiracies theories: 'I had looked after my consistency very well, brought Balrampur in prominence in parliament.' Congress supporters, with help from officials at the polling booths, had misled and confused voters about the colour of the Jan Sangh's ballot (which had led to eight thousand votes being declared invalid).[103] The allegations were far-fetched, but he had surely been unlucky. In the assembly elections held simultaneously, three out of five Jan Sangh candidates in Balrampur had romped home. The showstopper wondered how those obscure candidates 'were able to cross the river' while 'I got drowned midstream'.[104]

Even so, Vajpayee had gathered more votes in total than the fourteen winners of Lok Sabha seats from the Jan Sangh – mostly upper-caste north Indian men; one Dalit, no women. He was duly rewarded. Rajya Sabha elections were held only three weeks later. On the basis of the party's improved performance in the assemblies – 119 as compared to 51 in 1957 – for the first time the Jan Sangh was able to send two candidates to the upper house. He was nominated from UP, where the party had won forty-nine seats.[105] It was a consolation prize: the Rajya Sabha did not exercise a veto on most legislation.

Meanwhile the communal situation was worsening, and it was not inside parliament but rather at the second NIC in early June where, against the backdrop of the communal riots in Aligarh and Malda, Vajpayee made a forceful defence of the Sangh Parivar. Rajasthan chief minister Mohan Lal Sukhadia made a reference to small children being 'poisoned' by communal outfits like the RSS. Vajpayee responded:

> I have been connected with the RSS right from my childhood. I am proud to say that whatever measure of patriotism, spirit of selfless service, concern for the suffering of fellow citizens I have in me, I owe it entirely to the RSS … Christian children are brought up under Christian *samskars*, Muslim children are bred under Islamic *samskars* … but it becomes a crime when Hindu children are sought to be imbued with Hindu *samskars*! You may disagree with the views of the Rashtriya Swayamsewak Sangh. But it isn't an index of a healthy mentality that a diverse opinion should be looked on as 'poison'?[106]

The performance had a touch of melodrama. Having been outmanoeuvred by the Congress in Balrampur, he carried a poster printed during the election by the Congress in Punjab declaring the Jan Sangh 'Gandhiji's murderer' and speculating if its workers were being 'trained for Nehruji's murder too'. His voice trembling, Vajpayee challenged Nehru: 'If you feel we are engaged in a conspiracy for your murder, then I must say that the proper place for us would be not this Council, but a prison-cell instead'. Contrary to what Nehru and leftist Congressmen believed, Vajpayee insisted that communal riots were 'essentially a law and order question and ought to be dealt with on that level'. Thus the second NIC too ended 'beating its wings in a void', as the *Times of India* succinctly put it, 'like an ineffectual angel of unity'.[107]

Without Vajpayee, the Jan Sangh failed to put up an impressive show in the Lok Sabha. In fact, with most of the prominent opposition members losing the elections – socialists Archarya Kripalani and Asoka Mehta, communist S. A. Dange, Swatantrite N. G. Ranga – some of the action had moved to the Rajya Sabha. Vajpayee missed the vibrancy and energy of the lower house, but was grateful to the chairman of the Rajya Sabha, Vice President S. Radhakrishnan, for allotting him a seat in the first row. Despite his party's low strength, now he was 'hardly ever denied a chance to speak'. Expectedly, Vajpayee used many of these occasions to needle the government about the incursions on the northern border.

China had continued to build posts, roads and airports in the western sector. By the end of June 1962, the answer to Vajpayee's repeated queries in the Rajya Sabha on whether there had been fresh incursions was often a yes: the government had sent a 'protest note', in reply to which the Chinese had 'fortuitously admitted' having established posts.[108] But neither the prime minister nor the defence minister expected a full-blooded confrontation. On 25 July, a seething Vajpayee wrote to Nehru, demanding to know why the defence minister was frequently out of the country at a time of tense standoff at the border. Nehru replied the same day, calmly defending Menon: he had been away for the Geneva accord on Laos, with which India had been involved since the beginning; the defence chiefs were ably monitoring the border situation in Ladakh.[109]

Three weeks later, Vajpayee grilled Menon as to why 'despite our protests the Chinese aircrafts continue to violate our space'. Menon replied, less earnest and more sarcastic, that it was beyond his power to decide where diplomacy stopped and war began: 'I might, however, submit that this aircraft penetrated into our territory 18 miles. By the time we took any action if we so wished the aircraft would have gone back to its territory.'[110] In the first week of September, Vajpayee once again badgered Nehru about the pointlessness of the proposed talks between Chinese and Indian officials, given that China had resolutely refused to withdraw from what it now called 'the line of actual control'. Nehru chided him for a 'rather amazing' suggestion on a serious matter: talking 'is always good whether it is accepted by the other party or not'.[111]

In the second week of September 1962, Vajpayee and eight other MPs were sent by the government to Ladakh 'to acquaint themselves with the conditions there'. But because of the bad roads and rough terrain (with the hills completely covered in snow), they could not be shown any check posts or allowed to meet any soldiers on the border. Vajpayee came back disappointed.[112] While he was in Ladakh, trouble had begun, unexpectedly, on the eastern front of the NEFA. A conflict ensued over the Dhola-Thagla ridge: India claimed the ridge was south of the McMahon Line; China, which had always raised doubts about its legality, insisted that the ridge fell on their side.[113]

After the first exchange of fire on 20 September, the two sides clashed intermittently to push back the other. On the night of 19–20 October, the Chinese simultaneously launched an invasion in the eastern and western sectors. For one month, the two sides fought bitterly. But with better resources and prior planning, the Chinese overran multiple Indian positions in both Ladakh and NEFA.[114] Nehru now admitted his failure in foreseeing such a situation, resulting in poor defence preparedness. The Americans were approached for arms, and they promptly despatched more than forty aircraft carrying equipment.[115]

On 26 October, the government declared a national emergency. That day Vajpayee, along with some of his Jan Sangh colleagues, called on the prime minister to request an immediate convening of parliament.[116] On 8 November, the two houses were summoned. In the meantime Nehru, at long last, sacked his defence minister Menon, which was to Vajpayee a 'most welcome piece of news'.[117] When Vajpayee rose to speak in Rajya Sabha on 9 November, the air was thick with humiliation and hurt:

> We have gathered here in the shadow of a great national crisis. Our very existence is at stake. The Communist China has put forward its bloody paws to erase all we hold dear and pious … This is for us a matter of life and death, and we shall emerge out of it victorious. But the first prerequisite for victory is introspection.[118]

Was it not a matter of shame, Vajpayee asked, that fifteen years after independence, India was not able to manufacture its own automatic rifles? That its soldiers did not have proper uniforms to protect them from the cold? He made the old Jan Sangh plea on national security that Nehru had earlier mocked: 'To tackle the 25-lakh-strong [Chinese] army, we need to militarise the country'. As earlier, Vajpayee differed from Nehru in that China's expansionist aims were not a result of extreme nationalism: the aggression really was part of a larger communist design to take over the world. After all, why had the communist world not condemned China's antagonism: 'Can the USSR and its fellow-travellers not see that China is the aggressor?' The interpretation mattered because closely hinged on it was the fate of non-alignment, India's chief gift to the theory and practice of foreign policy.

> Non-alignment is not a subject of worship; it is a policy, not a principle … the day it no longer serves the national interest, it should be discarded as one would an old, torn garment … And, by accepting weapons from the west, and thanking them for their aid, we have proved that we are hostage to no policy dogma.[119]

Vajpayee was certain that that the war had to be continued for as long as possible: no peace talks should be held 'until we evacuate India's land from the Chinese on the strength of [military] power'. For even if China withdrew itself behind the pre-8 September line in NEFA, how would it help Ladakh? 'Would we compromise in NEFA by giving up our territory in Ladakh – something the Chinese have been trying all along? Would not that be incentivising the invader for yet another attack?' It was another way of making a case for a prolonged acquisition of military aid from the US.

Significantly, even though Vajpayee held Nehru guilty of not preparing for an almost pre-destined war, he did not question Nehru's leadership at the toughest time of the prime minister's career.

> Today the country stands firmly behind the Prime Minister. He is a veteran of our fight for independence, our messenger of peace. But perhaps history wants to test whether or not a man who could lead in peace can withstand this rain of fire and rescue the nation to the banks of victory. This is not a test merely of our soldiers, but each of India's citizens, which includes our Prime Minister. The need is to creatively use the heightened consciousness of our people so everyone knows what is expected out of them in such a difficult condition.[120]

Nehru may have been relieved to hear such empathetic words from an adversary, but he rejected Vajpayee's arguments for continuing the war rather than negotiating: the war could go on indefinitely 'sucking the blood of the country', and therefore India would be willing to talk to the Chinese if they withdrew to positions held before 8 September.[121]

Vajpayee's guarded praise of Nehru was in contrast to the opinions of most people in the RSS–Jan Sangh.* A few days later, Home Minister Lal

* Soon after Vajpayee, B. D. Khobragade, a young Dalit MP of the Republican Party, pointed out the duality in the Jan Sangh: he was 'rather moved by the speech' but he quoted a sentence from *Organiser* about Nehru's 'decadent philosophy and anaemic politics' having debased a proud ancient nation 'to a flock of contemptible sheep'. And to transform Indians into the lions that their ancestors were, the mouthpiece wanted 'a leader other than – NEHRU'.

Bahadur Shastri complained in parliament about receiving 'somewhat depressing reports' about Jan Sangh's rank and file. While Vajpayee himself had proved to be an 'important and sober' voice during the war, in Shastri's own assessment, many in the Jan Sangh had been demanding 'a wartime leader'. Shastri asked rhetorically: what was the 'distinction between a peacetime leader and a wartime leader'? He answered the question himself, that the Jan Sangh:

> had not really suffered for the country and they do not know what determination we had shown under the leadership of Gandhiji to fight the British imperialism ... And is there any other better leader in this country, any other man, who has stood by these principles during the last fifteen years since Gandhiji's death except Pt. Jawaharlal Nehru?[122]

Among the non-communist opposition asking for the prime minister's head were Nehru's friend-turned-foe Acharya Kripalani, who had been defeated by Krishna Menon in the Lok Sabha election. On some occasions, Vajpayee spoke against Kripalani's demand for a change in the national leadership. Since it was wartime, Vajpayee argued, 'all of us must strengthen the hands of the present leadership'.[123]

Irked, Kripalani declared Vajpayee to be a Nehruvian in Jan Sanghi garb. At a rally held by the non-communist opposition on 7 November, Kripalani warned the Swatantra Party leader Minoo Masani: 'Don't trust that man, he is essentially a Nehruite, and not one of us.'[124] This was sheer prejudice on the Acharya's part. In reality, Vajpayee's differences with his own partymen, as well as with other opposition figures like Kripalani, were more semantic than qualitative. Vajpayee simply felt that to ask Nehru to resign – in the middle of a war, and only six months after he had been returned to office with a two-thirds majority – was a fatuous, impractical proposition.

Vajpayee and Nehru clashed again on 21 November, the very day China declared a unilateral ceasefire. The Jan Sanghi felt the Chinese ceasefire was a trap 'to confuse world opinion, and lull India again into complacency' and, that before arriving at a decision on the ceasefire offer, Nehru should conduct a public debate 'so that the decision may be a national decision as such'. A mildly annoyed Nehru wrote off the referendum as 'a very remarkable suggestion which will be quite unique in diplomatic history'.[125]

At the Bhopal annual session in late December 1962, most Jan Sanghis demanded the manufacture of nuclear weapons. Now Vajpayee conceded the demand. But there was a difference of opinion about the policy of non-alignment within the party while passing the foreign policy resolution.[126] Unlike his provocations on the floor of the house, Vajpayee thought that non-alignment still had its uses; seeking help from Western countries did not amount to its eschewing: India could secure 'massive aid, including air protection' from the US without giving up on non-alignment.[127] As Russia had taken a neutral stand in India's conflict with China, 'it would surely be imprudent to do anything that will push Russia actively with China against India'. It was advantageous, therefore, to continue to remain non-aligned with either of the two world blocs.[128] The party passed a resolution for the complete integration of NEFA with Assam, freedom to people from other areas to settle in NEFA, and direct administration by the centre of Ladakh.*

Vajpayee was vehemently opposed to the 'Colombo proposals' – an initiative taken by the prime minister of Sri Lanka, along with five other non-aligned countries, to mediate between Delhi and Peking. When he and other opposition leaders called on Nehru on 20 January, 'tempers rose on both sides' during the discussions. While the Colombo proposals asked China to vacate the territory occupied after 8 September, it was given the right of setting up civil posts even in those areas. The non-communist opposition demanded, on the contrary, that the positions held by the Indian Army until 8 September in NEFA should be fully restored.[129] The non-aligned countries had adopted a neutral posture, and did not refer to China as the aggressor. Vajpayee called the proposals 'a

* Vajpayee unsuccessfully demanded resettling 'one lakh sturdy Punjabis, especially Sikh ex-servicemen' in NEFA, with the dual aim of 'assimilation of tribals and to dissuade the Chinese from coming again'.

diplomatic victory for China'. India must push the Chinese to the south of the McMahon Line – even if it took another war – and if before that Nehru 'goes to talk to the Chinese Prime Minister, he will have to walk over our chests'.[130]

India's gloom reflected in the restrained Republic Day celebrations, at which the usual pageantry and pomp were conspicuous by their absence. Instead, for the first time, all MPs marched solemnly past the saluting base. Schoolchildren, trade unions and other volunteer groups also marched down Rajpath; among the trade unions was a contingent of the Bharatiya Mazdoor Sangh.[131] The RSS managed to sneak in a contingent of 2,000 Delhi-based volunteers, 'in full uniform – white shirt, khaki knickers, belt, black cap and full boots – [who] formed the major highlight of the Delhi Citizens group'.[132] Decades later, Vajpayee and others in the Sangh Parivar would use this occasion to insist that Nehru, impressed by the RSS's patriotism during the China war, had personally 'invited' them to take part in the 1963 parade.

7

The Husband and the Lover

THE WAR WITH CHINA ESTABLISHED VAJPAYEE, NOW IN HIS LATE thirties, as the rare opposition voice that was influential yet sober. For the first time, there was also a semblance of stability in his personal life: as an MP he was entitled to a monthly salary, and assigned an official residence – 30 Rajendra Prasad Marg – in the heart of the city. But Vajpayee was insecure in other ways: he had lost five of the six Lok Sabha elections he had fought thus far. And though his differences with others in the party were clashes of temperament and personal egos, he was often referred to as ideologically amorphous – a 'double agent' of sorts.

At a low moment in late 1963, he opened up in an interview to the Hindi monthly *Navneet*. He retraced the chain of events after Mookerji's death that had made him plunge into politics, saying he now regretted the decision as the 'biggest mistake of my life'. This was the first occasion on which Vajpayee revealed his intimate self, and his responses offer rare insights.

> I had envisaged a life of scholarship, carrying forward the family tradition; take something from the past, give back something to the future. But in the slippery paths of politics I feel I have, far from earning something, frittered away everything I inherited from my ancestors. My peace of mind is dead; I never feel satisfied anymore; my life is inundated with a strange hollowness.[1]

16. *Atal (first from right) at a public meeting held for S. P. Mookerji in Lucknow, 1952*

17. *Atal with Prabhudatt Brahmachari in Lucknow (second and third from right), celebrating the UP government's ban on cow slaughter in February 1955*

18. *On the verge of stardom, Atal agitates a crowd of Goa Satyagraha supporters in Delhi, 1955.*

19. A close-up of the candidate for the 1955 Lucknow by-election campaign

20. Protesting the imposition of sales tax at the Lucknow Assembly House in April 1956

21. Awaiting the 1957 poll results at home in Gwalior, Atal found time to ruminate on life without Ma–Babuji

22. Syama babu's successor: A typical campaign photograph of Vajpayee from the late 1950s

23. The Jan Sangh protesting Nehru's invitation to Chou En-lai to discuss the border dispute, 17 February 1960. L to R: Vajpayee, Deendayal, Madhok

24. The first-term Jan Sangh MPs, Premjibhai Assar (L) and Vajpayee, chat up Vice President S. Radhakrishnan.

25. The rising political star flips through Panchjanya *more than a decade after he helped launch it in January 1948.*

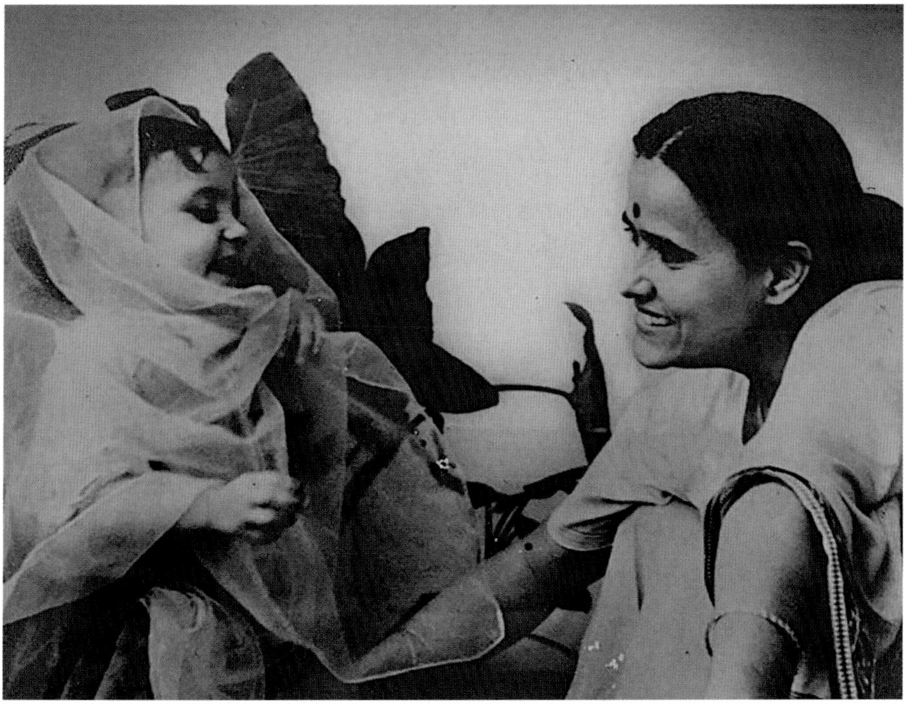

26. The toddler Gunnu with her mother Rajkumari

27. The fiery Subhadra Joshi pounded Vajpayee at the hustings in Balrampur in 1962.

28. Advocates of central law on cow protection gather at Prabhudatt Brahmachari's (first from right) ashram in Vrindavan, April 1965. L to R: Guruji Golwalkar, Deendayal, Atal

29. The Jan Sangh protesting the Kutch Agreement, June 1965

30. Shastri's all-party meeting in the midst of war with Pakistan, September 1965. Attendees included M. S. Golwalkar (third from right).

31. Deendayal Upadhyaya, the incoming Jan Sangh president, welcomed at Calicut for the 1967 session

32. Atal and (behind him) Balraj Madhok bid a tearful farewell to Deendayalji, whose presidential stint lasted all of forty-three days.

Without naming anyone, he bewailed the increasing strength of people in the Jan Sangh 'who revel in cheap gossip and cast doubt on other people's intentions'.

> Politics today demands glib speech-making, not conscience; it rewards publicity, not restraint. Far from respecting differences, the habit of tolerating differences is also getting extinct. Opportunism has replaced idealism. Even the differences of 'left' and 'right' have become more personal, less ideological … One has to compete for power not just with the opposition, but also with one's own party-men. To maintain power and prestige, one has to learn to manipulate and flatter and conspire. It has become dangerous to speak with clarity and fearlessness. Only by crushing one's soul can one rise ahead.[2]

Though the path of politics was slippery, where 'even a slight imbalance would lead to a mighty fall', he confessed that it was impossible to walk away from it: 'It's an obsession. The intoxication of reading your name in the morning newspapers refuses to leave you … then again, in a politics-dominated world – where everything, even culture and society, depends on the government's mercy – how does a politician escape self-publicity? It's a most extraordinary dilemma.'[3]

The interview revealed him as a man capable of frank introspection, not a trait common among full-time politicians. Even so, Vajpayee did not disclose that some of the hollowness in his life had to do with an unusually complicated love affair.

Despite being a rising political star, Vajpayee was emotionally a lonely, desolate man-child. The death of his parents in quick succession had stunned him. The trauma demanded closure, but there had been no time and there was no outlet. He had never been wholly averse to the idea of getting married. The RSS had made celibacy a necessity for its full-timers in the hope that it would help them channel their sexual energy into the selfless task of consolidating Hindus into a political unit. But the organization provided no spiritual framework to help them control their sexual urges.

In any case Vajpayee had never been a pracharak in a strict sense.

Also, by the early 1960s, many RSS full-timers were getting married – including party colleagues such as Madhok – without anyone judging them harshly. No one would have complained had he decided to settle down. But for someone brought up in a small town, Vajpayee was well past marriageable age (his university mates had been married for a decade). Besides, within the Sangh Parivar ecosystem in Delhi, there were hardly any women. It was in these circumstances that he first met 'Mrs Kaul'.

Born in Ujjain on 13 September 1925, Rajkumari Haksar was the eldest of five children of Govind Narayan Haksar from his second wife Manmohini.[4] The Haksars were Kashmiri Pandits who had for generations been a part of the Scindia bureaucracy in Gwalior: Govind was a small-time bureaucrat with the education department. The family lived in a bungalow called Lal Kothi in the affluent locality of Morar. Govind's father-in-law Roop Narayan Kaul was the indenting agent in India for Guest Keen Williams in Delhi. Each summer Rajkumari, with her siblings and mother, would stay with her maternal grandparents at their haveli at Chitli Qabar in Old Delhi.

The chronology of how Atal and Rajkumari met is hazy. Decades later, an account gained ground that they had fallen in love in college; and due to circumstances beyond the lovers' control, she ended up marrying someone else. Victoria College maintains no records of its past students, though Rajkumari had probably joined the college during the 1942–43 session. She may have had a fleeting acquaintance with Atal, her senior by a year. But neither Atal's close friends from college nor anyone in his family were aware of his acquaintance with Rajkumari. Atal in fact had a crush on another batchmate of his who, soon after graduation, married and settled down with a handsome Brahmin Marxist from Morena. At best Atal and Rajkumari may have spoken during college a few times. They were most certainly not lovers.

Significantly, too, they came from contrasting social classes: the Haksars were privileged enough to send their daughter to college in a buggy at a time Atal's family did not even own a bicycle. As against the Haksars' Lal Kothi in Morar, Atal's family lived in the humbler Shinde Ki Chhavni, where they queued up to draw water from a public well. The subsequent narrative about the two being lovers separated by misfortune was mostly fiction – floated by the couple themselves to make their affair seem less scandalous.

On 6 November 1947, Rajkumari's marriage was arranged to Brijmohan Nath Kaul, who came from a Kashmiri family settled for generations in Balrampur. Older than Rajkumari by nine years, Birjan Kaul had attended university at Allahabad and recently joined Ramjas College in Old Delhi as a lecturer of philosophy. Soon after they were married, the couple was blessed with a baby girl nicknamed 'Nanhi', little girl – who would later be named Nandita. In 1951, Ramjas was moved to the northern part of the city to join a group of other elite Delhi University colleges at the 'north campus'. In 1957 Gangaram Shastri, a faculty member who was also the warden of the Boys' Hostel, suddenly died. The responsibility was transferred to Kaul.*

The young couple moved into the warden's quarters, sprawled over 2,000 square feet inside the college campus. The garden had mango and guava trees, and enough open land for the family to grow vegetables, in which they were assisted by the government-deputed gardeners. For a while there were complaints from hostellers and non-teaching staff that Shastri's ghost had been sighted on the hostel grounds at night, but the ghost never harassed anyone.

The impression Dr Kaul wanted to create was that of a disciplinarian always on watch. At the beginning of every academic year, the warden would address the new hostellers: 'Remember, a hostel is not home, but nor is it a hotel.' This was to apply a brake in the minds of students for whom a college hostel brought freedom from the restrictions previously imposed by school and family. Kaul's tough exterior would with time crack to reveal a man who was considerate and tender. Every once in a while, he would come to the mess and ask students if the food tasted alright. If someone had an important message for their family, he would take the student to the only telephone the college had in that academic block. For any problem that a student encountered, Kaul saheb offered a solution. He would be immaculately dressed on formal occasions. On

* Kaul was selected for the job perhaps because he had less rigorous working hours. He was the lone faculty of the philosophy department. Ramjas did not offer an honours in philosophy; the course was only offered to BA (Pass) candidates.

other days the warden, his long Kashmiri nose perpetually pink, would roam around the campus in his hawai chappals.

In all probability, it was Birjan Kaul who first came to know the young new MP from his hometown. Through him Vajpayee met the warden's wife, and discovered their past association. To outsiders, the Kauls did not appear to be an unhappy couple: they had a young daughter; the marriage may have turned a bit dull, but it was nowhere close to imploding.

It is easy to appreciate why the bachelor politician was enchanted by the warden's wife: in her mid-thirties, Rajkumari was attractive, affable, kind, articulate. Unlike women in Vajpayee's extended family, she spoke elegant English. Married off at twenty-two, her perspective on life was still evolving. After almost a decade of quietly managing a household, she had begun to informally involve herself in college administration: 'She was popular among the college non-teaching staff,' an old student recalled. 'She had struck good equations with the administration of St Stephen's Hospital nearby, and if someone needed medical help, she would take them there.'[5]

A part of Vajpayee's appeal was his conviviality and rising celebrity. But some of it also had to do with the shared memories of the Gwalior of their childhood – a now-vanished world upon which many of Scindia's former employees and their families looked back with considerable nostalgia.

Rajkumari's embarrassed family tried convincing her to save her marriage by letting go of the new man in her life. She refused. There are no clear answers as to why she did not divorce her husband and formally marry Vajpayee. Was it because of Nandita, who was now approaching adolescence? Was it that the ensuing scandal would have hurt Vajpayee's career – as the face of a rising conservative party that preached the sanctity of family life?

Most of all, what did she have in mind when she went ahead with having a second child with Vajpayee eleven years after the birth of Nandita? Baby 'Gunnu' was born in early August 1960. As she grew older, Gunnu's facial features began to resemble her father's. On paper, she was to be the warden's daughter: Namita *Kaul*. Vajpayee may have felt the void of not being able to officially call himself a father, though Gunnu began calling him 'Baapji'.

He occasionally dropped hints of the tumult in his private life in his prose-poems, the themes of which had evolved over the years from Veer Ras to unpompous, self-reflective, melancholic lines on the human condition: they were almost entirely autobiographical. On his birthday in December, he felt that in 'worrying endlessly about past and future' he had 'lost track of the ongoing present'. That even though the mela of life was crowded, all his 'loved ones went away one by one living me alone'. Life had 'slipped past' without him quite realising.[6]

With time the trio arrived at an equilibrium of sorts. Rajkumari made genuine efforts to balance her care between the husband and the lover. Most people who knew the couple found the wife adequately devoted to the husband. She continued to live with Kaul saheb, who, after the early hurt and shock, learnt to make peace with the new arrangement. Some Ramjas alumni close to him speculated that Kaul saheb might have an alternative sexual orientation. After all it was uncommon in the 1950s to have only one child. Birjan Kaul was barely in his early forties when his wife met Vajpayee. Someone else in his position – handsome, popular, well settled in his career – might have walked out of the marriage to find another partner.

Vajpayee visited Ramjas as often as he could. If parliament was in recess, he would sometimes stay on campus for days on end. The hostel mess had a crew of cooks from Almora, one of whom would be persuaded to grind bhang for him.[7] Often hostellers close to Kaul saheb came for chai in the evening. The celebrity MP enjoyed chatting with the young students, discussing with them everything from current affairs to career options: 'he would try to convince us that the academics offered a good career', and sometimes even 'promised to help us get jobs'.[8]

When news of the affair reached Gwalior, Atal's family was suitably scandalized. For a while no one knew how to broach the subject. On one of his visits, Atal himself brought it up. Ma had, on her deathbed, divided the family jewellery among her daughters-in-law, keeping a share for Atal with Sada Behari's wife. Atal now asked his sister-in-law for his share, confiding that he wanted to give it to Rajkumari. On another trip, Rajkumari came along to see Atal's ancestral house. But this was a rare occasion. For many years, Rajkumari's contact with the Vajpayees remained minimal.

Atal went home for festivals and, increasingly, for the wedding of a niece or nephew. Sometimes he also brought gifts from foreign trips. But with so many nephews and nieces quarrelling for a piece, Chachaji would eventually prepare chits and draw a lottery. On Diwali nights, the three brothers would sit down to play cards. If a niece was getting married, Atal eagerly participated in mundane chores like chopping potatoes or shelling green peas even as he cracked silly jokes to keep the youngsters entertained. On some occasions the entire family, more than two dozen now, would walk to the nearby cinema hall to catch a night show.

With the Jan Sangh, however, he continued to be cagey about his private life. People in the upper echelons of the Sangh Parivar knew about this development, but it was mostly discussed in hushed tones. Decades later, Madhok would make an exaggerated claim that Vajpayee had reduced his MP bungalow 'to a haunt of adultery, with new women coming there every other day … I called up Atal at my house, and in a closed-door talk confronted him … I then suggested him to get married – else he will certainly harm his personal reputation, but may also hurt party's image.'[9]

This newly compartmentalized life was not entirely of his choosing. Oddly, though, it unburdened him from conjugal chores, while still lending him emotional security. With the Kauls raising his daughter, Vajpayee could afford to focus entirely on politics.

8

Missing the Lok Sabha's Spark: The Shastri Years

WITH THE MAHASABHA AND THE RAM RAJYA PARISHAD DYING SLOWLY, the Jan Sangh found it opportune to collaborate with the Praja Socialist and Swatantra parties to take on a physically and psychologically enfeebled Nehru.[1] In May 1963, they jointly fought the by-elections for four Lok Sabha seats, and won three. One of the winners, Acharya Kripalani, moved for the first time ever a no-confidence motion against the prime minister in mid-August. Initially the Jan Sangh, which was keen to integrate the non-communist opposition in parliament into one block, promised its support. The leader of the Jan Sangh group in the Lok Sabha, U. M. Trivedi, rose to support the motion.[2] But at the time of voting two days later, they vetoed Kripalani's motion.[3]

Acharya's motion was quashed 61–343, with a heated discussion preceding the vote. But the Jan Sangh's U-turn remains a mystery. All through, Vajpayee had been negotiating with the non-communist group in parliament to consolidate themselves as one party. But the socialists were hesitant about dissolving their identity; the move failed.[4] Perhaps this was the reason the Jan Sangh did not issue a whip for the no-confidence motion – with the result that many of its MPs were missing during the voting – and eventually decided to vote against it. It is possible that Nehru had a private word with Vajpayee – who, as a Rajya Sabha member, would not have a chance to vote in the lower house – to convince his Lok Sabha MPs to vote against the motion.[5]

To inject new life into the grand old party, K. Kamaraj, the Tamil Nadu chief minister, proposed that all senior Congressmen resign from their ministerial posts to devote themselves to strengthening the organization. This was not Nehru's idea, but that did not stop the opposition from floating wild theories. Six cabinet ministers were made to resign from their posts, including a few whom Nehru was happy to shed, such as the finance minister Morarji Desai. Vajpayee speculated that under the guise of the Kamaraj plan, Nehru wanted to 'get rid of ministers who were anti-communist'.[6] He gave notice for a privilege motion in the Rajya Sabha, which was denied.[7] He was informed that it was the prime minister's prerogative to appoint or dismiss ministers.*

In mid-April 1963, following a working committee meeting in Delhi, Balraj Madhok informed the American embassy that the Jan Sangh was, if only reluctantly, ready for the partition of Kashmir. Even though the party believed that legally all of Jammu and Kashmir was Indian territory, the country needed assistance from the US. Since the Americans considered Pakistan to be the aggrieved party, he conceded that 'India must yield' on Kashmir. Pakistan would get 'all of the area north of the Vale which is now on the Indian side of the ceasefire line; most of Baramulla district … and some areas in Poonch and Jammu but not to the extent of control of the sources of the Chenab'. Madhok assured the American embassy that his party did not want a 'status quo, a condominium, or a plebiscite'.[8]

Even if conveyed in private, this was a significant concession from a party that dreamt of undoing the partition. Of course Madhok's proposal meant little, because neither of the two governments risked selling a compromise on Kashmir to their citizens. Soon after, President Kennedy was shot dead, and his successor Lyndon Johnson, being less friendly towards India, put the military assistance programme on the back burner.

* On his travels, Vajpayee informed his Jan Sanghi cadres that the reshuffle would 'neither improve the administration nor strengthen the Congress party', that weakening the administration to strengthen the party, at a time the country faced foreign aggression and internal subversion, was not a wise move.

Feeling betrayed, Vajpayee mourned that the US was 'not prepared to give supersonic planes to India'; nor had the American government or its citizens criticized Pakistan for its 'unholy alliance' with China.[9] The Jan Sangh revoked its proposal for the partition of Kashmir.

The release of Sheikh Abdullah, who had been behind bars now for almost a decade, alarmed the Jan Sangh.* The prime minister wanted to make one final effort to include Abdullah in solving Kashmir. After walking out of Jammu jail on 8 April, Abdullah spent the next few weeks travelling in the Valley, where he demanded frequently that India and Pakistan must 'ascertain what the Kashmiris wanted' before deciding its fate. For Vajpayee such talk was sacrilegious, for it meant reopening settled questions – such as the accession of J&K to India.

On 28 April, the eve of Abdullah's arrival in Delhi, the Jan Sangh led a demonstration in front of the Parliament House. Vajpayee bragged to the crowd that the Jan Sangh had dropped the proposal to stage a black-flag demonstration against Abdullah so as to allow Nehru to meet him peacefully.[10] But the prime minister would have to tell Abdullah that Kashmir's integration with India had been a settled fact for seventeen years.[11] Significantly, by now many among the Congress senior leadership too agreed with the need to maintain status quo in Kashmir. Swatantra stalwarts Masani and Rajagopalachari, on the contrary, favoured engagement with Abdullah. On a trip to Gaya in the second week of May to attend the annual session of the Bihar Jan Sangh, Vajpayee criticized the statements of Rajaji and Masani (and others with similar opinions, such as Jayaprakash Narayan).[12] This drama had yet to reach its climax when, on 27 May 1964, Nehru passed away, three days after Sheikh Abdullah arrived in Pakistan to carry out his peace mission.

This was not wholly unexpected. Three months ago, when Nehru was recuperating from a stroke, Vajpayee had complained in the Rajya Sabha that the succession struggle was affecting administration, and had put across a proposal for a deputy prime minister for the time being.[13] He attended the funeral, marking the end of an unusual relationship.

* Nehru had always felt convinced that the charges against Abdullah – of receiving arms and funds from Pakistan and inciting communal discord in J&K – were mostly fictitious.

Speaking in the Rajya Sabha two days later, he paid a magnanimous tribute. He had spent the last few months bitterly attacking the prime minister. Now, he gracefully stepped back to assess Nehru's long career in public service.

> A dream lies shattered, a song silenced, a flame has vanished in the infinite … Bharat Mata is stricken with grief today, she has lost her favourite son … The curtain has come down: the lead actor on the world stage has finally bid us farewell … In the Ramayana, Maharshi Valmiki had said that Lord Rama brought the impossible together. In Panditji's life too we see a glimpse of it: he was a devotee of peace, yet the harbinger of revolution; he sought non-violence, but advocated every weapon to defend freedom and prestige of the country; he was an advocate of individual freedom, and yet was committed to bringing about economic equality; he was never afraid of a compromise, but he never compromised out of fear … The Indian democracy he established, and made a success of, is faced with a doubtful future … The loss to Parliament is irreparable. Nor would Teen Murti be ever graced by a resident like him. His persona, his exuberance, his ability to carry even the detractors along, his refined gentlemanliness – we may not again see in the near future. In spite of differences, we have nothing but respect for his ideals, integrity, love for the country, and an indomitable courage … I pay my and my party's humble homage to that great soul.[14]

In retrospect, the eulogy was more a quick, generous tribute than a careful assessment. Homage paid, Vajpayee went back to being an adversary. In mid-June, he would leave for East Asia as part of a parliamentary delegation: their most important destination was Formosa (later Taiwan). Some weeks prior, he had asked in the Rajya Sabha whether, given the hostilities with Communist China, the Indian government had any intention of recognizing Chiang Kai-shek's government in Formosa. Nehru had chipped in a quick no: both Communist China and the Formosa government were 'claiming authority over the whole of China'.[15]

The delegation spent a week as Chiang Kai-shek's guests in Formosa, where Vajpayee and fellow delegates were stunned to hear him too refer to Tibet as an 'integral part of China'. The delegation tried to impress on the eighty-year-old general that Nationalist China should support India's case in Kashmir, that such a posture by Formosa would strengthen their friendship as nothing else could.[16] The meeting produced nothing substantial. The general was well past his prime; the Americans who had supported him earlier were no longer confident that he could win back China from the communists.

For Madhok, who was also among the delegates, the highlight of the Formosa trip was a tiff he had with Vajpayee at the posh hotel near Sun Moon Lake where they were staying. Unbeknown to Vajpayee himself, he had a stomach ulcer, due to which excessive drinking sometimes gave him a severe stomach ache. On one such occasion, Madhok 'rushed to his room [as he was] he was crying in pain'. It was long past midnight, but a doctor came and administered an injection 'which made Atal feel better'. The next morning Madhok informed Vajpayee of the doctor's advice – to cut down on alcohol – and enquired why he drank so heavily. Vajpayee retorted: 'What else should one drink?' Annoyed, Madhok suggested, 'if you can't live without it, maybe drink only as much as you can digest'.[17]

Nehru's death may have been a 'national calamity', but the Sangh Parivar was infinitely relieved.[18] At the same time, their expansionist plans produced some strains between the parent body and its political progeny. After the new prime minister Lal Bahadur Shastri settled into office, Golwalkar paid a visit to Delhi in mid-August: he met Shastri and many of the cabinet ministers. In these talks, Golwalkar deplored the absence of a great goal and a sense of high mission in the country, and vaguely suggested that the government patronize the RSS. The partnership did not take off in a major way: the ban on RSS volunteers joining the Congress was never revoked. But Shastri was more deferential to Golwalkar than Nehru, and the visit helped the Sangh Parivar rehabilitate itself. Its mouthpieces were immediately given better access to newsprint and government advertising: the new minister of information and broadcasting, Indira Gandhi, was asked to write to the *Organiser* for 'specific ideas and suggestions' on 'reorganising and revitalising' the branches of her ministry.[19] In his exaggerated generosity, the RSS chief promised to support the government against the ongoing food agitation – and 'agitational politics in general' – embarrassing the Jan Sangh.[20]

A bigger crisis built up towards the end of the year over the selection of the party president. Traditionally, even though party presidents in the Jan Sangh had mostly ornamental roles, and were often parachuted to the post from outside, the final decision to appoint them was taken by Nagpur. One such outsider was the Congressman Raghu Vira – a renowned linguist and former member of the constituent assembly – who had crossed over to the Jan Sangh over differences with Nehru's China policy in 1961. But Raghu Vira's independent working style irked the RSS. After he died in a car accident while campaigning for Ram Manohar Lohia during the 1963 by-elections, the parent body decided to nominate only insiders to the post. They went overboard in nominating the next president: Bachhraj Vyas, head of the Nagpur district Jan Sangh, was not even a member of the central working committee. By the end of 1964, a majority of Jan Sangh units wanted to elect Deendayal as the president. Their popular choice being vetoed led to serious heartburn among the top leaders who regarded Vyas not fit to be raised to all-India leadership.

Missing the spark of the lower house since 1962, Vajpayee was keen to move up the ladder in the organization and be appointed the president. He had sulked when a newcomer like Raghu Vira was exalted to that position. Vajpayee was never openly combative, but insiders could sense the cold war brewing between him and the newcomer. The RSS elders thought it more useful to retain Vajpayee 'as the face – to travel, give lectures – rather than tying him down with organisational responsibilities'. Vajpayee's personality may have been another reason: even though he was wedded to the Sangh, he was 'non-conformist and freedom-loving';[21] he had a convoluted private life; there were also occasional complaints about his eating and drinking habits. All of it meant that the parent body did not as yet trust him enough to make him the president. But when Deendayal – a man wholly devoid of personal ambition – was denied the post, Vajpayee decided to protest. He boycotted the party's annual session in Vijayawada in January 1965, where Vyas was to formally take over as president. By not turning up for the annual session he combatted, for the first time, an RSS decision in public.

He was mollified. But the confrontation gradually assumed a sharp, urgent form over the language question. On 26 January 1965, the fifteen-year notice period of English as India's official language was ending. Subsequently Hindi was to be used as a full-fledged national language (encompassing all communication between the centre and the states). As the day approached, riots broke out across Madras State. On Republic Day, two young DMK workers set fire to themselves and died for the cause of Tamil. In early February, the violence escalated leading to a dozen-odd deaths and the resignation of two cabinet ministers from Madras. The Jan Sangh units in many states – openly in Madras State and West Bengal, quietly in Andhra Pradesh and Karnataka – rebelled too: instead of Hindi, they wanted to use their respective regional languages, along with English as the official language at the centre. The party refused to appreciate that people in non-Hindi speaking states saw English 'as a means of competing on equal terms with the large group of Hindi speakers for the prizes in administrative, professional and economic life'.[22]

As on many occasions in the past, Vajpayee treaded a tightrope. In the last week of February, outside the prime minister's residence, he led a demonstration of a thousand citizens of Delhi, demanding 'immediate freedom from the slavery of English' and a 'rightful place for Hindi as the official language'.[23] Privately, though, seniors like Vajpayee and Madhok felt they ought to – given the party's desperation to expand beyond the Hindi belt – moderate their stand. But the orthodox wing refused to be swayed by the unrest. The same week, a group of rampaging hoodlums from the RSS–Jan Sangh went about Delhi tarring English road signs.

Speaking in the Rajya Sabha on 22 February, Vajpayee boasted that if the DMK could stoke violence in the name of Tamil, the Jan Sangh could do the same for Hindi. He confidently asserted that the immolations in Madras were choreographed: 'Their entire body got burnt, but the letter [in their pocket] survived. That letter had been planted later.' Refusing to believe his fellow MPs that anti-Hindi feelings were widespread in many states, Vajpayee wished to pit English against the native languages. He argued that only the privileged elites in Madras and Bengal continued with English to ensure their domination, even though the Queen's language had obstructed the growth of Tamil and Bengali; and that these regional elites found a convenient bogeyman in Hindi. Predictably, he was assailed by many. The most delicious takedown came from a Congress MP from Madras State, T. S. Pattabiraman.

> Mr. Vajpayee has no objection to travel by a French Caravelle or to eat American wheat or Bangkok rice or to use machinery from Czechoslovakia or to plough with Russian tractors or to have a Swiss wrist watch and a transistor from Japan. Then why object to the English language? As a matter of fact, we must eliminate everything foreign, including English. But till we can replace them with something we have to keep them. I do not think Mr. Vajpayee will go to the extent of saying that we must not get American arms or Czechoslovakian machinery and that we shall have nothing but Indian weapons and nothing else. In pure logic it is *reductio ad absurdum*.[24]

Two weeks later, Vajpayee clashed with the DMK founder C. N. Annadurai. Responding to Annadurai's maiden speech in the Rajya Sabha in May 1962, Vajpayee had written off the Dravidian's demand for self-determination as a polite way of calling for the nation's disintegration – and at a time when the border situation was tense.[25] After the China war, the DMK had put the self-determination demand in cold storage, but it was wholly opposed to any compromise on the language issue.

Presently, Annadurai repudiated his party's complicity in the language riots, and said it 'neither instigated, nor welcomed, nor encouraged the students' agitation'.[26] By turn the Tamilian praised and taunted Vajpayee, even as he called for preserving the status quo of English as the official language, until the country arrived at a stage when all of its fourteen major languages (recognized by the eighth schedule of the constitution) could become official languages. While he loved to hear Vajpayee's graceful Hindi with its rich vocabulary and minimum use of English words, the majority of MPs spoke the language very poorly. Therefore,

'I would say that we are not only not prepared for Hindi but Hindi itself is not prepared to become the official language … with such a defective language you want to bulldoze all other languages? Even Pakistan tried [imposing Urdu] and failed.' Whereas Vajpayee thought Hindi should have been made a link language at the inception of the republic in 1950 itself, Annadurai wanted to leave the matter to posterity to decide: 'You should work in such a way that Hindi becomes de facto link language before you think about making it the de jure link language in course of time.'

Meanwhile, he wanted Vajpayee to 'learn Tamil and drink deep into the nectar of Tamil classics', convinced that if the Jan Sanghi did that, 'he will select Tamil alone as the link language'. He visualized a future India where 'my grandchildren will be learning Hindi alphabets and muttering Hindi phrases', while Vajpayee's grandchildren would speak Tamil. But for that to happen, the Tamilian requested Vajpayee to 'please get married [to a woman] from another language group'.[27] While he respected Annadurai's pride for Tamil, the heartland Brahmin retorted, the DMK founder should not forget that 'we too are proud of Hindi'.[28]

Thereafter, the debate gathered dust for thirty months. In late 1967, the government realized it could no longer delay passing the Official Languages (Amendment) Bill. In the run-up, a parliamentary committee had recommended using the regional languages as the medium of education up to the highest level, besides replacing English with Hindi as the link language. This was close to the Jan Sangh's demand. But Hindi as a link language was still vigorously opposed, for good reason, by the four southern states and West Bengal.[29]

Vajpayee participated in the tempestuous thirty-five-hour debate that took place over eight working days. But before the final vote was cast on 16 December, upon realizing that the government had succumbed to the pressure, he stormed out of the chamber in a fit of rage. The legislation allowed the continued use of English 'as long as the non-Hindi-speaking people did not desire a change'.[30]

On 23 February 1965, Vajpayee was among the first MPs to ask a question in the Rajya Sabha about a clash between border patrols in the Rann of Kutch: was it true that 'Pakistan had encroached 13,000 acres of land?'[31] He did not receive a reply immediately, as the government was still gathering facts. In the din of the language controversy, for a while skirmishes on the border had received less attention than usual.

The Rann of Kutch is a large but remote salt marsh which shares a border with the Pakistani province of Sindh. For a large part of the year it remains submerged under the tidal waters of the Arabian Sea and the Gulf of Kutch. At the time of independence it had no real value apart from its salt resources, and neither side attached much importance to it. By 1965, though, the two sides differed over 9,000 square kilometres; a confrontation began in January when an Indian patrol bumped into a patrol from Pakistan. In early April, the clash escalated to a battle of tanks and armoured cars on a scale previously witnessed only in Kashmir.[32] Shelling from their American tanks, the Pakistanis pushed the Indians back sixty-four kilometres, celebrating this achievement.[33]

With the situation going out of control, Shastri called a meeting with the opposition leaders on 5 May. By Vajpayee's account, the prime minister frankly admitted that the government had been caught on the wrong foot, and requested that 'nothing should be said by the opposition which would demoralise the people'. Shastri also assured the opposition that after the sea water receded in November, India would recover the lost territory.[34]

A few weeks later, the British prime minister Harold Wilson mediated a ceasefire: the two sides signed the Kutch Agreement on 30 June simultaneously at New Delhi and Rawalpindi. Almost immediately, demonstrators led by Vajpayee and Deendayal marched to protest at the Ministry of External Affairs, demanding the scrapping of the agreement, failing which Shastri should resign. Vajpayee was livid that 'without showing the courtesy of even consulting the opposition, and behind the parliament's back', Shastri had agreed to third-party mediation. They also rejected the agreement that both India and Pakistan would restore status quo as in January 1965. According to Indian reports, Pakistan had been patrolling across fifty square kilometres of Indian territory even before the recent incident. Thus, Vajpayee alleged, the end result was 'not status quo *ante* aggression but status quo *post* aggression'.[35]

Forty-two Jan Sangh workers, including Vajpayee, were arrested in front of the Central Secretariat while trying to break a police cordon to reach the MEA. But he 'did manage to burn a copy' of the ceasefire agreement before he was shoved inside a truck.[36] They were taken to Tihar Jail, and released three days later. The next day in parliament, Vajpayee demanded 'the publication of the correspondence between India, Pakistan and Britain on the Kutch cease-fire agreement'.[37] The Jan Sangh had also observed 4 July as Anti-Kutch Agreement Day. Vajpayee spoke at Gandhi Grounds, charging Shastri with having betrayed the promise he had made to the opposition on 5 May, declaring he was 'determined to fight the pact inside Parliament and outside it'.[38]

Vajpayee was wrong on several counts, but accurate on one. Far from improving relations, the Kutch Agreement would bolster Pakistan's confidence in further misadventures. In early August, militants from Pakistan crossed the ceasefire line to blow up bridges and police stations in Kashmir, hoping to make it appear a popular uprising against India. After the bad publicity on the Kutch Agreement, Shastri was under pressure. When the opposition leaders met the prime minister on the evening of 15 August, the two-hour meeting was 'marked by sharp exchanges' between Shastri and Vajpayee, especially when the latter taunted that 'there was a general feeling that the central leadership was weak and unable to cope up with the situation'.[39] Vajpayee and others also offered some unsolicited advice: 'India should attack the bases from where infiltrators had come; otherwise it would be difficult to stop further infiltration.' Shastri kept his action plan from the opposition, but he had already discussed his alternatives and taken his cabinet into confidence.

The next afternoon Jan Sangh members packed the square in front of Parliament House. Even by RSS–Jan Sangh standards, it was a most humongous demonstration: meticulously planned over the last few weeks, it had a turnout of anywhere between one and five lakhs. Leaders from other parties too came to address the rally. But the star was Vajpayee, who began with a Mahabharata analogy. At the battle of Kurukshetra, Lord Krishna had to manifest his 'viraat roop' to shake the despondent and crestfallen Arjuna out of his inertia. 'We hope,' he said amid cheers, 'that the virat roop that the people have demonstrated today will similarly arouse the Shastri government from its passivity. My only fear is that this kaliyugi Arjuna may prove too inert and obtuse.' If India ceded any further territory in Kutch or Kashmir, he dared Shastri, 'the Jan Sangh would demand dissolution of parliament, and [call for] fresh elections'.[40]

Significantly, this was the first time the size and fervour of a Jan Sangh demonstration was applauded even by their detractors. The Bombay weekly *Blitz* lauded the party for giving 'expression to the popular upsurge on such a sensitive, emotional issue': 'We call upon all other leftist and democratic parties to emulate the Jan Sangh's praiseworthy lead.'[41] According to the *New York Times*, the demonstration had played a part in forcing the government to announce the same day that 'it had ordered its troops across the ceasefire line to retake the disputed Kargil posts'.[42]

India mounted an impressive counter-offensive by crossing the LoC and blocking all the major entry points for infiltrators. Pakistan in turn responded by sending its regular troops to capture the strategically located Akhnoor, near Jammu, which would have sealed off J&K from India. Fearing the loss of J&K Shastri, on 6 September, permitted the army to cross the LoC in Punjab and head towards Lahore and Sialkot. This was primarily to force Pakistan to spend its energies outside of J&K, thereby weakening its onslaught there.[43]

Representatives from all parties gathered at a meeting convened by the prime minister. The attendees included the RSS commander-in-chief – an unthinkable proposition during Nehru's regime.[44] Golwalkar promised 'unconditional support' for the war efforts. The same day the Jan Sangh suspended its anti-Kutch-pact agitation 'in view of the new situation'.[45] Soon, their volunteers were regulating traffic in parts of Delhi; they took part in civil defence services – from arranging night-watching shifts to setting up virtual Air Raid Precautions corps; they were also encouraged to take part in blood donation camps. The gesture was not wholly unpartisan, but helped the Sangh Parivar establish its credentials.

With the first full-fledged war on the western border, it was possible to talk about issues that were earlier discussed in hushed tones: Vajpayee wanted the government to openly come out and say that Pakhtoons – an ethnic group in Pakistan, whose calls for provincial autonomy had been brutally quashed – had every right to demand a separate homeland, and that the Indian government would help in every possible way.[46]

During the war, China repeatedly alleged border violations, even as it had publicly avowed its total support to Pakistan. On 16 September, the Chinese almost threatened to wage war, accusing India of building up military structures near Sikkim border. The west viewed China's diplomatic offensive with alarm: Harold Wilson, who had mediated the Kutch ceasefire only two months earlier, issued a statement promising India help from the US–UK alliance just in case China jumped into the fray. On 20 September, the UN Security Council adopted a strongly worded resolution demanding that the two sides declare a ceasefire immediately, and withdraw to positions held before 5 August. The war came to a halt three days later. Initiating a discussion in the Rajya Sabha the next day, 24 September, Vajpayee was miffed that the UNSC resolution had not condemned Pakistan for initiating the invasion; and that it was only after India crossed the LoC in Punjab, on 6 September that the UN was stirred to desperately hunt for a solution.[47] Therefore, India should refuse to revert to the old ceasefire line that existed until 5 August: what was the point of recognizing the UNSC-mediated ceasefire line if it was bound to be violated by Pakistan again and again?

Earlier that afternoon, he had done something more theatrical. One of China's many accusations during the Indo-Pak war had been that Indian troops had kidnapped four Tibetan herdsmen along with a flock of 800 sheep and 59 yaks near the Sikkim border. The MEA had issued a statement denying this, but the Chinese were unconvinced. In response, Vajpayee led one of the 'strangest and rarest processions the capital had ever seen'.[48] Around 800 sheep 'trotted this afternoon to the Chinese Embassy on the Lytton Road with placards round their necks saying "humko khao, duniya ko bachao"' – eat us, but please spare the world. 'Thousands of laughing citizens of Delhi lined the route of the procession. Expectedly, the Embassy officials refused to accept the sheep that Vajpayee offered as a mock compensation. In true Jan Sangh tradition, copies of the memorandum were then pasted on the Embassy walls.'[49] Two days later, China shot off an angry letter to the Indian Embassy in Peking complaining about Vajpayee's protest. The government clarified that it was only a 'spontaneous, peaceful and good-humoured expression' against Chinese bullying on 'trumped up and trivial issues'.[50]

Soon after the ceasefire, the government came up with a plan to send delegations abroad with the aim of explaining India's stand on its conflicts with China and Pakistan. Vajpayee was to be part of the four-member Parliamentary Goodwill Mission to East and Central Africa – a potentially useful exercise given the increasing strength of newly independent African nations in the UN and the Commonwealth. The delegation reached its first destination, Nairobi, on 31 October. By the mid-1960s, the RSS had opened branches in many parts of Africa under the name of Bhartiya Swayamsevak Sangh. Beginning at Nairobi airport, wherever the BSS had arranged a reception for the delegation, its volunteers followed – Kenya, Uganda, mainland Tanzania, Zanzibar, Zambia, Malawi. All these countries had a sizeable and economically well-off Indian diaspora, whose relationship with the native governments – representing citizens with a heightened racial consciousness (often looking at Indians as outsiders) – was now tense.[51]

Wherever he went, Vajpayee divided his time between formal occasions (where the delegation called on ministers and heads of states) and addressing BSS units. He apprised the governments about the facts of India's conflict with Pakistan and China. The delegation also beseeched the governments to protect the lives and property of Indians who had chosen to become citizens of their countries. At BSS gatherings and elsewhere, he spoke of 'an India bubbling with confidence and pride … determined to shake off all crutches of foreign dependence'; the united response Indians had given to the Sino-Pak challenge, in which differences of province, language and creed had melted away.[52]

Not everyone was thrilled with India sending a delegation for propaganda. On 4 November, the *Daily Nation* of Nairobi asked: 'Why should foreign nations try to import their domestic problems into this country instead of pursuing their diplomatic duties?' Without naming him, the editorial criticized Vajpayee for saying at a private reception that the Kashmir episode should 'infuse a new spirit into the Indians of east Africa' and that it was 'wrong for them to think they have been forgotten'. The editorial asked whether the inference was that 'Indians here should take up a hostile attitude to nationals from Pakistan and whether it meant that Indians should not give their complete loyalty to Kenya'.[53] A chastised Vajpayee responded appropriately: while he had begun his trip by rousing Indians to spread Hinduism in Africa, towards the end of the visit, in the last week of November, he was confident that 'if there was any threat to the freedom and integrity of Kenya, the BSS will make all sacrifices to meet it'.[54]

He returned Delhi to be informed that Shastri and Ayub Khan were to meet in the first week of January 1966 at Tashkent, for a summit mediated by the Russian premier Alexei Kosygin. The Jan Sangh opposed the talks, apprehensive that 'international pressure might force the Indian side to return Haji Pir and Tithwa, the two important posts captured by the Indian Army in Pakistan-occupied Kashmir'. Their suggestion to Shastri was to instead import modern arms, besides increasing indigenous production and the size of the army to 2.5 million, and manufacture atomic weapons. The last because the Chinese, who had produced the atom bomb the previous year, had done so 'not for using it against America or Russia but against India'.[55]

Even so, as the leader of the Jan Sangh's parliamentary group, Vajpayee wished Shastri the best of luck to withstand international pressure at Tashkent and win the diplomatic war.[56] He was among the opposition leaders who called on Shastri before his departure for Tashkent. As earlier, Vajpayee sought from the prime minister two assurances: to retain the key posts captured in PoK during the war, and to extract a no-war pact. Shastri – tiny and old, wise and equanimous – refused to give any such assurances. He said he would try, but talks would continue even if Ayub Khan did not agree to all of India's demands. The conversation drifted to the frigid weather in Tashkent. In a light-hearted moment, Vajpayee questioned the adequacy of Shastri's sartorial outfit in the Soviet city: 'It will be real cold, why not churidars this time?' Shastri replied: 'This time, I think, I must have my dhoti.' Only later did it occur to Vajpayee that Shastri's refusal may have had something to do with Ayub Khan's jibe: 'How can a dhotiwala fight a battle?'[57]

For an entire week in Tashkent, Shastri and Khan bickered and bargained and compromised. On the afternoon of 10 January, they arrived at a text that each could sell to his countrymen. The armies of both sides were to withdraw to the pre-August 1965 positions: this meant India had to return Haji Pir and Tithwa. Pakistan did not agree to a no-war pact, but rescinded its old demand for international arbitration in Kashmir. Expectedly, Vajpayee found the news from Tashkent 'shocking'. He spent much of his energy over the next few weeks wailing that Shastri had betrayed the 'solemn assurances given to Parliament and the people' in agreeing to withdraw from captured areas in return for an ambiguous assurance not to resort to arms to settle Kashmir.

Meanwhile, in a tragic turn that would generate for posterity much mystery and misinformation, on the night of 10 January 1966, Shastri died in his sleep of a heart attack. Speaking at the condolence ceremony two days later at the Ramlila grounds in Delhi, Vajpayee was dignified enough not to use the occasion to talk about Tashkent. Instead, he credited Shastri for vindicating the national honour and restoring the prestige of the armed forces after the shameful 1962 defeat with China. In 1965, the 'world realised that India could take up arms if circumstances so required'.[58]

One of the conspiracy theories was that Shastri had been poisoned. Vajpayee too believed this. A few weeks after Shastri's death, the foreign minister Swaran Singh made a statement in parliament stating there was no conspiracy whatsoever; that Shastri had had a heart attack in the recent past, and the next one had proved fatal. Besides, at the time Shastri suffered the attack, he had been surrounded by doctors. Vajpayee rose to say that he had read the last thing Shastri took before going to sleep was a glass of milk: 'I should like to know who was the person who offered that glass of milk.' Swaran Singh did not know 'whether he took milk as the last thing and I do not know who administered it. It has nothing to do with the present statement.' The Jan Sanghi pressed on: 'It might have something to do. Let the Minister find out whether a glass of milk was offered to Shastriji before he went to sleep.'[59] He was the lone member of the Rajya Sabha to vote against the motion approving the Tashkent declaration.[60]

9

SVD: A Stillborn Coalition

AS THE JAN SANGH'S CENTRAL LEADERSHIP MET IN KANPUR IN mid-January 1966 to take stock of the new political situation, manoeuvres in Delhi were in full swing. Vajpayee casually mentioned to a Kanpur crowd that, so far as his party went, it mattered little 'whether it was a Shriman or a Shrimati': 'The Jan Sangh would judge Shastri's successor by the policies he – or she – adopts.' He was in fact following developments with interest, and sharply criticized the misuse of All India Radio 'to create an atmosphere in favour of a particular candidate in these elections': Indira Gandhi. When the results were declared on 19 January, he wished Nehru's daughter 'every success', even as he advised her to be pragmatic and 'steer clear of the right and the left' dogmas.[1]

Despite having taken up the I&B ministry after her father's death, Indira Gandhi, widowed five years ago, had been unsure of a career in politics. The forty-eight-year-old took oath as the head of an almost entirely all-men cabinet. Fellow party members saw her as the least contentious candidate for the job at present. She would continue as prime minister until the general elections due early next year, and then perhaps be replaced by a man more adept at administration and guile.

Almost immediately, Mrs Gandhi proved a harder nut to crack than the old partymen had expected. Two of her decisions during her first year in office also irked the saffron brotherhood. One was to concede to the Akali demand for a Sikh-majority state. After the regional formula of 1956 divided Punjab into Punjabi- and Hindi-speaking zones, the Akalis had over the years kept up their fight whereas the Congress governments at the centre and in Punjab had lost steam. Their new leader Fateh Singh – who had once been an acolyte of Tara Singh but since broken away and replaced his master as the most prominent Sikh voice – was frequently threatening to immolate himself if the demand was not considered.

In September 1965, the government constituted a cabinet sub-committee to examine the proposal. Mrs Gandhi was one of the three members. She had supported the division of Bombay State five years ago, and now saw no harm in bifurcating Punjab. By this time, varied groups in Haryana and Himachal too demanded separate states. Another vital reason for conceding a Sikh-majority state was to acknowledge the important role played by Sikh soldiers and officers in the 1965 war. On 9 March 1966, the Congress Working Committee accepted the demand, giving the government a go-ahead.

The same day Yagya Dutt Sharma, secretary of the Punjab Jan Sangh, began a fast unto death at a roadside tent in Amritsar – mimicking Fateh Singh who was on a similar fast in another part of the same city. Significantly, Sharma had begun his fast without consulting the central Jan Sangh leadership, who were still groping for a coherent strategy. The problem was compounded now by intra-party differences: some Jan Sangh members from Haryana were beginning to think of a separate state of Haryana as a lucrative proposition. Riots had erupted in many parts of Punjab; the Jan Sangh MP from Rohtak resigned, complaining that the party was fanning violence in the region.

By now Vajpayee, his party's chief trouble-shooter, was certain that the decision on bifurcation was not going to be reversed. He tried finding a face-saving device that could make Sharma break his fast. On 18 March, he warned the Rajya Sabha that if Sharma was arrested – as rumoured to be the government's plan – and allowed to die in jail, 'there would be a riot in the Punjab'. Defending his partymen against charges of rioting and arson, Vajpayee instead blamed 'police excess' for the violence in Haryana. He brought along for everyone to see the bloodstained clothes of a twelve-year-old boy who had been killed in the police firing while inside his house.[2]

During a private conversation with Vajpayee, Home Minister

Nanda suggested that he might try and persuade the prime minister to reconsider some of the controversial clauses. After hectic negotiations, the government assured the Jan Sangh that 'common links as found feasible will be provided' and that 'the legitimate rights and interests of the minorities will be safeguarded' on both sides.[3] But this assurance evoked, on 21 March 1966, an angry reaction from Fateh Singh, who announced that he would not tolerate any common links. Apprehensive that the Akali rejection might unnerve the centre, Vajpayee rang up the prime minister's secretariat and drew its attention to the Akali leader's statement. He insisted that the government must give renewed clarifications before the Jan Sangh high command could finally request Sharma to end his protest. The reply came swift and firm: 'We have made a promise and we stand by it. If the Sant opposes, we will face him. Please see that the fast ends today as promised.'

Sharma, who had lost ten kilograms in thirteen days, was to break his fast at 9 p.m. that evening with juice that was to be ceremonially offered to him by Vajpayee. However, Vajpayee left for Amritsar too late in the afternoon to be able to reach on time. Sharma's self-imposed ordeal had exasperated him. Making the defeat sound like a victory, Vajpayee coolly informed the media in Amritsar the next day that the government's assurances had substantially 'met our main demands'.[4]

Partly to rejuvenate its Punjab unit, which was depressed after losing the battle against bifurcation, the party decided to hold its annual session in Jullundur in the last week of April 1966. The senior-most Punjabi in the party, Balraj Madhok, was made the president. 'There were reservations about making Madhok president, but Deendayalji said "let us for once and all feed his ego and see if it helps."'[5] One of the first decisions the party took at Jullundur was dissolve the old working committee whose members' interests were now divergent from each other: three ad-hoc committees (one each for Punjab, Haryana and Kangra) were appointed. Vajpayee, Madhok and Sundar Singh Bhandari were tasked to mentor the new committees. That apart, it was decided that the partition of the state would be downplayed and the focus shifted instead to other pet peeves such as national security.

The prime attraction at the session was Bibi Amar Kaur, sister of the revolutionary Bhagat Singh, who had been appointed president of the Ferozepur district's Jan Sangh. She led a procession of women through the city chanting, 'Qaum na haari, fauz na haari, haari hai sarkar humaari' – the army had won the war, it was the government that lost the diplomatic battle in Tashkent.[6] A *New York Times* correspondent who attended the Jullundur session found the atmosphere there 'strikingly different' from the Congress annual sessions: 'the Congresswallahs clogged the aisles, argued loudly, drifted in and out to the tea-room while the speakers droned on virtually unheeded. But at Jullundur, Jan Sangh delegates, ranged in neat rows under the awning, listened quietly and intently to the proceedings on the platform.'[7]

Vajpayee drew the party's attention to two crucial subjects. The first was his traditional obsession with the strategic failures: Why was the army unable to throw out Pakistanis from Akhnoor (which eventually escalated the war)? Why could the army thereafter not capture Lahore and Sialkot? Why was the new prime minister opposed to manufacturing nukes? Indira Gandhi will be 'discharging a filial obligation by taking that Nehruvite stand, but is she discharging her duty to the nation's security?'[8] His more important pronouncements on the upcoming elections were marked by less bravado. He expressed his 'personal view' that the party need not take a rigid attitude in regard to adjustments with other parties. This basically meant: no truck with the communists or (obviously) the Muslim League of Kerala, but there should be no bar to others such as Swatantra or Samyukta Socialist Party. He drew sharp comments when he posed to the delegates – inviting their free opinion – whether the Jan Sangh should rule out adjustments with Swatantra in Kerala only because the party might be in alliance there with the Muslim League, or with the SSP in some states because the latter might be hand in glove with the communists there.[9] The final decision was left for later discussion.

Meanwhile, Fateh Singh continued his antics over the Suba demand. In response, Vajpayee occasionally threatened to launch a 'direct action to force the government to fully implement its assurances' to his party.[10] He was miffed that even though the Boundary Commission recommended granting Chandigarh to Haryana, the government, under pressure from the Akalis, did not abide by this: Chandigarh was now to be made a union territory serving as capital to both the states. When the Constitution (18th Amendment) Bill, 1966, approving the linguistic bifurcation of Punjab was debated, Vajpayee was among the few in the Rajya Sabha who bitterly opposed it and refused to vote.[11]

At the beginning of the 1967 election campaign, the Jan Sangh embroiled itself in a controversy whose costs and benefits it had never clearly assessed. In the past, the party had supported the RSS's agitations to force the government to make laws to ban the slaughter of cows; at least in Uttar Pradesh they had been successful. At the same time, the Jan Sangh had never, even during the Mookerji years, considered the banning of cow slaughter a strong enough plank for a countrywide agitation. By late 1966, most states had partially or fully banned it. But the cow-protection groups were keen to make a last-ditch attempt for a comprehensive legal ban by the central government, something Nehru had resolutely opposed all through his fifteen years in office. In the last week of September, a motley bunch came together to form the All Party Anti-Cow-Slaughter Campaign Committee – Sarvadaliya Goraksha Maha Abhiyan Samiti: SGMS. It had members belonging to the Congress, RSS–Jan Sangh, Arya Samaj, Mahasabha, some independent MPs, as well as sadhus and religious leaders.[12]

The timing was crucial: the Hindu nationalists resented the bifurcation of Punjab, but there was something to emulate in the way the Akalis had held the centre to ransom. The SGMS president Prabhudatt Brahmachari threatened that if no agreement was reached by 20 November, he and others would begin fasts unto death that very day. Vajpayee later declared at an election rally that it was only near the time of elections that the Congress government could be forced to listen: it 'becomes deaf to the grievances of the public once it comes to power'.[13] Of course, if the movement succeeded, the Jan Sangh secretly hoped to benefit from it in the elections due in two months.

Vajpayee's engagement with the cause was mostly emotional. He was busy with other matters. In the last week of September, he travelled to Ottawa as a delegate to the 12th Commonwealth Parliamentary Conference.[14]* Back in Delhi, he busied himself negotiating seat adjustments with the non-communist opposition party allies for the election. By the end of October, the Jan Sangh had decided to contest 'almost all the seats' in north Indian states; they made adjustments in Gujarat, Rajasthan and Orissa with Swatantra, and on a smaller scale with the SSP and others in the remaining states.

In the last week of October, he was in Maharashtra to combine campaigning with a general council meeting in Nagpur. In Thane, he complained about the 'latest Chinese intrusion into the Southern Chumbi valley in Bhutan'. It was 'useless to debate whether India should or should not have atom bomb when China's atom bomb was trained against her'.[15] In Poona the next day, he disclosed that the election strategy of the Jan Sangh would be to 'cut the Congress to size' in the Lok Sabha and 'smash its monopoly of power' in the assemblies. Significantly, though, he said his party would not do anything to encourage violent agitations.[16] This was a misleading claim: Vajpayee had cautioned his party colleagues to not get overly involved in the cow agitation.[17] But the boundaries between the Jan Sangh and the RSS were fluid; the line between mere sympathy and active involvement was blurred.

Adding to the ambiguity was the party's assurance to the SGMS, at the general council meeting in Nagpur during 3–5 November, of 'complete cooperation'. The SGMS had planned an ambitious rally in Delhi on 7 November, at which Vajpayee was also scheduled to address the crowd. The general council warned the central government of 'very deep feelings on the matter of the cow. If on any occasion this widespread public resentment goes out of control, the consequences would be serious and their responsibility will be completely on the government.' The general council recommended the banning of cow slaughter 'by amending the constitution in the present session of parliament'.[18]

Around 12:30 on the afternoon of 7 November, Vajpayee emerged from the Rajya Sabha to join the procession outside Parliament House.

* He had been sullen with Britain since they had supported Pakistan during the UNSC debate on ceasefire the previous year. When he got a chance to speak, he launched – for all it was worth – 'a vigorous attack' on Britain's Rhodesia policy.

The crowd here, anywhere between one and seven lakhs, had been gathering in Delhi for days in advance. This included many sadhus in their saffron robes, flaunting tridents and spears; many protestors also carried flags bearing the cow emblem. SGMS members and prominent MPs like Vajpayee sat on a makeshift stage. The leaders spoke in turn and, for the first hour, the protest proceeded as it had on previous occasions. Then came Swami Rameshwaranand's turn.

Rameshwaranand was a well-known Arya Samaji of the Punjab who had won the 1962 election on a Jan Sangh ticket from Karnal, partly because the sitting Congress MP Subhadra Joshi had been shifted to Balrampur to vanquish Vajpayee. This morning, the swami had requested the speaker to adjourn the proceedings of the house, urging the speaker to instead meet the protestors. The speaker rejected what was really a bizarre demand. When Rameshwaranand persisted in disturbing the proceedings, the speaker suspended him 'from the service of the house for the rest of the session'. The Karnal MP had to be physically dragged out.[19] Rameshwaranand emerged seething and proceeded to join the demonstration. Around 1:30 p.m. he rose to speak. He informed the crowd of his humiliating exit and egged them on: why were they sitting quietly when they could gherao the Parliament House and prevent the ministers from coming out?

Taking his cue, a group of protestors – including fifty–sixty sadhus – started moving towards Parliament House, hoping to force their way in. Vajpayee grabbed the mike to dissociate himself from Rameshwaranand's statement and to dissuade the crowd. Suddenly, a sadhu climbed the dias and 'slapped me on the head, and snatched the mike from my hands'.[20] By this time the protestors and the police were clashing near the gates – the former flinging sticks and stones at the police, the latter responding with tear gas and rubber bullets. Soon after, the police lobbed a tear gas shell at the dais and cut the loudspeaker wires. In the mayhem that followed, the protestors gave vent to their anger by setting on fire hundreds of vehicles on the premises of government offices nearby. Some of them torched Congress president Kamaraj's bungalow. At least seven protestors were killed in police firing. The centre clamped down with a forty-eight-hour curfew; the army was brought in to patrol important locations in the capital.

Vajpayee's response to this orgy of arson and mob violence was ambiguous. He issued a statement deploring the 'undesirable elements, who resorted to violent activities in the demonstration against cow slaughter, had done a great harm to the pious cause'.[21] The same evening in the Rajya Sabha, as one of the few eyewitnesses to the event, he exonerated his fellow RSS–Jan Sangh members and instead blamed the police for the escalation of violence. Rameshwaranand had made a provocative speech, but 'had the police arrested those sadhus [trying to enter the Parliament House] and got them out of the way, the later incidents could have been avoided'. Specifically, by hurling a tear gas shell at the stage, 'the Delhi Police made the five-lakh strong crowd leaderless; the absence of a leader made the crowd hysterical'.[22] He requested the government to conduct a judicial enquiry into the incident. Over the next few days, hundreds of RSS–Jan Sangh activists were arrested. Vajpayee complained that the government was taking 'political advantage of an unfortunate situation', and warned that his party would not take it lying down.[23]

When the subject was discussed in detail in the Rajya Sabha on 16 November, Vajpayee distanced his ideological family from the demonstration. They had organized many demonstrations in the past, but none of them had turned violent. With a straight face, he said the Jan Sangh was 'not a part of that Samiti, nor indeed is any other political party. Yes, my people did participate [in their individual capacity], and they have full freedom to participate'.

In evidence once again was the oldest Sangh Parivar technique of absolving the organization in case of a disaster. If it was proved that members of the Jan Sangh had indulged in violence, Vajpayee burst out melodramatically, 'I am prepared for any penalty. I will quit Jan Sangh, I will retire from politics. I can't stay in a party that incites violence.' Since Congressmen were chiding his party, he lodged a bizarre counter-allegation: either the government or the police had planted some unruly sadhus so as to enable the police to retaliate and disrupt the protest. He even cited instances to substantiate his claim. How was it that Kamaraj's house was attacked even before the police opened fire on the procession? Vajpayee said he had gone looking for the sadhu who had snatched the mike from his hands and had later been handed over to the police: 'Where is he now? … I know him by face, but he is not in police lock-up, nor in jail. Was he a man of the police? Was he a man of the Delhi administration? Or was he a man who wanted to malign [the home minister] Nandaji?'[24] Nanda had been unceremoniously fired from his job by Indira Gandhi for being seen as sympathetic to cow agitators.

For the first time, he was heckled inside parliament by Congressmen and communists alike. The sharpest attack came from the leftist Congressman I. K. Gujral, who argued that the sadhu who hit Vajpayee on the head and took away the mike may have been an RSS man. Vajpayee's was a 'voice of sanity as his generally is' and therefore friends of his 'who draw inspiration from Nagpur and not from the Jan Sangh wanted to remove him from the mike'.

> Unfortunately in the Jan Sangh politics he does not belong to the inner core. He is himself in a minority … the real politics is controlled by the inner core of the R.S.S. to which Vajpayee has no access … wise and sane people like Vajpayee try to give a cover to those sinister designs behind which is the R.S.S. hand and which is trying to undo all that this country stands for.[25]

As a remedy, Gujral suggested that the RSS 'should either be declared political or it should be banned'.[26] The newly appointed home minister Yashwantrao Chavan too charged the Sangh Parivar as being among the key players responsible for the violence: 'It cannot be denied that he [Rameshwaranand] is a representative of the Jan Sangh in Parliament. I am only referring to the minimum facts.'[27] Vajpayee defended the indefensible all day.

The debate on the 7 November violence typecast Vajpayee in an image he would come to be remembered by: of a wise, sane, moderate man who was forced to defend hoodlums and fanatics in parliament. His responses hinted that he did not particularly relish this double role. But the impression he had inadvertently made was already helping him. His party president Madhok (who was not even in Delhi on 7 November) was now lodged at Tihar Jail. On the other hand Vajpayee (who was on the rostrum when the violence broke out) was not only spared, but allowed to vociferously defend the Sangh Parivar. Two weeks later, with the campaign in full swing, he featured on the *Times of India*'s front page, addressing an election rally in Bombay.[28] There too Vajpayee impressed on his audience that his party men were implicated in a conspiracy by a section of the government that had not spared even its own home minister, that Nanda's exit marked the 'slaughter of the only cow in the cabinet'.[29]

For much of December 1966 he was on the road: Rajasthan, Vidarbha, Karnataka, thereafter briefly touching parts of Kerala and Tamil Nadu. At many of these places he was presented purses by party folks. Later, the *New York Times* would claim that the CIA had contributed to the Jan Sangh's election funds.[30] The leftist weekly *Blitz* claimed to have identified the organization which provided '$18,000 in crisp American greenbacks' to Vajpayee shortly before he began his campaign.[31] The furore died down, probably because there were also allegations of Russia's KGB having funded the DMK, communists as well as leftist Congressmen.[32]

Like every shrewd politician, Vajpayee tailored his speech to suit the audience. In a public meeting at Jodhpur, from where came one of the Jan Sangh activists who was killed in the 7 November firing, he repeated an eye-witness account of the afternoon: 'According to my information,' Vajpayee proclaimed, 'hired goondas had come from outside and a deliberate plot to murder Kamaraj had been hatched.'[33] In Jaipur, he claimed that his party stood for a non-communal state and the minorities would have nothing to fear if it came to power. In Hubli he emphasized that he had raised in parliament the matter of Karnataka requiring a steel plant at Hospet: 'I told the Government that Karnataka should not be neglected only because Karnataka was not represented in the cabinet.' At another venue in Karnataka, Shimoga, his speech was translated on the spot by the editor of *Vikram,* the RSS's Kannada mouthpiece. 'I speak in Hindi, you listen in Kannada,' Vajpayee said. 'Let not English stand as an obstacle in between us.'[34]

Inaugurating the Delhi Jan Sangh's election campaign on the first day of 1967, Vajpayee felt confident that the Congress would be toppled in several states. Speaking at Raebareli – the UP constituency chosen for Prime Minister Mrs Gandhi from which to contest her maiden election – he informed his audience that the Jan Sangh had invited Sardar Bhagat Singh's mother to fight the election from that constituency. She had accepted, but her doctors had advised complete rest in view of her indifferent health.[35]

He was still bitter about losing the previous election. Having witnessed two wars and the deaths of two prime ministers during his Rajya Sabha term, he would later look back on 1962–67 as 'the most significant period in the life of independent India'.[36] This time he was desperate to win. It was a measure of the Jan Sangh's confidence that, unlike on previous occasions, the party did not feel the need to field Vajpayee from more than one seat. Though Uttar Pradesh returned eighty-five members to the lower house – the largest for any state – only about half a dozen seats were keenly contested: Balrampur was the site of the biggest 'prestige fight' between two old rivals.[37]

On 26–27 November 1966, Subhadra Joshi had staged a 'Ban RSS' meeting thinly disguised as an 'Anti-Communalism Convention' in Delhi.[38] There were rumours that Joshi had been lobbying for a ticket from a safer seat in either UP or Delhi, but internal rivalries in provincial Congress units foiled her chances. She was entrapped but could not walk out.

Joshi had her advantages. She had nursed the constituency assiduously for five years. She had visited it almost every month, trying her best to get roads built and schools opened, parched lands irrigated. She had also been distributing pamphlets against the RSS–Jan Sangh, condemning them for exploiting the cow-slaughter issue for election purposes. In urban areas, she advocated nationalization of banks and control over other key sectors of the economy.[39]

On the other hand, Vajpayee, who had visited the constituency less often after his 1962 defeat, hoped to compensate with his eloquence. A journalist who followed the 'neck-and-neck race' between the duo in Balrampur, reported the contrast in their approach:

> He uses innuendos, satire, understatement and ridicule with deadly effect ... like other Jana Sangh propagandists, [he] fully uses the cow issue and appeals to the sentiments, but he concentrates his fire on the policies which have resulted in a steep rise in the prices of essential commodities. He is listened to with rapt attention as he talks of corruption and inefficiency in high places and of the Government's inability to deliver the goods in any field of life. As a speaker, Joshi does not fly on the wings of eloquence as Vajpayee does, but she is almost as effective as he. He appeals to emotion, she to reason. He sweeps the audience off its feet. She persuades it to accept her point of view. She raises electioneering to the level of political education.[40]

None of the top UP Congress leaders – not even Sucheta Kripalani, fighting from nearby Gonda – came to campaign in Balrampur. Fortunately the prime minister came to Joshi's rescue, hoping to bring the luck that her father's presence had last time. Given Vajpayee's popularity and more or less untainted resume, Mrs Gandhi chose to instead attack his ideological forbears. She made a sensational claim: during the Indo-Pak war, the Jan Sangh in Delhi had planned to create communal disturbances; the government's vigilance had foiled their designs. To Vajpayee's constant refrain about the humiliation in the 1962 war, she responded that the Congress was still the only party that the 'big powers wanted to form the government in the interests of world peace and progress'. As a woman campaigning for another woman – an old friend and a feisty colleague – the prime minister exhorted women to turn up in large numbers on election day to defeat the feudal Jan Sangh.[41]

Balrampur was among the areas worst affected by droughts and floods over the last decade, leading to severe scarcity of food and drinking water. But in a pattern that would often repeat itself across Hindi heartland – whereby the most distress-ridden areas became sites of larger ideological battles – addressing the structural problems of Balrampur seemed to be a top priority for neither side. An instrumentalist approach was more convenient: representatives of the Tharu tribe were summoned to meet the prime minister so she could be photographed with them. She promised that if Joshi won again, they would be declared a Scheduled Tribe and given all privileges accorded to that group.[42]

By the end of February, a little over half of the twenty-five-crore electorate had gone to the polls and voted out their frustration over drought, food shortages, soaring prices, unemployment and a variety of other unfulfilled expectations. At the end of the first day of counting, the Jan Sangh workers were relieved to hear on AIR that Vajpayee was leading by over 5,000 votes; eventually, he won by a comfortable margin of 32,000. A bigger surprise was the party's stupendous performance: winning thirty-five seats in the Lok Sabha and 268 in assemblies across twelve states.* Overall, though, the 1967 mandate was essentially negative in character: the Congress was punished for its inability to solve the problems. At the same time, in most of the northern state assemblies where the Jan Sangh did its best – ninety-eight in UP (out of 425), seventy-eight in MP (out of 296) – voters did not display a clear left or right trend.

The Jan Sangh busied itself with luring power-hungry Congressmen to defect from the parent party in the states, where the Congress now had governments with narrow majorities. Before long, the opposition had success in four states – UP, Haryana, Bihar, MP. The coalition was named SVD – Samyukt Vidhayak Dal, or United Legislators Party. It included, apart from Jan Sangh members and Congress defectors, legislators from Swatantra, Socialist and other local parties. The Jan Sangh joined the governments everywhere, except Haryana, where it gave the coalition outside support. In Punjab the Jan Sangh allied with its bêtes noires, the Akali Dal (faction led by Fateh Singh) and the CPI.

The party was bitterly divided at every level on whether or not it should collaborate with communists or other communal parties like the Majlis-e-Mushawarat (in UP) and the Akali Dal. Vajpayee had Deendayal's quiet, cautious backing. The party president Madhok was less than enthusiastic.

* It fetched 1.4 crore votes in the Lok Sabha polls, still a distant second to the Congress's 5.9 crores.

His original wish had been to form governments in states by collaborating with Swatantra and wooing the rightist elements in Congress to defect. But Swatantra had performed badly in the states, and a majority opinion was that the electoral adjustments with Rajaji's party had paid no dividends.[43] Madhok had no choice other than to reluctantly agree to Vajpayee's plan.*

On 21–23 April, the Jan Sangh's 900 General Council members descended on Delhi to deliberate on the new developments: their chief target of attack was Vajpayee. Expecting hostility, the third-term MP had carefully prepared a resolution to amplify his position: 'Coalition Governments and Jan Sangh'. He tried to persuade his colleagues that the 1967 elections had radically altered the political map of India, and that the party could not stick inflexibly to its pre-election attitudes. The decision to join or support the governments in several states had been 'prompted by a desire to bring relief to the common man oppressed by twenty years of Congress misrule'. Prior to the elections, he said, it was customary among the Congress leaders to assert that the Congress could not lose. Now that the elections had proved them wrong, they had started saying that these coalition governments could not last: 'Let the Jan Sangh prove the Congress wrong a second time ... The Congress is disintegrating so rapidly,' he impressed upon the anti-coalitionists, 'that it no longer presents a meaningful choice.'[44]An association with the communists did not mean the party had given up on ideology: it was a tactical move forced by circumstances, whereby the party retained freedom of action and could walk out of the coalition whenever necessary. But the point of the Sangh Parivar entering politics was to capture power and, as such, they should not practise untouchability: 'after all the Communists are also sons of the Bharat Mata'.[45]

---

* Even so, there remained considerable opposition from the middle tier too, some of it legitimate. Many argued that the new governments would, under pressure from the communists, be forced to adopt radical measures, such as state trading in food grains, which were in fundamental conflict with the Jan Sangh's policies. Other hardliners felt that the party should wait for another five years, get a clear mandate in 1972, and only then form a government.

In mid-July 1967, Vijaya Raje Scindia – the dowager of Gwalior – led a dramatic coup in Madhya Pradesh.* She got thirty-six Congress MLAs to defect, forcing the Congress chief minister D. P. Mishra to resign.† For a while the Rajmata had been struggling to maintain a working relationship with Mishra. She quit the party shortly before the election, partly because she had not been consulted about the choice of candidates. When Mishra became chief minister for the second time in March 1967, she was desperate to bring about his downfall. Operating alongside the Rajmata behind the scenes was her loyal lieutenant (and rumoured lover) Sardar Angre and the Madhya Pradesh Jan Sangh president, Brijlal Verma. The most popular of the defectors was Govind Narayan Singh, a small-time maharaja whose father had briefly served as the chief minister of Vindhya Pradesh (before the region was merged into MP in 1956).

Whether or not Vajpayee was involved in plotting the coup, he blessed its smooth execution. He celebrated Mishra's fall as 'good riddance'.[46] The new government was formed and, in the first week of August, Vajpayee arrived in Bhopal to bargain with Singh and the Rajmata for important portfolios on the Jan Sangh's behalf.[47] The coup briefly made the party overconfident. At a press conference in Bombay on 13 August, Vajpayee boasted that considering the 'pathetic disarray' the Congress was in, a Madhya Pradesh might be enacted in New Delhi. Mrs Gandhi's days were numbered; the rickety Congress might crash before the 1972 elections. It was for the opposition to start thinking of providing an alternative: 'If the right communists [CPI] could change themselves (and they had occasionally given the impression of being responsive to popular sentiment and an urge to break away from the Marxist dogma and extra-territorial attachments), the opposition might become the mainstay of the alternative government.' There was no reason why Congressmen who had no faith in Indira Gandhi's leadership should 'stifle the voice of their conscience and become a party to the drift and inertia'.

The Congress rebutted, calling Vajpayee a daydreamer. They were right: during the presidential election in May 1967, the opposition had failed in

* Jivajirao Scindia died in 1961, leaving behind a young widow and five children.

† D. P. Mishra had rejoined and rehabilitated himself in the Congress, and was dispatched as the chief minister of Madhya Pradesh in September 1963.

their attempt to arrange large-scale defections in the Lok Sabha.[48] Vajpayee believed that while ideological differences would be relevant to form a coalition at the centre, bringing desperate non-Congress parties together might be easier in the states. Soon he would find out that there were real limits to the extent of ideological differences even states could withstand.

Considering the lure of power was the prime motivation for the rainbow coalition to stick together, the SVD governments were beset by factionalism from day one. To keep the Congress at bay, each side compromised for some time. Before long it became apparent that the governments were not going to last. Instead of resolving their differences, each party then wanted to extract the maximum gains from being in power, besides ensuring that their own political prospects would improve in the course of their tenure. These sectarian aims were incompatible with the government's day-to-day functioning in the meantime. The Sangh Parivar was among the chief culprits.

This was the first time the Jan Sangh was formally getting a chance to spread its tentacles inside the state apparatus. In UP especially, it used its education portfolio to promote the RSS's Saraswati Shishu Mandir schools and to pack the managing boards of schools and colleges with its own nominees; similarly, the party used its cooperative portfolio to load the committees and administrative posts with RSS men.[49] Occasionally socialists and communists in UP and Bihar clamoured for Urdu to be given the status of a second official language; the Jan Sangh threatened that it would be a dealbreaker. The Jat leader Charan Singh's defection from the Congress was meticulously arranged by Nanaji Deshmukh. But his government had been 'in difficulties ever since it took office' and, by early August 1967, Chaudhary Charan Singh was confessing that 'virtually all its energies have been consumed in internal infighting'.[50]

The advocates of coalition inside the Jan Sangh believed that the mid-term elections in the SVD states would further improve its tally. In public, the Jan Sangh claimed that there was no threat to the SVD governments' stability. But privately Vajpayee admitted that the party leadership regarded the coalition government as a short-term investment, and that 'his party would welcome, and were already preparing for mid-term elections'.[51]

In October 1967, the first major difference among the constituents surfaced on the question of abolition of land revenue in UP. The Jan Sangh had in the past too called for this abolition, but its commitment had been vague. Now it wanted the abolition to not remain confined to uneconomic holdings – which is what the SSP and CPI demanded – but to all landholdings, which would help the rich peasants from whom the Sangh Parivar drew their support. Given its potentially explosive consequences, all sides made the subject of land revenue abolition a prestige issue.[52] For over a week, the administration in UP remained virtually paralyzed.

In mid-October, Vajpayee was visiting Bangkok as part of a parliamentary delegation when he was informed that the veteran socialist Ram Manohar Lohia had passed away after a botched prostate gland surgery. For a while he was 'speechless and bereft of senses, as if struck by a bolt'.[53] With the key bridge between the Jan Sangh and the SSP gone, it was yet another bad omen for the survival of SVD governments. Later that month the Delhi leadership, along with twenty-three Jan Sangh ministers from five states, gathered in Bhopal for a threadbare discussion on their brief experience of sharing power. With the UP crisis as the focal point, a resolution was adopted appealing the SSP and communists in UP and Bihar to give up their 'mock heroics over the issue of land revenue' and to generally stick to the common programme.[54]

The leadership also privately discussed other fundamental changes in the party. For the first time in 1967, more than half the legislators in state assemblies and parliament who returned on Jan Sangh tickets had no RSS background. Its old vested interests and new social base pulled the party into two conflicting directions, lending its thoughts and actions a confusing duality. In order to ensure RSS control over the party, mostly legislators from the Sangh background were appointed ministers. It was assumed that they would work under the guidance of the central Jan Sangh. But the ministers owed their loyalty primarily to Nagpur; they acted independently. The Delhi leadership had theoretically agreed to a programme of land reforms in Bihar. In practice the state leadership obstructed the implementation of the legislation conferring tenancy rights on sharecroppers.[55]

Even so, the Bhopal gathering was the first-of-its-kind in the party's history. A group photo clicked at the end of the conference gives the appearance of a big, happy family that had grown steadily over the last fifteen years to become a force in national politics. Some ministers squat in the front while others stand in the last row. Seated on chairs in the second row and flanked by Deendayal, Nanaji Deshmukh and Sunder Singh Bhandari, Vajpayee and Madhok occupy the centre. And these two central figures were now embroiled in a quiet tussle for the party presidentship (in Madhok's case being allowed another term). Over the next few weeks, the quiet drama played out.

Unlike in the late 1950s, the Jan Sangh president was no longer a mere figurehead. Vajpayee's old desire to become president was now more than a personal milestone: he wanted an official stamp for his political line of non-Congress coalitions, including left-dominated state governments. Even though he had successfully had his way thus far, many in the RSS were wary of the non-conformist Vajpayee gaining a total grip over the party. Madhok was unequivocally sceptical about the future of non-Congress coalitions. He had been publicly running a campaign for an immediate break with the communists even if it brought down the SVD ministries. Vajpayee and Deendayal were convinced that the time for a rightist coalition (of the Congress–Swatantra–Jan Sangh type) was not yet ripe. Even though the SVD coalitions were in tatters, there was no harm continuing as long as the arrangement lasted. As the brain behind the coalitions, Vajpayee did not want the Jan Sangh to be held responsible for their collapse. Disloyalty to non-Congress fronts, whatever the pretext, would undermine the popular base of the party.

Significantly, Deendayal was losing patience with Madhok on organizational grounds. The incumbent president had created awkward situations by taking positions differing from the party's official stand. Their joint opposition effectively blocked Madhok's ambition to remain president for a second term. Ultimately Deendayal, who had in the past refused the office, accepted it.[56]

The annual session in Calicut in late December 1967 was an out and out Deendayal Upadhyaya show. The choice of the location had to obviously do with the party's desperation to expand in south India. (In the assembly elections for the four southern legislatures in early 1967, the party had to be content with a total of seven seats – less than one in hundred.) In consultation with Deendayal, Vajpayee drafted the language resolution, calling for the full flowering of the regional languages, but with a carefully tucked-in caveat that 'Hindi must grow on the basis of voluntary acceptance'.[57]

Deendayal had never been as excited about the SVD coalitions as Atal, but he defended his protégé from the attack by hardliners. When some delegates continued to taunt the party for sharing power with the CPI, Deendayal quietly countered: 'Kharbooja chaaku par gire ya chaaku kharbooje par, katega toh kharbooja hi' – whether the melon falls on the knife or the knife falls on the melon, it is the melon that gets sliced.[58] Madhok's suggestion that the meeting pass a resolution declaring that the non-Congress coalitions were going to collapse soon and the Jan Sangh was ready to form alternative coalitions – if necessary, with the Congress – was rejected.

Though unobtrusively, the Calicut session marked the outgoing president's fall from grace. This was tragic because Madhok had an impeccable resume. As a young pracharak in J&K in the early 1940s, he had helped erect the RSS network there from scratch. He had played a key role in founding the Praja Parishad in Jammu in late 1947 and, later, the Jan Sangh in Delhi in 1951. Unlike most partymen, Madhok was now married and held a day job as a history lecturer at the PGDAV College in Delhi. But as someone famed for his ideological convictions and sharp intellect, the Jan Sangh president was also fast acquiring a reputation for an acerbic tongue, a fragile ego and inflexibility in the face of opposition. Deendayal had been upset with Madhok not so much due to their differences over the direction the Jan Sangh ought to have taken after the elections, rather because of his frequently taking positions – in public – that went against the majority opinion in the party, thereby causing embarrassment and confusion. For these reasons, Madhok was demoted twice over. He was not given back the role of the northern zone's secretary, which he had held before taking over as the president. During discussions on foreign policy, his suggestion of unequivocal support to the US in the Vietnam war was rejected too.[59]

On yet another key question, the new president displayed optimism and flexibility. For a section of the Jan Sangh leadership, the 1965 war had brought a slight change of heart towards Muslims. If saving Kashmir for India had once been Vajpayee's criterion for loyalty, most Muslims – including some Kashmiris – had passed it. In July 1966, four popular Muslims from Old Delhi had enrolled themselves in the Jan Sangh. Welcoming them at a gathering held in front of the Jama Masjid, Vajpayee had hoped that the 'thick wall of misunderstanding' between Muslims and the Jan Sangh would be 'entirely demolished'.[60] This had helped blunt some of the Muslim opposition to the Jan Sangh, contributing to the party's 1967 clean sweep of all three Delhi elections – Lok Sabha, Municipal Corporation and Metropolitan Council. At Calicut, Deendayal laid out a plan to 'welcome more and more Muslims to join' the party fold.[61]

Before dispersing, the delegates gathered to take a group photo. This was the first day of the new year 1968. Each delegate was happy to see their new president – quiet-spoken and universally loved – at the centre, getting the attention he deserved. Unbeknown to them, this was the last time they would be seeing Deendayalji.

On the morning of 11 February, Vajpayee and other Jan Sangh MPs had gathered at the new party office at 1 Feroze Shah Road to draw up plans for the budget session which was to commence the next morning. The discussions had hardly begun when there was a brief, cryptic telephone call from Lucknow. A dead body with a crushed skull and fractured ribs had been found lying beside a track near the Mughalsarai railway yard; a crowd had gathered around the place, some people suggesting it resembled Deendayal Upadhyaya. The gathered MPs got frightened, for the previous night the Jan Sangh president had boarded a train in Lucknow bound for Patna. Vajpayee and Madhok rushed to the house of the railways minister, who rang up Mughalsarai station and confirmed that the dead body was in fact Deendayal's. Home Minister Chavan arranged a special air force plane for them to reach the spot and bring the body to the capital. Vajpayee, Madhok and the office secretary J. P. Mathur left by an Ilyushin troops carrier. By the time they flew back, it was past midnight.

The body was placed in one of the rooms at Vajpayee's residence: 30 Rajendra Prasad Marg came closest to what Deendayal – an orphan who was also, like most others in the Sangh Parivar's top leadership, a bachelor – had for a home. The MP had requested his mentor a few years ago to move into his spacious bungalow. Deendayal was frequently travelling but, when in Delhi, the two spent a lot of time together; which partly explains why there was never a communication gap between them.

All through the night thousands of well-wishers and Sangh Parivar cadres queued up for a last glimpse of the man.[62] Early next morning, the president and the prime minister came to pay their tributes. Even though he had been awake all night, Vajpayee went to parliament to speak briefly about Deendayal's death: 'I find darkness all around. For me all light has extinguished.'[63] It was not a case of death by accident, he informed the house. Evidence indicated that Deendayal may have been killed in a conspiracy, and the central government should conduct a high-level enquiry. The journey from Vajpayee's residence to Nigambodh Ghat, where the last rites were performed, was a moving spectacle – almost as grand as a state funeral. The body, carried atop a tractor-trailer, was 'virtually buried under a mass of flowers'.[64] Sitting on the hearse, Vajpayee was reminded of the triumphant presidential procession at Calicut six weeks ago when flowers had been showered upon a faintly smiling Deendayal.[65]

At Deendayal's funeral, there were signs that the Jan Sangh was beginning to shed its communal tag and acquire respectability. The Gandhian socialist Acharya Kripalani was expectedly present among the mourners who walked down to the ghat, but to everyone's surprise there was also the former J&K chief minister Bakshi Ghulam Mohammad. Even the CPI in Delhi had adopted a condolence resolution. And at a public gathering held at Ramlila Maidan to pay homage to Deendayal Upadhyaya's memory, the CPI's Hiren Mukherjee extolled him as an 'Ajaatashatru' – a man without an enemy – whose 'quest to search [for] the real roots of Indianness' he admired despite their many ideological differences.[66]

On the morning of 13 February, the bereaved Working Committee sat for an emergency meeting to choose a new family head. The presidents of the state units and the leaders of the Jan Sangh's legislature parties were also present. There was shock and disbelief on every face. Vajpayee had drafted the condolence resolution. As he began to read it, he broke down. The rest of the resolution had to be read by the vice president Pitambar Das, who proposed Vajpayee's name for the vacant presidency. Everyone unanimously agreed. A teary-eyed Madhok stood up, embraced Vajpayee and led him to the presidential seat. In this moment of crisis and grief, their differences had waned.

Vajpayee already held three key posts: leader of the parliamentary group; chief spokesperson of the party; and leader of the committee which looked after the affairs of the various Jan Sangh assembly parties. Why then was he allowed by Nagpur to wield more power and responsibility as the president? As Deendayal's most trusted lieutenant, he represented, more than anyone else, the policies enunciated by the late president. No other leader carried prestige and authority with the non-RSS elements in the party, who now accounted for half the total strength of legislators in parliament and the assemblies. Thirdly, after the meltdown in the winter of 1965–66, Vajpayee had laboriously repaired his links with the RSS leadership; the latter too had begun to show greater consideration for his capacity as a mass leader. In fact, Deendayal had himself played a role in smoothening his protégé's relationship with Nagpur.[67]

In a distracted state, Vajpayee attended parliament. But he mostly busied himself with overseeing and, where required, performing the rituals associated with Deendayal's last rites – such as taking the urn containing Deendayal's ashes which were to be scattered in the Ganga at Allahabad. A special tourist coach was attached to the Toofan Express for the purpose. The urn had been so placed on a pedestal as to be visible through the windows, so Jan Sangh supporters on the way could come and offer their tributes. At dozens of stations on the way, Vajpayee addressed the gatherings briefly, voiced their grief and anguish, and reiterated the party's resolve to withstand the tragedy. The next morning in Allahabad, on 18 February, a boat procession reached the sangam – the confluence of rivers where a clearly discernible watery line divides the fast-moving and clear waters of the Ganga from the deep blue-green waters of the Yamuna. As Vajpayee inverted the urn in order to immerse the ashes, the crowd shouted a tearful 'Pandit Deendayal Upadhyaya, Amar Rahein'.[68] Later that day in Allahabad, the party pledged to raise eleven lakh rupees to erect a memorial in Deendayal's name.

Around this time conspiracy theories began circulating. Many in Sangh Parivar circles were vaguely pointing fingers at communists and Muslims, especially one Dr A. J. Faridi of the Majlis-e-Mushawarat in Lucknow. Faridi's Majlis had been part of the SVD government in UP, but unhappy with the Jan Sangh's growing influence and aggressive attitude, he had withdrawn his support. The Home Ministry panicked at the possibility that the mourning might provoke communal disturbances. But the Jan Sangh leadership had passed instructions to restrain their local branches from reacting violently. To everyone's relief, the call was heeded.[69]

On the other hand, a section of the Urdu and leftist press alleged that Deendayal had been liquidated by the extremists in the RSS–Jan Sangh. In hushed tones, some even speculated the involvement of Vajpayee and Madhok. To be sure, Deendayal's rising clout on the organizational front was beginning to make some in the top brass in Nagpur insecure. But there was no evidence of an insider plotting a murder. When asked about the rumours about his involvement, Vajpayee said he had not cared to contradict them because they did not merit his contempt: 'It is like saying that Nehru and Patel had hired Godse to murder Gandhiji.'[70]

He was not wrong. Not only had the deceased party president actively promoted Atal's career in the past, Deendayal also posed no threat to his future ambitions. If anything, Atal desperately needed Deendayal to continue shielding him in the face of vociferous opposition from hardliners on most issues.

It was also a deeply personal loss. Deendayalji had been one of the few links in the party with Atal's past life. On his trips to Gwalior in the early 1950s, Deendayal had on several occasions stayed at Atal's house, and got to know Ma–Babuji well. Elders in the party joked about how one winter night Babuji had forced Deendayal, a light eater, to drink a tall glass of hot milk post dinner.

Living together at 30 Rajendra Prasad Marg, Deendayal may not have approved of Atal's complicated private life or even – as someone who strictly kept onion and garlic out of his diet – his drinking and meat-eating habits. With time and his rising celebrity, Atal too had been outgrowing his mentor and, occasionally, even disagreed with him. Nonetheless, Atal was at all times conscious of the mellowing, moderating influence Deendayalji had on people around him, as well as his knack for resolving disputes inside the party and, of late, building bridges with other parties.

Acquiescing to popular demand, the government appointed a one-man enquiry commission. In his report, Justice Y. V. Chandrachud categorically denied any political vendetta whatsoever: 'Undoubtedly, he had political rivals but his death is the rash and extempore handiwork of mere thieves.' Chandrachud concluded that Deendayal had been pushed out of the running train, and he had dashed against the traction pole and died an instantaneous death. The murder 'was accompanied by an immediate theft, which shows that the two are part and parcel of the same transaction'.[71] Lacking spice, the report satisfied neither side.

Its chief strategist gone, the Jan Sangh's incoherencies spilled out into the open. With the Vajpayee's SVD experiment foundering and Deendayal no longer present to mediate, the hardliners' opposition risked becoming further fratricidal. The incoming president, prophesied *Time* magazine, 'will need all of his political skills to keep his party extremists in line'.[72]

Part Three

In the Shadow of Shrimati Gandhi 1968–77

10

The Incoming Party President

WITHOUT DEENDAYAL BY HIS SIDE, VAJPAYEE BEGAN REGRESSING almost immediately. Whereas the situation demanded radical new initiatives, the incoming president only clutched to old obsessions. The party drifted aimlessly.

His first assignment came out of the rekindling of an old controversy. The international tribunal to establish the Indo-Pak boundary in the Rann of Kutch had rendered a mixed verdict. Though 90 per cent of the disputed territory was awarded to India, approximately 900 square kilometres were to go to Pakistan, which included some sites of strategic importance.[1] In a joint letter to the prime minister, Vajpayee and the SSP's Madhu Limaye regretted that 'the tribunal had exceeded its jurisdiction' and awarded Indian territory to Pakistan 'on political, rather than judicial, considerations'.[2] Mrs Gandhi was herself not thrilled, but India was bound by a prior commitment to accept the award; doing otherwise would hurt its standing in the world. On 28 February 1968, the Lok Sabha spurned the Jan Sangh-sponsored censure motion 203–72.[3]

By this time, the Jan Sangh and the socialist parties SSP and PSP had declared a countrywide agitation.[4] Over the next few weeks, the new Jan Sangh president travelled to Patna, Jaipur, Bombay, Bhopal and Calcutta to chalk out a plan. Everywhere he lambasted the government for meekly accepting the tribunal's recommendations. After all, Kutch might serve as a dangerous precedent; Pakistan or China might demand similar tribunals in Kashmir and elsewhere.[5] While rejection might 'not only infuriate

Britain but also the US and the Soviet Union',[6] saving India's territory was cause enough to risk the wrath of the big powers.* In the second week of April, Vajpayee undertook a tour of Gujarat towns, exhorting the local population to support the satyagraha.[7] At a press conference in Rajkot, he challenged the prime minister to fight a by-election against him from her own constituency of Raebareli on the Kutch award issue.[8]†

On 21 April, the first batch of volunteers marched from Khavda (in Bhuj) to enter the prohibited territory on the Kutch–Sindh border. The satyagrahis, which also included MPs and former SVD ministers, shouted slogans: 'Seema ki raksha kar na sake jo, woh sarkaar nikammi hai' – a government which can't protect its borders has no right to govern. They symbolically violated the ban by entering the prohibited area without a permit. But overpowered by a large police force stationed there, they were packed into vans and sent back to Indian territory to be locked up for a few hours.

Vajpayee did not offer himself for satyagraha, but frequently made speeches before seeing off the satyagrahis at Bhuj. He had been threatening that the satyagraha would force the prime minister to resign. Turned out the show was not nearly successful enough. The Jan Sangh had promised to send 15,000 volunteers; the final tally was barely a fifth of this number. The satyagraha fizzled out, and was disbanded after eighteen days. Experts from the two countries had already gathered in Kutch to demarcate the new boundary.

Meanwhile in UP, Charan Singh had resigned after his prolonged clash with the Jan Sangh and SSP factions. President's Rule was imposed, even as the Congress candidate C. B. Gupta unsuccessfully tried to recover

---

* If the government was not intrepid enough to outright refuse the award, Vajpayee suggested, there were at least two other alternatives. The first was an opinion poll; he repeatedly referred to the referendum in Goa in January 1967, wherein the Goans had chosen to continue as a union territory rather than merge with Maharashtra. The other option was to seek advice on the matter from the Supreme Court. Otherwise 'not even a square inch of the Kutch territory could be gifted away to Pakistan'.

† A local Congressman from Raebareli attempted a deflation by inviting Vajpayee to instead fight the upcoming UP assembly by-polls from one of the five constituencies there, 'not against Mrs. Gandhi, but against an ordinary citizen of the Prime Minister's constituency like me'.

control of the state for the Congress. On 15 April, the president issued a proclamation dissolving the UP assembly. The next day, most of the opposition led by Vajpayee walked out of the Lok Sabha in protest. UP was the fourth state – after Rajasthan, Haryana and West Bengal – where Mrs Gandhi had toppled the government by imposing President's Rule. Vajpayee cried himself hoarse, reminding the house that Dr Ambedkar had hoped that Article 356 would remain 'a dead letter'.[9] Soon the Bihar and Punjab assemblies too found themselves dissolved.

In MP, the chief minister Govind Narayan Singh bickered with Rajmata Scindia on the one hand, and with Jan Sangh leaders on the other. Singh alleged that the Rajmata had been acting as the super chief minister: a mere telephone call from Jai Vilas Palace in Gwalior was enough to change cabinet decisions – 'even if it was a call from only a palace clerk'.[10] On the other hand, all seven Jan Sangh ministers had resigned, complaining that they were 'utterly disgusted' with Singh's interference. The trigger was the transfer of certain senior officials without prior consultations with the ministers concerned.[11] On some occasions, Singh sat down with the Rajmata and Vajpayee to settle differences. The Jan Sangh had barely rejoined when the Congress managed to lure back some of its defectors, forcing Singh to resign.

By mid-1968, Vajpayee was privately grieving that while the SVD coalitions had 'served the purpose for a time of keeping the Congress out of power', they had 'achieved nothing else'. He perpetually complained of being 'short of money'.[12] In fact the Jan Sangh's finances had marginally improved. In all SVD coalitions, its men had infiltrated multiple government departments. Less visibly, the Sangh Parivar had used the brief stint to acquire real estate everywhere. In the capital, where the Jan Sangh governed the Delhi Metropolitan Council, the combined clout of the party and the RSS's labour wing Bharatiya Mazdoor Sangh ensured that top industrial houses (like Birla) contributed lakhs of rupees to the party fund.[13] It was a sign of financial prosperity that the party mouthpieces were streamlined: *Panchjanya* moved from Lucknow to Delhi. In the winter of 1968, the RSS spent more than ₹10 lakhs to float its first English daily: *The Motherland*.[14]

Mid-term polls in four states under President's rule were announced for February 1969. The euphoria of working together in a non-Congress coalition had turned into intense rivalry, especially in UP between Charan Singh's new party Bharatiya Kranti Dal and the Jan Sangh. Projecting itself as representing the middle castes, the BKD hoped to eat up some of UP's rich peasant base that had begun voting for the Jan Sangh. In his speeches, Vajpayee now described the Jat leader as a casteist and an opportunist.[15]

The Jan Sangh's bumper performance in the previous assembly elections had to do with a section of Dalits voting for the party, apart from its traditional Brahmin-bania voters: twenty-nine out of ninety-eight Jan Sangh MLAs in UP were Dalits. Addressing the Jan Sangh-sponsored UP Scheduled Caste conference at Lucknow on 2 December 1968, Vajpayee crowed that his party stood firmly for social justice and equality: 'We want to see a Harijan as chief minister in one of the states.'[16]* For the first time, the party also fielded a Muslim candidate in UP.

But the campaign had fatal flaws that Vajpayee underestimated. Till 1967, the elector had judged the grand old party by its performance and the opposition by their promises. For the first time, the Jan Sangh was going to be judged for its brief stint. The fellow SVD constituents alleged corruption; as earlier, Mrs Gandhi condemned the Jan Sangh as 'a menace to national unity'.[17] Also, unlike C. B. Gupta for Congress or Charan Singh for the BKD, the Jan Sangh did not have a figure as chief ministerial candidate. The party was thrashed in UP (winning only forty-nine seats, half of its previous strength) and West Bengal (zero). In Punjab and eventually in Bihar, the Jan Sangh joined the government as a junior partner. The by-polls undid many of the changes brought about in the country's electoral geography two years before.

A poor debut did not sully the president's reputation. Vajpayee was given a rousing reception on 21 April as he drove into Bombay in an open jeep for the fifteenth annual session. Between Dadar and Girgaum Chowpatty, thousands of admirers rushed forward to shower him with

---

* Winding up the conference, however, Nanaji Deshmukh clarified that he 'disfavoured reservation of jobs etc. for Harijans and that such provisions smacked of separatism. Harijans should consider themselves not beggers but masters in the country and cease to depend on others for petty concessions.'

rose petals.[18] The many layers of fiction introduced to his resume over time were bearing fruit as good press: one talked admiringly of his role in the freedom movement, even as 'he kept the balance between politics and studies so well that he never missed a first class throughout his career'. And that 'he ascended the Jana Sangh *gaddi* last year, after having twice refused his party's highest honour'.[19] Vajpayee's presidential speech calling for an end to untouchability and dowry was praised the president's 'new radicalism'.[20]

At the annual session, a committee was set up to negotiate with the BKD and Swatantra for future collaboration. The SVD constituents had fallen apart only to soon realize the message: they could only ever tackle Indira's juggernaut by coming together. In the past, Jan Sangh and Swatantra elders had sat together on several occasions to discuss the possibility of a merger. Balraj Madhok was especially keen on it, and he wasn't being wholly unreasonable. With forty-two Lok Sabha seats, Swatantra was the largest opposition group. If they merged, the new unit would be officially recognized as the opposition party.[21] In UP similarly, had the Jan Sangh and BKD fought together, they could have outperformed the Congress (which had a bare majority, its vote share being 33.7 per cent against Jan Sangh–BKD's joint 39.3 per cent).

But when the initiative for a merger came from Charan Singh, Vajpayee was sullen. He commented to an interviewer that he did not understand why people first 'form new parties and then start discussing merger'.[22] Even so, he agreed to discuss the exploratory talks on working together. Charan Singh wanted nothing short of a quick, complete merger. In late May, with Vajpayee admitted at AIIMS for an ulcer surgery – after sharp stomach pain on a Delhi–Bombay flight – they traded insults.[23] The three parties, he suggested, first ought to form a united block in parliament and state legislatures: 'How can there be a merger without agreement on fundamental principles?'[24] Vajpayee was not sure if the Jan Sangh, with its large, dedicated band of volunteers, would derive any medium-term benefits from joining hands with Swatantra and the BKD who had nothing comparable to offer in return.

Privately, the Jan Sangh considered the BKD a caste-based party 'of very little significance' and expected its disintegration 'any time'.[25]

Vajpayee would have liked to wean away from Swatantra some of its inexhaustibly wealthy maharajas. At the same time, he was wary of his rapidly expanding party being tagged as one with vested interests or subscribed to economic rightism. The Jan Sangh was taking the cause of labour more and more seriously, borne out by the party's support to the strike by central government employees in September 1968.

Most of all, though, he had been smelling treason against the prime minister among a section of the Congress's senior leadership: he wanted to wait for the new trend to reveal itself clearly before making up his mind. He was in Munich on 4 May when he received news of President Zakir Hussain's death. Given Hussain's past affiliations – he had served as vice chancellor of Aligarh Muslim University – the Jan Sangh had attempted unsuccessfully to thwart his election two years ago. Now, from Munich, Vajpayee extolled Hussain as 'a great educationist, a thorough gentleman'.[26]

Back in Delhi, the opposition leaders were invited by the prime minister to informally discuss the choice of Hussain's successor. She was exploring the possibility of a consensus candidate. In Vajpayee's recollection, her first preference was Defence Minister Swaran Singh, followed by Vice President V. V. Giri.[27] But Mrs Gandhi was tentative about Giri due to his old age; she ruled out Agriculture Minister Jagjivan Ram due to his deep attachment to politics; the 'unpredictability of his views' put Jayaprakash Narayan out of the running.[28]

Strong rumours emerged that the Jan Sangh and Swatantra were conspiring with the old Congress guard (known as the 'Syndicate') to dislodge Mrs Gandhi. The Syndicate decided to nominate the former Lok Sabha speaker Neelam Sanjeeva Reddy as the Congress's official candidate for president. Indira knew that Reddy's sympathies lay with the old guard and feared they could collude at some later date to force her to resign. At the AICC meeting in Bangalore in the second week of July 1969, Mrs Gandhi opposed Reddy's candidature and declared her support for the septuagenarian vice president Giri, who was contesting independently. Another major event in Bangalore briefly took the limelight away from the president's election: Mrs Gandhi proposed a radical economic idea that had been talked about often: nationalization of the country's major commercial banks. Soon after she returned to Delhi, she fired the finance minister Morarji Desai – also deputy prime minister – who was ideologically opposed to the idea.

In early August, the Congress president Nijalingappa sought the support of the Jan Sangh and Swatantra for Reddy. Despite the merger fiasco, the Jan Sangh–Swatantra–BKD triad had fielded the former finance minister C. D. Deshmukh as their candidate, but Vajpayee privately promised to 'cast our party's second preference votes for Reddy'.[29] With Nijalingappa seeking support from rightist factions began a season of mudslinging within and across parties. While Mrs Gandhi's supporters, Jagjivan Ram and Fakhruddin Ali Ahmed, interrogated Nijalingappa on the 'ugly rumours' about the conspiracy to remove the prime minister,[30] an agitated Vajpayee declared it was no crime for the president of a party to canvass votes for his own party candidate. He described Desai's removal 'an act of sheer personal vendetta', [31] and called Jagjivan Ram a hypocrite for lobbying with the 'Schedule Caste members of all opposition parties, including ours, to vote for Giri'.[32] The communists accused Vajpayee of being 'a high-powered propagandist for the syndicate'.[33]

Ultimately, the coup failed. Though a majority of Congress legislators in Delhi as well as the states voted for Reddy, Giri pulled off a narrow win with support from motley opposition groups. A few weeks later the Congress split, with the prime minister being expelled from the party. The Congress members aligned themselves either for or against Mrs Gandhi. While she lost her majority in parliament, she survived mainly with support from the DMK, Akalis and the two communist parties. Her party was now called Congress (Requisitionist), as against the Congress (Organization) of Nijalingappa and Morarji Desai. For Vajpayee, this 'radically new situation' in the aftermath of the SVD debacle held 'immense possibilities.[34] His optimism was misplaced.

Perhaps inevitably, Indira Gandhi's economic radicalism divided the Jan Sangh. The debate on bank nationalization revealed its economics to be ad hoc and deliberately vague. In the first week of September 1969, the party's central working committee met at Ghaziabad. The BMS founder Dattopant Thengadi – also a Rajya Sabha MP now – introduced a resolution in favour of bank nationalization. Madhok opposed it, pointing to the 1967 election manifesto which clearly mentioned that the party was opposed to the nationalization of banks. 'During the lunch break,' Madhok recalled, 'Vajpayee came to tell me that Thengadi's proposal had come from the RSS.'[35] By now, Vajpayee and most others concurred with Thengadi. Though he had at first called the move 'anti-people' in parliament, the Jan Sangh president had realized its great mass appeal. Even small businesses, which formed the core of the party's base in north India, felt they were likely to gain from the shift in credit policies.

The muddled take revealed itself in a pamphlet issued by the Jan Sangh to explain its stand. First it cited Upanishads to show that Bharatiya culture had no place for unbridled private capitalism. Private banking had refused to render adequate assistance to agriculturalists and small-scale industrialists. Nevertheless, it 'could not be denied that the ordinance was promulgated with undue and indecent haste'. Then it rambled across the world – from Marx to Adam Smith – to finally propose that state monopoly was no panacea. If there was need for a shift from private ownership, it was more desirable to widen the participation of people in bank management and ownership rather than hand the banks over to the government.

Taking a middle ground, the pamphlet hoped to iron out the differences in the party – between the Vajpayee-led majority and the smaller faction of ideologically steadfast men like Madhok who wanted the party to counter Mrs Gandhi's populist turn.[36] Vajpayee was convinced that her motivation was 'not at all economic' – choosing between nationalization and free enterprise – but 'essentially political, personal', a means to survive in office. He did not think it prudent to swim against the populist current.[37]

Madhok's differences with Vajpayee, then, were only partly ideological: they were mainly clashes of style, tactics, timing. Coming from the Sangh Parivar that had secrecy as one of its trademarks, Madhok began to be undone by his sharp tongue and indiscreet behaviour. After being removed from major organizational roles, the former president had frequently begun to use the press to air his grievances: the latest was a detailed leak on the differences within the party at the Ghaziabad meeting. Madhok was warned 'to be cautious in his public utterances'.*

Keen to quell all rumours of a split, Vajpayee clarified that he had 'no personal differences' with Madhok; that in fact he felt 'great regard' for the former president, but then 'everybody has to abide by the party discipline'.[38] Even so, they had gradually lost the old affection and warmth for each other. Madhok was fond of shooting off in public that he was ideologically closer to the RSS than Vajpayee, and that the latter was exploiting the presidentship to fuel his personal ambition.[39]

There was some truth to the charge. 'Kya hota tha ki I was caught in a crossfire between these two gangs,' recalled *Panchjanya* editor Devendra Swaroop. 'Atalji would come to *Panchjanya* office, hand me over a slip to be passed off as an editorial.' Madhavrao Muley, the joint general secretary of the RSS, would tell Swaroop, 'You don't need to take sides between the two of them.'[40] Vajpayee's personal temperament, however, ensured that he had many more supporters in the party than Madhok: he was pragmatic, adaptable, balanced, more concerned with the preservation of the party's physical identity over economic ideology, which had in any case never been the Sangh Parivar's primary concern.

When the party met in Patna in the last week of December 1969, everyone's morale and confidence were, thanks to the Congress split, stronger than in Bombay.† But the occasion foregrounded once again the painful dilemma: how to retain the party's traditional support system while widening its base. Vajpayee felt an effective strategy would be toning down the party's anti-Muslim propaganda and adopting a relatively radical

---

* The Parliamentary Board held a meeting – which Madhok skipped – to remind the former president of his recent lapses which were spoiling the party's public image: his opposition to the one-day strike led by the central government employees in September 1968, on the grounds that it was led by communists; filing a writ petition with Minoo Masani in the Supreme Court challenging the validity of the bank nationalization ordinance without consulting the party.

† Patna was significant in that there were, for the first time, 600 delegates from the tribal areas of south Bihar. They paraded in their traditional costumes. The marchers shouted slogans, the loudest of which was 'Atal Behari bol raha, Indira shaasan dol raha' – Atal Behari's call has shaken the Indira government.

economic programme. Madhok thought this fatuous: the Jan Sangh could not outdo Mrs Gandhi or the communists in this competition and would end up looking like an inferior cousin of the Congress (R), confusing its cadres without winning any meaningful support.

To counter nationalization in the economic domain, the Jan Sangh came up with its own cultural and political policy: 'Indianization' – as the 'subordination of all narrower loyalties', in particular 'those with extra-territorial loyalty or allegiance, overt or covert, to the two-nation or the multi-nation theory' – hinting obviously at Muslims and communists. When Vajpayee insisted on deleting a sentence that contained a specific reference to Muslims, an incensed Madhok packed his bags and left the conference.[41]

Around this time, Vajpayee occasionally sought guidelines from Guruji Golwalkar. The president argued that an ideological party would not manage to capture power, though it could happily exist as a powerful pressure group. The Jan Sangh's only real option was to compromise ideology for power. Once they had attained power, they could mould the body politic as per their desire. At one such meeting in Delhi, Guruji responded that an ideological party could, in theory, come to power. Quoting the example of the Labour Party in England, he argued that it took them twenty-nine years to become a partner in a coalition, and yet another decade to fetch a majority. In the Jan Sangh's case, it might take more or less time depending on the circumstances. But where the mentee wanted a clear direction, Guruji offered none.[42] The crisis sagged.

By early 1970, when Indira Gandhi completed her fourth year in office, her transition into a consummate politician was total. Belying Vajpayee's frequent boast that it was 'not impossible to topple' her, the prime minister had held her flock together rather tightly.[43] A mix of economic radicalism and renewing the party's engagement with Muslims had worked well for her. By April 1970, she had won nine out of the thirteen parliament seats contested since the split. She may have been heading only a minority government, but there was a surge in her self-confidence:

for the first time she seemed in command of the political situation. Two of her strategies in 1970 were calculated to hurt the opposition, the Jan Sangh in particular. One was to expose the party by denouncing it at every forum as communal and fascist; the other was to revoke the privy purses promised to the maharajas at Independence.

Her speeches were now punctuated with wisdom and humour, similes and sarcasm. If ever she had been one, she was no longer the dumb doll the opposition had once declared her to be. She attacked Indianization as 'a masquerade to disguise the face of reaction': the world remembered vividly the havoc unleashed when some Germans declared their fellow citizens to be 'un-Aryan and, therefore, un-German'.[44] Vajpayee was hiding 'dangerous thoughts behind his smiling face and mellifluous Hindi'.[45] When the Jan Sangh president tried to undercut her, she coolly responded: 'If I may quote Shakespeare, it seems the lady protesteth much.' The Lok Sabha went wild with laughter. She heaped further insult, saying the Jan Sangh president 'acted only as a kind of a make-up man to Madhok's ideas'.[46]

The Jan Sangh had no strategy in sight. In the first week of May 1970, on the day of Shivaji Jayanti, riots erupted in Bhiwandi, a town of weavers fifty kilometres north of Bombay. Hindus and Muslims had clashed, leading to widespread arson and 250 deaths – more Muslims than Hindus. The government held responsible the recently founded Rashtriya Utsav Mandal – the majority of whose members belonged to the RSS–Jan Sangh – for bringing the tensions to a boil (later confirmed by a commission of enquiry).[47] Vajpayee, on the other hand, was informed that the riots had been pre-planned by a group of Muslims who had 'laid down conditions to regulate the Shivaji Jayanti processions'. Had the police arrested them, he argued, the mischief could have been nipped in the bud.[48]

Vajpayee sought a date for a parliamentary debate on the subject, which was granted. His body language and tone on the afternoon of 14 May showed that he had come meticulously prepared. He began by quoting a recent Home Ministry report to answer the fundamental question of 'who starts these riots'. Reviewing the twenty-three major instances of communal incidents over the previous fifteen months, the report charged Muslims with providing the provocation on twenty-two occasions.[49] Evidently then, while a majority of Muslims were patriots and peace-lovers, 'there is certainly a class of Muslims – and there is a need to say this without mincing words – who like to spread communal feelings in the country.' The cause established, he proceeded to neatly explain the effect:

> Our Muslim brethren are becoming more and more communal, and as a reaction Hindus are turning more militant. Hindus were not militant earlier … If you want to give us [the RSS–Jan Sangh] the credit, I'll take it … We have received enough beating in the last 700–800 years. But now in this country, sir, the Hindus refuse to get beaten up.[50]

'Ab Hindu maar nahi khaayenge.' Amid loud interruptions from the two sides, Vajpayee and Mrs Gandhi began to lambast each other. She rose to point out that Vajpayee's speech was 'going to create a bad atmosphere in the country'. Vajpayee bluntly asked the prime minister to 'keep quiet, madam: how come you were never ashamed to collaborate with Muslim League [in Kerala]? … You resign and get out … Someone who just broke her own party has the audacity to talk about the nation.'[51] When a Congress MP demanded a ban on the Jan Sangh, Vajpayee said that threats did not bother him: 'We are not here at the Prime Minister's pleasure, we are here in spite of her.'

Mrs Gandhi interrupted again to criticize Vajpayee's body language, saying the Jan Sangh president spoke 'with his hand raised in the old Hitler style'. Vajpayee's response to this, expunged, was: 'Well, madam, I have never met anyone who speaks with his feet raised.'[52] When she got her chance to retaliate, the prime minister insisted that the RSS–Jan Sangh activists were often responsible for communal violence: every time they travelled somewhere, 'riots erupt in the surrounding areas; this is a strange coincidence'.[53]

For a decade, Vajpayee had been popular among parliamentarians and the media – including sections of the left-liberal press – as well as liberal Muslim intellectuals such as M. C. Chagla and Hamid Dalwai: they routinely praised Vajpayee for his moderation, realism, tough balance.[54]* In June 1969, the progressive Hindi weekly *Dinaman* had put his face on its cover. The Atal–Indira spat sparked, for the first time, a debate on Vajpayee's moral and political character. Some felt Vajpayee's was a speech 'calculated to incite communal feelings' in the Hindu community at an extremely tense time.[55] Others believed that he went off the rails deliberately to preserve his position intact in the party – vis-à-vis Madhok and other hardliners. To be sure, there was nothing in Vajpayee's speech that he had not said at other public fora. But addressing a crowd of Jan Sangh sympathizers was one thing; a hostile Lok Sabha – with a prime minister who had recently begun to display her debating skills – was quite another.

The most scathing response to Vajpayee's diagnosis of the communal situation was a cover story in the June 1970 issue of the monthly *Secular Democracy*, run by his chief baiter Subhadra Joshi: 'A. B. Vajpayee: Mini-Hitler or Golwalkar's Puppet?' Joshi accused Vajpayee of having 'sedulously cultivated an image of being different' from the rest of the Sangh Parivar.[56] She chided the 'good-hearted Liberal Democrats' who hoped Vajpayee would someday recast his party 'in the secular, democratic mould'.

> The thought never crossed any democratic mind that Vajpayee was only acting the liberal to provide cover to the RSS so that this fascist machine could gain time it needed to build adequate strength. Golwalkar's preference for Vajpayee was obviously based on his ability to be a better actor than Madhok who, because of his ebullience, usually gives away the game. Every political party has its mermaids – fancy politicians who waffle eloquently about the have-nots and the downtrodden – whose primary function it is to make sweet noises, to seduce the people to their den ... The most generous construction that can be put on his behaviour

* In a November 1967 profile, Dalwai had praised Vajpayee's support for investigation against soldiers of the Rajasthan armed constabulary who had been charged with committing atrocities against Muslims living near the border at Barmer during the 1965 Indo-Pak war. He hoped that upcoming Muslim leaders would follow Vajpayee's lead and start 'viewing matters without the blinkers of minority and majority politics'.

> is that there is conflict in his mind, that the RSS oriented outlook is at odds with his other understanding about India and its problems.[57]

Vajpayee took issue with being cast as 'a master of doubletalk'. He had always visualized his roles as a swayamsevak and a democrat to be perfectly compatible: Hindutva needed to be updated for the changing times, but it was the only genuine model of secularism.

Less than a week after his controversial speech, he was re-appointed chairman of the Public Accounts Committee for 1970–71 by the Speaker.[58] At the same time, Jan Sangh workers distributed one million copies of Vajpayee's 14 May speech throughout the country. Its title was the most controversial line of his speech: 'Ab Hindu maar nahi khaayenge' – now the Hindus refuse to get beaten up.[59]

The prime minister's calculated fury against Vajpayee led many to compare Indira with her father. Faced with a similar situation, Nehru, some observers felt, would have invited Vajpayee and others in opposition to visit Bhiwandi with him to defuse the tension.[60] Nehru's daughter had no such desire. Amid rumours of an impending ban on the RSS–Jan Sangh, Vajpayee travelled to Bhiwandi, telling the media there that the problems had to be solved 'peacefully and politically … not by outlawing this or that organization'.[61] In case of a ban, 'we will fight the issue in the Supreme Court', and Mrs Gandhi 'must be ready for confrontation'.[62] As in the past, the government failed to find a way to legally implicate the Sangh Parivar.

Pending a legal ban, Mrs Gandhi prohibited the use of parks and public places for the RSS's drills and exercises. Based on the previous year's hate speech charges, Madhok was arrested. However, Madhok 'surrendered himself to the police amidst such an ostentatious show from hundreds of his supporters that so far from his arrest being a blow for secularism it became the occasion of an arrogant triumph.'[63] In her public meetings now, the prime minister never missed a chance to tell her audience that one of Vajpayee's ideological kinsmen had killed Mahatma Gandhi. A bit dramatically, she also began to talk of a Jan Sangh plot to kill her.[64] One of her ministers claimed that the RSS had paid someone 'four lakh rupees to assassinate Mrs. Gandhi'.[65] (The charge was never substantiated.)

The Jan Sangh chief also carefully evaded the facts, arguing that his party was not even born when Gandhi was assassinated.[66] Next, he claimed that there was 'no relationship' between the Jan Sangh and the RSS.[67] Vajpayee also questioned her silence on the 'Naxalite menace' which openly threatened to tear down the Indian state: 'The PM dare not touch them because she depends on Marxists for the security of her chair.'[68] But he knew that some of the mud slung by Mrs Gandhi had stuck.

He was still hopeful that in the next elections the opposition could pull off a coalition at the centre. For the first time, the foreign media speculated Vajpayee's name – a '5'6", 200 lb thorn' – to replace Mrs Gandhi. The Jan Sangh 'will be helped into power by … [yet another] split in Congress'. Vajpayee himself was happy to fuel these casual speculations.[69]*

A more rigorous assessment would have shown that a sustained collaboration was marred due to unbridgeable differences. A large chunk of Congress (O) members supported the nationalization of banks and insurance, while Swatantra was opposed to it and the Jan Sangh continued to vacillate. In private, Vajpayee did not yet have a high opinion of Swatantra and the BKD. As for the Congress (O), he was half-hearted about having a common programme: while he respected Morarji and a few others, he felt the party had too many old, discredited men who might eventually prove a liability to the Jan Sangh. At the party's Chandigarh meeting in mid-July 1970, the hardliners vetoed a collaboration with the Congress (O) in states like Gujarat, where the two parties were pitted against each other. Even as Vajpayee struggled to think of ways to bring together the non-communist opposition, Mrs Gandhi used another arrow from her quiver to shoot them down: she decided to revoke the privy purses and privileges promised to the maharajas at Independence.

* Vajpayee insisted that the Jan Sangh had altered its base from urban to rural: 'Our cadres have been active in the countryside working among the small shopkeepers, farm workers and landless peasants.' He denied that his party was anti-Muslim: 'My party controls the Delhi Metropolitan Council and not a single riot has occurred in the capital.'

The tax-free annual purses paid to hundreds of maharajas may have been morally abominable for a poor democracy, but they were arrived at through honourable negotiation before signing the instrument of accession, and therefore had constitutional sanction. The amount was not sufficient to relieve India of all its economic ills, but it was large enough to quietly squeeze the finances of the Swatantra and Jan Sangh. Most of the maharajas were affiliated to these two parties, and had beaten several Congress candidates in the 1967 elections.

When the matter was first discussed in Ghaziabad in September 1969, the Jan Sangh was divided, with some members supporting the abolition of titles and purses. Eventually, it was decided to 'leave the matter to Atalji': 'Jan Sangh was not in favour of the privy purse abolition because of Rajmata, and a few other maharajas.'[70] So far the Rajmata had been supporting the party from the outside. But in February 1970, at a ceremony in Gwalior attended by Vajpayee, her Oxford-graduate son Madhavrao formally joined the Jan Sangh. Coming on the heels of the government's decision to do away with the purses, the move was expected to create a formidable force in MP politics where the right-wing party shared political influence with the Gwalior durbar.

On 1 September, with the scions of many dynasties watching the proceedings from public galleries, the Lok Sabha passed the historic bill seeking to efface traces of monarchy by a two-thirds majority. By now Vajpayee was publicly favouring the retention of purses, and wrote it off as a pathetic move; having failed to usher in socialism, this was Mrs Gandhi's attempt to maintain her popularity on the eve of elections. He asked the government to consider the repercussions such an act would have in Bhutan and Sikkim, with whom India had treaty relations. If the abolition of privy purses was the 'people's demand', let there be a referendum on the matter. After all, many princes had been returned to the house with popular support.[71]

He was thrilled when, three days later, the Rajya Sabha defeated the privy purses bill by one vote: 'Upper houses are expected to reflect an ideal blend of change in continuity and act as a brake on hasty legislation' and, on this occasion, the upper house had 'fulfilled this role with credit'.[72] Vajpayee's joy was short-lived. After an emergency meeting of the cabinet the same evening, on 5 September, Mrs Gandhi got the president to 'derecognize' the princes with immediate effect. The Jan Sangh president deemed the presidential decree 'contempt of parliament and a fraud on the constitution'.[73]

Madhavrao Scindia took the lead in challenging the presidential decree in the Supreme Court. But given the uncertainty of opposing a populist move, the Jan Sangh needed a face-saver: Vajpayee released a statement claiming his party had suggested that the Concord of Princes come forth with an announcement: if the Supreme Court decided in favour of the maharajas, they would use the occasion to voluntarily relinquish their privileges.[74] The apex court gave its verdict on the privy purses case on 15 December, finding the presidential decree to be unconstitutional and invalid. (Bank nationalization had similarly run into legal tangles on the issue of compensation.) Vajpayee was happy to see the Supreme Court administering 'a slap in the face' of the government.[75] The indignant prime minister was now considering seeking a fresh mandate in order to have a more 'committed judiciary'.

Fearing a snap poll, Vajpayee hit the road to campaign. From Ahmedabad he wrote to the president, requesting him to 'use his discretion and judge whether any purpose or interests would be served by a mid-term poll'.[76] In Pune, he floated wild theories about the emergence of a 'New Syndicate' in the ruling Congress which would 'definitely go against' Mrs Gandhi after the election (with Finance Minister Y. B. Chavan, backed by Congress MPs from Maharashtra, making a bid for the prime ministership).[77] On the evening of 27 December, while Vajpayee was on his way to Bombay from Pune by road, the prime minister finally announced on All India Radio the dissolution of the Lok Sabha: the president had acted 'merely as a rubber stamp', and was 'liable for impeachment'.[78] He forgot that parliament would not be convened again until after the elections.

Vajpayee calculated that an openly rightist combo would no longer fetch more than 150 seats, and that the Jan Sangh ought to assume the role of a right-of-centre party with its doors open to all non-communist parties. After weeks of wrangling, five parties joined hands – Congress (O), SSP, PSP, Swatantra and Jan Sangh – to declare themselves a 'Grand Alliance'. They decided to forgo a common programme, concentrating instead on the division of seats to field a common candidate against the ruling party.

This too proved hard. Even when the top leadership agreed, the local units vetoed the adjustments. The Congress (O) wanted more seats in Maharashtra and Gujarat based on its superior performance in 1967 – which the Jan Sangh's local units resisted. Similarly, the Jan Sangh's UP unit demanded more seats. A satirical column pointed out the confusion: 'If [Tarkeshwari] Sinha [of Congress (O)] tells me to vote for her, actually she means that I should vote for [George] Fernandes [of SSP]. And if Fernandes tells me to vote for him, he means that I should vote for Vajpayee.'[79] They bickered right until the last day before elections.

Whatever doubts he may have had, in public Vajpayee made a case for multi-party governments. He would point towards Italy and West Germany (he had visited the latter the previous year), which 'rose to its present phenomenal economic status under a coalition government'. As for the SVD disasters, he contended that the differences were 'more temperamental than ideological', and that past mistakes wouldn't be repeated.[80]

Titled 'War on Poverty', Jan Sangh's 1971 election manifesto was essentially economic. It tried to ape the ruling party's 'Garibi Hatao' slogan. It demanded a nation-wide program of public works to absorb unemployment. Apart from the traditional Keynesian methods such as building roads and a house for every family, it also bizarrely included a nuclear weapons programme to absorb the educated unemployed.* But

* The party elders did not pause to think that India, growing at less than 2 per cent per annum, had neither the funds nor the administrative capacity to undertake such a mammoth employment guarantee task. Vajpayee's own macroeconomic ideas were ad-hoc and adventurist: he drew upon his experience as chairman of the public accounts committee to argue for lower incidence of tax: 'If incomes up to Rs.7,500 are exempted from taxation it would lead to no loss of revenue because the loss would be more than balanced by the saving in expenditure'. But what about black money, which was running as a parallel economy? 'In order to unearth the hoarded black money,' Vajpayee answered, his party would 'forthwith demonetise high-denomination currency.'

this egalitarianism was careful obfuscation: the manifesto declared the party's opposition to any lowering of land ceilings, which showed it keen to woo medium and large farmers rather than the landless labourers.[81]

Formally launching the campaign at the Ramlila grounds in Delhi on 24 January, Vajpayee mocked Mrs Gandhi's attempt to turn herself into royalty through democratic process: her approach to life was 'heads I win, tails you lose, and the rest belongs to my father'.[82] On his travels, he presented the prime minister as an enemy of all that was sacrosanct about India's democracy: when the party did not accept her choice for president, she broke it up; when parliament did not pass the bill for the abolition of privy purses, she abolished them through a presidential order. When the Supreme Court quashed the presidential order, she dissolved parliament. If the lady dictator had her way, she would perhaps dissolve the Supreme Court!

Vajpayee exerted himself more than his body could allow. Given the uncertainty about mid-term polls, he had been travelling incessantly all through 1970 so as to be prepared for a sudden announcement. With an undisciplined diet and no physical exercise, he had been overweight for a while. (Even the odd newspaper cartoon lampooning the Jan Sangh president showed him with a considerable double chin.[83]) A year after the ulcer operation, he was diagnosed with a kidney problem.[84] On 10 December, Vajpayee was on the way to his constituency when he began to feel giddy, followed by profuse bleeding from his nose. The entourage returned to Lucknow where, after a check-up, he was advised complete rest. But there was no time to convalesce. He bitterly complained that while the prime minister was touring the country in an Air Force plane, he found it difficult to even book an ordinary seat on an Indian Airlines flight – which were also often mysteriously delayed by hours.[85]

On 3 February – the last day for filing nominations – Vajpayee filed his from Gwalior. Asked why he had suddenly run away from Balrampur, he joked that the Congress had insulted him by setting up a 'light-weight' candidate there; he had moved to his hometown to fight a 'heavier' rival.[86] The real reasons were more complicated. Some of the local Jan Sanghis who looked after the Balrampur constituency for the party president were tainted with corruption charges: Pratap Narayan Tewari, who had won the assembly election there in 1967 and briefly served as the whip of the SVD government in UP, was accused of black-marketing sugar.[87] The party had fared badly in the subsequent by-polls. Vajpayee possibly smelt risk there.

It is tempting to see the shift also as a compromise by the Jan Sangh to showcase the Gwalior durbar in a positive light. Early in his campaign, Vajpayee had been urging the maharajas to do away with frivolous gestures like 'accepting gun salutes at ceremonial parades and displaying of special number plates on their cars'. Giving away purses and privileges would endear them to the people: 'I am sure the princes are alive to the pulse beats of the times.'[88] But despite the Supreme Court verdict in Madhavrao Scindia's favour, Jai Vilas Palace did not – contrary to Vajpayee's earlier promise – seem keen to relinquish any of their privileges.

Instead, the Rajmata granting one of her former subjects the most coveted constituency under her fiefdom would serve as a symbol of the Scindias turning democratic. (The ex-queen herself stood from Bhind, Madhavrao from Guna.) Vajpayee's friend Narayan Krishna Shejwalkar, the former Jan Sangh mayor of Gwalior, volunteered to be his election manager; Shejwalkar's house became the focal point of his campaign.

Vajpayee's bodyguard-cum-secretary Shivkumar and old friend Appa Ghatate accompanied the native son for filing the nomination. Both camped there until polling was over. 'He would be travelling in other constituencies,' recalled Appa, 'but kept coming every week or so.' The Rajmata's men had swept the five assembly seats of Gwalior constituency in 1967; all five MLAs were summoned to canvass on behalf of the Jan Sangh president. Most top leaders from the ruling Congress – Mrs Gandhi, Jagjivan Ram and others – arrived to foil his chances. But 'it was a safe seat'. Gwalior went to the polls on 1 March. 'We knew he is winning, Congress also knew.'[89]

In Delhi the next day, Vajpayee became the target of the ruling party's casually vindictive campaign. In the afternoon, he was addressing a crowd of government servants on the Boat Club grounds. He had barely begun when a yellow two-seater airplane hovered over the meeting and dropped multi-coloured propaganda leaflets. This was the prime minister's elder son Rajiv's plan. Rajiv Gandhi flew Indian Airlines planes for a day job, and had a reputation for looking handsome and suave and being uninterested in his mother's line of work. At first Vajpayee mocked the attempt to disrupt his rally. Let their pamphlets hang in the air, he quipped, 'I am here to collect your votes.' But as the plane showed no sign of leaving – it took a total of twenty-three sorties – a ruffled Vajpayee denounced the fouling of public life with low-level tactics. He gestured towards the plane and asked his audience: 'Is this democracy?'[90]

11

Loose Ends, New Beginnings

VAJPAYEE'S PREDICTIONS WERE WILDLY OFF THE MARK. HE HAD BEEN preparing himself for a graceful defeat, but was surprised to find the Grand Alliance routed at forty-nine. The Jan Sangh tally came down from thirty-five to twenty-two, the votes mostly from the feudal pockets of MP and Rajasthan where the former maharajas still held sway. It won barely seven seats in the rest of the Hindi-speaking states.

The party president himself won safely by more than 70,000 votes. He obliquely admitted the ideological confusion: the rank-and-file workers in many parts of the country did not relish the association the party had acquired by giving tickets to princes and business tycoons. But this had been necessary to get the funds which it badly needed.[1] When the Jan Sangh high command sat down to introspect, he refused to apologize for having joined the Alliance: the verdict had to be accepted 'in a sporting spirit'.[2] Vajpayee deemed the Congress victory a mere 'passing phase'.

Riding on a mix of personal charisma and populist measures, Indira Gandhi was returned with 350 seats – almost a two-thirds majority, although her party secured only 44 per cent votes. Vajpayee was right in attributing some of her success also to 'greater resources, solid Muslim support'.[3] But the causes did not matter, the consequences did. Far from Vajpayee's speculation about a cabinet coup, Mrs Gandhi now had complete control over her party and the government. Such starkly unequal authority in a populist democracy meant more mudslinging and empty rhetoric.

The election had stripped the opposition of some of its most eloquent speakers: the socialist Acharya Kripalani, the Swatantra veterans N. G. Ranga and Minoo Masani. For its first few days, the fifth Lok Sabha appeared devoid of life and colour. In the last week of March 1971, Vajpayee and a few others enlivened it with discussion of a tragedy unfolding on the eastern border with Pakistan.

Pakistan had held its first major general elections in December 1970, in which the Awami League, led by Sheikh Mujibur Rahman, had secured a majority. The Awami League was based in East Pakistan, whose Bengali-speaking residents had often complained of economic and cultural prejudice by the western wing. With his newfound majority, Mujib hoped to achieve a modicum of self-determination for his people. But the military chief General Yahya Khan and Zulfikar Ali Bhutto, leader of the People's Party (which had captured most of the seats in the western wing), collaborated to prevent Mujib from taking over power. His Awami League responded by calling a massive indefinite strike across East Pakistan. By late March 1971, the Pakistani army was crushing the rebellion by shooting dead thousands of people suspected of supporting the League – university students, writers, journalists – besides indulging in arson and rape. The East Pakistan regiments mutinied; Mujib was arrested and carted off to a secret location in West Pakistan. Before long, lakhs of refugees were pouring across the border into Assam and West Bengal.

Even though the Jan Sangh's genesis lay in the refugee crisis of East Bengal two decades before, the present crisis was several notches higher in magnitude. The refugees included both Hindus and Muslims, though the former were more numerous. While the Sangh Parivar did not hold much sympathy for the Muslim refugees, they were thrilled to see Jinnah's 'land of the pure' self-destructing. Addressing a public meeting in Bombay on 28 March 1971, Vajpayee appealed to the government to support Mujib and recognize 'Bangladesh' – whose flag Mujib had first raised five days ago. In the true tradition of an RSS volunteer, he wanted the government to 'allow the willing youths to cross the border and help the people of East Bengal in their hour of crisis', saying he would be 'the first to enroll himself as a volunteer'.[4]

Earlier that day, Vajpayee had demanded in the Lok Sabha a resolution in support of Bangladesh. This found favour from all groups, including the Marxists. The prime minister accepted the demand even as she took care to point out that, given the diplomatic tangles, she was against making frequent statements on East Bengal. She advised the opposition to be reticent.[5] The carefully worded resolution assured East Bengal of India's 'whole-hearted sympathy and support', without any mention of Bangladesh.[6] Later that day, Vajpayee and other opposition MPs demonstrated outside the Pakistan high commission, recording 'our complete solidarity with the heroic people of Bangladesh'.*

In the second week of April, Vajpayee toured the districts of West Bengal, Tripura and Assam adjoining the border with Pakistan, to see hordes of refugees in pitiable conditions. A few weeks later, Mrs Gandhi had a tense three-hour meeting with the opposition, at which Vajpayee accused her of 'vacillating' under pressure from the big powers. Based on his travels, he suggested that the government help the Mukti Bahini – a group of select refugees trained in guerrilla warfare – by declaring territory adjacent to the Indian border as a Liberated Zone. The government's response was: how can we aid Bangladesh so long as we do not recognise it?[7]

Pressure from the opposition escalated after an eleven-man Indian guard post on the East Pakistan border was overrun by the Pakistani army. On the morning of 24 May, Vajpayee led a crowd marching to Parliament House. With more than a touch of melodrama, he held up a Bangladesh flag and swung it about. Addressing the crowd, he rued that Pakistan had waged a war against India without even firing a bullet. The influx of refugees, some of whom were feared to be Pakistani spies, had put the economy in grave danger. The only way out was to recognize Bangladesh.[8] That day, the entire opposition walked out of parliament after the Speaker

* The MPs were accompanied by Jan Sangh demonstrators carrying anti-Yahya Khan placards. For a while, the Jan Sanghis also held a rally outside the Chinese embassy protesting against the country's 'aiding and abetting of the reactionary military clique of West Pakistan'.

rejected Vajpayee's contention for an adjournment motion on the subject. Over the next few weeks, Vajpayee demanded that the Indian Army be moved along the 1,349-mile border with East Pakistan, replacing the paramilitary Border Security Force. The government replied that it would use the army when necessary.

Soon, everyone in Delhi was discussing the possibility of a 'five-day war' with Pakistan. Vajpayee was found talking 'of a blitz liberation of Bangladesh as if it would be as easy a walkover as Goa or Hyderabad operations'.[9] At its annual session in Udaipur, the Jan Sangh decided to launch a mass satyagraha during 1–12 August to force the government to recognize Bangladesh and give it all material and moral support. By this time, more than ten million refugees had crossed the border into India. 'India cannot permit Pakistan to endanger our economy and political stability,' Vajpayee thundered, 'because of its own problems.'[10]

The government was wary of China's full-scale support to Pakistan.[11] Mrs Gandhi had been advised by the army chief to avoid a war until the onset of winter, when it would be difficult for the Chinese to cross the snow-laden Himalaya.[12] Even so, by June the cabinet had decided to covertly provide training to the Mukti Bahani. A war with Pakistan could no longer be avoided.

In the first week of July 1971, Henry Kissinger – National Security Advisor to the American president Richard Nixon – alighted in Delhi as part of a South Asian tour. When he met Nixon in 1960, Vajpayee's impression was that the Republican would be friendlier to Islamabad than to Delhi. He was right. But whereas America's earlier tilt towards Pakistan had to do with consolidating anti-communist allies, in the summer of 1971 Nixon had another reason to favour Pakistan: it played mediator in American relations with communist China, whom the Americans had yet to officially recognize.

Kissinger's evasive replies convinced Mrs Gandhi and her team that the American attitude to the refugee crisis was unsympathetic. Vajpayee queried in parliament whether 'Dr. Kissinger had been invited to visit refugee camps'. Yes, but Kissinger had excused himself, citing a 'busy' schedule.[13] This schedule included a trip to Pakistan, from where he was secretly flown to China to lay the ground for a visit by Nixon himself. The Americans did not want an India–Pakistan war anytime soon. For if South Asia exploded, China would get involved and, in Kissinger's words, 'everything we have done [with China] will go down the drain'.[14] Over the next few weeks, the Americans repeatedly warned India against attacking Pakistan.[15] Soon enough, the news of Kissinger's trip to China reached Delhi.

Vajpayee no longer peddled his old two-China policy – backing Chiang Kai-shek, long after the Americans had come to think of the general as a dead duck. But he was pained to see America overhauling its China policy. On 19 July, he made an impassioned, broad-brush speech on the irrelevancy of non-alignment the way India had pursued it. Why was India not an attraction for the global powers, he asked.* His argument that India had to be self-reliant – manufacture an atom bomb, pull itself economically – before it could have a voice in global affairs was true but unhelpful in the immediate context of the refugee crisis. Someone should also have educated the Jan Sangh chief that China's economic and military might had to do with changes in social structure brought about by violent revolutions which had wiped out monarchy many decades ago. He was, on the other hand, still vacillating on the abolition of purses to maharajas.

In the first week of August, volunteers converged in Delhi from across the country for the Jan Sangh satyagraha on the issue of Bangladesh. Each day about 500 volunteers shouted slogans on the roads, and got arrested for defying the prohibitory orders promulgated in the capital. Unbeknown to Vajpayee and other organizers, the agitation coincided with what they had feared – India entering into a treaty with the USSR. The two foreign ministers were to sign the agreement on the morning of 9 August.

---

* This was not entirely accurate: the Soviet president Podgorny had admonished Yahya Khan in a letter at the beginning of the refugee crisis (which had provoked the Chinese to support Pakistan). And while Nixon was keen to cut aid and cause 'mass famine' in India, public opinion in the US was swinging decisively against Pakistan.

Vajpayee had earlier disapproved of India taking 'shelter under Moscow's wings'. Expressing an exaggerated fear of India becoming a 'Soviet satellite', Vajpayee had argued that 'if we allow Bangladesh to become another Vietnam, the whole of our eastern region will be lost'.[16] On the other hand, in case India recognized Bangladesh, he was certain that 'China would not intervene or attack India at least until the China-US summit was over'.[17] The Indian government was less confident. The treaty now secured Moscow's written promise that the USSR would back India in the event of Indo-Pak hostilities. Most MPs welcomed the alliance.

On the last day of the agitation, 12 August, Vajpayee described the treaty communiqué as a 'stab in the back of Bangladesh'. By referring to Pakistan as the 'third party', the treaty implied 'the indivisibility of Pakistan and carefully avoided the term Bangladesh or even East Bengal'. He wondered how Mrs Gandhi, herself a woman, could be so complacent in the face of unprecedented physical and sexual violence against women in Bangladesh. The crowd shouted: 'Bengal ki naari roti hai, Indira Gandhi soti hai' – as the women of Bengal sob, our prime minister slumbers.[18]

At a recent rally, Mrs Gandhi had accused the Jan Sangh of exploiting the crisis to whip up communal passions. There were rumours that the Jan Sangh was motivated by a desire for the merger of East Bengal with India. Vajpayee's clarification was not helpful: only the citizens of the newly created Bangladesh would have 'the right to decide whether or not their country should merge with India'.[19] Some of the Congress MPs complained about the suspicious manner in which the RSS was collecting funds for Bangladesh refugees.

Vajpayee understood the prime minister's restraint on Bangladesh, but he had no great incentive to publicly empathize with the woman who had just emphatically defeated his party. The creation of Bangladesh seemed inevitable sooner or later. By raising its voice now, the Jan Sangh might later claim some of the credit. When the party's general council met at Ghaziabad in the last week of November 1971, Vajpayee cautioned that the Congress was sure to gain politically in case of a war: the Jan Sangh might have to brace for more electoral shocks.[20]

With the two armies standing eyeball to eyeball, the prime minister took the initiative to call a truce with the opposition: Vajpayee met her on the afternoon of 22 October. Two days later she was to leave on a trip to Europe and the US to make a last-ditch effort to rouse support in the West. The half-an-hour-long meeting commenced on a rather tense note: the prime minister said she knew what was going to happen in East Pakistan; she was going to ensure, with or without a war, that the refugees returned with honour and safety. Vajpayee was sceptical, which annoyed her: 'I am not concerned with whether you believe me or not, I am concerned with what is going to happen.'[21] Calmly she continued, 'Once I take a decision, I see to it that it is implemented. I will see to it that the refugees go back.'[22] After a while the air cleared, as Mrs Gandhi emphasized the need for unity and high morale in the country over the next few months.[23] The Jan Sangh chief assured his party's 'unreserved support' in case of a war.[24]

Indira Gandhi's trip to the West proved futile. Nixon, who hoped to postpone the war at least until his China visit was completed, was particularly unsympathetic about the seriousness of the refugee crisis.[25] Back in Delhi, Mrs Gandhi ordered the army to establish bases in East Pakistan to eventually lay siege to Dhaka on 4 December 1971. She was relieved when, on 3 December, Pakistan formally initiated the war by bombing Indian airfields in the western sector. At a meeting with opposition leaders, Vajpayee found her 'a picture of worry and concern' as she informed them of the army's march into Bangladesh.[26]

Over the next two weeks, a hyperactive Jan Sangh president divided his time attending parliament and addressing crowds in Delhi and elsewhere. In a clownish statement, he informed his audience that, at long last, 'Indiraji is following Jan Sangh policy'. But he also appealed for wholehearted support to the government.* When the Russians vetoed an American resolution in the UN Security Council calling for a ceasefire, Vajpayee took a sharp U-turn to thank the USSR: 'Whoever stands by us in our present crisis is our friend. We can resume our ideological battles

* Vajpayee suggested that traders and consumers ought to avoid hoarding to check price-rise; and that the Jan Sangh workers should come forward, as they had during the 1965 war, for blood donation and civil defence jobs.

later.'[27] He was 'happy that Smt. Gandhi is out to teach a lesson' to Yahya Khan. Here was a historic opportunity to 'liquidate the theocratic state, or at least cut it to the smallest possible size'.[28]

By the second week of the war, India seemed poised to capture Dhaka. Vajpayee urged the government to not accept a ceasefire 'before the occupied Kashmir was liberated'. At one such gathering, he shared the stage with Krishna Menon, old foe turned friend, who now agreed with him. To scare India, the Americans had dispatched a ship with a nuclear warhead to the Indian Ocean: Vajpayee thought the presence of the US Seventh Fleet 'should not alarm us'.[29] In parliament, he unsuccessfully demanded that Mrs Gandhi share her communication with the US and China, given that 'attempts were being made to force a ceasefire'.[30]

It was in fact Soviet Russia that was keen for India to withdraw without causing Pakistan further humiliation in the west, lest China and the US, so far only barking, might bite. On 16 December, India captured Dhaka and the West Pakistan forces surrendered. The prime minister's advisors were divided on whether or not to call for a unilateral ceasefire on the western front. That evening she announced to a jubilant parliament that Dhaka was now the 'free capital of a free country'. Since 'our objectives were limited', the Indian armed forces would not remain in Bangladesh any longer than necessary.[31]

It is widely believed that on the evening of 16 December, Vajpayee praised Mrs Gandhi as an incarnation of Durga – the goddess of feminine strength who was forced to kill the demon king Mahishasura.* In actual fact, that evening he was missing from parliament: he was either travelling or indisposed (for earlier that afternoon he had also missed a meeting of opposition leaders with Mrs Gandhi to discuss the ceasefire plans). The next morning, an agitated Vajpayee tried unsuccessfully to convince the speaker to allow the house to discuss his reservations on the ceasefire. When the prime minister made a statement thanking 'all political parties' for her decision, the Jan Sangh president immediately rose to refute her: 'We don't want a ceasefire, we want to put an *end* to

* Asked later by Pupul Jayakar, a close friend and later biographer of Mrs Gandhi, Vajpayee vehemently denied ever referring to Indira as the reincarnation of Durga.

hostilities' for all times – for which it was necessary to continue the war in the western sector.[32] The speaker refused permission for discussion. With the exception of the Jan Sangh and Socialist Party, the entire house was in favour of the ceasefire. The speaker chided Vajpayee, saying he should 'not be so grim' on an auspicious occasion.

Two days later, a joint sitting of the two houses was held in the Central Hall to felicitate Mrs Gandhi. Certain that it was going to be an Indira-worship show, Vajpayee skipped, this time perhaps strategically. With the war over, the assembly elections would be held on time in March 1972. For the previous two months, he had extended his wholehearted support to the ruling party, but to unconditionally praise the government further was not going to help his party. For the sake of formality, he sent a letter to be read out by Pitambar Das, the Jan Sangh's leader in the Rajya Sabha.[33]

He left for Bombay to address a 'victory rally' – the first to be organized by any political party in the city – at Shivaji Park, his arrival at the venue marked by the bursting of firecrackers. His Hindu heart swelling with pride, Vajpayee declared that 'the country has not experienced in centuries' so glorious a triumph. The main architects of this victory were the armed forces, but he also praised Mrs Gandhi's 'calm and unruffled, fully confident' leadership through the two-week war. Vajpayee devoted a sizeable portion of his speech to explaining the military and strategic implications of the win – a theme he would repeat at election rallies and press conferences over the next few months. He emphasized that his party had voiced its apprehensions about a unilateral ceasefire. But now that the government had gone ahead, India should exchange the territory captured in the western sectors (Sindh and Sialkot) for Pakistan-occupied Kashmir.* India ought to be firm at the negotiating table: 'We have won the war, we must now win the peace.'[34]

Soon enough, elections for sixteen states assemblies were announced. Vajpayee's fears proved right: the ruling Congress was keen to make 'party capital out of a national victory'.[35] A reporter following his campaign

* Vajpayee felt that areas such as Kargil posts in Pak-occupied Kashmir, crucial for the defence of India's supply line to Leh, ought not to be returned. In 1965 too, India had captured these posts, but they were returned as per mandates in the Tashkent agreement.

closely saw the Jan Sangh president struggling to appeal to the electorate 'to distinguish between national and local issues' and to choose their MLAs carefully. Unfortunately, 'the people are in such a mood of buoyancy that they are unlikely to heed appeals to parochialism. What is more, there are no major local issues anywhere that might engender emotion.'[36] For all his desire to delink national issues from local ones, Vajpayee was himself unable to resist the temptation of talking about India's great victory every now and then. He spent eight days touring Andhra Pradesh and Karnataka, claiming 'war was not an election issue' in south India.[37]

By the time the campaign climaxed in late February, his brief camaraderie with the prime minister was all but lost. Vajpayee was especially irked that she had no kind words on the clean administration provided by the Jan Sangh-ruled Delhi Metropolitan Council during 1967–72. Instead, she went around saying that the saffron party had done nothing 'except changing the names of roads and colonies'. Vajpayee responded by counting the prime minister's failures during the war: 'The showdown came a little too late, the ceasefire a little too early.'[38] Since she was desperate to grab all the credit for Bangladesh's independence, maybe she should also take the blame for the (eight-month) delay which led to the butchering of lakhs of people and rapes of thousands of women. Further, the premature ceasefire was effected due to Soviet pressure and without properly consulting even the service chiefs, when another few days of fighting would have broken the back of the Pakistani army.[39]

None of this helped. The Congress captured a majority in fourteen out of sixteen state assemblies. In Kerala and West Bengal, it formed governments with its submissive partner CPI. Mrs Gandhi now commanded more power than her father had at his peak.

When the party gathered in Bhagalpur in early May to introspect, Vajpayee owned full responsibility for the debacle. He stood up and stepped aside, requesting the vice president's chair for the session so that delegates would not hesitate to criticize him.[40] The delegates obliged. At a closed-door session, they tore into the senior leadership while the high command sat impassively. Due to Vajpayee's wholesome praise for

Mrs Gandhi during the war, many remarked that they had had a tough time convincing voters to go against the ruling party. But this was still a minor factor compared to the ideological dilemma that preceded the war. Some delegates said equivocating on pro-poor stances such as privy purses and bank nationalization had kept the party cadres and the public confused, adding to the Congress's advantage.

The government had recently amended the constitution to abolish the privy purses of the erstwhile monarchs. Vajpayee no longer went to the extent of openly opposing the bill, but even his suggestion for consultation with the Supreme Court was flogged by 378–25 amidst a crescendo of 'shame, shame'.[41] The steel minister Mohan Kumaramangalam, the brain behind the constitutional amendments, likened Vajpayee's performance to that of 'a boxer, who feints here, who ducks there, who moves out of the way, but never comes to grips with his opponent'.[42]

In many ways, Vajpayee personified the Jan Sangh's doublespeak. One of Mrs Gandhi's election promises was to amend the constitution to lower ceilings on land ownership so as to make land available for distribution among the landless peasantry. On his first day in Bhagalpur, Vajpayee had avowed the party's opposition on the pretext that it denied compensation for the acquired land at market rates.[43] But given the bottom-up pressure to respond adequately to the prevailing radical mood, the leadership was forced to modify the statement to propose land ceiling at a 'level that could yield an income of Rs. 1,500 a month per family of five, including three minor children'.[44] This too was an evasion.[45]*

But Bhagalpur energized the party enough to launch agitations, clutching at any issue it could find. For years the Jan Sangh had charged the government with utilizing All India Radio for disseminating Congress propaganda. During 4–11 June, the party staged demonstrations demanding to convert the AIR into an autonomous body. Else they

* A newspaper editorial expressed it succinctly: 'Who was to determine how big a holding will earn a family of five an income of Rs. 1,500 a month, especially when the agriculture output itself depends so much on the quality of land and the amount and quality of inputs on the one hand and the hard work put in by the farmer and his family on the other? In any case, agricultural prices fluctuate so much and so often that a farm which earns Rs. 20,000 in one year may bring in only half that amount in the next.'

would install their own transmitters to launch 'Janata Radio'. Vajpayee and 300 others were taken into custody for defying prohibitory orders.[46]

A week later he sat down, in an ultimately hollow gesture, at Bombay's Hutatma Chowk to conduct a token twenty-four-hour fast. Two Dalit women had been disrobed and paraded naked in a Maharashtra village because they had dared to drink water from a well. How deep could his commitment be to annihilating caste when he had only recently opposed the redistribution of land? Sometime later, he bared his heart to an American interviewer. For the Jan Sangh to bounce back, it had to break 'its former image of representing the shopkeeper class' and 'create the image of standing with the common man'.[47] Clearly, Vajpayee's solution had to do with images, symbols, postures rather than social justice.

Meanwhile, Mrs Gandhi had begun negotiations with a dismembered Pakistan. Her chief concern was Mujib's safe release. In return, President Zulfikar Ali Bhutto was keen that she release 93,000 of its soldiers presently lodged in India in prisoner-of-war camps. Pakistan was also desperate for the withdrawal of Indian troops from areas of west Punjab and Sindh captured by India during the December war.

Vajpayee kept a close watch. As he saw it, the release of POWs and withdrawal of troops in Punjab and Sindh ought to follow the return of Pakistan-occupied Kashmir, since New Delhi had the moral right to extract a victor's price from Islamabad. Mrs Gandhi was acutely conscious of not humiliating Pakistan any further. India had a vested interest in ensuring a stable South Asia, which would not be possible unless Pakistan had a democratic government.

Like Vajpayee, the prime minister and her advisors were keen to settle Kashmir once and for all. But unlike Vajpayee, who wanted Bhutto to surrender all of Pakistan-held Kashmir – an unrealistic demand – Mrs Gandhi was keen to simply convert the ceasefire line into a formal line of control that would evolve into the international boundary. All through summer, Vajpayee swore his party's strong opposition to accepting the ceasefire line in Kashmir as the permanent international boundary.[48]

By the time the news broke about a forthcoming summit in Simla, the Jan Sangh had more or less given its verdict. On 28 June, as the two sides began their talks, Vajpayee arrived in Simla 'to feel the summit'. Given the VIP presence, a ban was enforced there under Section 144 CrPC. Even so, the Jan Sangh president was allowed to address a public meeting (perhaps the government wanted to impress on its visitors the immense pressure under which it was operating). Once Pakistan had given back all of Kashmir, Vajpayee casually fantasized, there would be no impediment to a confederation in South Asia. On his way back to Delhi, he proposed an agreement under which 'the armed strength of Pakistan should be limited to one-sixth of India's, since its size had shrunk' to India's one-sixth.[49]

The summit ran into a stalemate. India agreed to withdraw its troops from West Pakistan territory and return the 5,000 square miles of territory occupied there during the war. But the question of POWs had to wait as Bangladesh was keen to try some of them for war crimes. As earlier, the negotiations got stuck over Kashmir.* Eventually, on the last day, the two executive heads had a one-on-one chat in which both made crucial concessions. Bhutto agreed to rename the December 1971 ceasefire line in Kashmir as the 'line of control', with the implication that it would finally become the international boundary, thus settling Kashmir's fate.† He also agreed to negotiate over Kashmir bilaterally, without the interference of the UN or the two power blocs.

Reactions were positive. Except the Jan Sangh's: Vajpayee was 'shocked' at another Tashkent-like patchwork; Simla was 'nothing short of a sell-out'. His primary grouse obviously was that India had agreed to return

---

* Bhutto was coaxed into agreeing verbally to the proposal for declaring the ceasefire line as the international boundary. But he refused to commit himself on paper. Apparently he pleaded the risk of being overthrown by the army: no Pakistani head of state could hope to give away the claim to Kashmir and hope to survive in office. Apart from refusing to dilute Pakistan's stand on Kashmir, Bhutto also cited domestic constraints in his refusal to sign a no-war pact.

† The accompanying text was phrased in a way that would allow both to sell to their constituents whatever story they wished: 'In Jammu and Kashmir, the line of control resulting from the cease-fire of December 17, 1971 shall be respected by both sides without prejudice to the recognized position of either side.'

territories in West Punjab and Sindh without obtaining Pakistan-held territories in Kashmir. Besides, allowing 'other peaceful means' in Kashmir kept the door open for foreign interference.* Nehru's daughter had allowed herself to be 'duped', and 'once again pushed India into self-deception' where peace would 'mean nothing more than mere pious chants'.[50]

Mrs Gandhi thought the Jan Sangh was 'look[ing] with a microscope for things they can rake up'.[51] The party made elaborate plans to greet her with black flags at the Safdarjung airport on her return from Simla. In response, the ruling party workers stoned the Jan Sangh's central office.[52] The police rained lathis and tear-gas shells on both situations, injuring many in the melee.

Ideally the fracas should have ended here. But determined to whip up public anger, the Jan Sangh called an emergency meeting of the Working Committee to send volunteers to physically oppose the pact.[53] On the evening of 23 July, a crowd followed Vajpayee from Chandni Chowk to the railway station, while he boarded the train for Barmer. From Barmer he was to cross the Rajasthan border to enter Gadra city in Sindh, captured during the war, which was to be handed back to Pakistan as per the Simla agreement. It's not clear what exactly Vajpayee was expecting out of this symbolic agitation. Maybe the gymnastics of travelling to the border on an emotive issue would keep the party's hardcore cadre motivated and engaged.[54]

Once there, he took along three dozen-odd satyagrahis (which included some Jan Sangh MPs and MLAs) across the international border. Chanting slogans that the government had nullified the sacrifice of the armed forces – 'Desh na haara, fauj na haari, haari hai sarkaar hamaari' – they walked four kilometres on kuchcha roads, braving the scorching sun and sandstorms, to enter Gadra city.[55] They had spent three hours in an old temple there when the army arrived and huddled everyone onto trucks and transported them back to the Indian side.[56] They made another attempt the next evening (possibly to avoid the unbearable day

* The text read: 'The two countries are resolved to settle their differences by peaceful means through bilateral negotiations or by any other peaceful means mutually agreed upon between them.'

temperatures). Along with sixty-four satyagrahis, Vajpayee was stopped by the army barely 180 metres into the occupied area. The satyagrahis sat down, refusing to move to the waiting trucks after an army major announced their arrest. Among the volunteers were four women, who posed a problem as the army had no women to deal with them. Vajpayee complicated matters by announcing that the men would not move until the women did. The stalemate continued for three hours, after which the major called their bluff and ordered the women to choose between walking to the trucks themselves or being lifted in by men. The threat worked.[57]

The spectacle invited coverage and cartoons in the media, but beyond that it had no great effect. Yet the Jan Sangh did not want to retreat. Back in Delhi, on 31 July, the first day of the monsoon session, Vajpayee went to and fro between the Lok Sabha and the Boat Club, a few hundred yards from the circular parliament building. He enquired whether 'a hotline call with the Kremlin on the last day' had broken the stalemate at Simla.[58] Some Jan Sangh MPs tore up copies of the agreement inside the house.

So far she had ignored the Jan Sangh's smear campaign. Now the prime minister got up to repudiate. Only a person 'suffering from some deep inferiority complex' could make such an allegation, she said. 'Are we going to listen to the voice of the crores or are we going to listen to the voice of the small, whining minority?' Vajpayee's squat on the sands of Gadra city was a 'tamasha' – a gimmick. She recalled that Vajpayee had spent much of the previous year lampooning her:

> Can Vajpayee deny that there is Bangladesh today? Can Vajpayee deny that the refugees have gone back to Bangladesh? Still he says 'I do not believe you'. Let him not believe me, it matters little to the people of India ...[59]

While Simla might not guarantee peace for all times to come, it had helped create a situation whereby 'the capacity for Pakistan acting against us is minimised'. She stressed that, despite Bhutto's domestic exigencies, he was doing his best to live up to the terms and spirit of the agreement: 'I think it is in our interest to turn the face of Pakistan from its past hatred and bitterness to a new future of peace and friendship.'[60] It was a masterly performance, at once unsentimental politicking and statesmanship.

Constant bickering rather than an intellectual appraisal of situations was hurting domestic politics. Mrs Gandhi's whiplash gave the subject a much-needed closure. Vajpayee would continue to blow hot and cold on Simla, but the controversy ultimately fizzled out.

Vajpayee was now emotionally more stable and fulfilled than ever before. Yet, he assiduously cultivated the public image of being an ascetic. Youngsters who idolized him said they were inspired by Vajpayee's 'lack of family and material comforts'.[61] In fact, on his election campaigns, the celebrity found ways to talk about his bachelorhood. Many of Vajpayee's fellow MPs in Lok Sabha were aware of his ambivalent private life; on numerous occasions, his apparent singledom had been a matter of light banter.* Rumours circulated privately about how, despite having a stable partner, he indulged in occasional flings.

Meanwhile, a major change had taken place in his domestic arrangements. It was triggered by unforeseen events at Ramjas, which was gradually acquiring the dubious distinction of being, depending on how one saw it, the best among the worst colleges or the worst among the best colleges of Delhi University. Though Birjan Kaul had been

* During a discussion about irregularities in the 1971 electoral rolls, Vajpayee complained that at many places 'the husband's name was in the rolls, while the wife's was missing and vice-versa'. The speaker G. S. Dhillon, a Congressman with whom he got along well, remarked cheekily: 'Why are you worried about others' wives?' Sometimes Vajpayee inflicted the joke upon himself. Denouncing the AIR's airing the news of film star Dilip Kumar's marriage with Saira Bano as trivial, he sarcastically asked the minister of information and broadcasting whether the news of the weddings of bachelor MPs like himself would also be broadcast. Justifying the coverage, the minister added that if Vajpayee got married that news would be broadcast too. During the discussion on privy purses in August 1971, the Indira-loyalist Siddhartha Shankar Ray sarcastically remarked on the Jan Sangh's history of opposing even the most basic social reforms: 'I understand Shri Vajpayee is a bachelor,' but his partymen had opposed the Hindu Marriage Act in 1955 because they secretly fancied marrying 'a thousand wives'.

given a permanent appointment as hostel warden, in 1970 the college authorities decided to assign the job to faculty members by rotation for briefer periods. Kaul saheb gracefully accepted the decision, but it meant that the family would have to vacate their spacious house. The college arranged alternative accommodation, a three-bedroom flat, a few hundred metres from Ramjas. The family moved without enthusiasm into the new house, even as Kaul saheb continued his hunt for a larger one. Hostelers were obviously sad to see the family leave; now they could not drop in unannounced for a cup of chai, or to request Gunnu to bring pickles from her mother.

Vajpayee had, after Deendayal's death, moved from 30 Rajendra Prasad Marg to 1 Ferozeshah Road – swapping his residence with the Jan Sangh's parliamentary party office. One option for the Kauls was to move into his bungalow; Rajkumari had already been dividing her time between the two places. There were fresh complications too: while the warden's quarters at Ramjas was secluded from public view, Vajpayee – now popular enough to be recognized on the streets – visiting the new flat on the university premises attracted unwanted attention.

Eventually, Kaul saheb reluctantly moved with the family into the MP's bungalow. At the same time, he did not vacate the flat allotted to him by the college. Given Vajpayee's fragile fortunes, he wanted to have a home as back-up. If the Jan Sanghi lost an election tomorrow – or retired from politics, as he was threatening to do – he would have to vacate the bungalow. The celebrity bachelor could easily find another place for himself and Rajkumari, but where would the aging philosophy lecturer go? To take care of his flat, he deputed a Ramjas student to live there. And even though he now took a U-special bus to college, Kaul saheb did not change his university postal address.

With time Vajpayee's definition of family had evolved. As the Jan Sangh's most popular face, he was at all times welcome in Sangh Parivar households across the country. The new MP from Gwalior began to visit his hometown more frequently than before. He took good care of his extended family, helping his grown-up nephews in Gwalior obtain jobs, sometimes even going to the extent of requesting the Scindias to intervene.[62] But while he visited Shinde Ki Chhawni every once in a while, now he did not stay over. Besides basic inconveniences – the road there was not wide enough for a car to pass – he was also emotionally outgrowing the conventional family ties. Now he lived at the spacious house of his friend Narayan Shejwalkar. The Shejwalkars were a well-off Marathi-speaking family of Gwalior: Narayan's father had been Gwalior's RSS sanghchalak in the past; the son had followed his father into the law, but had eventually plunged full-time into politics.[63]

In Bombay he stayed at party worker Ved Prakash Goyal's house. 'He was always simple, undemanding,' recalled Goyal's wife Chandrakanta. Vajpayee never brought up his personal life, but loved playing with the couple's children, who were 'always excited to see Atalji'. At first, their toddler son 'Happy' (Piyush) was terrified of his bodyguard Shivkumar's thick moustache. But as he grew older, Happy became so fond of Atalji that he would often sit in the car and refuse to come out, with the result that he would accompany the Jan Sangh chief on his tours in and around Bombay.[64]

Wherever he went, the local RSS–Jan Sangh network competed to serve him. He was uninterested in money matters as long as his needs were fulfilled. (Vajpayee's only major material possession was an Ambassador car, purchased after the 1969 ulcer operation.) If he needed something, he demanded it. One of his attendants on Bombay trips was Swarup Goyal, who divided his time between running a suiting business and raising funds for the party. Every time Goyal went to meet Vajpayee, the latter would ask: 'Kya laaya hai, Swarup?' Aware of Vajpayee's fondness for bhang, Goyal often brought fresh thandai for him. On one occasion Vajpayee was going abroad, and demanded that Goyal get him a smart suit stitched: 'Suit sila ke do ek badhiya sa, America ja raha hoon.'[65]

Through the same Sangh Parivar network, Shiv Shankar Pareek too had entered Vajpayee's life. A native of Rajasthan, 'Shivkumar' had come to Delhi to practise at the Supreme Court, but continued dabbling with politics on the side. Both of the Jan Sangh's popular presidents had died mysteriously and, as a fan, Shivkumar was worried about the physical security of the new president. The Brahmin Shivkumar fancied himself in the role of a Kshatriya warrior – with his broad chest and thick moustache twirled in the Rajasthani style. Even though he only had a slight acquaintance with Vajpayee, Shivkumar offered to stay with him at all times – as a cross between a secretary and a bodyguard.

Vajpayee dodged the suggestion, saying he was a bachelor who had chosen a life of public service. If he was destined to die a horrific death, he would embrace it gracefully: 'Maut aani ho toh aa jaayegi. Parantu akaal mrityu ho, usmein aap kya karenge?' When Shivkumar persevered, he refused again, though he was moved by the gesture. Hoping to deter Shivkumar, Vajpayee said: 'Look, I cannot afford to pay you, nor can the party.' When Shivkumar insisted that he would serve as an unpaid volunteer, the celebrity president relented.

For the next four decades, Shivkumar would follow him everywhere like a shadow. Apart from being a secretary and bodyguard he also, when required, acted as Vajpayee's cook, driver, election campaigner. But the boss always treated the unpaid employee with dignity. He would introduce Shivkumar as a young lawyer who had sacrificed a thriving practice to assist him: 'Supreme Court ke vakeel hain, mere saath lage huwe hain.'[66]

For a while, hardliners had been incoherently grumbling about Vajpayee taking on too many roles. The president had often quelled such protests by declaring his desire to retire from electoral politics, saying he had completed fifteen years in parliament and would not seek re-election. He would rather 'devote himself to organisational work' in the party. Though barely in his late forties, his health was deteriorating, and he had been advised by doctors to travel less often. For many years he had also unsuccessfully tried 'to do some writing' and now hoped that being a backroom worker would fetch him more time for his literary pursuits.[67]

After his stomach ulcer resurfaced, Vajpayee underwent another major operation at AIIMS in early October 1972. As he recovered, he began to actively persuade colleagues to let him step aside from the presidentship, though he was keen to continue as the party's leader in parliament.[68] Hoping to make a bid for the top job, the Gwalior Rajmata joined the party formally, at long last giving up her independent kingmaker stance.

But despite their deep affection and gratitude for the Scindias, the senior leadership felt that her feudal past would prove to be unwanted baggage. Two back-to-back electoral showdowns – the abolition of privy purses being one of the key issues – were proof enough.

Obsessed with the right image and symbols, the party eventually chose a compromise candidate: the wiry, spectacled and rapidly balding L. K. Advani. The amiable, hard-working Sindhi refugee, now forty-six, had quietly moved up the ladder. After assisting Vajpayee with his parliamentary work during 1957–62, he had done brief stints as an editor of *Organiser*, president of the Delhi Jan Sangh, and chairman of the Delhi Metropolitan Council during 1969–70. Advani had been rewarded with a Rajya Sabha seat in 1970. He had also taken time out to get married and had, unlike most pracharaks, a stable emotional life. With his unique curse – the lack of a homeland, and thus the absence of a sizeable Sindhi vote bank anywhere in the country – he also did not threaten anyone's personal ambitions. At the Kanpur annual session in early February 1973, Vajpayee readily handed over the charge to his lieutenant.

Asked about his five-year-long stint, though, the outgoing chief had 'mixed feelings in my heart'. He felt 'light at being relieved from a massive responsibility, but also a bit strange'. Referring to the electoral debacles, he said maybe his stars were not aligned well: 'Now that I am no longer the President, I am sure Jan Sangh will once again see better days.'[69] Vajpayee's answer, when asked for suggestions on the party's future, was a reminder of the Jan Sangh's never-ending intellectual confusion: 'People at the receiving end of social discrimination and economic exploitation will be staking their claims sooner than later. If we can align ourselves to their interests, we will be able to rejuvenate the country based on Indian value systems.'[70] How exactly were Indian value systems, which had for centuries resisted the idea of equality and justice, going to tackle caste-class discrimination? Predictably, while the conference devoted three hours to a debate on what should be done 'to end the disability of Harijans', there were tense exchanges about the party moving too far away from its traditional moorings.[71]

With the external frontier peaceful, the conference devoted its attention to the economic situation. The oldest agent provocateur lambasted his colleagues for the leftist turn the party had been taking. On 7 February, Madhok submitted to the working committee an elaborate note accusing the party of 'deviating from its principles, the leadership of being gutless, and the organisational structure as being undemocratic and boss-ridden'. During the discussions, he argued that the Jan Sangh's role in Indian politics was that of a rightist party and on economic matters there was not much difference between the policies espoused by Swatantra and those of the Jan Sangh. On this Madhok was unanimously opposed by the General Council. Feeling humiliated and cornered, he left Kanpur in a huff, but not before leaking his note of dissent to the press.[72]

Responding two days later, Vajpayee declared that Madhok was alone among the party elders in his desire to opt for economic rightism (in reality, many delegates, including some maharajas, shared this desire). As earlier, Vajpayee ridiculed the idea of a merger with the Swatantra: the Jan Sangh would not function 'as a lobby for vested interests'; and while it was opposed to concentration of economic power in the hands of the state, it did not subscribe to a market-based economy, where the state confined itself to looking after law and order. In a vast country like India, with its complex problems, the state had to intervene in the economy's management.[73]

By now Madhok's relationship with his party colleagues had broken beyond repair. After losing the 1971 Lok Sabha election, he had gone back to his old ways. With more time on his hands, he was writing books and columns, dangerously injuring the Sangh Parivar's credentials in public. He would tell everyone that the 1971 election had been rigged by Mrs Gandhi with help from the USSR.* And that Vajpayee was one of the rare 'Soviet-approved candidates' from the opposition allowed to win, whereas deserving ones like him lost. Even Madhok's well-wishers in the party thought this a serious flight of imagination.[74]

The most lethal was a story from mid-1972. It was about a notice from the Income Tax Department sent to the RSS headquarters demanding

---

* He had floated a grand theory about chemicalized ballot papers that had an invisible stamp of the Congress (R)'s cow-and-calf symbol which became visible after a few days, even as the chemical made the stamp placed by voters at the booths disappear – contributing to Mrs Gandhi's two-thirds majority.

income tax on its 'guru dakshina' collections. The IT notice had unnerved most of the RSS leaders, and Golwalkar apparently directed Vajpayee to use his influence and see that the notice was withdrawn. Vajpayee met Mrs Gandhi twice and promised a softened RSS attitude towards the ruling party on the condition that the notice be rescinded.[75]

Madhok threatened to expose the matter to the assembled delegates at Kanpur. There may have been some truth to the story, but they would have been fatal to the cadre's morale as well as the party's fast-sagging public image. By the time the party met in Kanpur, Madhok's expulsion looked certain; even his supporters were now fed up of his fratricidal ways.

After he left the annual session mid-way, the party slapped a show-cause notice on him. Advani dropped him from his new working committee. There ensued a protracted correspondence between Advani and Madhok. Far from bridging the communication gap, it led to more name-calling and countercharges. 'Your inflated ego has clouded your judgement,' Advani wrote to Madhok in his final letter on 13 March 1973. The next day Madhok was, after nearly five years of confrontation, expelled from the party.[76] Asked about this at a press conference, Vajpayee responded that the 'Madhok chapter is closed now forever'.[77]

Balraj Madhok's awkward attempts in the future to rehabilitate himself would prove futile. All his life he would curse the RSS, Vajpayee especially, for using 'the boneless wonder' Advani (who had 'no constituency nor independent opinion') to throw him out of a party he had helped birth.[78] His unacknowledged life would be enlivened occasionally by the publication of books – including a three-volume memoir, in which he gleefully mixed facts with fiction, pausing occasionally to declare himself a saint crucified.

A more consequential generational shift was underway at the Sangh Parivar high command. Over the last few years, Golwalkar had occasionally attempted getting in touch with Mrs Gandhi.[79] But like her father – and unlike Shastri – she was unresponsive to the effort of the intermediaries. In early 1970, the RSS chief noticed a lump on the left side of his chest. He consulted doctors only after the lump swelled up further, causing him pain. A biopsy revealed that he was suffering from chest cancer; the doctors advised immediate operation. Atal learnt about it when Guruji was about to be operated upon in Bombay.

Hardly 10 per cent of the Sangh swayamsevaks were thirty years or older, which meant they had not even been born when Golwalkar took total control of the organization: he had helped set up from scratch a major political party and a wide range of other affiliates.* There was an impression in the minds of many pupils that Guruji was a god incarnate, that he possessed divine powers. His hagiographers had informed the readers of Guruji's ability to withstand prolonged hunger, high fever and even a scorpion sting.[80] As in Atal's case, such myths had spread easy and wide, helped by the Sangh's strategic employment of secrecy and misinformation.

But the news of a potentially fatal ailment, the news that Guruji was not after all above mortality and old age, could not be hidden forever. Presently the mouthpieces played down the severity, saying the tumor was only 'skin-deep'.[81] In private the doctors insisted that he had no more than three to five years. Soon, the illness incapacitated the RSS chief, making it impossible for him to travel. There arrived a morning when he could not even walk outside his room to offer the prayers along with fellow residents of Hedgewar Bhawan – a ritual he had performed every day since taking over as the RSS chief three decades ago.

In late May 1973, he began feeling breathless due to inflammation in his lungs. He warned everyone that the 'last bell was tolling'. Atal rushed to Nagpur, where he was surprised to see that Guruji still had a sharp memory and was playfully attentive. When tea was served, Guruji recalled that Atal's ulcer would prevent him from drinking any: 'Atal chai nahi peeta, doodh lao,' he asked the server. The disciple noticed that Guruji's feet were swollen: 'I moved my hands towards his feet, so I could press them a bit' – a gesture of affection. He refused: 'Iski aawashaykta nahi.'[82]

* This included the ABVP (1949), Vanavasi Kalyan Ashram (1952), BMS (1955), and the Vishwa Hindu Parishad (1964).

Later that day, when Guruji was unable to breathe, he had to be put on oxygen support. Atal had barely returned to Delhi that night when he was informed of Guruji's passing. The next morning, an aircraft from Delhi flew all the seniormost Sangh Parivar leaders to Nagpur for a last darshan of the man who had been their supreme authority since 1940. His mortal remains were consigned to the flames in the presence of 30,000 people.[83] At a condolence ceremony organized in Delhi, Atal sat morosely in a corner. Guruji had lived his life like Bhishma in the Mahabharata, he told a newsman, his eyes welling up; like Bhishma, he was granted death at a time of his choosing.[84]

Whereas Hedgewar declared Golwalkar his successor barely a few minutes before he died, this time the choice had been settled months in advance. It was to be Balasaheb Deoras, the general secretary since 1964, whom Atal knew well as the elder brother of his mentor Bhaurao.* In fact, Balasaheb had himself spent some time in UP as a young pracharak. Between the two siblings they held considerable sway, and so it came as no surprise when Atal and his colleagues in UP and Bihar successfully backed the elder Deoras' claim. As Golwalkar faded, Balasaheb gradually took over his decision-making tasks.

In contrast to Golwalkar's short frame and flowing beard, the incoming RSS chief was taller, broad-chested, clean-shaven. Looking at his handsome build and appearance of good health, one could not guess that Balasaheb was, at a relatively young age of fifty-five, severely diabetic. For long he had had a slightly tense relationship with Guruji – especially on the matter of how deeply the RSS and its affiliates ought to involve themselves with the Jan Sangh. Golwalkar's unfulfilled wish

---

* Even though Balasaheb's resume had a major flaw – during 1948–50, in the wake of the crackdown following Gandhi's assassination, the Deoras brothers had left the RSS and started a shop in Nagpur – he had rehabilitated his image and outshone rival pracharaks like Eknath Ranade, the chief of the Vivekanand Rock Memorial Society, who had been away from organization duties for very long; Dr Bhai Mahavir, whose Rajya Sabha membership and outsider status as a Punjabi in an organization where few non-Maharashtrians occupied the top positions, marred his chances; and especially Madhavrao Muley, a personal favourite of the outgoing chief, who had served as the organizer of the North-Western zone at the time of partition.

had been simply to be appointed as the rajguru, advisor, to the prime minister. His successor was instead desperate to play kingmaker. Unlike Golwalkar, Balasaheb had no interest in spirituality, nor did he put on any intellectual airs: he was an out and out political beast. Though he had limited control over running the Jan Sangh, the incoming RSS chief encouraged other affiliates to feel their way through political movements. Which, at a time like this, meant stepping on a landmine.

33. Vajpayee and Nanaji Deshmukh at a conference of the party's women's wing

34. Women of the Bombay Jan Sangh greet the party president with a chandan teeka at the 1969 session.

35. Embracing Gandhi's fads but none of his virtues: the Organiser *cover on the Mahatma's centenary*

36. Vajpayee (sitting, left) at a 1971 party rally in Calcutta in support of Bangladesh's independence

37. 'Is this democracy?' A plane hovers above Boat Club to disrupt Vajpayee's 1971 campaign rally.

38. Sit-in at Gadra to protest the return of such territories captured during the 1971 war

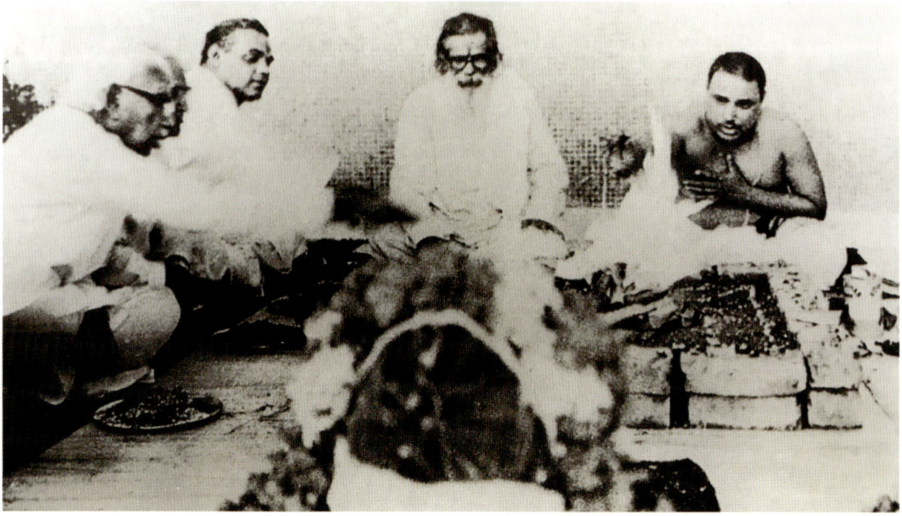

39. Atal with a cancer-ridden Guruji at a yagna to lay the foundation for the Deendayal Research Institute, Delhi, 1972

40. The Jan Sangh's cold feet over appointing Vijaya Raje Scindia as the president cleared the way for the compromise candidate, L. K. Advani. R to L: Advani, Scindia, Vajpayee

41. Feeding the multitudes at the 1973 Kanpur session, where Madhok's fratricidal ways stole the limelight

42. Riding a bullock cart to Parliament in November 1973 to remonstrate the rise in the price of petrol

43. The incoming RSS chief Balasaheb Deoras felicitates the Sangh Parivar's most popular face on his fiftieth birthday in December 1974.

44. JP at the 1975 session: 'If the Jan Sangh is fascist, then I too am a fascist.'

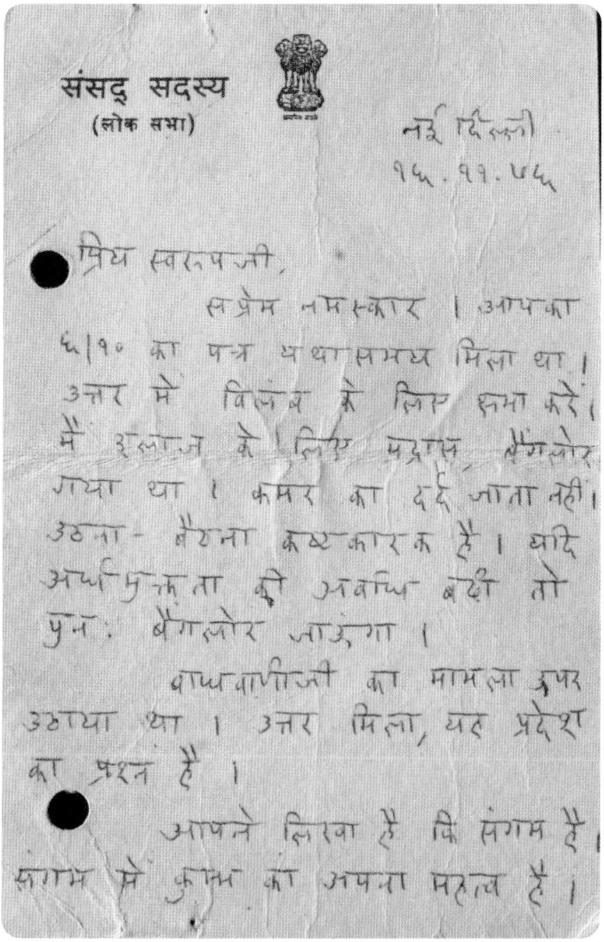
संसद् सदस्य
(लोक सभा)

नई दिल्ली
१५.११.७६

प्रिय स्वरूपजी,

सप्रेम नमस्कार। आपका ५/१० का पत्र यथासमय मिला था। उत्तर में विलंब के लिए क्षमा करें। मैं इलाज के लिए मद्रास, बैंगलोर गया था। कमर का दर्द जाता नहीं। उठना-बैठना कष्टकारक है। यदि अर्धमुक्तता की अवधि बढ़ी तो पुन: बैंगलोर जाऊंगा।

वाधवाणीजी का मामला ऊपर उठाया था। उत्तर मिला, यह प्रदेश का प्रश्न है।

आपने लिखा है कि संग्राम है। संग्राम में कुम्भ का अपना महत्व है।

45. (a) and (b) November 1976: Letter to a 'MISA detenue, Arthur Road Central Jail'. The postcard, brief and tangential, was a typical means of correspondence during the Emergency.

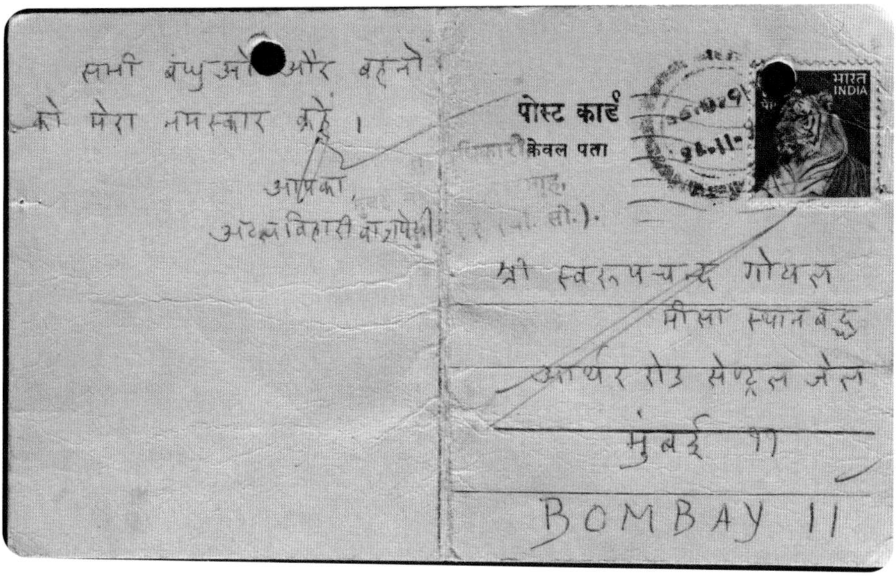
सभी बंधुओं और बहनों को मेरा नमस्कार कहें।

आपका,
अटलबिहारी वाजपेयी

पोस्ट कार्ड
केवल पता

भारत INDIA

श्री स्वरूपचन्द गोयल
मीसा स्थानबद्ध
आर्थर रोड सेण्ट्रल जेल
मुंबई ११
BOMBAY 11

46. March 1977: Anxiety and excitement on the eve of the Janata Party's swearing in; Vajpayee stayed mostly quiet. L to R, sitting: JP, Kripalani, Desai, Vajpayee

47. The external affairs minister on his first day in office on 26 March 1977

12

1974: A Reactionary Revolution

JUST WHEN SHE HAD EVERYTHING UNDER HER THUMB, INDIRA GANDHI began to fall apart. The nationalization of industries for political (rather than economic) reasons had drained resources. Being capital-intensive, they produced few jobs. India's industrial output grew sluggishly. The two wars had imposed financial burdens, worsened by America suspending economic aid. Soon after, an erratic monsoon had led to food shortage, met partly by high-priced grain imports.[1] The government printed money to finance its expenditures, which led to a price rise – 20 per cent for necessary goods – affecting the poor majority. It had no money to finance its 'Garibi Hatao' promises.

Her attempts at social reform fared worse. In contrast to China and East Asian countries, India had criminally neglected investment in education and health. And despite constitutional amendments and high-flying rhetoric in Delhi, implementing land reforms in rural areas had proved impossible. The age-old Hindu equilibrium tired out Indira's radical coterie (those like Mohan Kumaramangalam, the Cambridge-educated minister of steel and mining).[2]

During the winter of 1972–73, Vajpayee travelled to agitate across the country – on rising prices, growing unemployment, galloping corruption. The citizenry 'could no longer be fed empty slogans'.[3] In Delhi, he sat on dharnas (twice outside the prime minister's residence), led walkouts from parliament (after being disallowed adjournment motions). He was arrested twice.

The food situation was deteriorating everywhere. Often fair-price shops had no stock, while the government had banned the sale of wheat in the open market. At many places, such as Sinnar in Maharashtra, crowds looted the ration shops, and the police retaliated by firing. Speaking at Shivaji Park in the last week of April 1973, Vajpayee expressed his solidarity with the looters: 'If the government cannot give food, it is no crime for the people to break shops.'[4] In parliament, he complained that the rations offered to cardholders in Maharashtra were 'not enough even as sparrow feed'.[5] On another occasion, he pulled out a packet containing a sample of the rations issued at Gadra Road in Rajasthan to illustrate the poor quality of supplies.[6]

Corruption permeated every layer of public life. Sometimes, the Congress MPs and MLAs were selling food grains meant for ration shops in the black market. Vajpayee relished narrating the story of a chief minister who complained to Mrs Gandhi that 'his government had to pay to the Food Corporation of India Rs 35 for every truck of foodgrains'. While the chief minister was grateful to the centre for its food grains, he did not know how to account for the bribe.[7]

Soon, corruption and nepotism took hold in the prime minister's own household. A day after her younger son Sanjay turned twenty-six, in mid-December 1972, the opposition demanded a debate on his pet project to manufacture small cars in the country: he had set up a factory in Gurgaon, a village on the outskirts of Delhi.[8] Vajpayee alleged that Sanjay had been allotted land, raw materials (steel and coal), telephone connections even, at dirt-cheap rates.* Maruti Limited was in fact 'corruption unlimited'.[9] By turn, the ministers of industry as well as defence production brushed aside the charges, claiming cockily there was 'nothing shady' about the Maruti's transactions.[10]

The outcry died down until March 1973, when the opposition dug up a graver substantiation. There was an ammunition depot near the site,

* In a well-researched speech, Vajpayee accused the Haryana government of cheating the Gurgaon farmers while acquiring more than 300 acres of land for Maruti. As against the market rate of ₹40,000 per acre, they were paid barely ₹11,000. And the speed at which Maruti secured 6,000 tonnes of steel and thirty-five rakes of coal was nothing short of a miracle.

and the land had been allotted to the prime minister's son – in violation of the Works of Defence Act – ignoring objections from the authorities. The opposition raised privilege motions against two union ministers for having deliberately misled the house earlier, the rejection of which led to walkouts once again.[11] Vajpayee demanded an enquiry, otherwise 'people would assume there was something fishy'.[12] No enquiry was held. Mrs Gandhi accused the opposition of maligning her through her son.

Simultaneously, the two sides brawled over the appointment of A. N. Ray as Chief Justice of India, superseding three judges senior to him. It was a political decision to further the cause of a 'committed judiciary', whereas the unbroken convention had been to elevate the seniormost judge of the Supreme Court to the post. On 26 April, Vajpayee sought an adjournment motion charging the government with creating an impression that only the judges who favoured it would get rapid promotions.* The speaker refused. The law minister H. R. Gokhale maintained that 'the appointment was fully, in letter and spirit, in conformity with the Constitution'.[13]

The three who were passed over resigned. On 3 May, a conference was held at the Constitution Club in which they were felicitated for 'upholding the principle of an independent judiciary'. In the middle of his speech, Vajpayee took a mock oath mimicking the 'committed' judge: 'Whatever I say shall be according to Mohan Kumaramangalam's social philosophy.'[14] Allowed a discussion in parliament the next day, he packed a strong punch: 'Tomorrow it will be said that the Chief Election Commissioner and the chairman of the UPSC should also have the same social philosophy as the government. Would this rule apply to the armed forces too?' Laws could not be made by a 'galaxy of yes-men', only by an independent judiciary.[15] The ruling party MPs lambasted him as a discredited reactionary: 'Mr. Vajpayee's view has

* There was a personal tinge to Vajpayee's bitterness. In May 1971, he had introduced a private member's bill to amend Article 124 of the Constitution to ensure that the seniormost judge of the Supreme Court was made the chief justice. His motion was prescient, but the bill did not get priority and it came up for debate thirty months too late, in November 1973. Then again, when the bill was put to vote, the Congress and CPI came together to crush it.

been overthrown by the people, he has no right to express his opinion in this House.'[16]

A global oil shock towards the end of the year aggravated the economic situation. After the fourth Arab–Israeli war in October 1973 – which Israel won, though less spectacularly than on previous occasions – the Organization of Arab Petroleum Exporting Countries doubled the price of crude oil in a punitive move against the West, who were considered Israel's backers. India, which supported half of its crude oil requirements with imports from the Arab world, had been steadfast against Israel all along, but became an unintended recipient of the OPEC's ire. The government responded by passing an ordinance, almost doubling the price of fuels.

After fighting two wars, the non-communist opposition frequently slammed the government for its refusal to extend diplomatic relations to Israel: if Arab countries can be friends with our enemies Pakistan and China, they argued, why should India continue to shun Israel (out of an imaginary fear of offending native Muslims)? In September 1967, three months after the Six-Day War, Vajpayee had travelled to Israel as a state guest on a goodwill visit. He was keen to understand Israel's remarkable victory over the numerically superior Arab nations.[17] Meeting politicians and army commanders, he was told that Israel would be happy to establish trade ties even without insisting on diplomatic relations. He was gratified to see that, just as there was a 'very strong current of support' in India for Israel despite the official stand, there was equal support for India 'over the Kashmir question and in relation to China and Pakistan', even though Israeli media never openly expressed it.[18]

Whereas in the 1930s the RSS–Mahasabha had admired the totalitarian regimes in Italy and Germany, by the mid-1960s they were awestruck by the economic successes of Japan and, especially, Israel. In the psychological universe of Hindutva, India and Israel shared a common enemy: Islam. The way Jews in Israel had resurrected their language, Hebrew, was an inspiration for Sanskrit and Hindi zealots. At the peak of the language debate, Vajpayee had responded to Annadurai in the Rajya Sabha: 'If

Israel can dig up Hebrew from its grave, run its administration in that language, conduct scientific research in that language, there is no reason why we can't develop our 14 languages' without English.[19]

Accompanied by Israeli officials, he had 'walked around the old city of Jerusalem and through the market in Gaza talking to ordinary people, but nowhere did I detect traces of hatred or ill feeling which one expects three months after a war. The man in the street here, Arab and Israeli alike, wants to go about his business.'[20] Vajpayee saw what he wanted to see, even though a mass exodus of Muslims to Gaza during the last two decades had made it a poor, overcrowded city. After spending a week, Vajpayee was convinced that a durable peace was possible only after the Arab countries had 'reconcile[d] themselves to the independence of Israel as a nation'.[21]

Six years and another Arab–Israeli war later, even the progressive left-wing *Economic and Political Weekly* thought there were no clear angels and devils there, and New Delhi issuing 'statements of blind support to Arab actions is not going to win us support either in Arab policymaking or elsewhere.' Vajpayee chipped in: 'By rushing to hold Israel responsible for the present war our Government has destroyed what little possibility there was for the play of constructive diplomacy.'[22] The Jan Sangh working committee met in Rajkot in early November 1973, to castigate the government for pouring 'oil on the leaping flames of inflation'.[23] But in a slight departure from the past, a resolution demanded 'the return of all Israeli-occupied territories to the Arabs', provided Israel was guaranteed the right of sea navigation on all sides.[24]

It took everyone a while to understand the wider consequences of the oil shock. Apart from pushing inflation, it was also going to hurt food production. Hoping to inspire the country into an austerity drive, Mrs Gandhi made some token appearances around the capital in a Victorian-style buggy. In response, the Jan Sangh decided to demonstrate against her in its own pastoral way. On the opening morning of the parliament's winter session, Vajpayee climbed onto a bullock cart at the party's parliamentary office at Rajendra Prasad Marg. Following the cart drawn by two white bullocks were Advani and a dozen-odd other MPs, each of whom rode a bicycle and carried placards protesting the recent increase in petrol and kerosene prices (the latter was now used widely in rural India for lighting and cooking). Workers carrying the Jan Sangh's saffron flags and shouting slogans made up the rear of the procession, which took about twenty-five minutes to cover the one-kilometre distance to Parliament House. There were jams along the route, holding up the morning's peak-hour traffic. The processionists were stopped at the parliament's entry gate, but Vajpayee entered the portico in his bullock cart. Inside parliament, the government was interrogated on the propriety of raising fuel prices through an ordinance when the house was due to meet only a week later.[25]

Widely adjudged India's worst year since independence, 1973 ended with another spectacle. To commemorate the silver jubilee of Independence, the government had engraved a 'time capsule' to be buried in the foreground of the Red Fort. The opposition demanded to be shown the contents of the capsule. Vajpayee was certain that it did not say kind things about him or his ideological predecessors. A few weeks ago, releasing a book on the life of V. D. Savarkar in Pune, he had declared Savarkar to be the 'greatest personality of the last 100 years', whose prescience on the need for adequate militarization had been proven by the four wars since 1947. Vajpayee was confident that the capsule did not mention Savarkar's contribution: 'Is it not a matter of shame?'[26]

When the government declined to reveal the contents, Vajpayee and the Congress (O) leader S. N. Mishra threatened to dig up the capsule. On the morning of 23 December, the duo addressed a crowd at the Red Fort calling the capsule 'a fabrication of Indian history'.[27] Watched by a crowd of supporters, they proceeded to dig the earth with pickaxes. They had hardly dug six inches when the police arrived with a warrant for their arrest, on grounds of 'breach of peace'. After being released later that day, Vajpayee was adamant about making another attempt to dig up the offensive capsule.[28] (A satirical columnist suggested alternatives to the time capsule that the opposition could use – including a photo album showing Vajpayee's theatrics 'in various poses and at various ages'.[29]) But soon he became weighed down with a responsibility that would for a while keep him away from the Red Fort, and from Delhi.

All through the year, the Jan Sangh had vacillated on whether or not to collaborate with others for the UP assembly elections to be held in early 1974. The Congress (O) and the Socialist Party proposed that Nehru's septuagenarian sister Vijaya Lakshmi Pandit 're-enter politics and confront her niece' by fighting as a candidate of the joint opposition there.[30] Pandit was more than willing, but the BKD and Jan Sangh politely rejected the idea.[31]

The consensus in the Jan Sangh was to go alone and form post-electoral coalitions if necessary. It declined the offer of a common minimum programme with a common flag and symbol.[32] The party was keen on declaring Vajpayee its chief ministerial candidate. The candidate was certain of an anti-Congress wave sweeping the country. Subduing the ruling party in the largest state would be 'a turning point' in India's political history.[33] At the same time, Vajpayee was wary of his own candidature. In private, he whined that it was Nanaji's trap to denigrate him to provincial leadership.[34] He declined to contest the assembly election, for it would have been a demotion for the man who had been sent to parliament as Mookerji's replacement. A mid-way solution was found: he would lead the campaign, but the 'choice of the CM would be made only after the election'.[35]

Releasing the election manifesto in mid-January, Vajpayee vowed to repeat 'Delhi's efficient administration' of 1967–72 in UP.[36] In keeping with its U-turn on unitary states, the Jan Sangh had recently declared UP 'too unwieldy to handle its manifold problems', demanding its break-up into four smaller states.[37] To tackle food shortage, the Jan Sangh came up with a 'dual-pricing policy'.*[38] Perpetually short on funds, the party strained its resources to fight most of the 450 seats. It summoned teams from other states, dispatching them to different parts of UP.[39]

Vajpayee issued appeals for donations, hoping that his party could command 'at least a fraction' of the amount that the ruling Congress had been throwing into the campaign. The Jan Sangh had 'the best candidates

---

* It promised to give the weaker sections wheat, for example, at ₹0.86 a kilogram, at the same time fixing the procurement price from farmers at ₹1.05. Asked how he would raise resources to meet the 19-paise-deficit, Vajpayee naively suggested eliminating corruption and inefficiencies as the solution.

– and the finest workers … We have pitted cycles against their caravans of jeeps – and are getting the better of them … You can help us win many many more seats by sending your donation … Send a minimum of Rs. 11 today. And more, the better.'[40] Shortages in paper and yarn had also made electioneering costlier. Also, whenever the prime minister was passing through an area with a modicum of support for the Jan Sangh, the police tore up the saffron party's flags, banners and posters so that these would not irritate her eyes.[41]

Conscious of its waning popularity, the ruling party cynically deployed government machinery and populist methods. By early December 1973, it announced dozens of development works in the state, sometimes re-laying foundation stones for projects that had been half-completed (such as the bridge over the Ganga near Haridwar).[42] In vain, the Jan Sangh appealed to the Election Commission to ban the inauguration of new projects on the eve of elections.[43] Soon, Vajpayee was complaining that the Congress had collected ₹50 crore from industrialists – vegetable oil manufacturers, textile magnates, sugar mill owners – towards its election funds for the UP and Orissa polls. He undertook to 'substantiate the charge' if an enquiry was set up.[44] Even unbiased observers felt the Congress campaign to be 'dangerously close to unfair practice'.[45] Some minor irritation stemmed from Madhok, whose rag-tag startup Loktantrik Jan Sangh – pitted against the 'fascist' Jan Sangh wrecked by 'communist infiltrators' like Vajpayee – hoped to confuse the Sangh Parivar cadres.[46]

In a departure from convention, some Congress veterans decided to take down Vajpayee personally. Hoping to cast aspersions on his moral character, the UP chief minister Hemvati Bahuguna occasionally titillated his audience with details of Vajpayee's domestic arrangements. Deeply disturbed to find the Kauls dragged into a fracas they had nothing to do with, Vajpayee privately urged the Congress elders to respect boundaries.

A more substantial hatchet job was attempted by the Bombay communist tabloid *Blitz*. Early in his campaign, Vajpayee had visited Bateshwar and, speaking at the annual cattle mela, made exaggerated claims about his role in the Quit India movement. Weaving together some past documents with interviews, the weekly published a story charging Vajpayee with having 'betrayed the 1942 movement'. Filed by an acolyte of Subhadra Joshi, it was timed (26 January 1974 issue) so as to wreck Vajpayee's delicately constructed reputation.

Blitz was accurate about Vajpayee's unheroic role in the sabotage at Bateshwar. But the insinuation that he had 'acted as informer' was factually incorrect.[47] The tabloid was unaware of a documented fact – that Vajpayee had indeed participated in the Quit India protests in Gwalior, as a result of which Babuji had been threatened by the durbar. The Jan Sangh presented its own witnesses to counter-charge *Blitz*'s claims. The party slapped a legal notice, demanding an 'unconditional apology' and further threatening a criminal defamation suit. The case dragged on, but the damage was done. Given how over the years he had inflated his resume, Vajpayee had mostly himself to blame.[48]

By the end of the polls, he was hoping that the opposition might pull off enough seats to form a coalition government.[49] The results proved him only slightly off the mark: the four opposition parties managed a respectable 182 – BKD 106, Jan Sangh 61 – with the Congress (helped by the CPI) winning a slim majority at 231.

But this fourth consecutive electoral reverse broke Vajpayee in some fundamental way. He had downgraded himself by entering state-level politics, and had still been rejected. A few months earlier, he had been asked whether the opposition should start boycotting all elections, since the Congress was anyway going to win. He had responded that despite all its might, in 1971 the ruling party secured less than 50 per cent of the votes, 'so there is no reason to get disheartened'.[50] Now he *was* disheartened, though the Congress had only 32 per cent of votes.

In his reply to the motion of thanks after the president's speech in the Lok Sabha, Vajpayee's bitterness was apparent. He ridiculed parliament as a 'comedy' where a party that received a lower proportion of the votes made laws as per its whims, ignoring the protests of the opposition that had a mandate of over 60 per cent. The same party selected a president who arrived in parliament at the beginning of every budget session by way of a garish ceremony, made a dull speech 'prepared in advance', then returned contented 'to his posh residence'. The discussions that followed too were 'wholly removed from the reality of the lives of the majority of citizens'. The Lok Sabha, envisaged as the house of the people, 'no longer reflects the popular will of masses' but was merely 'a coveted jewel of the power-hungry'.[51]

Having no alternate ideas to offer, the opposition relied on theatrics and outdated slogans. Now they had a slight advantage: lack of social reforms and economic stagnation, coupled with a fast-rising population, meant overcrowded cities filled with unemployed migrant youth. It was a recipe for anarchy. India's problems had over time piled up so high that a credible opposition face, even one devoid of original ideas, could fire up a large-scale movement.

While Vajpayee was busy in UP, in Gujarat a student-led agitation against corruption, inflation and non-availability of grains had forced its Congress government to resign. In the second week of February 1974, Mrs Gandhi had dissolved the assembly and imposed President's Rule in the state. She alleged a conspiracy by participants as disparate as the CIA and the RSS, though it never became clear how deeply either of the two was involved.

Events in Gujarat spurred the Chhatra Sangharsh Samiti, a non-communist opposition group of students, to launch protests in Bihar, hoping for similar results. Here the ABVP – and covertly the RSS, encouraged by its new boss Balasaheb Deoras – played a prominent role. On 18 March, clashes with the police in Patna killed three students. The veteran Gandhian socialist Jayaprakash Narayan was persuaded by the CSS to give up his neutral stance in favour of leading their movement. So did his old friends – the celebrated Hindi poet Ramdhari Singh Dinkar, and Ramnath Goenka, owner of the *Indian Express,* who had debuted in politics by winning the 1971 general elections, with the Jan Sangh's support, from Vidisha.*

* Dinkar, who had previously been a critic of the Sangh Parivar, delivered the opening speech at the ABVP's 20th annual session in December 1972. A friend of the Nehru family, he agreed only after Vajpayee convinced him that the 'ABVP has nothing to do with the Jan Sangh. But I saw there many of the party's supporters. I was gratified, however, to witness the enthusiasm and discipline of the Vidyarthi Parishad.' Dinkar naively hoped that 'all

Jayaprakash Narayan was reluctant. JP had been a close friend of Nehru, and was a well-wisher to his daughter 'Indu'. In some of their informal meetings in the early 1970s, JP had lectured Vajpayee on decentralized development (he had a term for it: 'Gandhian socialism'). Only a few weeks ago, he had extracted a promise out of the Jan Sanghi to bridge his communication gap with the government. JP was to be in Delhi in late March, and he wanted to discuss with Vajpayee 'how, as an opposition party, you can help the prime minister and her administration'.[52] This meeting never took place, for JP allowed himself to be persuaded to lead the Bihar agitation.* Obviously any plan that JP came up with had to include the Sangh Parivar.

Dislodging the Congress through ballot box was a futile exercise, but Vajpayee was sceptical of Gujarat- or Bihar-type agitations – which led to civil unrest and violence – as a countrywide model to counter the ruling party. When the general council met at Ujjain in early April, many copies of a resolution proposed by Vajpayee advocating peaceful agitation were torn to pieces by delegates. Ram Prakash Gupta, the former deputy chief minister of UP, and many others demanded a boycott of all elections. Finally Nanaji Deshmukh rewrote the draft, endorsing confrontational tactics, calling for 'action committees' to be set up in all districts by 15 May.[53]

Vajpayee soon gave in to the demand. This had mostly to do with JP, who was now demanding the dissolution of the assembly in Bihar. Things had come to such a pass that, when India exploded an underground nuclear bomb on 18 May, the party's reaction was decidedly restrained, evasive even. Everyone knew that Mrs Gandhi had once again preempted their ultranationalism: 'the nuclear blast has blasted the guts out of Jan Sangh,' a friend of the prime minister noted in her diary.[54] On a trip to Kolhapur, Vajpayee 'praised the Indian atomic scientists for enabling the country to join the club', but was careful not to compliment the prime minister.[55]

---

such forums are a journey towards the national unity'. By some accounts, soon before his death in April 1974, he had applied himself to cajoling JP to lead the anti-Indira movement.

* Goenka also arranged for JP's prostate gland operation in Vellore in April 1974.

The test was 'more of a physics experiment than a workable bomb design'.[56] But worried about international reaction, the government lied, calling it a 'peaceful explosion'. Vajpayee criticized the government for trying to be apologetic: India 'owed no explanation to anyone', especially since each of the superpowers had nuclear arsenals of their own.[57] Besides, 'in view of the Chinese threat India should not bind itself to any commitment that she would not use nuclear energy' for military purposes.[58]

In the summer of 1974 JP, the last hope of the non-communist opposition, attempted to formulate his ideas into a coherent movement. Apart from demanding fresh elections in Bihar – which Mrs Gandhi resolutely opposed – and electoral reforms, it entailed an overarching transformation of national life. On the evening of 5 June, JP addressed a crowd in Patna and called for a grand 'Sampoorn Kranti' – Total Revolution – to rid India of the social, economic, cultural and moral ills that had plagued it since independence.

Even at the launch, confusion reigned among his key supporters about the exact blueprint and stages of this non-violent Gandhian movement. Moreover, was the septuagenarian leader suffering from multiple ailments going to live long enough to be able to steer his abstract ideas to fruition? A more fundamental paradox was the location of the movement in Bihar. The state's upper-caste elites, from whom came many of JP's supporters, had little interest or incentive to change the status quo. Bihar's failure at land redistribution since independence was adequate indication of the state's refusal to accommodate even a modicum of social justice. How then was Sampoorn Kranti to be achieved?

The Sangh Parivar was divided about JP's movement.[59]* Vajpayee was

* When K. N. Govindacharya, a young pracharak in Patna, chirpily explained JP's lofty vision to Balasaheb Deoras, the new Sangh Parivar honcho snapped saying Govindacharya was being over-optimistic: 'Dekho, itna sab kuch nahi niklega'. However, Deoras conceded that if JP managed to put some social deterrents on the conduct of politics, that itself would be a mammoth contribution.

convinced that 'JP has emerged as the symbol of people's revolt against a barren political system', a 'revolutionary situation is developing just now in India', and 'with a constructive approach, the country can be lifted out of political and economic morass and slough of despondency'.[60] By early August 1974 he had, in consultation with JP, devised a tentative three-tier programme for the opposition.

First, the opposition should make optimum use of parliament. This meant no frequent disruption of parliamentary procedures: 'Even a weak opposition can keep the ruling party on its toes if the members do their homework properly and are vigilant to exploit the opportunities.' Second, they had to simultaneously mobilize the 68 per cent of masses who had voted against the ruling party, for a prolonged war of attrition through civil disobedience and no-tax campaigns.[61] Third, constructive programmes had to be put before the people – as was done in the Gandhian struggle for independence.[62]

In the second week of September, 250 Jan Sangh workers selected from across the country met in Hyderabad for a five-day study camp. The idea was to brainstorm how to put these vague ideas into practice and prepare the party for a peaceful but long-term confrontation with the establishment. Both Advani and Vajpayee claimed that the Jan Sangh was 'not looking for shortcuts to power, the petty politics of jockeying for a few seats here and there'.[63]

For the first time Vajpayee invoked Gandhi in a positive light. Was this exhibition and opportunism, or a genuine change of heart? The primacy of society over state had been an overlapping theme between the otherwise polarized worldviews of Gandhi and the Sangh Parivar. But it is difficult to ascertain the extent of Vajpayee's commitment. In the absence of basic rights, how was 'love and service' in semi-feudal rural India, with its economy in tatters, going to fetch the poor land, employment, dignity? Vajpayee may not have been insincere, but what of the many Sangh Parivar elders, upper-caste conservatives, who privately squirmed at JP's naive fantasies of a bloodless revolution?

Back from Hyderabad, Vajpayee undertook a five-day tour of Bihar. Beginning on 2 October, the Mahatma's birth anniversary, the demand for the dissolution of the assembly was to be intensified into a three-day

Bihar bandh. In Patna, Vajpayee warned the protestors against blasting rail tracks and roads: 'Any change brought about with the help of violence was short-lived and required violent means to sustain it.'[64] He left for the districts, addressing meetings to spread JP's message.

On 24 September, Vajpayee was arrested in Motihari. He had sought permission to meet the Jan Sangh workers arrested under the controversial MISA – Maintenance of Internal Security Act, 1971 – at Motihari jail. Permission was granted, but when he came out after meeting the detenus, he himself was served with an order of detention.* Soon after, a group of demonstrators protesting his arrest were caned and Section 144 CrPC imposed upon the sleepy town.[65] Vajpayee was kept as an X-category prisoner – 'prisoner of a more dangerous type' – in a cell where there was no light or fan or latrine. At 11 p.m., he was just preparing to sleep when an order arrived that he was to be transferred to Hazaribagh jail 400 kilometres away. The journey, in a private rickety bus, lasted fifteen hours, where there was little space to stretch one's legs. Vajpayee's most recent ailment had been a slipped disc, for which he had recently undergone traction treatment at AIIMS.[66] He had been strictly advised against long journeys.

Hazaribagh jail shocked Vajpayee. He met undertrials who had been rotting inside for years – some for petty crimes like stealing fruits, while blind men had been charged with murder and dacoity – without any hopes of being presented before a magistrate in near future. It was considered a model prison, but Vajpayee found it crowded and lacking in elementary facilities. Thankfully he was released the next afternoon. On his way back, he addressed press conferences in Patna and Delhi: the 'law of the jungle' prevailed in Bihar's jails, he lamented; why else would a civilized government treat a political prisoner like himself as a criminal?[67]

---

* There was to Vajpayee's arrest in Motihari an absurd irony. Motihari (earlier Champaran) had been the site of Mahatma Gandhi's first major satyagraha against colonial rule. Now, the ruling party proclaiming 'non-violent radicalism' was haphazardly caning protestors, arresting them under MISA. The protestors themselves belonged to a school of thought that had been implicated in the Mahatma's murder, but were now championing a non-violent total revolution.

A few weeks later, with Vajpayee away in Tokyo on a parliamentary delegation, the Bihar bandh became a tremendous success. The protest moved to the Patna secretariat on 4 November. Three days prior, in the course of a long meeting in Delhi, Mrs Gandhi had offered to dissolve the Bihar assembly, provided JP did not demand the pulling down of yet another state government.[68] JP refused what was in fact a sincere effort at compromise by the prime minister. Vajpayee was 'glad that the talks had failed': this would give JP the chance to show the strength of his movement.[69]

On 4 November JP, accompanied by Nanaji Deshmukh, was on his way to the secretariat when his jeep was attacked by a posse of policemen. The lathis hit him thrice, on his left ribs and right arm. Before they could do further damage, Nanaji came forward to shield JP.[70] The Bihar Congress chief, Sitaram Kesri, privately confessed that 'had something happened to JP, it would have hurt the Congress as much as Gandhi's death had hurt the RSS and Jan Sangh'.[71] The next day, photos of a collapsing JP and Nanaji fending off the lathis appeared prominently on the front pages of many newspapers. Except that most of the captions did not name Nanaji, who, despite being a Sangh Parivar powerbroker, was virtually unknown to the media. JP was obviously moved by the gesture, and it certainly helped the Jan Sangh win his trust.

During the parliament's winter session, Vajpayee alleged a Congress conspiracy to assassinate JP.[72] By now Mrs Gandhi had been speaking of JP and Vajpayee together, recklessly calling them fascists, reactionaries, CIA agents. Whatever Vajpayee may have thought about the epithets, he felt honoured to be mentioned alongside JP. As 1974 closed, Vajpayee was certain of 'a mid-term poll before March'.[73] But there were complications.

Seven parties – prominent among them PSP and Swatantra – had recently merged into Charan Singh's BKD: it was now renamed Bharatiya Lok Dal. When JP convened a meeting of the opposition leaders in Delhi during 25–26 November, Charan Singh proposed that the charismatic old man lead them in the elections. JP refused: 'I do not visualise the People's movement as one of a united front of political parties.' But he promised to exert himself to unite the opposition.[74] Vajpayee concurred. Sounding self-deprecatory, he reasoned that the credibility of politicians like him had sunk to an all-time low, whereas 'Jayaprakashji wields a tremendous influence'.[75]

During the winter of 1974, JP was briefly overshadowed by the rakshasa of Licence Raj hitting back at the Congress. The railway minister L. N. Mishra had, in his earlier avatar as foreign trade minister, issued import licences supposedly in exchange for a hefty bribe. In a less crony and more trade-oriented economy, such imports (scientific equipment etc.) should have been freely allowed. For now, the opposition was content to use the import licence scandal to its benefit. Significantly, too, given Mishra's role as the party's fundraiser-in-chief, it was impossible to segregate his personal corruption from his contribution towards the Congress treasury.

With Watergate at the back of his mind, Vajpayee hoped this scandal would similarly lead to high-profile resignations.[76] The government instituted a CBI enquiry, whereas the opposition demanded an all-party parliamentary committee to probe it. Vajpayee derided the agency for being a *Committed* Bureau of Investigation. Independently pursuing the case, he concluded that the CBI was colluding to efface traces of Ram's involvement.[77]

Disenchanted by parliament and enamoured by JP, Vajpayee was more and more tempted to take to the streets. In Rajasthan's Ganganagar on 8 December, he called a press conference announcing his resignation from the Lok Sabha. It was primarily 'to rouse the consciousness of my Congress colleagues', a majority of whom were in favour of a thorough enquiry but lacked the courage to defy the Congress whip.[78] Predictably, Mrs Gandhi's loyalists deemed him 'a sacrificial goat' for the reactionary combine.[79] By and large, however, the press sympathized with him: the parliament 'needs more and not less, men and women of integrity and caliber'.[80]

It was mostly a pressure tactic, for Vajpayee continued to attend parliament. Apparently the party was making up its mind on whether to let him go. The parliamentary board eventually 'declined to permit' him to resign.[81] Prolonging his stunt, Vajpayee was adamant that he was 'not going to contest the next election'.[82]

A week later, L. N. Mishra was blown up by a bomb while inaugurating a railway line in Bihar's Samastipur. The opposition convinced itself that Mrs. Gandhi had got rid of Mishra as he had outlived his utility. On her part, the prime minister blamed the 'cult of violence' sponsored by JP's agitation, going a step further to claim that Mishra's killing had been a dress rehearsal for her own assassination.[83] Vajpayee was pained that even a ghastly tragedy had 'failed to move Congress into introspection'. With the villain dead, the scandal petered out; a bit tragicomically, the opposition now demanded a probe into the Samastipur explosion.[84]

In early 1975, JP and the Jan Sangh agreed on all things urgent except for one: Kashmir. JP had been an early advocate of autonomy for Kashmir within the democratic framework. Dethroned in the wake of Mookerji's death in 1953, Sheikh Abdullah had spent the previous two decades in the wilderness, for the most part either inside a prison or under house arrest. India had fought two wars, and Abdullah knew his best hope now lay in returning as chief minister and bargaining for as much autonomy as was possible. Aided by considerable rigging, the Congress had won a majority in the J&K's previous election. After prolonged negotiations, the two sides finally signed the 'Kashmir Accord'.

Vajpayee's demand for the abrogation of Article 370 was countered in parliament by one of the more eligible participants in the debate. Karan Singh, the son of Maharaja Hari Singh of Kashmir who – notwithstanding his father's secret ties with the RSS – had joined the Congress; he was currently the minister for health. Singh thought Article 370 to be 'a simple problem but Atal Bihari ji has been making heavy weather of it'. The Himalayan state was already integrated with India: '92 out of 97 entries in the Union List and 20 out of 47 entries in the Concurrent List have been extended' to J&K. Abdullah was 'tallest of all the Kashmiris, both figuratively and literally. He is a mass leader of considerable stature', and ought to be trusted. The junior maharaja thought it 'a strange coincidence' that two of the 'most unhappy people after this agreement were Vajpayee and Bhutto'.[85] Vajpayee's demand was whipped 191–8.[86]

The Jan Sangh virtually had no base in the valley; the only three seats it won in the 1972 elections were all in the Jammu region. Vajpayee's recent speech in Srinagar to mark Mookerji's twentieth death anniversary was disrupted by Sheikh's supporters flinging stones at the dais, forcing him to duck.[87] With the negotiations between the centre and Sheikh at an advanced stage, he made an empty threat to begin an agitation. He knew that, with the borders peaceful, it might not pick up momentum. Besides, now the Jan Sangh had, logistically and emotionally, thrown itself at JP's feet, and it would be embarrassing if their differences on Kashmir surfaced in public. A few weeks later, JP was to be the chief guest at the Jan Sangh's annual session in Delhi.

The venue would be a football ground renamed 'Ambedkar Stadium'. A dais was erected against a canvas backdrop showing people on the march and a line from a Ramdhari Singh Dinkar poem: 'Singhasan khaali karo ki janata aati hai' – vacate the throne for the people are arriving.[88] During JP's late November meeting with the opposition, the only proposal unanimously endorsed was to gherao Parliament House and the AIR to present the opposition's demands. The date finally set was 6 March; the annual session was timed to precede it.[89]

The highlight of the session was JP's attendance on the last day. The Gandhian strategically avoided any mention of Kashmir.* At Ambedkar Stadium both sides had a common focal point: uninstalling Mrs Gandhi from office. The Gandhian expressed his gratitude for the support the party had given to his movement in Bihar. Jan Sangh workers had braved lathis and bullets during the movement, he said, and Nanaji had saved his collarbone by deflecting a lathi blow.

But the highlight of JP's seventy-minute address was his effusive verdict on the party's character after having worked with them for one year. JP said the Jan Sangh was neither communal nor reactionary: 'How can any party which had lent its support to a Total Revolution be called reactionary or fascist?' In the heat of the moment, JP went overboard: 'If the Jan Sangh is fascist, then I too am a fascist.'[90]

---

* Abdullah had recently called on JP before leaving for his oath-taking ceremony in Srinagar, and the old friends had hugged each other warmly. In turn, while Vajpayee called for an energetic campaign against caste, dowry and purdah, he had quietly dropped his earlier demand for a uniform civil code.

The next day JP, sitting in an open jeep and draped in spotless white khadi, led a march of nearly a million people from the Red Fort to Parliament House. Senior opposition figures – Vajpayee, Charan Singh, Raj Narain – followed him in three other open jeeps. After addressing the crowd at the Boat Club, where he demanded Indira's resignation, JP and others went into parliament to present the speaker with the seven-point charter of people's demands: electoral, educational, economic and political. Fresh elections in Gujarat and Bihar were among the few pointed demands.[91] Convinced that JP's following was growing by the hour, Mrs Gandhi attempted an awkward reconciliation. She made gestures to revise the electoral laws and dissolve the Bihar assembly. JP refused to talk until all his demands were fulfilled.

All this while, the opposition parties had struggled to fortify their unity. The Jan Sangh had authorized Vajpayee to hold consultations to form a united front in parliament, and to field 'Janata candidates' on a common symbol and an agreed-upon Minimum Programme in all the upcoming elections.[92] The Congress (O), initially adamant on fighting Gujarat alone, was coaxed to give up its anti-alliance stand.[93] Charan Singh wanted nothing short of a merger of the Jan Sangh with BLD, before he would commit himself to anything else. There were other differences too: Vajpayee welcomed JP's suggestion that the front-rank leaders should keep themselves away from elections in order to guide the masses from outside the legislatures. To Morarjibhai and Charan Singh, though, this may have come across as too clever by half. Vajpayee was still young at fifty, but the two septuagenarian leaders had no great desire to end their careers so unceremoniously.

Vajpayee blamed Charan Singh's 'personal ego' as the hurdle for opposition unity although, by not committing to a merger, he was himself responsible too.* The Jan Sangh wanted to avoid a merger to

* At the annual session, Vajpayee again lashed out at the BLD chief: 'A merger could not be ruled out in future, but how could it take place unless the cadres first learn to work together at the grassroots for the JP movement.'

ensure enough room for manoeuvre in a fast-changing situation. Between the Jan Sangh, ABVP and (covertly) the parent body RSS, the Sangh Parivar was providing more sinew and muscle to JP than other opposition groups; they were keen to use it in order to gain maximum advantage for themselves. Vajpayee also wanted to tread slowly because, for all his swank in public, he privately thought there was 'no chance Mrs. Gandhi could be defeated in the next elections'.[94]

In the first week of April 1975, everyone's attention shifted to Morarji Desai. It had been more than a year since President's Rule had been imposed in Gujarat: in Ahmedabad the Congress (O) veteran began an indefinite fast on 6 April, demanding immediate assembly elections. He also pressed the government to revoke the 'national emergency' – especially the Defence of India Rules imposed during the December 1971 war – something Vajpayee too had been demanding for years.*

By the fifth day, the seventy-nine-year-old Morarjibhai's health seriously deteriorated. 'Will you hold the elections in May or let Desai die?' Vajpayee screamed in parliament, as the opposition held up routine work for three hours before walking out.[95] Vajpayee and Advani joined fourteen other non-CPI opposition parties in signing a petition charging the government with discovering 'the convenient pretext of drought for delaying elections' in Gujarat.[96] Arriving in Ahmedabad two days later, Vajpayee warned that if Desai were to die, 'more people would stake their lives' demanding the same.[97] The next day, the government agreed to hold elections in June. A jubilant Vajpayee congratulated Desai on his 'successful' fast.[98]

On 14 April 1975, JP arrived in Delhi to convince the opposition that the time was ripe to dissolve themselves and form a federal party. Attending the meeting on behalf of the Jan Sangh, Vajpayee and Nanaji

* The war had been over in a fortnight and, having signed a treaty in Simla, by August 1974 the government returned the territories captured as well as the POWs. Its excuse was that the country was now going through a severe 'economic emergency'. The opposition argued that the Constitution had a separate provision for economic emergency, Article 360, and that it should revoke Article 352, meant to fight external aggression or internal disturbance. The DIR could be invoked to curb the freedom of speech as well as association and movement of all kinds. Indeed, the government used it to break the railway strike. The makers of the Constitution would not have approved the use of DIR during peacetime.

agreed in principle, but the party's working committee decided to defer its mechanics until after the Gujarat elections.[99] JP may have been hurt by this backstep after his recent endorsement of the Jan Sangh. In one of his subsequent meetings, he doubted whether the Sangh Parivar secretly wished not so much for a social or economic transformation but to simply capture power by dethroning Indira Gandhi. In December 1974, he had expressed similar concerns in Banaras after witnessing the ABVP's desperation to capture the CSS in UP. Of Vajpayee and Charan Singh, he had then rued, 'Total Revolution will come about only when they get the Prime Ministerial throne.' Vajpayee had called it his 'misfortune' not to have won JP's complete trust: 'I don't know how much more effort it would take us.'[100] But these were minor quibbles in a mutually beneficial relationship that promised to deliver results.

During the negotiations on Gujarat seat distribution, the Jan Sangh, BLD and Socialist Party acquiesced to playing junior partners to the Congress (O). The crucial difference was that on previous occasions, each party had fielded its candidates without consulting others. This time the senior leadership of the front sat together to unanimously select candidates. In case of conflicts, the final decision was left to Morarji.[101] Unlike the 1971 alliance, the Janata front now had a common programme.

By mid-May, every major leader was touring Gujarat. Wherever she went, Mrs Gandhi attracted the largest crowds. In her eleven-day tour, she covered almost every constituency in the state.[102] She toned down her radical slogans, relying instead on the need for a stable government.[103] Often she attacked the Jan Sangh: its involvement in riots; the RSS's training of young boys in wielding lathis and knives; she mocked Vajpayee as a soapbox orator who knew nothing about running an administration.[104] The Congress campaign in Baroda used cinema slides at local theatres. Intended to portray the government's achievements, the ads also named India's enemies: Vajpayee stood shoulder to shoulder with Bhutto, BLD's Piloo Mody was paired with Mao.[105]

JP was the crowd's second favourite. Then came Vajpayee, who had used every occasion to advertise his decision to not contest the next Lok Sabha: India's fate was to be decided on its streets now, not in parliament.[106] Travelling together on some occasions, JP briefed his listeners that he was leaving some tricky subjects for the Jan Sanghi to handle, 'for it seems to me that goddess Saraswati sits on his tongue'.[107] Close on Vajpayee's heels came the native son Morarjibhai, who had in the recent past struggled to pull large crowds.[108]

Early in his campaign, Vajpayee was presented a purse of ₹11 lakhs in Bombay raised by the local Jan Sangh – a sign that the party's participation in the JP movement had swung its morale upwards. In Bombay, Vajpayee claimed that the Congress had raised money from the jailed gangster Haji Mastan to finance its campaign. Everywhere Vajpayee refuted the prime minister's charge that the Janata front was attempting the revival of the SVD or the Grand Alliance: there would be no repetition of past mistakes; soon after the Gujarat win the front was going to be merged into a single party.

Often, he ridiculed the nationalization of banks. He demanded that a commission be set up to inspect their bad debt write-offs at the instance of VIPs.[109] With new information on the Maruti controversy, Vajpayee accused Mrs Gandhi of using her office to further her incompetent son's business prospects. The chiefs of Punjab National Bank and the Central Bank of India had been fired for their refusal to bail out Maruti – which had so far not produced even a single car – by sanctioning fresh loans. There was some truth to the accusation, for Vajpayee's Baroda speech on Maruti, issued by three news agencies, was killed on the orders of I&B minister V. C. Shukla.[110]

As earlier, he occasionally passed off casual sexism as good-natured banter. At some of Mrs Gandhi's rallies, the crowd had hurled stones at the dais. Alluding to the prime minister's Gujarati-style sari drapes and description of herself as a daughter-in-law of the western state, he said, the 'boys who threw stones at her would be her brothers-in-law, she should not mind a few stones'.[111] After winding up his campaign, he was certain of the front scoring a victory, for the climate was 'not only anti-Congress but pro-Janata front'.[112] He may have been less sure in private.

After a month of rough travel, Vajpayee went to Srinagar to cool down, and also to appraise Kashmir under Abdullah. He fell sick there and was convalescing when the result was announced on the afternoon of 12 June: the Janata Front won eleven seats more than the Congress and, after a few weeks of wrangling, managed to form a government.[113]

Three hours later that day, a bigger thunderstorm descended upon Allahabad. Raj Narain, who had lost to the prime minister in 1971 from Raebareli, had filed a case against her in the Allahabad High Court for violating election rules. After months of hearing, the court declared the prime minister's election nullified. This meant she might have to resign. An ecstatic Vajpayee declared she had been 'snubbed by both, her maika [parents' home – Allahabad] and her sasural [in-laws' home – Gujarat].'[114]

Mrs Gandhi was allowed twenty days to appeal in the Supreme Court. Emboldened, Vajpayee shot off a statement from Srinagar asking her to 'resign forthwith' lest people 'rise in revolt'. If the apex court's verdict went in her favour, she would be entitled to return. But to continue in office 'on the ground that the High Court has given a stay order is to take shelter behind the letter of the law, while doing away with its spirit'.[115] Vajpayee called on the President F. A. Ahmed, who was coincidentally also in Srinagar, beseeching him to use his authority to persuade her to step down.[116] Back in Delhi, he joined opposition MPs to call on the Lok Sabha speaker, petitioning him to summon the house to discuss the judgement.

Thereafter, Vajpayee left for Bangalore to attend a meeting of the Joint Select Committee of parliament regarding a legislation against defections. On 24 June, the Supreme Court rejected Indira Gandhi's appeal, giving only a conditional stay. Now there was growing consensus, in the media and even among her party elders, that Mrs Gandhi should step down. In Bangalore that night, Vajpayee assured a crowd at the Town Hall that there was going to be 'no let-up in the opposition demand': Indira Gandhi's fate 'will continue to hang in the air'.[117]

The following day in the capital, the entire opposition (other than the CPI) sat together with JP to plan the next step. A People's Struggle Committee – Lok Sangharsh Samiti – was set up with Morarji as president and Nanaji as convener. Beginning on 29 June, the LSS would mobilize public support to force the prime minister to resign.

In the first week, satyagrahis would gherao her residence and the AIR premises. Overstretching himself in an extra-constitutional move, JP urged the armed forces, police and other public-sector employees to defy government orders, given Mrs Gandhi's refusal to quit office despite adverse court verdicts.[118]

The judiciary and the legislature had sealed her fate. But Indira Gandhi still wielded executive veto, and she acted fast and clever. The conflict had reached its climax. It demanded a resolution.

13

Emergency: The Lion and the Monkey

ON THE MORNING OF 26 JUNE, AT AROUND 7:45, ADVANI BURST into Vajpayee's room at the MLAs' hostel in Bangalore. They were there for the Joint Select Committee meeting along with two other opposition MPs: S. N. Mishra of the Congress (O) and Madhu Dandavate of the Socialist Party. Advani informed Vajpayee of a phone call he had just received from the local party office. Before sunrise, the top opposition leaders – JP, Morarji, Raj Narain – had been picked up by the police. The arrests were to continue; the police could be arriving any moment to apprehend them too. The confirmation came fifteen minutes later when Mrs Gandhi declared emergency on All India Radio. By this time most Sangh Parivar leaders – Nanaji, Bhandari, Thengadi – had hidden themselves.

The four opposition leaders decided to take the next flight to Delhi; perhaps they calculated that it would be better to be locked up in Tihar than in a jail 2,000 kilometres from home. Vajpayee was keen to have some breakfast, before packing up and leaving for the airport. Even as they were eating in the hostel canteen, the Bangalore police arrived. They were all arrested not under the MISA, but under section 151 of the IPC 'for apprehended breach of the peace'. This was a stratagem employed by the police to take them into custody without any arrest warrant or written order.[1]

A local Jan Sangh worker who went to meet them at the hostel found Vajpayee sitting in a chair 'with the benign smile of Ganesh'. Like a tourist 'in search of a good hotel', Vajpayee asked him about the 'best jail' in Bangalore: 'I shall ask the police to take me there.'[2]

The four leaders were taken to the High Grounds police station. Someone brought them a small transistor so that they could listen to updates while in prison. They were made to wait at the police station all day; the state authorities were not sure what kind of detention order was to be slapped on them. Vajpayee was bored but sat stoically. Thousands of his partymen had been arrested or roughed up across the country. In a small town in Madhya Pradesh, for example, a batch of Jan Sangh workers protesting against the imposition of Emergency that afternoon were beaten up. Thereafter, they were commanded by the superintendent of police to take out another procession – this time shouting death to their leaders: 'Jai Prakash–Atal Behari, murdabaad-murdabaad.'[3]

Around 8 p.m., the four leaders were sent to Bangalore Central Jail under Section 3 of MISA. Advani and Vajpayee were to share a large oblong room. The authorities informed them that the recently constructed room had so far not been occupied: Vajpayee–Advani were going to 'inaugurate' it. Vajpayee had in the past spent time inside five jails – Agra, Balrampur, Motihari, Hazaribagh, and Tihar in Delhi. But they had felt more like 'a brief stay at the house of in-laws'.[4] He sensed that this stay was going to be longer.

With state censorship in full swing, the newspapers became dull and insipid overnight. Hardly any had carried the news of Vajpayee's arrest. Soon there would be no mention of opposition leaders at all, as if they had never existed. The four VIP detenus relied on foreign radio broadcasts – BBC, Voice of America, Radio Pakistan even. And it was on the radio that Vajpayee heard, on 4 July, that the RSS had been banned. The Jan Sangh had been spared, but with Vajpayee and Advani in jail and others in hiding, the party had become headless. In a *New York Times* story on the Emergency, a reporter recounted telephoning the Jan Sangh's central office, only to be told: 'I am the clerk. Nobody else is here. They're all in jail.'[5]

With all the time and solitude in the world, Vajpayee read and wrote prose-poems more profusely than ever before. He even gave himself a clever pen name, 'kaidi-kavirai' – the prisoner-poet. For a while, he also documented his stay in the jail:

> 27 June 1975, day one: Borrowed two books from the library – Manto's *Rajo* and *Miss Faria.** Manto is a painter of naked realism. If you are looking to discover an ideal society, you will be disappointed. He shows a mirror, in whose reflection you would see people on the margins – the abandoned, the low-paid, the oppressed. Manto's craft – his storytelling skills, his grip on the subject, his subtle descriptions, his satire, and boldness – they are unmatchable.[6]

Suffering no great personal inconvenience, the prisoners began to settle in. Vajpayee volunteered to supervise the cooking in the jail mess. In his prison diary, Advani praised his old mentor for ensuring that the culinary arrangements were 'as perfect as they can be in a jail. Our food is simple but wholesome and delectable.' Sometimes the four of them played cards. Coming from different ideologies they also, for the first time, exchanged ideas unencumbered by immediate electoral exigencies.[7] Dandavate found the Jan Sangh duo so likeable that he was soon reading literature on the Sangh Parivar by Deendayal Upadhyaya. He wrote to his wife concluding, a tad simplistically, that the Jan Sangh 'are nearer to Gandhi than we, the socialists'.[8]

Mishra, who had seen better days under Nehru as his minister for planning, was perpetually angry at his fate. Yoga helped him stay sane. Harping upon the miracles it had wrought on his body and soul, Mishra convinced Vajpayee to use his time in prison to take up the practice. Except for his routine morning walk, Vajpayee had never been a fitness enthusiast. For an unagile man with a pronounced professorial paunch, and recently hospitalized with a backache, Vajpayee should have taken it slow. Perhaps out of restlessness, he began to attempt a headstand after a few days of his initiation into yoga.† Soon, he developed pain in his

---

* In recent years, Vajpayee had started reading Urdu literature. It was an unusual development if one considers his background: all through his years in journalism, he had shunned words of Arabic origin. 'The ghazals of Ghalib and Bahadur Shah Zafar are as good as anything else in world literature,' he updated *Panchjanya* in February 1973. But he still felt that 'Urdu writers should write in Devanagari script, that way their work would reach many more millions of Indians.'

† More than a decade ago, he had teased Nehru in parliament that the prime minister's opinion of the Jan Sangh was inverted because he spent too much time doing yoga and, especially, standing on his head.

back and the lower part of his abdomen. He went to the jail hospital a few times only to be told that it was nothing serious.[9]

On 10 July, Appa Ghatate came to meet Vajpayee in a lawyer's capacity. Appa was shocked to find his friend in prison clothes. Vajpayee joked: 'Now Indira Gandhi will feed me and give me clothes, I am not going to spend a penny from my pocket.' Appa informed him that most opposition leaders had decided to not file a petition challenging their arrests. He disagreed: 'This is 1975, not 1942. The courts are ours. We must make the judiciary face the acid test.'[10] On behalf of the four VIP detenus, Appa filed a habeas corpus in the Karnataka High Court.

Two days later, Vajpayee felt an acute pain in the stomach after lunch. He was shifted to Victoria Hospital. On the way, he noticed at the Bangalore crossroads billboards of Indira explaining her newly launched twenty-point economic programme. After doctors struggled for a day to diagnose the cause of his pain, the head of surgery at the hospital concluded that he was suffering from acute appendicitis: an immediate surgery was necessary. Things went downhill from here: the doctor who was to operate had a tiff with the anesthetist. During surgery, the colon got accidentally perforated, leading to faecal contamination of the peritoneum. Far from being relieved of his stomach pain, Vajpayee now had hiccups, vomiting and a high fever.

While he lay half-conscious in his bed after the botched operation, the petitions challenging the bona fides of the Emergency and the validity of the detentions were being debated at the nearby High Court. Keen to have the petitions dismissed, Home Minister Brahmananda Reddy had filed an affidavit saying he had personally satisfied himself that the detention of the four opposition leaders was necessary. The attorney general Niren De himself appeared to wage a fierce battle on behalf of the government. But the intrepid Karnataka High Court overruled the government's arguments. The central government decided to move the four VIP prisoners out of its jurisdiction.

On the afternoon of 17 July, the Advani–Dandavate–Mishra trio was packed into a special Air Force plane and hurriedly transferred to Rohtak jail in Haryana. Since Vajpayee was under medical care, the state home commissioner had no choice but to seek medical opinion. The hospital staff may have been willing to oblige with permission to move their patient. But when the bandage over Vajpayee's stitches was removed, it was stained with blood; the wound had not healed. On the insistence of some doctors, he was retained at the hospital.[11]

The next day, an application was filed in the High Court on behalf of Vajpayee, contending that the transfer order was a malafide act. The High Court promptly issued orders restraining the central government from transferring him. Meanwhile at the hospital, Vajpayee was shocked to find that he had been cut up unnecessarily. The pathologist's report showed an 'appendix with normal mucosa'. The cause of Vajpayee's abdominal pain had been the same old slipped disc. The exertion of hectic touring during the JP movement, followed by over-enthusiastic yoga sessions, had exacerbated the old symptoms. He wanted to be transferred to his old retreat, AIIMS. On 6 August, he was brought in a special plane directly to the hospital in Delhi.[12] But with the caveat that after being discharged, the government could detain him 'in any place it deems' appropriate.[13]

At AIIMS, Vajpayee was isolated on the fourth floor of the hospital in room 401, outside which hung a name plate: 'UNKNOWN'. He was soon transferred to room 402 with its smaller windows, lest the VIP attempt to escape – never mind that the kaidi-kavirai was unable to even stand erect. Policemen took turns to guard his room, its windows now fitted with wire netting.

He had few clothes or articles and little money left on him; and complained about not being given newspapers, or even objects of basic personal toilette like oil and soap.[14] When he asked for shaving cream – shaving had come to be one of Vajpayee's non-negotiable daily rituals – he was rebuffed. Why did he need to shave, he was asked – he was not addressing the parliament or a crowd. Family and friends struggled to meet him. The process involved getting clearances from both the Home Ministry and the PMO before the file could be sent to the Additional District Magistrate's office for final orders.[15] At the last step, the magistrate would once again call his higher-ups to ask whether or not permission to meet 'our friend in room no. 402' was to be granted.[16]

Equally awful was the raw physical pain. Some days Vajpayee's backache became so severe that he 'did not get a wink of sleep all night'.

He would watch the nurses and policemen on duty in deep slumber. Restless and suffocated, he would desperately wait for the morning to arrive.[17] For the first time in his life, he had no one by his side to provide tender care or share in his anguish.

The only antidote to his misery was reading and writing. He wrote about celebrating Independence Day at AIIMS 'amid new-found slavery'.[18] At the end of August 1975, Patna was ravaged by floods. Vajpayee cast the calamity in karmic terms, 'a consequence of JP being sent to the jail'. He made a modest contribution towards the relief fund.[19] On the evening of Dussehra, he watched from the rooftop of the ten-storey AIIMS building a giant effigy of the ten-headed Ravana going up in flames.[20] Three weeks later, he saw Diwali being celebrated in the distance, even though he was himself 'besieged by the darkness all around'.[21] Some of the poems were character sketches of leading netas: the Congress president D. K. Barooah (infamous for his 'Indira is India' remark) was rendered 'chamchon ke sartaaj' – sycophant-in-chief.[22]

As Vajpayee lay in bed disconnected from the world, a major change had occurred in the circles of power. In a double perversion of sorts, the power that had shifted over the years from cabinet to the Prime Minister's Office, now moved to the Prime Minister's Family and Friends: Sanjay Gandhi and his coterie had usurped much of the power wielded by Mrs Gandhi's top bureaucrats in the PMO. They would soon launch a programme to beautify the capital, for which they would demolish shanties, of mostly hapless Muslim households, around Turkman Gate in Old Delhi. Muslims were also disproportionately affected by the government's compulsory sterilization drive, to which Sanjay's hoodlums applied themselves with great enthusiasm. Vajpayee found out that Sanjay's lackeys had ensured that he was shown no special favour by the AIIMS staff. Maruti had failed to bring a single car to Delhi's roads, he wrote in a poem, but the scion's career was 'fast climbing Delhi's power corridors'.

> Sab sarkaron se bade, hain chhote sarkar;
> gaddi jinki chadh rahi, Dilli ke durbar...
> Kah kaidi-kavirai, lokshahi ki chutti;
> beta raj karega, peekar mugli ghutti.[23]

Nonetheless, Mrs Gandhi was still very much in command. Vajpayee heard it from the horse's mouth when the toothless foreign minister Y. B. Chavan came to see him briefly. Asked who was currently 'number two' in the government, an embarrassed Chavan 'went quiet for some moments'. Then he replied in a whisper: 'The lady is number one, the men are all at number ten.'[24]

In the last week of August 1975, Sheikh Abdullah made an undisclosed trip to Delhi to meet Mrs Gandhi. She had brought him in to mediate with JP. While JP did not mind endorsing the government's economic programme, he was 'not prepared to tolerate Mrs. Gandhi's continued leadership of the country'. Unfortunately, JP's core team also included Vajpayee, whose relationship with Abdullah had often been frosty. There is no record of whether Abdullah personally visited AIIMS, but Vajpayee's tepid response to the J&K chief minister was that he 'would have to consult his party'.[25] To capitulate would have deprived them of their martyrdom, which could fetch political dividends in the future. Mrs Gandhi shelved the reconciliation.

The government was irked by two of Vajpayee's other acts of confrontation. In mid-September, he had communicated to the Karnataka High Court his inability to be present in Bangalore due to ill health. No less an aggravation for Mrs Gandhi was that M. C. Chagla – the celebrated Bombay lawyer and her ex-cabinet colleague – had agreed to represent him. The case was at the heart of the Emergency, and its verdict would have repercussions across the country.

Aware that his letters were being intercepted, Vajpayee did away with envelopes altogether. He began to use postcards 'because it costs less, [faces] less trouble passing the censor'. He wrote letters in a tone stiffer than usual, for instance, addressing Appa as 'Dear Dr. Ghatate', with nothing more than essential facts for his ongoing hearing in Bangalore.[26] Occasionally, though, Vajpayee managed to smuggle out messages and letters to underground journals. The most popular of these was *Janvaani* – People's Voice. One of his visitors recalled pretending to use the toilet in his AIIMS ward to collect Vajpayee's letter tucked into a corner there.[27]

The external intelligence wing R&AW was closely monitoring all underground journals and, in all probability, word about his bylines had reached the PMO. Struggling to crush the underground movement, the government ordered that Vajpayee be 'speedily moved' from AIIMS to Tihar jail. This was averted, as his operation was still due. Some of Mrs Gandhi's advisors also discouraged her from sending an ailing VIP political prisoner to jail at a time when smugglers and criminals lodged at Tihar were out on bail citing health excuses.[28]

The day before he was to be operated upon, Vajpayee was granted a fifteen-day parole inside the hospital – meaning he would 'at least nominally not be in GoI custody'. At the same time, while he was being kept on traction, there was no staff 'to even ask for a glass of water'.[29] On 16 November, he had a complicated surgery to remove a disc from his spine. It began at 7:30 in the morning and continued until 2 in the afternoon.[30] The operation was successful. JP was also admitted at AIIMS, but Vajpayee's post-operative condition was not good enough to allow a meeting between them. None of this ever made it to the press.[31]

The parole was extended, but Vajpayee was placed under house arrest. When he returned home after four months, he was welcomed back at 1 Ferozeshah Road by Delhi Police constables. They maintained a register, and the kaidi-kavirai was amused to see his dog's name included in the list too. The terms of parole imposed restrictions he did not like: he could not take part in any political activity, overt or underground; he could not use a phone. Few old friends dared to visit; the vegetable vendors stayed away from the house; even the neighbourhood taxi drivers were reluctant to ferry the Kauls for fear of being interrogated by the police. Vajpayee's schoolgoing daughter Gunnu never forgot the humiliation of being 'treated as untouchables'.[32]

Nourished by warmth and care at home, by mid-December 1975 he was able to 'move about a bit'.[33] But for Vajpayee the political beast, life was otherwise depressing. Taking stock in a birthday poem, he wrote that 'the sun in the evening of my life has decided to set ... Words are devoid of meaning ... What was music once is now scattered noise.'[34] Birjan Kaul, who had to bear the ignominy of living under restriction for no fault of his own, understood the dilemmas of his wife's lover rather well. On the afternoon of 25 December, when a mutual friend came with a box of sweets to wish Vajpayee on his birthday, Kaul saheb took the visitor aside to treat him to a classic story:

> Once there lived a lion in a jungle. He had three servants – a cow, a jackal, and a monkey. One day, in a fit of temper, the lion killed and devoured the cow. Thereafter, the lion asked the jackal to tell him if his breath smelled fine. The jackal said his breath had the foul smell of meat. This irritated the lion so much that he then killed the jackal, and ate him too. He then he asked the monkey whether his breath still smelled foul. A shrewd judge of situations, the monkey excused himself: 'Sir, I just caught a cold, the zukaam has hampered my sense of smell.'
>
> That's Atalji's dilemma: he cannot speak, and he cannot remain silent. If he speaks, he will be put in jail – which in his present health he can't afford. But if he stays quiet for too long, he will lose whatever worth he has left as a politician.[35]

Vajpayee's birthday was a significant date for another reason. The Sarvodaya leader (and JP's colleague), Vinoba Bhave, who Mrs Gandhi occasionally sought out, was to break his maun vrat – vow of silence – that day. Opposition leaders who had approached him, hoping the Gandhian would rebuke the prime minister to end the Emergency, were told: 'Wait till the 25th of December.' This long list included the RSS chief Deoras. Between August and December 1975, Deoras had written two letters each to the prime minister and the home minister K. B. Reddy from his lodge in Pune's Yerawada jail. In his childlike handwriting, a chastised Deoras had beseeched them to unban the RSS, offering his organization's services to the government.

Indira Gandhi had ignored Golwalkar's advances in the past, and she did not deem the present RSS chief worthy of a response.[36] Disappointed, Deoras shot off a letter in the second week of January 1976 to Vinoba Bhave, with whom he had a slight acquaintance. He complained that the arrests of his innocent volunteers and full-timers were 'still continuing'. Once again no reply came forth. On hearing that the prime minister was to meet Bhave at his ashram in Wardha on 24 February, the RSS chief sent the acharya a second letter, begging him 'to do your best to remove the wrong impressions the PM is carrying about the Sangh'.[37] No response.

Why were the RSS chief's multiple letters to Mrs Gandhi, Reddy, Bhave (also apparently to some of Sanjay Gandhi's lackeys) all ignored? It had to do with the embedded ambiguity in the RSS's character, further amplified during the Emergency. Each of them knew that many of Deoras's claims in his letters – for example that the Sangh Parivar had not participated in the JP movement – were lies. It was common knowledge that the RSS–Jan Sangh provided shock troops for the Lok Sangharsh Samiti.

Formed the day before Emergency was imposed, the LSS was now coordinating its activities underground. With Morarji Desai under arrest, for the first few weeks Nanaji was the chief coordinator of the underground. He travelled across the country, with the party's Rajya Sabha MP Subramanian Swamy acting as his driver. Nanaji had given up his dhoti-kurta for a grey safari suit and dyed his greying hair black, taking on the appearance of an upstart businessman. Swamy pretended to be a Sikh (the most common disguise among RSS–Jan Sangh folk) from Tamil Nadu who could awkwardly mumble a few lines in his Tamil-tinged Punjabi. After Nanaji was surprised by a raid at his South Delhi hideout in late July 1975 and jailed, his place was immediately occupied by Congress (O) leader Ravindra Verma. After Verma was caught at a Bombay bus stop in December, the charge was taken by Dattopant Thengadi until he too was caught.

The underground thrived in the early months because the RSS pracharaks, full-timers, were trained for exactly such an event. There being no proper documentation of their identities, they were mostly obscure faces who could hide in a crowd or in a fellow volunteer's home as a relative. The more popular among them were reshuffled. Most of them remained at large.[38] In some cases, they were also helped by sympathizing police and intelligence officers.[39]

Few things about the Emergency depressed Vajpayee as much as the deaths of partymen in jail or hiding underground, some of whom were close friends. He had received news of the death of Baban Kulkarni, the Maharashtra Jan Sangh secretary, while he was awaiting surgery at AIIMS. He sent a condolence letter to Kulkarni's wife, which – possibly withheld by the censors – never reached her. He cried his heart out to Advani: 'Sometimes it seems unbelievable that I would not get to see Babanrao on my next Bombay trip; that he would never again be around with his cheerful face or quick-witted suggestions.'[40] 'Deeply shocked' by the premature death of another old colleague, he wrote to a mutual friend: 'How fragile our bodies are, how fleeting this life.'[41]

In his letters, he also stressed his colleagues' perseverance: 'How many of us have the great fortune of dying a martyr's death?' The apologists and defectors were a small minority: 'Friends who deserted us in this crisis deserve not hatred but pity ... It's strange that the fearful and greedy include mostly MLAs and MPs. The ordinary workers stand unwavering. It appears that the present parliamentary politics churns out only a hedonistic class which cannot take even minor blows to its pursuit of self-interest.'[42] He was referring here to the betrayal in Gwalior. At the beginning of the Emergency, Madhavrao Scindia had switched sides to join the ruling party. Worse, the son was emotionally blackmailing the Rajmata, recently released from Tihar jail, to quit the Jan Sangh. She would soon give in.

In reality, by early 1976 the underground movement of 'ordinary workers' had petered out. Between 14 November (Nehru's birth anniversary) and 26 January (Republic Day), the LSS had attempted a satyagraha across the country. The aim was no longer to bring down the government, but only 'to test popular response and their own powers of mobilization'.[43] But the headless satyagraha failed to take off, partly because the hardcore RSS–Jan Sangh–ABVP volunteers were either in jail or too afraid to risk being arrested. Coming mostly from petty traders' families, these sympathizers of Sangh Parivar had not expected a prolonged confrontation.

At this point, two major developments stunned the opposition. First, the government postponed the Lok Sabha elections, due to be held in the summer, by a year. Then, in the last week of April 1976, the opposition decisively lost the legal battle. In response to petitions by hundreds of detainees – including that of top-tier leaders like Vajpayee – a Supreme Court bench delivered its most shameful judgement ever. It ruled that during an Emergency, the government was empowered to suspend the fundamental rights to life and personal liberty. With the writ petitions quashed, Vajpayee's lawyer withdrew his High Court petition in Bangalore, 'not because the judgement of the Hon'ble Supreme Court was right but because it was final'.[44]

The message was loud and clear: the Emergency was here to stay. Mrs Gandhi's advisors were now informally facilitating meetings between the opposition members to make them sign a 'surrender document'.[45] Some leaders of the Janata front – Charan Singh, Ashok Mehta of Congress (O) – were released from jail so they could begin the negotiations.[46] Elders in the Sangh Parivar were on board. For the same reason, Vajpayee did not resign from the Lok Sabha (whereas the socialist Madhu Limaye sent his resignation from jail to protest the extension of its term). In fact, in coordination with the acting RSS chief Madhavrao Muley, Vajpayee advised Advani to file a nomination for his second term in the Rajya Sabha from Gujarat.[47] The largest number of the MISA prisoners came from the Sangh network. By summer, dozens had perished in jail or after their belated release. Pressure was mounting on Vajpayee to strike a deal.

Around this time, he had a slightly tense meeting with JP, who had been earlier released on health grounds and was briefly in Delhi. Vajpayee tried persuading the father of the LSS that it was not making an impact anymore: 'If you think the movement cannot be sustained, you should call it off.' The Gandhian was unimpressed. Charan Singh had disassociated himself, JP rebutted, but most of the BLD workers had not been released. Vajpayee tried to convince JP that 'the movement is in your name', and therefore the government thinks 'you alone can call it off'. Exasperated perhaps by the Jan Sangh leader's pusillanimity, JP put forward a proposal: if Vajpayee could convince Indira Gandhi to release *all* prisoners, he would call off the struggle: 'Main Sangharsh waapas lene ko taiyaar hoon.' But in the absence of democratic freedom, what choice did one have 'other than a movement of this kind'.[48] On realizing JP's reluctance to bow down, the government put the initiatives by others on hold.

A fellow visitor to AIIMS occasionally ran into Vajpayee, who went there for check-ups. He found Vajpayee 'totally disheartened. I had never before realised that the opposition had become so frustrated.' Vajpayee said he 'can now perfectly understand how the English could rule over us for more than two centuries: it was through fear and a little greed.' He was shocked that there was no mass uprising against the Emergency; the crowds that once thronged his meetings had stayed inert, some even celebrating the improvement in law and order and that trains and buses were running on time. When the two met on the first anniversary of the Emergency, 26 June 1976, there was nothing new to talk about: they exchanged views on Hindi novels they had been reading.[49]

The Emergency had further piled up the opposition's older anxieties on the merger. With JP's persuasion, the party representatives had first met in Bombay on 21–22 March. Shedding his earlier inhibitions, Vajpayee was now keen to 'bend every effort toward forming a one-party opposition to Congress'.[50] But as he was disallowed to travel, the Jan Sangh was represented by one Om Prakash Tyagi, a Rajya Sabha MP from UP who had been spared arrest. Tyagi was strictly a face, though, advised to never exceed his brief. Sitting at home, Vajpayee remote-controlled the parleys, and even wrote up press statements on behalf of the party. Some memos mention him as the 'top leader of Jan Sangh in Delhi who was out of the prison walls'.[51]

Apart from the miscellaneous differences (name of the new party, flag, symbol, president), the opposition also squabbled on other matters. The Congress (O) wanted four months' time to shed the psychological barrier. Some found it 'emotionally tough' to dissolve the party when they had spent 'the best portions of our lives under its banner'.[52] Others desired a reunification with the ruling party rather than joining a shaky startup.[53]

On 7 July, Charan Singh met Vajpayee in Delhi. The talk about the merger was cordial. But Vajpayee felt annoyed when the BLD chief set forth the condition that the proposed party should not take part in 'surreptitious activities': 'no member of the new party will be free to become a member of the RSS.' Vajpayee 'could not see his way to agree to this', whereupon the talks abruptly ended.[54] Charan Singh launched his tirade on dual membership at all subsequent meetings on the merger proposal. Soon, the BLD was hammering away at the Jan Sangh's doublespeak: 'On the one hand, the Jan Sangh as an organisation is part of the Sangharsh or the struggle that is going on. On the other [its UP unit says] it "would extend its full cooperation to the government in constructive programme and social welfare activities". The two hardly go together.'[55]

The socialist leaders complained about RSS–Jan Sangh detenus being 'desperate to be released at all costs'. Thousands of them had signed the government's twenty-point-programme memo, promising to 'not participate in activities prejudicial to the present Emergency'. This had a demoralizing effect on the other detenus.[56] They also found the Sangh Parivar detenus across jails being involved in whisper campaigns.*

All these reservations were passed on to the Janata commander-in-chief.[57]† At the same time, JP was also corresponding with the Sangh Parivar elders. The acting RSS chief Madhavrao Muley had recently assured him that the organization would consider amending its constitution to allow Muslims into their fold. The RSS also promised JP, rather insincerely, that the organization would consider – like the Jan Sangh – dissolving and merging with the volunteer organizations of other parties. But for that it was important to be unbanned first: could JP please 'write a letter to Vinobaji in this regard'?[58] (Muley was also

* As per one such account, Mrs Gandhi had sent her emissary P. N. Haksar to talk to Deoras at Yerawada Jail. But the RSS chief scolded Haksar saying he would not talk to a middleman, preferring to talk directly to Indira. A similar story claimed that all parties other than the Jan Sangh were desperate to attend parliament and it was only Vajpayee who firmly ruled it out: 'No, until every parliamentarian locked up inside prisons is released, we will keep the struggle going.'

† In early September 1976 Limaye wrote to JP – both of them Quit India veterans – that the behaviour of RSS–Jan Sangh prisoners in the jail 'made one hang one's head in shame'. Across states they had been parroting, 'what is the point of rotting in the jail; there is nothing wrong in supporting the 20-point programme and getting out'.

exploring other conduits, such as Mrs Gandhi's former media advisor, H. V. Sharada Prasad, for this purpose.) JP smelt 'some risk' on taking the RSS at face value, but his experience with the Jan Sangh in Bihar was 'satisfactory' and he hoped that 'working together will further foster unity'.[59] He was keen to give them the benefit of the doubt.

In October 1976, the Jan Sangh completed twenty-five years of its existence. The same month, parliament passed the 42nd Constitutional Amendment: Article 31D gave the government power to act against 'anti-national' activities or associations. With the communal organizations outlawed, the Jan Sangh wondered if it was their turn next. This existential threat unblocked whatever inhibitions the party had against the merger. The socialist H. V. Kamath, one of the key negotiators, asked Vajpayee his terms and conditions for the merger. Came a prompt riposte: 'No conditions: you can have any flag, any name.' The negotiator was relieved to have got 'a blank cheque'.[60]

In public, though, Vajpayee presented a different logic. 'As per the ashram tradition, a man begins the family life after 25 years,' he wrote to a friend. Similarly the Jan Sangh had to join other parties to become part of a large family. 'Dr. Mookerji had once laid the foundation for the Nationalist Democratic Front in parliament, now the time has come to give that historic process a final shape.'[61]

By this time, the government too seemed serious about breaking the stalemate. Now that the government had consolidated its position, it saw no harm in bargaining with an opposition whose teeth and spine had been broken; they looked so demoralized that Mrs Gandhi's advisors dropped the idea of making them sign a surrender document. She was also keen to improve her sagging image abroad.

Vajpayee's back had now improved sufficiently. An emissary who went to meet Vajpayee at his residence – the police was by this time 'mercifully inefficient' – was surprised to see that he 'walked comfortably from the inside of the house to the drawing room'.[62] In early December, Vajpayee wrote to the Home Ministry asking for an unconditional release instead of a parole extension. On the last day, 13 December, the Ministry released a statement agreeing to his demand.[63] Having received no personal communication, the kaidi-kavirai found out from the 6 p.m. bulletin of AIR which announced it. Two days later, he sat in a meeting of opposition leaders in the capital convened by M. Karunanidhi, the toppled chief minister of Tamil Nadu.[64] Vajpayee was made a part of two committees: to represent the opposition in discussions with the government; and to enable the constitution of the soon-to-be-born party.

Mrs Gandhi was still keen on JP personally announcing the dismantling of his LSS. But the kidney patient in Patna sulked over the opposition's capitulation. He wrote to Vajpayee: 'One should not fear to negotiate, but also one should not negotiate out of fear.' But the government was now earnestly responding to communications, as also gradually releasing prisoners. Vajpayee did not want to break the momentum. On the first day of 1977, he landed up in Patna to urge JP to agree that the Lok Sangharsh Samiti be transformed into a tame Lok *Shikshan* Samiti that would conduct awareness campaigns for the opposition, at the same time allowing JP a face-saver.

Hereafter things moved fast. On the afternoon of 18 January, Advani and Morarji were freed. After spending nineteen months incarcerated, Advani was peremptorily asked to leave Bangalore jail 'at the earliest, within an hour'.[65] That evening Mrs Gandhi declared on AIR, in a voice soft but firm, that she had decided to dissolve the Lok Sabha and conduct polls; the Emergency was to be relaxed and press censorship suspended.

Her intended beneficiaries were reserved. Vajpayee's knee-jerk reaction was to oppose the elections.[66] Coming barely two months after the extension of the Lok Sabha's term, the opposition (including the CPM) suspected a ploy. Some wildly speculated that Indira would rig the polls to further deepen her dictatorship. Amid the fear and suspicions, Vajpayee bemoaned: 'Most of our workers are still in detention, a pall of fear hangs over the country ... AIR and television are virtually out of bounds for even replying to wild charges. We are no less handicapped in funds as the industry and trade are held in tight leash by the government.' True, it was a most unequal contest. But now that elections had been declared, the opposition could not run away. Besides, given their minuscule presence in the current Lok Sabha, there was not much to lose by entering the ring. Vajpayee accepted the challenge 'to educate the masses about the grimness of the situation and to build up a viable alternative'.[67]

Soon, Morarji Desai's residence became the pivot of opposition activity. JP arrived to confer on the nitty-gritties of the new 'Janata Party'. Morarjibhai was made president, Charan Singh vice president. Avoiding the limelight, Vajpayee pushed Advani's name as one of the three general secretaries. He was for now happy being merely a national committee member.[68] On 28 January, Vajpayee joined Janata leaders to meet the prime minister with a demand that she ensure free and fair elections.[69] He urged Mrs Gandhi to immediately release all his partymen. When she replied that it might take time, Vajpayee quipped: 'You could maybe release them as speedily as you threw them into jail.'[70] But the RSS was still outlawed and, given their joint affiliation, most Jan Sangh prisoners were shown no mercy.

On the evening of 30 January, the Janata Party, yet to be formalized on paper, launched its campaign. Morarji and Vajpayee were to address the crowd at Ramlila grounds in Delhi.* The planners were nervous. When they pasted posters on walls announcing the rally, they did not know if the average Delhiite would be enthused or brave enough to come. Most media outlets had written off the Janata: the newly launched fortnightly *India Today* denigrated the party's hopes of winning the election as living in a 'fool's paradise', even as it fawned over the government's achievements.[71]

The Janata did not have its flags printed yet. For a while, Jan Sangh organizers mulled over whether they should ask workers to carry their own saffron flags at the rally. But for the police, the Jan Sangh flag was like a red rag to a bull; the idea was dropped. Arriving at the venue with opposition leaders, Vajpayee was relieved to find it jam-packed. This was significant

* JP launched the campaign in Patna; Charan Singh in Kanpur; the ex-Congressman Chandra Shekhar – who had spent the Emergency in jail and had now joined Janata – in Jaipur.

for a chilly January evening, made worse by a drizzle. 'Unlike at public meetings in normal times, when there is always a carnival atmosphere, there was a seriousness about this rally': it was as if the crowd 'had been waiting a long time' for this gathering.[72] Released two weeks ago, Desai was to be the showstopper. Vajpayee, the crowd-puller, would speak last. His turn came at 9:30 p.m. Climbing a stage after nineteen months, the artist felt a thrill: he knew the crowd was waiting for him in anticipation.

> No sooner did he reach the podium than the vast crowd stood up and started cheering. He began his speech with a verse that in simple words told the whole story of the pain and terror of the Emergency: 'Baad muddat ke mile hain deewane. Kehne sun-ne ko bahut hai nafsaane. Khuli hava mein zara saans to le lein, kab tak rahegi azaadi kaun jaane (It has been an aeon since we met. There are stories to tell and stories to hear. But, first let's relish our freedom, for who knows how long it will last)'. The applause began after the first line and by the last line the huge crowd seemed to go completely mad.[73]

There was silence as he spoke of how, since June 1975, India had become a vast prison camp in which humans were no longer humans. This election was a contest between democracy and dictatorship, and the opposition 'shall fight to the last breath' for democracy.[74] Janata would function as a united party keeping national interest above everything else.[75] Reading Urdu literature had subtly influenced his vocabulary. It was wholly suitable for the occasion, for his audience included Muslims from nearby Old Delhi. India's expanding population was a problem, he said, but he 'did not believe that human beings could be bundled into trucks like animals, sterilized against their will and sent back'.[76]

The Janata Party was starved of funds. While Vajpayee spoke, his party workers quietly went around the ground with cloth sheets, and donations poured in. By old Jan Sangh standards, it turned out to be a handsome amount: three lakh rupees; some men gave away their watches, women their silver bangles.

With life breathed into the opposition, Vajpayee sat down with former jailmate Madhu Dandavate to prepare the manifesto. They made tall promises, Vajpayee later confessed, because Janata did not expect to be voted to power. The final version that the party released on 10 February promised to usher in 'Gandhian socialism that will help the decentralisation of economic and political power and help build up a free and just society'.[77]

In the meantime Mrs Gandhi's agriculture minister Jagjivan Ram, who had been sulking over the Emergency for a while, jumped ship. But instead of joining Janata he floated a startup, Congress for Democracy, with help from the former UP chief minister Bahuguna and a few others. His exit gave the Janata a colossal psychological boost. With the tallest Dalit leader no longer by her side, Indira Gandhi was no longer unshakable.

On 7 February, JP and Ram shared the stage at Ramlila Maidan. The otherwise dull Doordarshan broadcast *Bobby*, a titillating teenage romance, to wean away the youth. But many, like Vajpayee's daughter Gunnu, paid no attention. On her way to hear the old men, Gunnu heard muffled sounds as her taxi neared the venue: the driver said 'it was the sound of people's feet. We had to get down and walk to the grounds.'[78]

Her father missed the thrill. The previous evening, Vajpayee had joined others in launching Janata's official campaign in Bombay: the artist performed at Shivaji Park for forty-five minutes to a one-lakh strong crowd. He was so energetic that it almost seemed as if he had exaggerated his spinal woes since early 1976 to extend his parole. If voted to power, the Janata Party's first priority would be to repeal the Emergency laws and restore the basic structure of the Constitution that had been 'mutilated' by the recent amendments. Janata would lift India out of the morass of low investment, low consumption, low production and low wages: 'We will provide jobs to all not just the son of one mother.'[79]

In Punjab's Gurdaspur and Jalandhar, the latter being the constituency of Defence Minister Swaran Singh, he narrated stories from his stay at AIIMS. While he was admitted there, a senior Congress leader – he did not name Y. B. Chavan – had come to see him. The minister 'wrote on a piece of paper that the room was bugged and therefore he could not talk freely'. Warning: if the audience committed the mistake of voting for the lady dictator, such restrictions on freedom would be imposed again.[80]

Time was drawing close for a crucial personal decision. So far Vajpayee had parried the question of whether he was going to contest the elections. He had 'yet to make up his mind' given his poor health and the promise he made two years ago not to re-seek election. Before 30 January, he may also not have been sure of pulling off a victory. In what was a mark of his current popularity, though, three of Janata Party's local units had invited him to fight – Balrampur, Gwalior and Rajkot.[81] A man of flexible principles, Vajpayee was finally coaxed in mid-February. He was eyeing Lucknow, but it was stolen by Bahuguna (whom he detested) while Vajpayee was still vacillating.[82] Eventually, he filed his nomination from the high-profile New Delhi constituency.

He was to lock horns with the Congress's Shashi Bhushan Bajpai, who had defeated Madhok in 1971 from the nearby South Delhi constituency.[83] Shashi Bhushan was a distant cousin of Atal's, the leftist MP being the only other Bateshwar boy who had made it big in national politics. There was little love lost between the two cousins, even though each knew the other's life intimately. (Not unlike Atal, Shashi Bhushan too had earlier scandalized his folks in Gwalior by marrying a Christian woman.) Since he was fighting from a new place under a new party's banner, Appa naively asked if Vajpayee was going to ask for votes in Morarji's name. 'Kyon, main apne naam par vote loonga,' he rebutted: his own name was good enough.[84] He may have been lying low, but Vajpayee knew he was, after JP, the Janata's biggest crowd-puller.

Other things went less smoothly. The merger in late January was a fait accompli. Amid murmurs, Vajpayee had advised the Jan Sangh Working Committee: 'Jab pralay aati hai toh jo kuch bhi bacha-khucha ho, usko sambhalna chahiye' – after the calamity, one should hold on to whatever is left behind; for all you know, you might lose even that.[85] With the gradual release of its partymen, though, the Jan Sangh hardened its stance. For example, Charan Singh wanted the Janata flag to be green – representing the farmers. Nanaji Deshmukh vetoed it, saying green was 'the colour of Pakistan's flag.' There were arguments on seat-sharing with Charan

Singh, especially in UP where the Jat leader was the final authority for allotting eighty tickets. BLD had kept forty for itself, giving Jan Sangh only fifteen, while Ram's CFD was accommodated on nineteen seats.[86]

Because there was no time for Janata to register itself and obtain a new symbol from the Election Commission, all its constituents fought on Lok Dal's symbol. It boosted Charan Singh's ego, who was surly for having to play a deputy to Morarjibhai.[87] Overall, though, the Jan Sangh faction extracted for itself around a handsome 120 Lok Sabha constituencies. 'I thought you had given a blank cheque,' H. V. Kamath grumbled to Vajpayee, but he eventually 'did not give even your signature'.[88]

Predictably, Mrs Gandhi wrote off the new Janata as 'a facade for the Jan Sangh and the RSS' – which had collaborated with the British, murdered the Mahatma. Everywhere, she and her lieutenants mocked the new party as a conglomeration of disparate elements with nothing in common, except their hunger to capture power. If Janata was voted to power, it was sure to collapse, lurching the country into political instability. As one of the Janata's star campaigners, Vajpayee was at the receiving end of Congress's ire and anxiety more than ever before. Was the man who had compared Indira to Durga and now branded her a 'dictator' to be trusted, asked the MP chief minister at a Jabalpur rally.[89] In Akola, the Maharashtra chief minister cautioned against Jan Sangh's communal character: was it not Vajpayee who had 'called for the Indianisation of Muslims in the country'?[90] Rafiq Zakaria, the revenue minister of Maharashtra, announced to Pune Muslims the immediate threat: a Janata victory would mean Vajpayee 'firmly installed in the Prime Minister's house'.[91] The sharpest critique came from the AICC general secretary, V. B. Raju, who mocked Vajpayee's 'latest revelation' on Gandhian socialism. Vajpayee had been awkwardly clarifying that the Jan Sangh had not accepted socialism earlier only because he believed it to represent statism. Raju said the clarification had come twenty-five years too late.[92]

On the afternoon of 1 March, Mrs Gandhi was booed by a hostile crowd at a Boat Club rally. She had accompanied the candidate Shashi Bhushan, who first took the mike.

> The audience was inattentive, their conversation continuing in lower key. Then after a while, he shouted, '*Bolo, Indira Gandhi ki...*' Silence. He repeated the cheer as it were, but to the same response. Bewildered and flustered, he thought the mike was out of order and he began pushing it around. 'Perhaps you can't hear me,' he shouted. This led to laughter and a waving of hands to indicate how well they could hear... Indira then went on undeterred ... '*Gow bachre ko vote dena,*' referring to the unfortunate Congress symbol, the cow and calf. 'No... No...' was the answer ... It was a defiant gesture which could cost them their jobs in case she returned.[93]

Visibly shaken, she went on the defensive, apologizing to the crowd for the Emergency's excesses. In retaliation her supporters dismantled the podium, which was to be used by the opposition rally in a few hours. The power for the speakers and microphones was also cut off at the last minute. In his speech, Vajpayee regretted the disturbances at the prime minister's rally and threatened to go on an indefinite hunger strike if it was repeated: 'Do you want me to die?' The friendly crowd – whose size was now 'claustrophobic and a bit frightening – the slightest disorganisation could lead to a stampede' – screamed 'no'.[94] Though declared a gallant gesture, Vajpayee was in fact wary that the government would use such trivial affronts as an excuse to tighten the Emergency. Earlier that day, while he was addressing students at Delhi University's north campus, a helicopter had hovered overhead. It was actually the R&AW trying to assess the size of the crowd.[95]

Near Jama Masjid later that evening, Abdullah Bukhaari, imam of the mosque and spiritual guide to Delhi's Muslims, sat at the rally with Vajpayee, shedding past animosity and suspicion. For the first time since independence, Muslim politicians and clergy were sharing platforms with Jan Sangh leaders.[96] A young reporter who was following him on this eventful day noticed that even though Vajpayee's acts on stage appeared natural, he took pains to at least 'mentally prepare his points in advance. He has the capacity to shrewdly assess his audience before his speech, and take up specific issues that they can identify with.' The reporter was surprised by the contrasting atmosphere of his residence: 1 Ferozeshah

Road was 'quiet, unruffled, unlike any politician's house. No crowds outside, no parties of people from his constituency.'[97]

As the campaign reached its climax Vajpayee, his voice hoarse, claimed for Janata nothing less than a two-thirds majority; a coalition would be a 'worst case' resort. Even so, 'if a coalition could work smoothly in West Germany, and at home in Kerala, why not at the Centre'.[98] Some of the surge in his confidence had to do with the fate of his opponent. In the beginning, the media had put them on an equal footing: a popular daily described Vajpayee as the Janata's 'glamour guy', while his cousin was a 'giant killer' who could gather a crowd for demonstrations in no time. But soon Shashi Bhushan, who had once advocated a 'limited dictatorship within the democratic structure', was being shouted down at his rallies. In the government servant-dominated New Delhi constituency, he focused on two things: a promise to increase dearness allowance; followed by the Jan Sanghi's apparent betrayal of the Quit India movement thirty-five years ago: 'Is this a man you can trust?' But his speeches had none of his usual lustre and conviction. Towards the end of his campaigning, Bhushan looked 'bone-tired and spiritless, deep grooves of fatigue criss-crossing his plump face'.[99]

Polling in Delhi done peacefully on 16 March, Vajpayee left the next morning on his last campaign assignment: a quick trip to Gujarat and Rajasthan. His first stop was Rajkot, partly to compensate for not fighting the seat himself. Privately he may still have had some doubts about the Janata's performance, for Vajpayee demanded Mrs Gandhi's assurance to not arrest newly elected MPs under MISA.[100] Jaipur the next day was made memorable by a bizarre incident of four snakes appearing from four corners of the ground. The agitated crowd started shouting 'Janata Party – Zindabad' and 'Congress – Murdabad'. It later became known that the snakes had their poisonous fangs taken out before they were let loose in the ground by the Janata workers themselves. Apparently someone had thought snakes were auspicious for catching votes.[101]

Votes were to be counted at the Union Public Service Commission building on 20 March. That morning, Vajpayee made the rounds of counting tables to pick up traces of rigging. As the day progressed, word got round that he was leading. Hundreds of Janata flags buffeted the pleasant March afternoon outside the building. In contrast, not one Congress supporter was in sight. Soon after sundown, it was confirmed that Janata candidates had swept all seven Delhi seats: Vajpayee had thrashed Bhushan by 80,000 votes. Rickety jeeps and rickshaws, flying the orange and green of Janata flags, took off carrying the news everywhere. A relieved and garlanded Vajpayee waved to the crowd as he left the counting centre. He felt it was 'more like a referendum than an ordinary election'.[102]

Soon came the thrilling reports of the defeat of the mother-son duo: Indira to Raj Narain in Raebareli; Sanjay to Ravindra Pratap Singh, an obscure young ex-MLA from the Jan Sangh, in Amethi. At 299 (out of 545), the Janata–CFD had managed a majority on its own; along with allies, they fell only a little short of a two-thirds majority.[103] In the Hindi heartland, the Congress was drubbed beyond its wildest fears. It got none out of 139 seats in Bihar and UP, and only two (one each) in MP and Rajasthan out of sixty-five. When the RSS men in Patna called on JP with a box of sweets, he nibbled some despite being severely diabetic.

On the evening of 23 March, the spiritual guide of the Janata victory slowly descended the ramp of the Patna–Delhi Boeing, clutching the handrail. Relieved to sink into a wheelchair, he was taken to a waiting car. He was driven to the Gandhi Peace Foundation where he was to decide which of the three men – Morarji Desai, Jagjivan Ram, Charan Singh – would lead the country's first non-Congress government.

Morarji Desai had served as the deputy prime minister twice, missing the top job by a whisker. He had vast administrative experience: he had led the Congress split in 1969; he had been chosen the president of Janata Party two months ago, before which he had quietly endured seventeen months of imprisonment. Jagjivan Ram too had three decades of administrative experience as cabinet minister across portfolios. More significantly, his support to Janata had proved crucial in swinging the mandate. But his resume had a fatal flaw. Until 1975, he had been among Mrs Gandhi's staunchest supporters. He had stayed with the ruling party all through the Emergency, resigning in an opportunistic move after he watched the Janata campaign receiving a sound response. Charan Singh, leader of the middle-caste peasants, had briefly served as the chief minister of UP, but never been in the central cabinet. Apart from having the weakest resume among the three, he had also ticked off the Jan Sangh faction during the campaign. After some ego massage, the Jat leader withdrew himself from the race.

Significantly, the Jan Sangh faction had the highest tally – ninety (against the BLD's fifty-five and the Socialist Party's fifty-one), a qualitative jump by all means.[104] This meant that Vajpayee could have at least made a nominal claim for the top job. But at fifty-two, he was still too young to be fighting alongside desperate old men. Unlike the three of them, he had never held a major administrative post. Vajpayee throwing his hat in the ring would also undermine the newborn party that had yet to be formalized in writing. Both strategy and idealism dictated he must remain content to be part of the historic experiment.

He had tentatively promised Jagjivan Ram his party's support. Morarji Desai often appeared uncompromising and self-righteous. Jagjivan Ram, on the other hand, would have been easier for the Jan Sangh faction to manoeuvre. Despite being adversaries in parliament, Vajpayee got along well with the mild-mannered Dalit leader. Backing him would have also boosted the Sangh Parivar's image among the downtrodden. Many in the Socialist Party also preferred Jagjivan Ram. Vajpayee would have preferred a formal vote, in which case Jagjivan Ram might have beaten Morarjibhai.

But the Jat leader had despatched a letter from his hospital bed, rejecting Jagjivan Ram 'outright'. Vajpayee was relieved to see Charan Singh's letter supporting Morarjibhai, 'since we were more confident of persuading Ram to work under Desai than of persuading Chaudhary Saheb or Desai to work under Ram'.[105] At the Gandhi Peace Foundation hall, Vajpayee saw JP and Acharya Kripalani confronting the leadership dilemma. They decided on Morarji Desai, but the duo also suggested a prime ministership by rotation: 'the person chosen as a leader should relinquish office after two or three years', and the other person should take over for the rest of the term.[106] None of this was formally documented.

The next morning, 24 March, JP took the entire herd of Janata MPs to Rajghat, where lay the mortal remains of the Mahatma. From his wheelchair, JP read out the pledge to follow the Mahatma's path. In parliament a few hours later, Desai was unanimously elected leader of the Janata Parliamentary Party amidst loud applause in the Central Hall. Raj Narain proposed Morarji Desai's name; Vajpayee seconded it. Mrs Gandhi had absented herself from the ceremony. Vajpayee said it was the Janata's good fortune to have many stalwarts, 'but we can have only one Prime Minister'.[107]

They left together for a Janata victory rally at the Ramlila grounds. The air was filled with hope and idealism. Declaring Vajpayee 'mere aziz bhai' – my beloved brother – Bukhaari of Jama Maszid exonerated the Sangh Parivar: 'This previous government was involved with all the disturbances caused here, not RSS or Jan Sangh.'[108] The incoming prime minister had just lifted the Emergency, and thousands of RSS workers were released from jail.

From a three-decade-old habit, Vajpayee referred to the Congress in his speech as the 'ruling party'. He paused to apologize with a faint smile, and gestured towards Desai and Ram sitting behind him, saying 'now *we* are the ruling party'. He congratulated the public for their wisdom, summing up the 1977 elections in a sentence: 'Lokshakti ki leher ne in loktantra ki hatya karne waalon ko itihaas ke kuredaan mein phenk diya hai' – the wave of popular mandate has consigned the murderers of democracy to the *dustbin of history*. It was an incongruous sentence spoken extempore, mixing metaphors, but the last phrase would be quoted for decades hereafter.[109]

He promised that the new dispensation would not be vengeful to its adversaries. Even though the Janata had done badly in the southern states, the new government would be fair and liberal in all centre-state matters. It seems Vajpayee had discussed the foreign relations of the new government with Morarji over the last few days. In a revealing U-turn, he declared that Janata would continue backing Palestine instead of Israel: 'Israel is an aggressor, and it must vacate all the Arab lands.' He said he was clarifying only because he came from a party discredited to be the enemy of Muslims: 'I am exceeding my brief, whoever becomes the new foreign minister will illuminate us more on it.'[110]

Ram was still hoping to receive a slight promotion – perhaps a deputy prime ministership. While he sulked, Morarji Desai distributed other portfolios. As the leader of the largest faction, Vajpayee was being poked by friends to bargain hard. But with Charan Singh around, he was resigned: 'Kahaan se Home milega, kaun dega?'[111] Morarji Desai asked him to pick either Defence or External Affairs. Vajpayee did not have to think hard before choosing the latter.

On the morning of 26 March, Vajpayee arrived at Rashtrapati Bhavan for the oath-taking ceremony, and quietly occupied a chair in the second row. The event was made awkward by Ram's refusal to attend. But fourteen other ministers were sworn in. Apart from Vajpayee, two other Jan Sangh men took oath: Advani as I&B minister, Brijlal Verma as industry minister. (Morarji Desai spurned the Jan Sangh's demand for Education.) The incoming prime minister had initially offered Industry to Nanaji, but as per Sangh Parivar strategy, he reluctantly excused himself to look after the organization. Brijlal Verma, who had been a minister in the MP SVD government, was rewarded for making Madhavrao Scindia bite the dust in Gwalior.

The local media praised Vajpayee for displaying through the critical period 'a degree of moderation, suavity and capacity to grasp issues and reconcile differences which cannot but serve him in good stead as Minister for External Affairs'.[112] Oddly, though, perception of him was less warm abroad. Much of this had to do with the Jan Sangh's past approach to foreign relations – instrumentalist, ultra-nationalistic, xenophobic even.

Soviet Russia's state-owned media was too stunned to respond, but it had in the recent past jeered the opposition as reactionaries. But even the Americans were unsure. A CIA cable pointed out that the Jan Sangh had 'consistently favoured a hardline in foreign policy, and has not been particularly friendly to the great powers'. Vajpayee's appointment was 'likely to cause concern in Islamabad, where many believe that the Jan Sangh favours the conquest of Pakistan'.[113] For the *New York Times*, Vajpayee's only major objective was 'to win recognition in the UN for

Hindi'.[114] Another American daily contrasted his past demand for nuclear weaponry with Desai's opposition to it, doubting whether Vajpayee would modify his past attitudes.[115]

Possibly sensing the distrust on all sides, he felt the need to make the Janata government's 'real non-alignment' policy clear. Holding a press conference on 30 March 1977, he stressed that there would be 'no immediate or major changes' in the country's foreign policy. The Janata coalition stood by all past commitments and ongoing negotiations. He calmly informed the media that he no longer held the extreme views he had expressed while in opposition. The relationship with Pakistan had to be strengthened further: 'There should be no apprehension that the new government will do anything to reverse the process.' He also hoped for quick improvement in relations with China, where India had reopened its embassy in 1976. The most significant clarification, though, was that India's first centre-right regime was committed to eschewing nuclear arms.[116]

The effect was soon evident. The foreign governments began to appreciate the import of a homegrown Indian cabinet with, for the first time, no Oxbridge alumni. Of this group, Vajpayee was one of the few who had 'so far visited 16 countries in total'. Even though 'not pro-western he is not, in private conversation, anti-British,' the British High Commission wrote back to London.[117] Another pen portrait clarified to the British Foreign Office that his surname was to be pronounced 'Badgepie'.[118]

For the incoming Indian foreign minister, such turnarounds were natural to his adaptable temperament and ability to appreciate all sides of a problem. Vajpayee now had a higher-ranked ministry than Syama Prasad Mookerji had ever held in his lifetime. But it was less easy for his ideological fraternity at Old Nagpur and Jhandewalan. Almost twenty-five years after the RSS launched its political wing, it had managed to grab power in the capital. The long route had involved hard work and perseverance, a strategic use of secrecy and misinformation, and a bullish, almost sinister, attitude to infiltrate Hindu society with its multiple affiliates. Where would the Sangh Parivar go from here?

In the early months of the Emergency, a senior RSS functionary had taken refuge in the house of a top intelligence official – an old friend, also Hindutva-leaning – in Banaras. The pracharak boasted that the Sangh Parivar would make 'a definite bid to share power at the centre after Indira was ousted'. But, the IB official asked, would it be possible for them to share power with ideologically divergent parties? 'Power is not a Hindu wife,' the celibate pracharak winked. 'It could be shared with the oddest bedmate, though only for a while. Such sharing alone, he felt, could prepare the Parivar for staking greater claims to the reins of the nation.'[119]

Acknowledgements

BETWEEN THE TWO VOLUMES, THIS PROJECT POSSESSED ME FOR eight years. I have come to owe a massive and lasting debt to several institutions and individuals, including (perhaps inevitably for such a project) those whose politics I disagree with mildly or bitterly.* Some people spoke with candour but requested anonymity. I have not acknowledged a few others simply because the second volume is to come out in December 2023 and it would be more appropriate to thank them there. The errors in the manuscript, if any, are mine alone.

First the institutions. Maulana Azad Library at the AMU. In Bhopal: the Directorate of Archaeology, Archives and Museums, especially Gita Subherwal; Madhav Sapre Sangrahalaya. In Chicago: Center for Research Libraries, Laura Ring at the UChicago library. In Delhi: Keshav Kunj at Jhandewalan, the National Archives, Ambedkar Central Library at the JNU. In Gwalior: Gorkhi Higher Secondary School, Maharani Laxmi Bai (formerly Victoria) College, the Scindia Archives. In London: the UK National Archives. In Lucknow: the (painfully and needlessly secretive) CID Archives, the *Rashtradharma* archives. In Maryland: the National Archives at College Park. The provincial State Archives in Calcutta, Lucknow and Patna. In Thane: Rambhav Mhalgi Prabodhini, especially Vinay Sahastrabuddhe and Dilip Navele. In Washington DC: the Library of Congress. The International Centre Goa for providing me a residency, especially Pushkar Sinha for his generous hospitality.

* I thank all such people for giving me their honest insights, and sometimes access to their network and private archives, despite being aware that my assessment was probably not going to be kind.

Thanks are due to a long list of dear friends and mentors, vague acquaintances and total strangers. Anubhav Agarwal, Zarin Ahmad, Mohammad Ali, Kumar Anand, Minnie and Walter Andersen, Pratinav Anil, Subhash Arya, Nisthasri Awasthi, Nethra P. B., Rukmini Banerji, Sandeep Bhardwaj, the late Shanti Bhushan, Arpita Chakravorty, Kumkum Chadha, Rohit Chandra, Dushyant Chawla, Sridhar Damle, Kinshu Dang, Aaditya Dar, Dilip Deodhar, Madhu Deolekar, Kanak Mani Dixit, Praveen Donthi, Raj Dutt, Ajitha G. S., Jatin Gandhi, Roman Gautam, the late Appa Ghatate, Meru Gokhale, K. N. Govindacharya, the late Chandrakanta Goyal, the late Swarup Goyal, Vijay Goyal, Shreya Gupta, Vinod K. Jose, Sanjay Joshi, Aashim Joy, Sudha Kanikicharla, Pralay Kanungo, Dileep Karambalekar, Kamini Kaul, Sanjeev Kaul, Aditya Kaushal, Krishn Kaushik, Sana Khan, Raj Kishore, Avina Kohli, Abhimanyu Kumar, Alok Kumar, Aman Kumar, Chandan Kumar, Jitendra Kumar, Mahendra Kumar, Prabhat Kumar, Saket Kumar, Shanta Kumar, Vikas Kumar, Ushinor Majumdar, V. K. Malhotra, Kanti Mishra, R. K. Mishra, Shruti Mohan, Srishti Narain (for her detailed feedback on the first draft), Ullekh N. P., Dinesh Narayanan, Ravi Nair, the late Kuldip Nayar, Kartik Nijhawan, Manisha Pande, the late Shiv Shankar Pareek, Pan Singh Patwal, K. Raman Pillai, O. Rajagopal, M. Rajshekhar, Ranveer (stringer for the daily *Hindustan* for his help in Bateshwar), M. K. Rasgotra, Arunabh Saikia, Tarushikha Sarvesh, Saibal Satyarthi, D. K. Sethi, Venky Selvaraj, M. R. Sharan, Sparya Sharma, Vivek Shejwalkar, the late R. P. Shukla, Abhishek Singh, Rahul Singh, Swadesh Singh, Pranay Sinha, the late R. R. Suresh, the late Devendra Swaroop, Rohan Todarwal, Vishwanath Tripathi, Ratnakar Tripathy, the late M. G. Vaidya, Deepak Vajpayee, Raj Kishore Vajpayee, Ramesh Chandra Vajpayee, Rahul Verma, Shivam Vij, Satyam Vyas.

Aunohita Mojumdar, who earlier edited *Himal Southasian*, for helping me get started in 2012. Aunohita gave me the freedom to write pieces – 'the longer the better' – mixing travel reportage with historical commentary, on a wide range of subjects. Robin Jeffrey, who apart from giving detailed feedback on the proposal, also kindly offered to write fellowship recommendations. Dipesh Chakraborty, for the grant that helped me travel to the US for field work.

Ramachandra Guha is a force of nature. He was the first person outside my circle in 2015 to encourage me to pursue this project vigorously; the second reader of all my chapters, lending them nuance and subtlety; the first to send an endorsement. I am grateful for his infectious energy, his casual generosity, his unwavering moral support all these years. As the founding custodian of the New India Foundation, he trusted me wholeheartedly to pull this book off. At that slightly vulnerable moment, it meant the universe to me.

The late Patrick French for his inspiration, and his magnanimity at crucial junctures. Patrick gave useful writing advice: at a 2013 workshop in Calcutta, when we travelled together during the 2014 Lok Sabha polls, over emails and, most pointedly, when I was writing the book proposal in 2016. He had recently flipped through the manuscript, and I was relieved to hear that it more than met his approval. 'What a thought that so soon ABV will be in print!' read his last message.

Without the NMML, this book could not have been conceived. After months of restlessness and confusion in 2015 – which included resigning from *Newslaundry* embarrassingly soon after joining – I decided to plunge into the research full-time. In retrospect, this was possible only because Teen Murti's rich archives had already given me enough material to convince myself that there did, after all, exist an original story. For large parts of 2016–19, it was my second home.

Chance meetings at Teen Murti have led me to pure magic: William Gould gave me the lead on accessing the British High Commission archives; Shilpa Sharma goaded me to explore ProQuest. I also felt enriched by informal interactions with people working on unrelated themes: Anumeha Yadav on the perils of the gig economy, Shaunak Sen on cinema. The place has far too many researchers and staff to be thanked individually, but I must mention Jyoti Luthra of the manuscripts section.*

Without the slightest doubt, this project would have been considerably worse off without the fellowship from the NIF. I am much obliged to the people who help run it: the high-spirited Yauvanika Chopra, Manish

* Not the least because she twice – pointedly, half-jokingly – warned me against missing her name.

Sabharwal, Srinath Raghavan. A special shout-out to Rivka Israel, the first reader of all my chapters, for her reassuring feedback and quiet encouragement over four years. Niraja Gopal Jayal was kind enough to find time out of her busy schedule to write an endorsement.

My deep and abiding gratitude to everyone who read the manuscript and sent an endorsement at short notice: Pankaj Mishra, Shruti Kapila, Sonia Faleiro, Christophe Jaffrelot, Sugata Bose, Walter Andersen and Zoya Hasan. I was blown away by the sudden effusive feedback after years of near-total seclusion.

My journey owes immensely to three journalists turned paratroopers of archives. Akshaya Mukul and Manoj Mitta have been my mentors and confidants and, on gloomy days, lone cheerleaders. Manoj is a walking encyclopedia on legal matters; and I envy Akshaya's extraordinarily wide reading across genres and languages, his resourcefulness, and his reservoir of news and gossip. Dhirendra Jha's sage-like disposition conceals his razor-sharp intuition on historical events. Dhiren finds it hard to stay in the archives and harder still to stay away.

I trusted the three of them with my excavations everywhere – even 'DOPE' folders. In turn they reciprocated with anecdotes, documents, striking new interpretations of their own. Perhaps we bonded over our shared handicaps. None of us was formally trained to turn cold, dead documents into lively beings with throbbing hearts; each was slogging away at an ambitiou book or two on a ridiculously low budget. (Mercifully, though, it spared us the more undesirable dogmas of academia.) We had each other's backs, and we were all much better off for it. If you are lucky enough to meet the right people, nothing succeeds like generosity.

The four of us also came to share a literary agent. Apart from taking care of the admin side of publishing and general handholding, Shruti Debi turned out to be a magnificent editor. Shruti's sharp, irreverent comments on the chapters – structure, tone, language – have elevated the manuscript.

I also leant on some old friends – friends who are not professional writers but sensitive to the sound on the page. I have exploited them for everything from becoming a sounding board for my ideas to a steady supply of the funniest and silliest memes. Even though they remain scattered across three continents, they are intuitively my most reliable recourses for 3 a.m. emergencies: Zahid Ali, Chinmaya Kumar, Leena Anthony and Kumar Rishabh, Anirvan Chowdhury, Mahati Sharma.

The good folks at Pan Macmillan/Picador India for bringing the book out into the world with enormous passion and conviction. Certainly Teesta Guha Sarkar in all her varied roles, but also Rajdeep Mukherjee, Vijay Sharma, Isha Banerji, Saburi Pandit, Ditsha Gupta, Shreya Gupta, and Haitenlo Semy for his elegant cover design.

Apart from being my closest friend, confidant and critic, Prashansa Taneja has also been a formidable in-house editor. Finally my extended family: the Choudharys on the paternal side (especially my sister Tunny, my cousin Lalit and his spouse Madhu), the Pandeys and the Sharmas on the maternal side. My parents, especially my mother Suneela – who trusted me enough to set me free. And (nani) ma, Ramkali, who died far too young and whose absence I often grieve. Boundless love from these two women is the source of what little perseverance and spark and empathy exists inside me. To them both I dedicate this book.

Abbreviations

ABVP: Akhil Bharatiya Vidyarthi Parishad
AICC: All India Congress Committee
AIGP: All India Ganatantra Parishad
AIIMS: All India Institute of Medical Sciences
AIMMM: All India Majlis-e-Mushawarat
AIR: All India Radio
AISF: All India Students' Federation
AMU: Aligarh Muslim University
BBC: British Broadcasting Corporation
BHU: Banaras Hindu University
BJP: Bharatiya Janata Party
BJS: Bharatiya Jan Sangh
BKD: Bharatiya Kranti Dal
BLD: Bharatiya Lok Dal
BMS: Bharatiya Mazdoor Sangh
BSS: Bhartiya Swayamsevak Sangh
CBI: Central Bureau of Investigation
CFD: Congress for Democracy
CIA: Central Intelligence Agency
CID: Crime Investigation Department
CPI(M): Communist Party of India (Marxist)
CrPC: Code of Criminal Procedure
CSS: Chhatra Sangharsh Samiti
DMC: Delhi Municipal Corporation
DMK: Dravida Munnetra Kazhagam

FIR: First Information Report
I&B: Information and Broadcasting
IB: Intelligence Bureau
IFS: Indian Foreign Service
IPC: Indian Penal Code
IT: Income Tax
J&K: Jammu and Kashmir
JSS: Joint Select Committee
KGB: Komitet Gosudarstvennoy Bezopasnosti
KMPP: Kisan Mazdoor Praja Party
LLB: Bachelor of Laws
LoC: Line of Control
LSS: Lok Sangharsh Samiti
MEA: Ministry of External Affairs
MISA: Maintenance of Internal Security Act
MLA: Member of the Legislative Assembly
MP: Madhya Pradesh
MP: Member of Parliament
NAI: National Archives of India
NATO: North Atlantic Treaty Organization
NEFA: North-East Frontier Agency
NIC: National Integration Committee
NMML: Nehru Memorial Museum and Library
OTC: Officer's Training Camps
PEPSU: Patiala and East Punjab States Union
PMO: Prime Minister's Office
POW: Prisoner of War
RRP: Ram Rajya Parishad
RSS: Rashtriya Swayamsevak Sangh
SAD: Shiromani Akali Dal
SGMS: Sarvadaliya Goraksha Mahaabhiyan Samiti
SRC: States Reorganization Commission
SSP: Samyukta Socialist Party
SVD: Samyukt Vidhayak Dal
UNO: United Nations Organization

UNSC: United Nations Security Council
UP: Uttar Pradesh (United Provinces during 1902–47)
UPSC: Union Public Service Commission
USA: United States of America
USSR: Union of Soviet Socialist Republics

Image Credits

1. Courtesy the author.
2. Courtesy *Jananayak* (Mumbai: Shri Gandharva-Ved Prakashan, 2001).
3. Courtesy *Jananayak*.
4. Courtesy the *Organiser* archives at Keshav Kunj, Jhandewalan.
5. Courtesy Unknown.
6. Courtesy *Jananayak*.
7. Courtesy *Gwalior Government Gazette*, 11 June 1938.
8. Courtesy Hamilton Studios, Mumbai.
9. Courtesy Deepak Vajpayee, Gwalior.
10. Courtesy Gwalior State Records, Madhya Pradesh State Archives, Bhopal.
11. Courtesy *Jananayak*.
12. Courtesy Unknown.
13. Courtesy *Panchjanya*.
14. Courtesy *Swadesh* of Bhopal, Atal Visheshank, 1999.
15. (a) Courtesy *Jananayak*.
    (b) Courtesy *Jananayak*.
16. Courtesy *Jananayak*.
17. Courtesy *Organiser*.
18. Courtesy *Jananayak*.
19. Courtesy *Organiser*.
20. Courtesy *Panchjanya*.
21. Courtesy Saibal Satyarthi.
22. Courtesy *Jananayak*.

23. Courtesy *Jananayak*.
24. Courtesy *Jananayak*.
25. Courtesy *Jananayak*.
26. Courtesy Unknown.
27. Courtesy NMML.
28. Courtesy Satyanarayan Goyal.
29. Courtesy *Jananayak*.
30. Courtesy DRI.
31. Courtesy DRI.
32. Courtesy *Jananayak*.
33. Courtesy *Jananayak*.
34. Courtesy *Jananayak*.
35. Courtesy *Organiser*.
36. Courtesy *Organiser*.
37. Courtesy *Jananayak*.
38. Courtesy *Jananayak*.
39. Courtesy *Jananayak*.
40. Courtesy *Jananayak*.
41. Courtesy *Jananayak*.
42. Courtesy *Jananayak*.
43. Courtesy *Jananayak*.
44. Courtesy *Jananayak*.
45. (a) Courtesy Swarup Goyal.
    (b) Courtesy Swarup Goyal.
46. Courtesy *Pictorial History of BJP* (New Delhi: Bharatiya Janata Party, 2005).
47. Courtesy *Jananayak*.

Notes

All translations in the book are by the author, unless otherwise specified.

Abbreviations

DEPI, CRL: Documentation of Emergency Period in India, June 1975–March 1977: Center for Research Libraries, Chicago
FOFIPA: Foreign Office Files for India, Pakistan and Afghanistan
GSR, MPSA: Gwalior State Records, Old Secretariat, Madhya Pradesh State Archives
JNSG Papers: Jawaharlal Nehru post-1947 Papers, NMML
JPNP: J. P. Narayan papers, NMML
NAUK: National Archives, UK
NAI: National Archives of India
WRPA, CID, UP: Weekly Report on Political Activities, C.I.D., United Provinces

Preface

1. Sagarika Ghose discussing her biography of Vajpayee, *Atal Bihari Vajpayee*, (Delhi: Juggernaut Books, 2021). Available at: https://www.youtube.com/watch?v=6fugJh4jwUI (accessed on 10 May 2022).
2. Vinay Sitapati, *Jugalbandi: The BJP Before Modi* (Gurgaon: Penguin Random House India, 2020), 56. For a book claiming to be scholarly, *Jugalbandi* is replete with serious errors of fact and interpretation.
3. I have borrowed this metaphor from Leon Edel's *Writing Lives: Principia Biographica* (New York: W. W. Norton & Company, 1987).

1. Bateshwar: The Second Banaras

1. Another legend says that the area around Bateshwar was the capital city of Suryasen, great-grandfather of the popular Hindu deity Krishna as well as of Neminath, the twenty-second Tirthankar of the Jains.
2. Dilip K. Chakrabarti, Archaeological Geography of the Ganga Plain: The Upper Ganga (Oudh, Rohilkhand, and the Doab) (Delhi: Munshiram Manoharlal Publishers, 2007), 204–05.
3. Report on the Batesar Horse Fair of 1880, Pro. A – January 1882, Nos. 539-43, Military Department, Simla Records, NAI.
4. File no. 3669–70, Annual Report of the CVD, 1899–1900, May 1901, Military Department, Veterinary Department, NAI. Available at: http://www.abhilekh-patal.in/jspui/handle/123456789/2735232
5. 'Annual Administration Report of the Civil Veterinary Department of India, 1894–5' quoted in Saurabh Mishra, 'Beasts, Murrains, and the British Raj: Reassessing Colonial Medicine in India from the Veterinary Perspective, 1860–1900', *Bulletin of the History of Medicine*, 2011, Winter, 587–619.
6. File no. 709-P-16/1-26: July 1918: Proposed construction of Agra Fort-Batesar Railway versus Dholpur-Rajakhera-Bah Railway, Project Branch, Railways Department, NAI.
7. Atal Behari Vajpayee, *Chuni Huwi Kavitaayein*, (Delhi: Prabhat Prakashan, 2007), 7.
8. Prem Behari Vajpayee, *Bateshwar ki Vibhuti: Pandit Shyamlal Vajpayee* (Gwalior: Kamal Prakashan), 13.
9. *Darbar Policy relating to the Department of Education and Municipalities (Gwalior State)* vol. 10 (Lashkar and Gwalior: Alijah Darbar Press, 1924) copy available at Jiwaji Rao Scindia Museum, Gwalior.

2. Coming of Age: Gwalior, Kanpur

1. Atal Behari Vajpayee, *Twenty-one Poems,* translated by Pavan K. Varma (New Delhi: Viking, 2001), 57.
2. Atal Behari Vajpayee, *Rashtriya Asmita ke Purodha,* edited by Ashok Kaushik (New Delhi: Anil Prakashan, 2001), 12.
3. Atal Behari Vajpayee, *Bindu-Bindu Vichaar,* edited by Chandrika Prasad Sharma (New Delhi: Kitabghar Prakashan, 1997), 16.

4. Vajpayee, *Twenty-one Poems*, 57.
5. Prabhat Jha ed., *Hamaare Atalji* (New Delhi: Prabhat Prakashan, 2015), 115.
6. Ibid.
7. Salil Mekaad, 'The speech that Vajpayee couldn't finish', *Times of India*, 17 August 2018. Available at: https://timesofindia.indiatimes.com/india/the-speech-that-vajpayee-couldnt-finish/articleshow/65432901.cms? (accessed on 15 July 2019).
8. Jha ed., *Hamaare Atalji*, 212.
9. Interview with R. P. Shukla, Gwalior, 24 December 2017.
10. Ibid.
11. Jha ed., *Hamaare Atalji*, 218–19.
12. Proceedings, January 1908, Nos. 19–26: 'Weekly Reports of the Director, Criminal Intelligence, and the Government of the Punjab on the Political Situation, during the Month of December 1907', Home Department, Government of India, NAI.
13. J. T. F. Jordens, *Dayananda Sarasvati: Essays on His Life and Ideas* (Delhi: Manohar Publishers, 2002), 186.
14. *Times of India*, 7 October 1902.
15. Apart from her name and the loss of her infant children, there is no information whatsoever available on Atal's grandmother.
16. 'Atalji rare speech at Tilak Puraskar: 1994 Pune', YouTube. Available at: https://www.youtube.com/watch?v=LIA7ApymYoA&t=1618s.
17. Francesca Orsini, *The Hindi Public Sphere, 1920–1940: Language and Literature in the Age of Nationalism* (New Delhi: Oxford University Press, 2002), 222–23.
18. Ibid., 188.
19. *Gwalior Government Gazette*, 11 June 1938, 87(24), 699.
20. Vajpayee, *Chuni Huwi Kavitaayein*, 9.
21. Kanhaiyalal Nandan ed., *Kya Khoya Kya Paaya* (Delhi: Rajpal and Sons, 2016), 125–26.
22. Tariq Ali, *An Indian Dynasty: The Story of the Nehru-Gandhi Family* (New York: Putnam, New York, 1985), 193.
23. File no 28/8/42 – POLL(I): 'Note on the organization, aims etc. of the Rashtriya Swayam Sewak Sangh', Home Department, Political (Internal) Section, NAI.

24. Vishwa Samvada Kendra, '"The Sangh is my Soul", writes Atal Bihari Vajpayee, the First swayamsevak who became Prime Minister', Samvad, 25 December 2014. Available at: https://samvada.org/?p=14271 (accessed on 15 July 2019).
25. File no 28/8/42 – POLL(I), 'Note on the organization, aims etc. of the Rashtriya Swayam Sewak Sangh'.
26. Ian Copland, *State, Community and Neighbourhood in Princely North India, c. 1900–1950* (London: Palgrave Macmillan UK, 2005), 109–10.
27. File no 28/8/42 – Pol. (I), NAI, 13.
28. Vishwa Samvada Kendra, '"The Sangh is my Soul", *Samvad*.
29. *Organiser*, 12 March 2006.
30. Jha ed., *Hamaare Atalji*, 189.
31. Ibid., 20.
32. From the personal collection of Deepak Vajpayee, Gwalior.
33. *Jayaji Pratap*, Old Secretariat, MPSA, Bhopal, 22 March 1945 issue.
34. Jha ed., *Hamaare Atalji*, 219.
35. Ibid., 192.
36. Ibid., 233.
37. Atal Behari Vajpayee, *Meri Ekyavan Kavitaayein* (New Delhi: Kitabghar Prakashan, 2017), 115–16.
38. Jha ed., *Hamaare Atalji*, 238.
39. Ibid., 7.
40. Ibid.
41. File no. 161 – P/41, 'Subversive activities of the students of the Victoria College, Gwalior', Political Department, Political Branch, NAI.
42. Ibid.
43. From a miscellaneous file dated August 1942: GSR, MPSA, Bhopal.
44. Nandini Gondhalekar and Sanjoy Bhattacharya, 'The All India Hindu Mahasabha and the End of British Rule in India, 1939–1947', *Social Scientist* 27(7/8), July–August 1999, 55. Available at: https://www.jstor.org/stable/3518013?seq=8#metadata_info_tab_contents.
45. From a miscellaneous file dated August 1942: GSR, MPSA, Bhopal.
46. *Frontline*, 7 February 1998 issue. Available at: https://frontline.thehindu.com/the-nation/article30160890.ece (accessed on 15 June 2019).
47. Ibid.

48. Ibid.
49. Amit Mukerji, 'Collective fines: A measure of suppression of the Quit India Movement in the Agra District', *Proceedings of the Indian History Congress* 52 (1991), 602.
50. Jha ed., *Hamaare Atalji*, 192.
51. Ibid., 188.
52. *Gwalior Government Gazette*, vol. 92 (51), 11 December 1943, 1614.
53. Jha ed., *Hamaare Atalji*, 67–70.
54. Ibid.
55. Ibid.
56. Ibid., 140–41.
57. Ibid., 110.
58. Jha ed., *Hamaare Atalji*, 68.
59. Vajpayee, *Chuni Huwi Kavitaayen*, 11–12.
60. Ibid., 129.
61. Ibid., 111.
62. Wendell L. Willkie, *One World* (London: Cassell and Company Ltd., 1943), 194.
63. Narendra Modi, 'Thanks to the National Archives …', Twitter. Available at: https://twitter.com/narendramodi/status/1027379399828627463/photo/1 (accessed on 25 July 2019).
64. Jha, *Hamaare Atalji*, 41–42.
65. Ibid.
66. Ibid., 146–47.
67. Jha, *Hamaare Atalji*, 219–20.
68. File no 50/2003, 'Durbar order regarding recovery of interest at the rate of 3% from scholars', Section: Education (Misc), GSR, MPSA, Bhopal.
69. Vajpayee, *Chuni Huwi Kavitaayen*, 13.
70. Siraj Qureshi, 'Almost a month after his death, Agra University finds Vajpayee's educational record', *India Today*, 1 September 2018. Available at: https://www.indiatoday.in/india/story/almost-a-month-after-his-death-agra-university-finds-vajpayee-s-educational-record-1329552-2018-09-01
71. *Times of India*, 2 August 1947.
72. File no: P – 108, part 1, 1947: Hindu Mahasabha Papers, NMML, 20.
73. Ibid., 21
74. Ibid., 11
75. *Times of India*, 2 August 1947.

76. File no: P – 108, part 1, 1947, Hindu Mahasabha Papers, NMML, 40.
77. Jha, *Hamaare Atalji*, 93.
78. Chandrika Prasad Sharma, *Atal Behari Vajpayee: Vichaar-Bindu* (New Delhi: Kitabghar Prakashan, 2000), 25.
79. Ibid., 24.
80. M. A. Sreenivasan, *Of the Raj, Maharajas and Me* (Hyderabad: Sangam Books, 1991), 220.
81. File no. 74-P/48, vol. 2, Ministry of States, Political Branch, NAI.
82. *Rashtradharma*, second issue, Bhadrapadi Purnima, Vikram Samvat 2004, Sadar Bazaar, Lucknow, 31.

3. Fear and Loathing in Lucknow

1. *Kavi Rajneta*, 81–82.
2. Pramod Majumdar and Ramshankar Agnihotri, *Bhaurao Ki Kahaani, Unki Hi Jabaani* (Lucknow: Lokhit Prakashan), 24.
3. Ibid., pp. 25–26.
4. Jha, *Hamaare Atalji*, 154.
5. Ibid., p. 153.
6. Ibid.
7. *Rashtradharma* (first issue), Shravani Purnima, Vikram Samvat 2004, Lucknow, 55–83.
8. Ibid.
9. M. K. Gandhi, 'The Afghan Bogey: 4 May 1921', *Young India (1919–22)* (Madras: S. Ganesan Publisher, 1924), 716–719. Available at: https://archive.org/details/in.ernet.dli.2015.211536/page/n783 (accessed on 10 September 2019).
10. M. K. Gandhi, *Young India* Microfilms, 18 May 1921, NMML, 156.
11. *Rashtradharma* (first issue), Shravani Purnima, 69.
12. Jha, *Hamaare Atalji*, 154.
13. *Rashtradharma* (second issue), Lucknow, September 1947, 31.
14. *Rashtradharma* (joint third–fourth issue), October–November 1947, 146–47.
15. *Rashtradharma* (fifth issue), December 1947, 35.
16. Shivkumar Goel, *Rashtriyata Ke Purodha: Sri Atal Behari Vajpayee* (Delhi: Surya Bharati Prakashan, 1999), 133–34.

17. *Times of India*, 8 January 1948.
18. *Times of India*, 23 October 1947.
19. Sankar Ghose, *Jawaharlal Nehru: A Biography* (New Delhi: Allied Publishers Limited, 1993), 170.
20. 'War with Pakistan Not Ruled Out'.
21. *Selected Works of Jawaharlal Nehru: Second Series*, vol. 4 (New Delhi: Jawaharlal Nehru Memorial Fund, 1949), 222.
22. File no 19(II): JNSG Papers, NMML, 246–47.
23. File no: 28/5/46 – Pol. (I): Home Department, Government of India, NIA: 'Volunteer organisations - Private Armies: Decision to Call For Monthly Reports from the Province', 2.
24. Shankar Prasada, Oral History Transcripts, NMML, 114–115.
25. An excerpt from Nisid Hajari, *Midnight's Furies: The Deadly Legacy of India's Partition* (New York: Houghton Mifflin Harcourt, 2015), 0547669216 (H) (accessed on iBooks); *Selected Works of Jawaharlal Nehru*, 330.
26. Ibid., p. 244.
27. Mountbatten to Ismay, 4 October 1947, Mountbatten Papers, MB1/E83A. Quoted in Nisid Hajari, *Midnight's Furies*.
28. Rajeshwar Dayal, *A Life of our Times*: (Hyderabad: Sangam Books Ltd, 1998), 93–94.
29. Hajari, *Midnight's Furies* (accessed on iBooks).
30. M. S. Golwalkar Papers, Microfilms Section, NMML., 38–40
31. M. G. Chitkara, *Rashtriya Swayamsevak Sangh: National Upsurge* (Delhi: A. P. H. Publishing Corporation, 2004), 263.
32. *Selected Works of Jawaharlal Nehru: Second Series*, vol. 4, 290.
33. D. R. Goyal, *Rashtriya Swayamsevak Sangh:* (New Delhi: Radha Krishna Prakashan, 1979), 98.
34. Govind Sahai, *RSS: Ideology, Technique, Propaganda* (Allahabad: 1 December 1948), 11.
35. Ibid. Also, File no. G-30/1946: AICC Papers, NMML, 55.
36. File no: 74 – P/48: Ministry of States – Political, NAI, 18–20.
37. File no. 138: Report by Kartar Singh on 9 December 1947: Delhi Police Record (Fifth instalment), NMML.
38. Ibid.
39. Goyal, *Rashtriya Swayamsevak Sangh*, 98–99.
40. *Times of India*, 19 December 1947.
41. *Selected Works of Jawaharlal Nehru: Second Series*, vol. 4, 418.

42. DO 133/93: Mahatma Gandhi's Fast: FOFIPA, 1947–64, NAUK, 40.
43. *Panchjanya*, 11 Paush Shukl, Year 1 Issue 2, Vikram Samvat 2005.
44. Ibid.
45. DO 133/93: Mahatma Gandhi's Fast: FOFIPA, 37.
46. Akhil Anand, 'Let the Old Man Die', *Mainstream*, 5 October 2002; Quoted in Ramachandra Guha, *Gandhi: The Years That Changed the World* (Gurgaon: Penguin Random House India, 2018), 869.
47. DO 133/93: Mahatma Gandhi's Fast: FOFIPA, 1947–64, 33.
48. *Panchjanya*, 11 Paush Shukl, Year 1 Issue 2, Vikram Samvat 2005.
49. *Panchjanya*, 11 Maagh Krishn, Year 1 Issue 4, Vikram Samvat 2005.
50. File no 74 – P/48: 'P' Branch, Ministry of States, NAI, 179.
51. File no 16(2) – P/49: 'P' Branch, Ministry of States, NAI, 74–75.
52. File no 74 – P/48: 'P' Branch, Ministry of States, NAI, 17–20.
53. Ibid., 49. [Emphasis added]
54. WRPA, CID, UP – 1948, for the week ending 6 February 1948.
55. L. K. Advani, *My Country, My Life* (New Delhi: Rupa Publications, 2008), 72.
56. File no 6: JNSG Papers, NMML, 46.
57. *Panchjanya*, Issue 4, February 1948.
58. *Panchjanya,* 6 Margshirsha Krishn, Vikram Samvat 2005.
59. File no. 406: Delhi Police Record, NMML.
60. WRPA, CID, UP – 1948, 20 February.
61. Ibid., 26 March–24 September.
62. File no 74 – P/48: 'P' Branch, Ministry of States, NAI, 61.
63. Interview with Devendra Swaroop, Bhiwadi, 8 January 2017.
64. Mauli Chandra Sharma Oral transcripts, NMML, 162.
65. Ibid., 173.
66. Durga Das ed., *Selected Correspondence of Sardar Patel, 1945–50*, vol. 6 (Ahmedabad: Navjeevan Publishing, 1973), 66.
67. *Panchjanya*, 6 Margshirsha Krishn, Vikram Samvat 2005, Bharat Press, Lucknow.
68. Interview with R. P. Shukla, Gwalior, 24 December 2017.
69. Patrick French, *Liberty or Death: India's Journey to Independence and Division* (London: Penguin UK, 1997), 246.
70. *Selected Correspondence of Sardar Patel, 1945–50,* vol. 6, 61–62.
71. Ian Copland, *The Princes of India in the Endgame of Empire*, 179–180.
72. File no 74 – P/48: 'P' Branch, Ministry of States, NAI, 41–74.

73. *Panchjanya*, 3 Margshirsha Krishn, Issue supplementary 26, Vikram Samvat 2005, Year 1.
74. Ibid.
75. Ibid.
76. Walter K. Andersen and Shridhar D. Damle: *The Brotherhood in Saffron: The Rashtriya Swayamsevak Sangh and Hindu Revivalism* (New Delhi: Vistaar Publications, 1987), 53.
77. File no. 74 (1) – P/48: Ministry of States – Political Branch; NAI, 44–47.
78. *Panchjanya*, 13 Bhandrapada Shukl, Vikram Samvat 2005.
79. File no: P-108, part two (1947): Hindu Mahasabha Papers, NMML, 308.
80. Interview with Devendra Swaroop, Bhiwadi, 8 January 2017.
81. Ibid.
82. WRPA, CID, UP – 1948, 1 October 1948.
83. WRPA, CID, UP – 1949, for the week ending 24 December 1948.
84. 'Varanasi se shuru huwi thi Atal ki shikhar yatra', *Navbharat Times*, 16 August 2018. Available at: https://navbharattimes.indiatimes.com/state/uttar-pradesh/varanasi/former-prime-minister-atal-bihari-vajpayee-lived-his-journalist-life-in-varanasi-uttar-pradesh/articleshow/65426837.cms (accessed on 15 November 2019).
85. File no 404: Delhi Police Record, Eighth instalment, NMML, 8.
86. Shankar Prasad, Oral History Transcripts, NMML, 165–168.
87. Interview with Vishwanath Tripathi, Delhi, 14 September 2018.
88. Ibid.
89. Rakesh Ankit, *Economic & Political Weekly*, 47(16), 21 April 2012, 71–78.
90. Ibid, 77.
91. Christophe Jaffrelot, 'Sardar and the Swayamsevaks', *Indian Express*, 7 December 2013.
92. *Times of India*, 1 November 2011.
93. Image no 160: India, Records of the US State Department Relating to the Internal Affairs of India, 1945-1949, Library of Congress, Washington DC, 16 April 1946 – 6 December 1949.
94. File no 16(2) – P/49: 'P' Branch, Ministry of States, NAI, 74–75.
95. Andersen and Damle, *The RSS: A View to the Inside*, 275.
96. Gopal ed., *Selected Works of Jawaharlal Nehru*, vol. 12, 453. Jha ed., *Hamaare Atalji*, 97–98.
97. File no 27 (II), JNSG Papers, NMML, 356–57.

98. Sheela Reddy, 'If I Weren't a Sanyasin, He Would Have Married Me', *Outlook,* 23 February 2004. Available at: https://www.outlookindia.com/magazine/story/if-i-werent-a-sanyasin-he-would-have-married-me/223036 (accessed on 15 September 2019); Hindustan Samachar report of 2 November 1949 quoted in *Panchjanya*, 12 Margshirsha Krishn, Vikram Samvat 2006. File no. 21 (I), JNSG Papers, NMML, 66–68.
99. Gopal ed., *Selected Works of Jawaharlal Nehru,* vol. 12, 13–14.
100. WRPA, CID, UP – 1949, for the week ending 15 July 1949.
101. Ibid., for the week ending 2 September 1949.
102. Clemens Six reaches a similar conclusion. Please see *Secularism, Decolonisation, and the Cold War in South and Southeast Asia*, Routledge Studies in the Modern History of Asia, (New York: Routledge, 2018), 89–123.

4. The Sangh's Most Loyal Son

1. WRPA, CID, UP – 1948, for the week ending 6 August 1948.
2. *Panchjany*a, 4 Margshirsha Krishn issue, Vikram Samvat 2006.
3. *Panchjanya*, 11 Margshirsha Shukl issue, Vikram Samvat 2006.
4. WRPA, CID, UP – 1949, for the week ending 25 November 1949.
5. *Times of India,* 17 November 1949.
6. *Panchjany*a, edit dated 2 Aashwin Krishn, Vikram Samvat 2006.
7. *Panchjany*a, 6 Maagh Krishn issue, Vikram Samvat 2006.
8. *Panchjanya*, 4 Paush Shukl issue, Vikram Samvat 2006.
9. *Panchjanya*, 5 Ashadh Shukl issue, Vikram Samvat 2007.
10. Shraddha Chigateri, 'Negotiating the "Sacred" Cow: Cow Slaughter and the Regulation of Difference in India', in *Democracy, Religious Pluralism and the Liberal Dilemma of Accommodation*, edited by Monica Mookherjee, Studies in Global Justice (New York: Springer, 2011), 142.
11. Department of Animal Husbandry and Dairying, Ministry of Fisheries, Animal Husbandry and Dairying. Available at: http://dahd.nic.in/related-links/chapter-i-introduction (accessed on 1 October 2019).
12. *Swadesh*, 24 September 1951 edit; Atal Behari Vajpayee, *Kuchh Lekh Kuchh Bhaashan*, edited by Chandrika Prasad Sharma (New Delhi: Kitabghar Prakashan, 1996), 202–03.
13. Rather farcically, though, this was carried out as per the economic logic

propounded by the conservatives. Article 48 elaborates the principle thus: 'The State shall endeavour to organise agriculture and animal husbandry on modern and scientific lines and shall, in particular, take steps for preserving and improving the breeds, and prohibiting the slaughter of cows and other milch and draught cattle.'

14. Ibid.
15. WRPA, CID, UP – 1949, 18 November 1949.
16. Andersen and Damle, *The RSS*, 194.
17. *Panchjanya*, 8 Magh Shukl issue, Vikram Samvat 2006.
18. *Panchjanya*, 3 Paush Krish edit, Vikram Samvat 2006.
19. Ibid.
20. Jha, *Hamaare Atalji*, 45–46.
21. *Panchjanya*, 6 Jyeshtha Shukl edit, Vikram Samvat 2007.
22. *Panchjanya*, 30 Ashadh Krishn, Vikram Samvat 2007.
23. *Panchjanya*, 6 Margsheesh Shukl edit, Vikram Samvat 2006.
24. *Panchjanya*, 13 Aasadh Krishn, Vikram Samvat 2007.
25. *Yugpravartak Dr. Hedgewar*: Sanskriti Jagran Mandal, Pune, 2014, 221.
26. *Times of India*, 23 December 1943, 4.
27. File no 14: JNSG Papers, NMML, 124–26.
28. File no 7: JNSG Papers, NMML, 185.
29. Vajpayee, *Kuchh Lekh Kuchh Bhaashan*,195.
30. File no. 13 (4) – P/50: Political Branch, Ministry of States, NAI, 162.
31. *Panchjanya*, 8 Kartik Krishn, Vikram Samvat, 2008.
32. *Panchjanya*, edit 19 Margshirsha Shukl 19, Vikram Samvat, 2007.
33. Balraj Madhok, *Portrait of a Martyr: A Biography of Dr. Shyama Prasad Mookerji* (New Delhi: Rupa Publications, 2001), 122–25.
34. File no. 54: Delhi Police Record (Fifth instalment), NMML, 77.
35. Ibid.
36. *Searchlight* (Patna), 22 November 1951, quoted in Ramachandra Guha, *India After Gandhi: The History of the World's Largest Democracy* (New Delhi: Pan Macmillan India, 2008), 136.
37. Bhartiya Jan Sangh: Presidential Speeches (1951–1975): Party Documents, 3.
38. *Times of India*, 22 October 1951.
39. File no. 54: Delhi Police Record (Fifth instalment), NMML, 53.
40. Interview with V. K. Malhotra, Delhi, 28 August 2017.
41. Jha, *Hamaare Atalji*, 76.

42. File no. 146: Delhi Police Record (Fifth instalment), NMML, 12–13.
43. Guha, *India After Gandhi*, 140.
44. File no. 146: Delhi Police Record (Fifth instalment), NMML, 12–13.
45. Jha, *Hamaare Atalji*, 22–23.
46. File no. 146: Delhi Police Record (Fifth instalment), NMML, 54.
47. Interview with Raj Dutt, Mumbai, 7 August 2017.
48. Madhok: *Portrait of a Martyr*, 146–47.
49. Ibid., 150.
50. File no. 142: Delhi Police Record (Fifth instalment), NMML, 17.
51. Ibid., 117.
52. Ibid., 93–96.
53. Mauli Chandra Sharma Oral transcripts, NMML, 196.
54. File no. 142: Delhi Police Record, 13.
55. Jha, *Hamaare Atalji*, 91.
56. *Praja Tantra*, Joint December 2014–January 2015 issue, Year 11, Issue 11–12, published from Bilaspur, 50.
57. Jha, *Hamaare Atalji*, 235.
58. File no. 142: Delhi Police Record (Fifth instalment), NMML, 93–96.
59. *Times of India*, 23 October 1951.
60. P. N. K. Bamzai, *Kashmir and Power Politics* (Delhi: Metropolitan Book Company, 1966) p. 202.
61. Srinath Raghavan, *War and Peace in Modern India* (Ranikhet: Permanent Black, 2009), 219.
62. Ibid.
63. File no. 55: Delhi Police Record (Fifth instalment), NMML, 89.
64. File no. 145: Delhi Police Record (Fifth instalment), NMML, 12.
65. Ibid., 11.
66. Ibid., 91.
67. Madhok, *Portrait of a Martyr*, 247.
68. Ibid., 153.
69. *Panchjanya*, 4 July 1955 issue.
70. Ibid.
71. *Panchjanya*, 8 Vaishakh Shukl, Vikram Samvat 2010.
72. *Panchjanya*, 25 Vaishakh Krishn, Vikram Samvat 2010.
73. Ibid.
74. *Panchjanya*, 8 Vaishakh Shukl, Vikram Samvat 2010.

75. *Panchjanya* 6 April 1953 issue.
76. File no. 52: Delhi Police Record (Fifth instalment), NMML, 12–13.
77. Ibid.
78. Advani, *My Country, My Life*, 834.
79. File no. 51: Delhi Police Record (Fifth instalment), NMML, 88.
80. Sarvepalli Gopal, *Jawaharlal Nehru: A Biography (1947-56)* vol. 2 (Delhi: Oxford University Press, 1979), 125.
81. Shankar Prasad, Oral History Transcripts, NMML, 225.
82. Ibid.
83. Norman D. Palmer, 'The Changing Scene in Kashmir,' *Far Eastern Survey* 22, 12 (1953), 157-63, Available at: 10.2307/3023853.
84. Madhok, *Portrait of a Martyr*, 287.
85. *Panchjanya*, 20 July 1953 issue.
86. Ibid.
87. File no. 47: Delhi Police Record (Fifth instalment), NMML, 1.
88. File no. 57: Delhi Police Record (Fifth instalment); NMML, 27–28.
89. Ibid., 10.
90. File no. 146: Delhi Police Record (Fifth instalment), NMML, 11.
91. Madhok, *Portrait of a Martyr*, 304–05.
92. *Panchjanya* 20 July 1953 issue.
93. Ibid.
94. File no. 43: Delhi Police Record (Fifth instalment), NMML, 79–80.
95. File no. 45: Delhi Police Record (Fifth instalment), NMML, 7–8.
96. *Organiser*, 14 September 1953 issue.
97. Ibid.
98. *Organiser*, 14 September 1953 issue.
99. Prabhat Jha ed., *Hamaare Atalji* (Delhi: Prabhat Prakashan, 2015), 97–98.
100. Ibid.
101. *Panchjanya*, 18 November 1953 issue.
102. File no. 44: Delhi Police Record (Fifth instalment), NMML, 61.
103. Ibid., 65.

5. An Implosive Sorrow

1. Andersen and Damle, *The Brotherhood in Saffron*, 161–62.
2. File no. 49: Delhi Police Record (Fifth instalment), NMML.

3. Christophe Jaffrelot, *The Hindu Nationalist Movement and Indian Politics: 1925 to the 1990s* (London: Hurst & Company, 1996), 122.
4. *Times of India*, 26 January 1954.
5. *Panchjanya*, 2 February 1954 issue.
6. Ibid.
7. *Panchjanya*, 23 October 1954 issue.
8. Aditya Balasubramanian, 'A More Indian Path to Prosperity? Hindu Nationalism and Development in the Mid-Twentieth Century and Beyond', *Capitalism*, Vol. 3(2), Summer 2022, 333–78.
9. *Organiser*, 6 December 1954 issue.
10. *Organiser*, 16 January 1955 issue.
11. B. D. Graham, *Hindu Nationalism and Indian Politics* (Cambridge: Cambridge University Press, 1990), 64–65.
12. *Organiser*, 16 January 1955 issue.
13. *Panchjanya*, 17 January 1955 issue.
14. Vajpayee, *Kuchh Lekh Kuchh Bhaashan*, 197–99.
15. *Panchjanya*, 17 January 1955 issue.
16. Ibid.
17. *Organiser*, 28 February 1955 issue.
18. *Panchjanya*, 28 April 1955 issue.
19. *Times of India*, 25 February 1955.
20. *Times of India*, 28 February 1955.
21. 'Details of Bye Elections from 1952 to 1995', Election Commission of India. Available at: https://eci.gov.in/files/file/2511-details-of-bye-elections-from-1952-to-1995/ (accessed on 21 November 2019).
22. Jha, *Hamaare Atalji*.
23. Ibid.
24. *Panchjanya*, 28 April 1955 issue.
25. Ibid.
26. Ibid.
27. Rashme Sehgal, 'Always Atal about His Roots', *Times of India*, 26 April 2003. Available at: https://timesofindia.indiatimes.com/home/sunday-times/deep-focus/Always-Atal-about-his-roots/articleshow/44589121.cms (accessed on 15 June 2020).
28. Interview with Kanti Mishra, Gwalior, 25 December 2017.
29. *Organiser*, 7 February 1955 issue.

30. *Panchjanya*, 22 August 1955 issue.
31. Ibid.
32. *Panchjanya*, 10 October 1955 issue.
33. *Panchjanya*, 3 October 1955 issue.
34. *Organiser*, 24 October 1955 issue.
35. V. S. Naipaul, *India: A Million Mutinies Now* (London: Picador, 1990), 169.
36. *Times of India*, 12 October 1955.
37. *Organiser*, 6 February 1956 issue.
38. *Panchjanya*, 20 February 1956 issue.
39. *Organiser*, 28 May 1956 issue.
40. *Organiser*, 4 June 1956 issue.
41. *Panchjanya*, 9 July 1956 issue.
42. *Organiser*, 2 July 1956 issue.
43. Jha, *Hamaare Atalji*, 220.
44. Ibid.
45. *Organiser*, 24 October 1955 issue.
46. *Organiser*, 2 April 1956 issue.
47. Interview with V. K. Malhotra, 2 April 2018, Delhi.
48. *Panchjanya*, 30 April 1956 issue.
49. *Organiser*, 30 April 1956 issue.
50. Based on an excerpt from Devika Sethi's *War over Words: Censorship in India, 1930-1960* (Cambridge: Cambridge University Press, 2019). Available at: https://scroll.in/article/926425/how-nehru-reacted-to-violent-protests-in-1956-demanding-withdrawal-of-a-book-about-religious-leaders (accessed on 15 May 2020).
51. *Panchjanya,* 24 September 1956 issue.
52. Ibid.
53. Ibid., Sethi, *War over Words: Censorship in India, 1930-1960*.
54. *Times of India*, 31 December 1956.
55. *Panchjanya*, 31 December 1956 issue.
56. Ibid.
57. Ibid.
58. *Panchjanya*, 31 December 1956 issue.
59. *Panchjanya*, 21 January 1957 issue.
60. *Panchjanya*, 25 February 1957 issue.

61. Vajpayee, *Kuchh Lekh Kuchh Bhaashan*, 197–99.
62. *Panchjanya*, 31 December 1956 issue.
63. *Panchjanya*, 28 January 1957 issue.
64. Ibid, Vajpayee, *Kuchh Lekh Kuchh Bhaashan*.
65. Ibid.
66. Dinesh Mishra, 'Memories of Atal's political nursery are scattered in Balrampur', *Navbharat Times,* 16 August 2018. Available at: https://navbharattimes.indiatimes.com/state/uttar-pradesh/others/memory-of-atal-bihari-vajpayee-from-balrampur-where-he-become-mp-for-the-first-time/articleshow/65426787.cms (accessed on 15 January 2020).
67. Dinesh Narayanan, *The RSS: And the Making of the Deep Nation* (Gurgaon: Penguin Random House India), Kindle edition.
68. Vajpayee, *Kuchh Lekh Kuchh Bhaashan*.
69. *Panchjanya*, 24 February 1993 issue.
70. *Panchjanya*, 8 April 1957 issue.
71. Ibid, 4.

6. Beloved Nemesis: The Nehru Years

1. Columns 450–452: Lok Sabha Debates, 15 May 1957. Available at: https://eparlib.nic.in/bitstream/123456789/1428/1/lsd_02_01_15-05-1957.pdf (accessed on 20 June 2020).
2. Columns 577–578: Lok Sabha Debates, 16 May 1957. Available at: https://eparlib.nic.in/bitstream/123456789/1398/1/lsd_02_01_16-05-1957.pdf (accessed on 20 June 2020).
3. *Times of India* (1861–current), Mumbai, 29 July 2001.
4. *Panchjanya,* 9 December 1957 issue.
5. *Times of India*, 1 June 1957.
6. *Times of India*, 21 August 1957.
7. *Panchjanya*, 10 February 1958 issue.
8. *Times of India*, 28 February 1958.
9. *Panchjanya*, 16 September 1957 issue.
10. Atal Bihari Vajpayee, *Four Decades in Parliament*, vol. 1, edited by Dr N. M. Ghatate (Delhi: Shipra Publications, 1996), 6-9.
11. *Panchjanya*, 9 December 1957 issue.
12. *Panchjanya*, 15 September 1958 issue.

13. *Panchjanya*, 22 September 1958 issue.
14. *Selected Works of Jawaharlal Nehru*, Second Series, vol. 41 (Jawaharlal Nehru Memorial Fund, Delhi, 2010), 640–641.
15. Ibid., 642.
16. Columns 1759–1760: Lok Sabha Debates, 19 August 1958. Available at: https://eparlib.nic.in/bitstream/123456789/1560/1/lsd_02_05_19-08-1958.pdf (accessed on 20 June 2020).
17. Gopal: *Jawaharlal Nehru: 1956-64 vol. 3* (Kindle edition).
18. Ibid, Columns 1759–1760, Lok Sabha Debates, 19 August 1958.
19. Gopal, *Jawaharlal Nehru: 1956-64 vol. 3* (Kindle edition).
20. Vajpayee, *Four Decades in Parliament*, xx.
21. Mikel Dunham, *Buddha's Warriors: The Story of the CIA-backed Tibetan Freedom Fighters, the Chinese Invasion, and the Ultimate Fall of Tibet* (New York: TarcherPerigee, 2004), 53.
22. Column 7708: 23 March 1959, Lok Sabha Debates. Available at: https://eparlib.nic.in/bitstream/123456789/1723/1/lsd_02_07_23-03-1959.pdf (accessed on 20 June 2020).
23. *Times of India*, 31 March 1958.
24. Guha, *India After Gandhi*, 301.
25. *SWJN, Second Series*, vol. 49, 5.
26. Vajpayee, *Four Decades in Parliament,* vol. 3, 159–62.
27. Record of Nehru's meeting with the Dalai Lama on 24 April 1959. Available at: http://www.archieve.claudearpi.net/maintenance/uploaded_pics/Talks_PM_DalaiLama_Mussorie.pdf (accessed on 20 June 2020).
28. *SWJN, Second Series*, vol. 49, 556–60.
29. Sarvepalli Gopal, *Jawaharlal Nehru: 1956-64*, vol. 3 (Delhi: Random House), (Kindle edition).
30. *Caravan*, April 2019 issue.
31. *Times of India*, 16 June 1959.
32. Interview with K. Raman Pillai, Trivandrum, 17 April 2018.
33. *Times of India*, 13 July 1959.
34. Columns 3384–3393: Lok Sabha Debates, Second Series, vol. 33 (13), 20 August 1959.
35. Vajpayee, *Four Decades in Parliament,* vol. 3, 163.
36. *SWJN, Second Series*, vol. 51, 457–59.
37. Vajpayee, *Four Decades in Parliament*, vol. 3, 163–66.

38. *SWJN, Second Series*, vol. 52, 235–39.
39. Column 6560: Lok Sabha Debates, 4 September 1959. Available at: https://eparlib.nic.in/bitstream/123456789/1840/1/lsd_02_08_04-09-1959.pdf (accessed on 20 June 2020).
40. Column 4871: Lok Sabha Debates, 28 August 1959. Available at: https://eparlib.nic.in/bitstream/123456789/1850/1/lsd_02_08_28-08-1959.pdf (accessed on 20 June 2020).
41. Advani, *My Country, My Life*, 102–03.
42. Column 6695: Lok Sabha Debates, 7 September 1959. Available at: https://eparlib.nic.in/bitstream/123456789/1834/1/lsd_02_08_07-09-1959.pdf (accessed on 20 June 2020).
43. Column 8108: Lok Sabha Debates, 4 September 1959. Available at: https://eparlib.nic.in/bitstream/123456789/1908/1/lsd_02_08_12-09-1959.pdf (accessed on 20 June 2020).
44. *Times of India*, 16 September 19595.
45. Ibid.
46. *Times of India*, 27 November 1959.
47. Ibid.
48. Ibid, 1.
49. *Organiser*, 25 January 1960 issue.
50. *Organiser*, 1 February 1960 issue.
51. Guha, *India After Gandhi*, 314.
52. Gopal, *Jawaharlal Nehru: 1956-64 vol 3* (Kindle edition).
53. *Organiser*, 22 February 1960 issue.
54. Column 1498-1499: 17 February 1960, Lok Sabha Debates. Available at: https://eparlib.nic.in/bitstream/123456789/55622/1/lsd_02_10_17-02-1960.pdf (accessed on 20 June 2020).
55. 'When Atal Bihari Vajpayee searched for Nehru', *Business Today*, 17 August 2018. Available at: https://www.businesstoday.in/current/economy-politics/when-atal-bihari-vajpayee-searched-for-nehru/story/281376.html (accessed on 20 June 2020).
56. *Organiser*, 29 February 1960 issue.
57. *Organiser*, 28 March 1960 issue.
58. *Organiser*, 4 April 1960 issue.
59. *Organiser*, 25 April 1960 issue.
60. Sarvepalli Gopal, *Jawaharlal Nehru: 1956-64*, vol. 3 (Kindle edition).

61. *Organiser*, 3 October 1960 issue.
62. Maharajakrishna Rasgotra, *A Life in Diplomacy* (Gurgaon, Penguin India, 2016), 154-55.
63. *Organiser*, 20 October 1960 issue.
64. *Organiser*, 24 October 1960 issue.
65. *Organiser*, 20 October 1960 issue.
66. Ibid.
67. Ibid.
68. Ibid.
69. *Organiser*, 31 October 1960 issue.
70. Interview with Maharajakrishna Rasgotra, Delhi, 6 March 2017.
71. Rasgotra, *A Life in Diplomacy*, 167–70.
72. *Organiser*, 19 December 1960 issue.
73. *Organiser*, 31 October 1960 issue.
74. Ibid.
75. *Organiser*, 5 December 1960 issue.
76. Ibid.
77. *Organiser*, 5 December 1960 issue.
78. *Organiser*, 24 October 1960 issue.
79. *Times of India*, 6 December 1971.
80. *Organiser*, 28 November 1960 issue.
81. Ibid.
82. Ibid.
83. *Organiser*, 5 December 1960 issue.
84. Sarvepalli Gopal, *Jawaharlal Nehru: 1956-64,* vol 3 (Delhi: Random House (Digital), 2014), (Kindle edition).
85. *Organiser*, 29 June 1959 issue.
86. Columns 99–105, 6 May 1961, Vol I – No. 2, Debates from the Joint Sitting of Houses of Parliament. Available at https://eparlib.nic.in/bitstream/123456789/55347/1/lsd_02_13_06-05-1961.pdf (accessed on 29 February 2020).
87. Vajpayee, *Four Decades in Parliament*, vol. 1, xxiv–xxv.
88. *Organiser*, 9 October 1961 issue.
89. *Organiser*, 20 November 1961 issue.
90. Columns 2940–54: Rajya Sabha proceedings of 5 December 1961. Available at https://eparlib.nic.in/bitstream/123456789/55542/1/lsd_02_15_04-12-1961.pdf (accessed on 20 June 2020).

91. *Times of India*, 19 December 1961.
92. *Times of India*, 29 March 1962.
93. Back cover of booklet titled *Know Your Election Law*, published by B. N. Atre (Bombay: BJS Bombay, 1961).
94. K. D. Malaviya, *The Dangers of Right Reaction* (New Delhi: A Socialist Congressman Publication, 1965), 35–36.
95. *Times of India*, 3 February 1967.
96. Sushil Manav, 'When Haryana woman MP humbled Vajpayee on his home-turf', *Tribune*, 17 August 2018. Available at: https://www.tribuneindia.com/news/archive/when-haryana-woman-mp-humbled-vajpayee-on-his-home-turf-638437 (accessed on 20 June 2020).
97. *Times of India*, 3 February 1967.
98. Vajpayee, *Four Decades in Parliament*, vol.1.
99. Krishna Pratap Singh, 'When the people of Balrampur taught a lesson to Atal Bihari Vajpayee for his indecent remarks', 2 April 2019. Available at: https://thewirehindi.com/76339/chunavi-baaten-when-atal-bihari-vajpayee-lost-his-balrampur-loksabha-seat/.
100. *Times of India*, 22 February 1962.
101. He had polled 1,02,260 against Joshi's 1,00,208; *Times of India*, 9 March 1962.
102. *Times of India*, 9 March 1962.
103. Ibid.
104. Vajpayee, *Four Decades in Parliament* vol. 1, State of the Nation, 20–22.
105. *Organiser*, 9 April 1962 issue.
106. *Organiser*, 11 June 1962 issue.
107. *Times of India*, 5 June 1962.
108. Columns 862–863: Rajya Sabha proceedings, 20 June 1962. Available at https://rsdebate.nic.in/bitstream/123456789/553150/1/PQ_39_20061962_S166_p862_p871.pdf (accessed on 20 June 2020).
109. Jairam Ramesh, *A Chequered Brilliance: The Many Lives of V.K. Krishna Menon* (Gurgaon: Penguin Random House India, 2019) (via iBooks).
110. Columns 2194–2195: Rajya Sabha proceedings, 20 August 1962. Available at https://rsdebate.nic.in/bitstream/123456789/551838/1/PQ_40_20081962_S443_p2193_p2195.pdf (accessed on 20 June 2020).
111. Columns 5053–5054: Rajya Sabha proceedings, 5 September 1962. Available at https://rsdebate.nic.in/bitstream/123456789/550740/1/PQ_40_05091962_S899_p5052_p5054.pdf (accessed on 20 June 2020).

112. *Times of India*, 14 September 1962.
113. Guha, *India After Gandhi*, 331.
114. Ibid., 332.
115. Srinath Raghavan, *The Most Dangerous Place: A History of the United States in South Asia* (Gurgaon: Penguin Random House India, 2018), 220.
116. Mani Shankar Aiyar, 'Vajpayee's Biting Criticism, at Age 36, of Nehru during a Time of War', *NDTV*, 12 October 2016. Available at https://www.ndtv.com/opinion/vajpayees-biting-criticism-at-age-36-of-nehru-during-a-time-of-war-1473003.
117. *Times of India*, 1 November 1962.
118. Columns 286–301: Rajya Sabha proceedings, 9 November 1962. Available at: https://rsdebate.nic.in/bitstream/123456789/549017/1/PD_41_09111962_2_p281_p426_5.pdf (accessed on 20 June 2020).
119. Ibid.
120. Ibid.
121. *Times of India*, 10 November 1962.
122. Columns 987–996: Rajya Sabha proceedings, 13 November 1962. Available at https://rsdebate.nic.in/bitstream/123456789/549149/1/PD_41_13111962_4_p859_p998_19.pdf (accessed on 20 June 2020).
123. *Times of India*, 19 November 1962.
124. Minocheher Rustom Masani, *Against the Tide* (New Delhi: Vikas Prakashan, 1981), 161.
125. Columns 1969–72: Rajya Sabha proceedings, 21 November 1962. Available at https://rsdebate.nic.in/bitstream/123456789/549341/1/PD_41_21111962_10_p1969_p1977_27.pdf (accessed on 20 June 2020).
126. *Times of India*, 1 January 1963.
127. *Times of India*, 25 March 1963.
128. *Times of India*, 31 December 1962.
129. *Times of India*, 21 January 1963.
130. *Times of India*, 25 January 1963.
131. *Times of India*, 28 January 1963.
132. *Organiser*, 4 February 1963 issue.

7. The Husband and the Lover

1. Vajpayee's interview in *Navneet*, December 1963, republished in Atal Bihari Vajpayee, *Rajneeti Ki Rapteeli Raahein*, edited by Chandrika Prasad Sharma (Delhi: Praveen Prakashan, 1997), 11–12.
2. Ibid.
3. Ibid.
4. 'Rajkumari Kaul (Haksar)', Geni.com. Available at https://www.geni.com/people/Rajkumari-Kaul/6000000011812394340?through=6000000017528412280
5. Interview with D. K. Sethi, Delhi, 11 August 2017.
6. Kanhaiyalal Nandan ed., *Kya Khoya Kya Paaya* (Delhi: Rajpal & Sons, 2016), 88.
7. Interview with Pan Singh Patwal, Delhi, 11 March 2018.
8. Kingshuk Nag, *Atal Bihari Vajpayee: A Man for All Seasons* (Delhi: Rupa Publications, 2016), 63–64.
9. Balraj Madhok: *Zindagi Ka Safar-III* (Delhi: Dinman Prakashan, 2003), 25.

8. Missing the Lok Sabha's Spark: The Shastri Years

1. Over the next few years, many of the Mahasabha and RRP elders crossed over to the Jan Sangh.
2. Column 1546: Lok Sabha Debates, 20 August 1963. Available at https://eparlib.nic.in/bitstream/123456789/2895/1/lsd_03_05_20-08-1963.pdf (accessed on 20 June 2020).
3. Column 2240: Lok Sabha Debates, 22 August 1963. Available at https://eparlib.nic.in/bitstream/123456789/2906/1/lsd_03_05_22-08-1963.pdf (accessed on 20 June 2020).
4. *Times of India*, 17 August 1963.
5. What we do know is that in December, when the Punjab home minister Mohan Lal casually alleged that the Jan Sangh had been collaborating with foreign powers to topple the Nehru government, Vajpayee threatened self-immolation. Eventually, Nehru intervened to wangle an apology out of Lal.
6. *Times of India*, 16 September 1963.
7. *Times of India*, 28 August 1963.

8. Airgram A-1248 from New Delhi to Department of State on 13 April 1963: Pol 32-1 India-Pak. Accessed at the Library of Congress, Washington DC.
9. *Times of India*, 31 December 1963.
10. *Times of India*, 29 April 1964.
11. Guha, *India After Gandhi*, 352.
12. *Times of India*, 12 May 1964.
13. Column 506: Rajya Sabha proceedings, 13 February 1964. Available at https://rsdebate.nic.in/bitstream/123456789/541478/1/PD_46_13021964_4_p429_p592_11.pdf (accessed on 20 June 2020).
14. Columns 91–93: Rajya Sabha proceedings, 29 May 1964. Available at http://164.100.47.5/Official_Debate_Nhindi/Floor/48/F29.05.1964.pdf (accessed on 20 June 2020).
15. *Times of India*, 29 April 1964.
16. *Organiser*, 8 May 1966 issue.
17. Balraj Madhok, *Zindagi Ka Safar-II: Swatantra Bharat Ki Rajneeti Ka Sankraman Kaal* (Delhi: Hindu World Publications, 1994), 140–41.
18. Lok Sabha Debates: Third Series, vol. 33, 1964/1886. Available at: https://eparlib.nic.in/bitstream/123456789/2962/1/lsd_03_08_29-05-1964.pdf (accessed on 15 January 2020).
19. Correspondence with Indira Gandhi: K. R. Malkani Papers, NMML.
20. Clipping from the *Patriot*, 20 August 1964, P. K. Malaviya Papers, NAI. Available at https://www.abhilekh-patal.in/jspui/handle/123456789/2690330? (accessed on 15 January 2020).
21. Interview with Madhu Deolekar, Mumbai, 24 February 2017.
22. Graham, *Hindu Nationalism and Indian Politics*.
23. *Times of India,* 24 February 1965.
24. Column 581, Rajya Sabha Debates, 22 February 1965. Available at: https://rsdebate.nic.in/bitstream/123456789/533515/1/PD_51_22021965_4_p539_p601_12.pdf (accessed on 20 June 2020).
25. Columns 1585-1594, Rajya Sabha Debates, 2 May 1962. Available at: https://rsdebate.nic.in/bitstream/123456789/553206/2/ID_38_02051962_11_p1500_p1642_11.pdf (accessed on 20 June 2020).
26. *Times of India*, 5 March 1965.
27. Columns 1991–2000, Rajya Sabha Debates, 4 March 1965. Available at https://rsdebate.nic.in/bitstream/123456789/533367/1/PD_51_04031965_12_p1975_p2104_4.pdf (accessed on 20 June 2020).
28. Columns 2024–28: Rajya Sabha Debates, 4 March 1965.

29. In a dramatic development, the foreign minister M. C. Chagla – who had previously served as the education minister – resigned in protest, calling the proposal for a rapid switch-over to regional languages 'unrealistic and impractical' and harmful to national unity.
30. http://www.indianlegislation.in/BA/BaActToc.aspx?actid=31961 (accessed on 20 June 2020).
31. *Times of India*, 24 February 1965.
32. Alastair Lamb, *The Kashmir Problem: A Historical Survey* (New York, Frederick A. Praeger, 1967), 116.
33. Guha, *India After Gandhi*, 396.
34. *Organiser*, 11 July 1965 issue (last page).
35. *Organiser*, 8 August 1965 issue.
36. *Times of India*, 1 July 1965.
37. *Times of India*, 5 July 1965.
38. *Organiser*, 11 July 1965 issue.
39. *Times of India*, 16 August 1965.
40. *Organiser*, 2 August 1965 issue.
41. *Organiser*, 5 September 1965 issue.
42. *Organiser*, 18 September 1966 issue.
43. Guha, *India After Gandhi*, 398.
44. Sudhir Nandgaonkar ed., *Rajneeti Ke Us Paar* (Mumbai: Rāmabhāū Mhāḷagī Prabodhinī, 2014), 107.
45. *Organiser*, 12 September 1965 issue.
46. *Times of India*, 22 September 1965.
47. *Organiser*, 3 October 1965 issue.
48. An excerpt from Probal Dasgupta's *Watershed 1967: India's Forgotten Victory Over China* (New Delhi: Juggernaut Books, 2020). Available at https://theprint.in/pageturner/excerpt/1965-china-accused-indian-troops-of-stealing-800-sheep-59-yaks/366554/ (accessed on 20 June 2020).
49. *Times of India*, 25 September 1965.
50. 'When Atal Bihari Vajpayee exposed China's designs with a flock of sheep', *Economic Times*, 5 July 2017. Available at http://economictimes.indiatimes.com/news/politics-and-nation/when-atal-behari-vajpayee-exposed-chinas-designs-with-a-flock-of-sheep/articleshow/59453326.cms (accesssed on 20 June 2020)
51. *Organiser*, 14 November 1965 issue.

52. *Organiser*, 5 December 1965 issue.
53. *Times of India*, 5 November 1965.
54. *Organiser*, 12 December 1965 issue.
55. *Organiser*, 2 January 1966 issue.
56. Column 4750: Rajya Sabha Debates, 10 December 1965. Available at https://rsdebate.nic.in/bitstream/123456789/528281/1/PD_54_10121965_27_p4746_p4760_29.pdf (accessed on 20 June 2020).
57. *Organiser*, 16 January 1966 issue.
58. *Times of India*, 13 January 1966.
59. Columns 300–12: Rajya Sabha Debates, 16 February 1966. Available at https://rsdebate.nic.in/bitstream/123456789/523738/1/PD_55_16021966_3_p300_p312_7.pdf (accessed on 20 June 2020).
60. *Times of India*, 23 February 1966.

9. SVD: A Stillborn Coalition

1. *Times of India*, 20 January 1966.
2. *Times of India*, 19 March 1966.
3. *Times of India*, 22 March 1966.
4. *Times of India*, 23 March 1966.
5. Interview with V. K. Malhotra, Delhi, 2 April 2018.
6. *Organiser*, 8 May 1966 issue.
7. *Organiser*, 18 September 1966 issue.
8. *Organiser*, 8 May 1966 issue.
9. *Organiser*, 8 May 1966 issue.
10. *Times of India*, 9 July 1966.
11. *Times of India*, 25 August 1966.
12. Akshaya Mukul, *Gita Press and the Making of Hindu India* (Delhi: HarperCollins, 2015), 302–7.
13. *Organiser*, 1 January 1967 issue.
14. *Organiser*, 16 October 1966 issue.
15. *Times of India*, 31 October 1966.
16. *Times of India*, 1 November 1966.
17. *Link*, 13 November 1966 issue.
18. Graham, *Hindu Nationalism and Indian Politics*, 151.

19. Column 1537: Lok Sabha Debates, 7 November 1966. Available at: https://eparlib.nic.in/bitstream/123456789/54772/1/lsd_03_16_07-11-1966.pdf (accessed on 20 June 2020).
20. Column 1449–59: Rajya Sabha Debates, 7 November 1966. Available at: https://rsdebate.nic.in/bitstream/123456789/520113/1/PD_58_16111966_7_p1425_p1497_9.pdf (accessed on 20 June 2020).
21. Guha, *India After Gandhi*, 413–14.
22. Ibid; Rajya Sabha Debates, 7 November 1966.
23. *Times of India*, 11 November 1966.
24. Columns 1449–59, Rajya Sabha Debates, 7 November 1966.
25. Column 1751–60, Lok Sabha Debates, 7 November 1966. Available at https://rsdebate.nic.in/bitstream/123456789/520136/1/PD_58_17111966_8_p1649_p1790_7.pdf (accessed on 20 June 2020).
26. Ibid.
27. Column 1771–75: Lok Sabha Debates, 7 November 1966.
28. *Times of India*, 28 November 1966.
29. Ibid.
30. Column 6309: Lok Sabha Debates, 12 December 1967 (Fourth Series), vol. 11(22).
31. FCO 37/36: 'India: 1967 Parliamentary election (Folder 2)': FOFIPA, 1965–71, NAUK.
32. Ibid.
33. *Organiser*, 11 December 1966 issue.
34. *Organiser*, 1 January 1967 issue.
35. *Organiser*, 8 January 1967 issue.
36. Vajpayee, *Four Decades in Parliament*, vol. 1, xxi.
37. *Times of India*, 8 February 1967.
38. *Organiser*, 4 December 1966 issue.
39. *Times of India*, 3 February 1967.
40. *Times of India*, 3 February 1967.
41. *Times of India*, 4 February 1967.
42. *Organiser*, 5 March 1967 issue.
43. *Link*, 30 April 1967 issue.
44. *Link*, 30 April 1967 issue.
45. *Link*, 31 December 1967 issue.

46. *Times of India*, 30 July 1967.
47. *Link*, 6 August 1967 issue.
48. *Times of India*, 16 August 1967.
49. Jaffrelot, *The Hindu Nationalist Movement and Indian Politics*, 225–26.
50. FCO 37/270: 'Political affairs of the Uttar Pradesh: 1967-1968': FOFIPA, 1965–71, NAUK.
51. Ibid.
52. Chaudhary Charan Singh Papers, NMML, Subject File 40, first instalment, 58.
53. Vajpayee, *Four Decades in Parliament*, Vol. 1, 728–29.
54. *Organiser*, 5 November 1967 issue.
55. *Link*, 31 December 1967 issue.
56. *Link*, 10 December 1967 issue.
57. *Times of India*, 31 December 1967.
58. Advani, *My Country, My Life*, 145.
59. *Link*, 14 January 1968 issue.
60. *Organiser*, 17 July 1966 issue.
61. *Times of India*, 1 January 1968.
62. *Organiser*, 18 February 1968 issue.
63. Columns 38–39: Lok Sabha Debates, 12 February 1968. Available at: https://eparlib.nic.in/bitstream/123456789/2432/1/lsd_04_04_12-02-1968.pdf#search=vajpayee%20atal (accessed on 20 June 2020).
64. *Times of India*, 13 February 1968.
65. *Organiser*, 18 February 1968.
66. Ibid.
67. *Link*, 17 March 1968 issue.
68. *Organiser*, 25 February 1968.
69. FCO 37/34: 'Internal political situation in India, 1968 (Folder 4)': FOFIPA, 1965–71, NAUK.
70. *Organiser*, 10 March 1968.
71. A. G. Noorani, 'How RSS Efforts to Prove Deen Dayal Upadhayaya's Murder Was "Political" Came Undone', *Wire*, 25 September 2017. Available at: https://thewire.in/history/deen-dayal-upadhyaya-death-mystery (accessed on 20 June 2020).
72. 'India: Growing Tensions', *Time*, 23 February 1968. Available at http://content.time.com/time/subscriber/article/0,33009,837939,00.html.

10. The Incoming Party President

1. J. Gillis Wetter, 'The Rann of Kutch Arbitration', *American Journal of International Law*, vol. 65 (2), April 1971, 348. Available at: https://www.jstor.org/stable/2199243 (accessed on 3 July 2020).
2. *Times of India*, 22 February 1968.
3. *Times of India*, 29 February 1968.
4. *Times of India*, 20 February 1968.
5. *Times of India*, 4 March 1968.
6. *Times of India*, 22 February 1968.
7. *Times of India*, 13 April 1968.
8. *Link*, 28 April 1968 issue.
9. *Times of India*, 19 April 1968.
10. *Link*, 14 July 1968 issue.
11. *Times of India*, 6 May 1968.
12. FCO 37/270: 'Political affairs of the Uttar Pradesh: 1967-1968': FOFIPA, 1965–71, NAUK.
13. Eklavya, 'How is RSS financed?', Sampradayikta Virodhi Committee, 1970.
14. S. No. 8, Writings/speeches by him, K. R. Malkani Papers, NMML, 1–2.
15. Vajpayee's edit, *Hindustan Times*, 28 January 1969.
16. *Organiser*, 14 December 1968 issue.
17. *Times of India*, 4 February 1969.
18. *Times of India*, 22 April 1969.
19. *Times of India*, 4 May 1969.
20. *Organiser*, 17 May 1969 issue.
21. *Times of India*, 31 December 1968.
22. Subject File 61, first instalment: Chaudhary Charan Singh Papers, NMML.
23. It was a complex surgery that involved vegotomy and gastrojejunostomy in order to treat a chronic duodenal ulcer.
24. *Times of India*, 30 May 1969.
25. FCO 37/363: India: Internal political situation and mid-term elections, 1969-70 (Folder 3): FOFIPA, 1965–71, NAUK.
26. *Times of India*, 5 May 1969.
27. *Times of India*, 15 August 1969.
28. *Times of India*, 29 December 1969.

29. *Times of India*, 15 August 1969.
30. *Times of India*, 12 August 1969.
31. *Times of India*, 17 July 1969.
32. *Organiser*, 23 August 1969 issue.
33. *Times of India*, 15 August 1969.
34. FCO 37/594: India: Congress Party (1970): FOFIPA, 1965–71.
35. Madhok, *Zindagi Ka Safar*-III, 48–49.
36. 'Jana Sangh on Bank Nationalisation: Party Documents', 2–22; *Times of India*, 6 September 1969.
37. *Organiser*, 23 August 1969 issue.
38. 18 September 1969: *Times of India*.
39. 12 September 1969: *Times of India*.
40. Interview with Devendra Swaroop, Bhiwadi, 8 January 2017.
41. *Times of India*, 31 December 1969.
42. Interview with K. N. Govindacharya, Delhi, 11 January 2018.
43. *Times of India*, 8 March 1970.
44. Columns 211–228: 4 March 1970: Fourth Series, vol. 37(11), Lok Sabha debates. Available at: https://eparlib.nic.in/bitstream/123456789/2615/1/lsd_04_10_04-03-1970.pdf.
45. *Times of India*, 5 March 1970.
46. Ibid.
47. Extracts from the report of the Justice D. P. Madon Commission of Inquiry into the communal disturbances at Bhiwandi, Jalgaon and Mahad in May 1970. Available at: https://www.sabrang.com/srikrish/annexure.htm.
48. *Times of India*, 1 June 1970.
49. *Organiser*, 31 May 1969 issue.
50. Columns 251–275: Lok Sabha proceedings of 14 May 1970. Available at: https://eparlib.nic.in/bitstream/123456789/2996/1/lsd_04_10_14-05-1970.pdf (accessed on 23 May 2020).
51. Ibid.
52. Interview with Shivshankar Pareek, Delhi, 29 April 2018.
53. Column 322: Lok Sabha proceedings of 14 May 1970.
54. Published in the *Rashtra Sevadal Patrika*, Diwali-special edition, 1967.
55. FCO 37/594, India: Congress Party (1970): FOFIPA, 1965–71.
56. After losing the 1967 election, Joshi had been devoting all her time to the Sampradayikta Virodhi Committee, whose chief task was to expose the

Sangh Parivar. Towards this end, the SVC organized seminars, published pamphlets and journals.

57. *Secular Democracy*, June 1970 issue, 36–39.
58. *Times of India*, 20 May 1970.
59. *Times of India*, 29 May 1970.
60. FCO 37/594: India: Congress Party (1970): FOFIPA, 1965–71.
61. *Organiser*, 6 June 1970 issue.
62. *South China Morning Post*, 15 July 1970.
63. FCO 37/598: India: Political disturbances (1970): FOFIPA, 1965–71.
64. *Times of* India, 19 July 1970.
65. *Times of India*, 2 November 1970.
66. *Times of India*, 21 July 1970.
67. *Times of India*, 24 July 1970.
68. *Organiser*, 20 June 1970 issue.
69. *South China Morning Post*, 15 July 1970.
70. Interview with V. K. Malhotra, Delhi, 2 April 2018.
71. *Times of India*, 2 September 1970.
72. *Times of India*, 6 September 1970.
73. *Times of India*, 9 September 1970.
74. *Times of India*, 13 September 1970.
75. *Times of India*, 16 December 1970.
76. *Times of India*, 26 December 1970.
77. *Times of India*, 27 December 1970.
78. *Times of India*, 28 December 1970.
79. *Times of India*, 10 January 1971.
80. *Economic Times*, 12 February 1971.
81. *Times of India*, 19 January 1971; *Economic Times*, 12 February 1971.
82. *Times of India*, 27 December 1970.
83. *Guardian*, 4 March 1971.
84. *Times of India*, 9 August 1970.
85. *Times of India*, 4 March 1971.
86. *Times of India*, 16 February 1971.
87. Bishan Kapoor, *The Dragon Unmasked: Role of the Jana Sangh in SVD Government in U.P.* (New Delhi: Sampradayikta Virodhi Committee, 1970), 15–16.
88. *Times of India*, 28 December 1970.

89. Interview with N. M. Ghatate, Delhi, 14 November 2018.
90. *Times of India*, 3 March 1971; *Organiser*, 6 March 1971 issue.

11. Loose Ends, New Beginnings

1. *Times of India*, 15 March 1971.
2. *Times of India*, 16 March 1971.
3. *Times of India*, 12 March 1971.
4. *Times of India*, 29 March 1971.
5. *Guardian*, 30 March 1971.
6. Katherine Frank, *Indira: The Life of Indira Nehru Gandhi* (London: Harper Perennial, 2007), 331.
7. *Organiser*, 10 July 1971 issue.
8. *Organiser*, 29 May 1971 issue.
9. FCO 37/955: Famine relief for Pakistani refugees in India, 1971 (Folder 7), FOFIPA, 1965–71.
10. *Irish Times*, 5 July 1971.
11. Guha, *India After Gandhi*, 454.
12. Frank, *Indira*, 334.
13. *Times of India*, 13 July 1971.
14. Raghavan, *The Most Dangerous Place*, 255.
15. Ibid.
16. *Times of India*, 25 July 1971.
17. *Times of India*, 26 July 1971.
18. *Organiser*, 21 August 1971 issue.
19. *Times of India*, 5 July 1971.
20. *Organiser*, 12 May 1972 issue.
21. Lok Sabha Debates, Fifth Session, 31 July 1972, vol. 17(1). Available at https://eparlib.nic.in/bitstream/123456789/2338/1/lsd_05_05_31-07-1972.pdf.
22. *Times of India*, 19 December 1971.
23. *Times of India*, 23 October 1971.
24. *Times of India*, 23 October 1971.
25. Raghavan, *The Most Dangerous Place*, 257.
26. Pupul Jayakar, *Indira Gandhi: An Intimate Biography* (New York: Pantheon Books, 1988), 176.

27. *Times of India*, 11 December 1971.
28. *Times of India*, 6 December 1971; *Organiser*, 11 December 1971 issue.
29. *Times of India*, 15 December 1971; *Organiser*, 18 December 1971 issue.
30. *Times of India*, 16 December 1971.
31. Columns 145–146: Lok Sabha proceedings of 16 December 1971. Available at: https://eparlib.nic.in/bitstream/123456789/1999/1/lsd_05_03_16-12-1971.pdf (accessed on 23 July 2020).
32. Columns 71–72: Lok Sabha proceedings of 17 December 1971. Available at: https://eparlib.nic.in/bitstream/123456789/1963/1/lsd_05_03_17-12-1971.pdf (accessed on 23 July 2020). (emphasis mine)
33. *Times of India*, 19 December 1971; *Organiser*, 25 December 1971 issue.
34. *Times of India*, 20 December 1971.
35. *Organiser*, 8 January 1972 issue.
36. *Guardian*, 21 January 1972.
37. *Times of India*, 11 February 1972.
38. *Times of India*, 9 March 1972.
39. *Organiser*, 4 March 1972 issue.
40. *Organiser*, 12 May 1972 issue.
41. *Times of India*, 5 August 1971.
42. Columns 227–229: Lok Sabha proceedings of 4 August 1971. Available at: https://eparlib.nic.in/bitstream/123456789/2327/1/lsd_05_02_04-08-1971.pdf (accessed on 23 July 2020).
43. *Times of India*, 4 May 1972.
44. *Times of India*, 8 May 1972.
45. *Times of India*, 9 May 1972.
46. *Organiser*, 20 May 1972 issue; *Hindustan Times* (evening news), 5 June 1972.
47. *Washington Post*, 28 March 1973.
48. *Times of India*, 17 June 1972.
49. *Times of India*, 30 June 1972.
50. *Organiser*, 8 July 1972 issue.
51. FCO 37/1149: Negotiations for a post-war settlement between Pakistan and India (Folder 4), 1972.
52. *Organiser*, 15 July 1972 issue.
53. *Organiser*, 22 July 1972 issue.
54. *Organiser*, 29 July 1972 issue.

55. This was also the slogan raised by Jan Sangh workers in Punjab after the Tashkent agreement.
56. *Times of India*, 26 July 1972.
57. *Times of India*, 28 July 1972.
58. Columns 269–270: Lok Sabha proceedings, 31 July 1972. Available at: https://eparlib.nic.in/bitstream/123456789/2338/1/lsd_05_05_31-07-1972.pdf (accessed on 23 July 2020).
59. Columns 304–312, Lok Sabha proceedings, 31 July 1972.
60. Ibid.
61. *Panchjanya*, 29 April 1973 issue.
62. Letter from Madhavrao Scindia to Vajpayee, 14/15 September 1970, from the collection of R. K. Mishra, Gwalior.
63. Jaffrelot, *The Hindu Nationalist Movement and Indian Politics*, 145.
64. Interview with Chandrakanta Goyal, Mumbai, 20 April 2018.
65. Interview with Swarup Goyal, Agra, 22 December 2017.
66. 'Exclusive Interview of Mr. Shiv Kumar, Atal Bihari Vajpayee's secretary', *First India News*. Available at https://www.youtube.com/watch?v=_86frahbJlk.
67. *Times of India*, 5 July 1971.
68. *Times of India*, 12 November 1972.
69. Vajpayee, *Rajneeti Ki Rapteeli Raahein*, 74–76.
70. Ibid.
71. *Times of India*, 19 February 1973.
72. Ibid.
73. *Times of India*, 10 February 1973.
74. Ibid.
75. *Everyman's*, 17 November 1973 issue, 1 and 16.
76. Ibid.
77. *Times of India*, 13 April 1973.
78. Madhok, *Zindagi Ka Safar*–III, 145–146.
79. Some of his utterings embarrassed the Jan Sangh. During the peak of the refugee crisis in mid-1971, the RSS chief praised Mrs Gandhi's handling of it – at a time when Vajpayee was heading the attack against the government. Whereas Vajpayee had been demanding a uniform civil code to disallow polygamy among Muslims, Guruji had confused his protégés by declaring it 'not necessary'; *Everyman's*, 17 November 1973 issue, 1 and 16.

80. *Secular Democracy*, September 1970 issue.
81. Ibid.
82. Nandgaonkar ed., *Rajneeti Ke Us Paar*, 111.
83. *Times of India*, 7 June 1973.
84. *Organiser*, 9 June 1973 issue.

12. 1974: A Reactionary Revolution

1. Francine Frankel, *India's Political Economy: 1947–2004* (Delhi: Oxford University Press, 2006), 514.
2. By the time the state legislatures – still dominated by landed castes everywhere – passed the laws, they were diluted. Then again, most states did not have the administrative capacity to implement them. Most importantly, though, the Congress in rural India was led by dominant castes, who had in fact frustrated efforts at redistributing land. With the party organization in decay – to which Mrs Gandhi had herself significantly contributed – the chances of success now were lesser still.
3. *Organiser*, 6 January 1973 issue.
4. *Times of India*, 23 April 1973.
5. *Times of India*, 25 April 1973.
6. *Times of India*, 25 July 1973.
7. *Times of India*, 8 August 1973.
8. *Times of India*, 16 December 1972.
9. *Organiser*, 30 December 1972 issue.
10. *Times of India*, 23 December 1972.
11. *Times of India*, 8 March 1973; *Times of India*, 9 March 1973, 10.
12. *Times of India*, 17 May 1973.
13. *Times of India*, 27 April 1973.
14. *Times of India*, 3 May 1973; *Organiser*, 12 May 1973 issue.
15. *Times of India*, 5 May 1973.
16. Columns 224: Lok Sabha proceedings, 4 May 1973. Available at: https://eparlib.nic.in/bitstream/123456789/892/1/lsd_05_07_04-05-1973.pdf (accessed on 23 July 2020).
17. With a much superior air force and army, Israel inflicted on them heavy losses: in less than a week, it had captured the West Bank (from Jordan) and the Gaza Strip and Sinai Peninsula (from Egypt), along with a few other territories.

18. *Times of India*, 20 September 1967.
19. Columns 2024–2028: Rajya Sabha Debates, 4 March 1965. Available at: https://rsdebate.nic.in/bitstream/123456789/533367/1/PD_51_04031965_12_p1975_p2104_4.pdf (accessed on 20 June 2020).
20. Ibid.
21. Ibid.
22. *New York Times*, 1 November 1973.
23. *Organiser*, 17 November 1973 issue.
24. *Times of India*, 19 October 1973; *Organiser*, 17 November 1973 issue.
25. *Times of India*, 13 November 1973.
26. Nandgaonkar ed., *Rajneeti Ke Us Paar*, 75–82.
27. *Organiser*, 29 December 1973 issue.
28. *Guardian*, 24 December 1973.
29. *Times of India*, 10 May 1974.
30. *Times of India*, 3 May 1973.
31. *Times of India*, 3 May 1973.
32. *Times of India*, 9 August 1973.
33. *Times of India*, 20 July 1973.
34. Madhu Limaye, *Birth of Non-Congressism: Opposition Politics, 1947–1975* (Delhi: B. R. Publishing, 1988), 434.
35. 4 January 1974, *Times of India*.
36. 26 January 1974 issue, *Organiser*.
37. 10 March 1973 issue, *Organiser*.
38. *Times of India*, 20 January 1974.
39. *Organiser*, 12 January 1974 issue.
40. *Organiser*, 16 February 1974 issue.
41. *Organiser*, 23 February 1974 issue.
42. *Times of India*, 20 January 1974.
43. *Times of India*, 20 January 1974.
44. *Times of India*, 5 February 1974.
45. Columns 214–215: Lok Sabha proceedings, 27 February 1974. Available at: https://eparlib.nic.in/bitstream/123456789/1227/1/lsd_05_10_27-02-1974.pdf (accessed on 10 September 2020).
46. *Times of India*, 28 April 1973.
47. *Blitz*, 26 January 1974 issue.
48. *Organiser*, 23 February 1974 issue.

49. *Organiser*, 23 February 1974 issue.
50. Vajpayee, *Rajneeti Ki Rapteeli Raahein,* 66.
51. Column 212: Lok Sabha proceedings, 27 February 1974.
52. Bimal Prasad, *Jayaprakash Narayan: Selected Works*, vol. 10, (Delhi: Manohar Publishers & Distributors, 2009), 249–250.
53. *Link*, 14 April 1974 issue.
54. Raj Thapar, *All These Years: A Memoir* (New Delhi: Seminar Publications, 1991), 379.
55. *Times of India*, 19 May 1974.
56. 'Looking Back: The 1998 Indian and Pakistani Nuclear Tests', Arms Control Association. Available at: https://www.armscontrol.org/act/2008-06/looking-back-1998-indian-pakistani-nuclear-tests.
57. *Times of India*, 2 June 1974.
58. FCO 37/1472: Indian nuclear test, 18 May 1974 (Folder 4): FOFIPA, 1972–80.
59. Interview with K. N. Govindacharya, Delhi, 3 January 2018.
60. *Organiser*, 17 August 1974 issue.
61. *Organiser*, 21 September 1974 issue.
62. An experiment of parallel government by people had to be tried in Bihar in a few blocks of, say, ten villages each, where the locals would manage the entire administration themselves and implement plans for employment through village industries, etc. Dalits and Adivasis, the underprivileged sections, must be 'absorbed into the mainstream with true love and service'; *Organiser*, 17 August 1974 issue.
63. *Times of India*, 16 September 1974; *Organiser*, 21 September 1974 issue.
64. *Times of India*, 22 September 1974.
65. *Times of India*, 25 September 1974.
66. In medical jargon, Vajpayee was suffering from neuralgic pain due to intervertebral disc prolapse.
67. *Times of India*, 28 September 1974; *Organiser*, 5 October 1974 issue.
68. Guha, *India After Gandhi*, 483.
69. *Times of India*, 4 November 1974.
70. *Times of India*, 5 November 1974.
71. S. No. 6, Writings/speeches by him, K. R. Malkani Papers, NMML, 2.
72. *Times of India*, 16 November 1974.
73. *Times of India*, 25 November 1974.

74. *Times of India*, 26 November 1974.
75. *Organiser*, 7 December 1974 issue.
76. *Times of India*, 10 September 1974.
77. *Times of India*, 29 November 1974.
78. *Times of India*, 9 December 1974.
79. Ibid.
80. *Organiser*, 21 December 1974 issue.
81. *Times of India*, 25 December 1974.
82. *Times of India*, 28 December 1974.
83. Guha, *India After Gandhi*, 484.
84. *Times of India*, 19 February 1975.
85. Columns 305–314: Lok Sabha proceedings of 3 March 1975. Available at: https://eparlib.nic.in/bitstream/123456789/1004/1/lsd_05_13_03-03-1975.pdf (accessed on 10 September 2020).
86. *Times of India*, 5 March 1975.
87. *Times of India*, 24 June 1973.
88. *Times of India*, 3 March 1975.
89. *Times of India*, 26 November 1974.
90. *Times of India*, 6 March 1975.
91. *Times of India*, 7 March 1975.
92. *Organiser*, 11 January 1975 issue.
93. *Times of India*, 24 January 1975.
94. 'Gandhi-Narayan Political Duel: New Notches': Declassified US Department of State. Available at: https://wikileaks.org/plusd/cables/1975NEWDE03608_b.html (accessed on 4 May 2020).
95. *Times of India*, 11 April 1975.
96. *Times of India*, 13 April 1975.
97. *Times of India*, 13 April 1975.
98. *Times of India*, 14 April 1975.
99. *Organiser*, 10 May 1975 issue.
100. *Panchjanya*, 18 May 1975 issue.
101. Ghanshyam Shah: *The 1975 Gujarat Assembly Election in India*: *Asian Survey* 16 (3), 1976, 270-82. Available at:10.2307/2643544 (accessed 24 August 2020).
102. *Times of India*, 21 May 1975.
103. Ibid.

104. *Times of India*, 31 May 1975.
105. *Times of India*, 29 May 1975.
106. *Times of India*, 7 May 1975.
107. *Times of India*, 9 June 1975.
108. *Times of India*, 6 June 1975.
109. *Organiser*, 7 June 1975 issue.
110. *Organiser*, 4 June 1977 issue.
111. *Times of India*, 28 May 1975.
112. *Times of India*, 6 June 1975.
113. Oddly, this time the Congress had won more votes than the Janata front. With help from, ironically, Chiman Patel – who, after his forced resignation, had quit the Congress and launched his own outfit – the front had enough numbers to claim its stake.
114. *Organiser*, 28 June 1975 issue.
115. *Times of India*, 13 June 1975.
116. *Times of India*, 15 June 1975; *Times of India*, 19 June 1975.
117. *Times of India*, 25 June 1975.
118. *Times of India*, 26 June 1975.

13. Emergency: The Lion and the Monkey

1. *Times of India*, 6 May 1978.
2. *Times of India*, 22 April 1977.
3. Reel 2: DEPI, CRL.
4. Atal Bihari Vajpayee, *Kaidi Kavirai Ki Kundaliyaan* (New Delhi: Saraswati Vihar, 2018), 117.
5. *New York Times*, 1 July 1975.
6. Chandrika Prasad Sharma ed., *Atalji Ke Pachchatar Padaav* (New Delhi: Bhartiya Prakashan Sansthan, 1999), 57.
7. There was a never-ending discussion about was the feasibility of a merger to oppose the Congress. Mishra favoured a federal rather than a unified party: 'One party – with Chaudhary Charan Singh? Only those like you do not know him can think of such a proposal. It is impossible to work in the same party with Chaudhary Charan Singh.'
8. Reel 3: DEPI, CRL.
9. Vajpayee, *Kaidi Kavirai Ki Kundaliyaan*, 118–123.

10. Ullekh N. P., *The Untold Vajpayee* (New Delhi: Penguin Random House India, 2017), 74–75.
11. *Organiser*, 20 June 1977 issue, 16.
12. *Organiser*, 20 June 1977 issue.
13. M. Rama Jois, *Historic Legal Battle* (Bangalore: M. R. Vimala, 1977).
14. Vajpayee, *Kaidi Kavirai Ki Kundaliyaan*.
15. Coomi Kapoor, *The Emergency: A Personal History* (New Delhi: Penguin India, 2015), 37.
16. *Organiser*, 13 June 1977 issue.
17. Sharma ed., *Atalji Ke Pachchatar Padaav*, 57.
18. Ibid., 91.
19. Ibid, 36–37.
20. Vajpayee, *Kaidi Kavirai Ki Kundaliyaan*, 131.
21. Ibid., 129.
22. Ibid., 85.
23. Ibid., 67. Mugli ghutti is an ayurvedic medicine prescribed for digestive disorders in infants and children.
24. Ibid., 79
25. FCO 37/1593: Political situation in India (Folder 6), 1975: FOFIPA, 1972–1980, NAUK, 318.
26. Interview with N. M. Ghatate, Delhi, 14 November 2018.
27. Interview with Subhash Arya, Delhi, 12 June 2017.
28. 'PMO Diary-II: The Emergency', 66–67.
29. Kapoor, *The Emergency*, 37–38. Available at: https://wikileaks.org/plusd/cables/1975NEWDE15290_b.html (accessed on 4 May 2020).
30. L. K. Advani, *A Prisoner's Scrap-Book* (Delhi: Prabhat Prakashan, 2014). Available at: https://play.google.com/books/reader?id=NcTfDAAAQBAJ&pg=GBS.PT73 (e-book).
31. FCO 37/1597: Political situation in India (Folder 10), 1975, 478.
32. Kapoor, *The Emergency*, 37–38.
33. Advani, *A Prisoner's Scrap-Book*. Available at https://play.google.com/books/reader?id=NcTfDAAAQBAJ&pg=GBS.PT276.
34. Nandan ed., *Kya Khoya, Kya Paaya*, 83.
35. Interview with a retired history lecturer of Ramjas College, Delhi, 16 June 2018.

36. Reel 6: DEPI, CRL. Also, *Frontline*, 21 August 2015 issue, 44.
37. Reel 2: DEPI, CRL.
38. Interview with Dileep Karambalekar, Mumbai, 23 April 2018.
39. Maloy Krishna Dhar, *Open Secrets: India's Intelligence Unveiled* (New Delhi: Manas Publication, 2005), 205.
40. Reel 6, DEPI, CRL.
41. Ibid.
42. Ibid.
43. The *Economist*'s 24 January 1976 issue mentioned in Reel 6: DEPI, CRL.
44. Jois, *Historic Legal Battle*, 55.
45. Telephonic interview with Ravi Nair, 3 May 2022.
46. Others, like N. G. Goray of the Socialist Party, had never been arrested.
47. Advani, *A Prisoner's Scrap-Book*. Available at: https://play.google.com/books/reader?id=NcTfDAAAQBAJ&pg=GBS.PT289.w.0.0.76_226.
48. Reel 6: DEPI, CRL.
49. 'PMO Diary-II: The Emergency', 368–90.
50. 'Opposition Unification Trend': Declassified US Department of State document. Available at: https://wikileaks.org/plusd/cables/1976NEWDE03492_b.html (accessed on 4 May 2020).
51. Reel 3: DEPI, CRL.
52. Important Correspondence: JPNP, IIIrd instalment NMML, 118.
53. FCO 37/1721: Internal political situation in India, 1976: FOFIPA, 1972–1980, NAUK, 3–4.
54. Reel 3: DEPI, CRL.
55. Ibid.
56. Important Correspondence: JPNP, third instalment, NMML, 46.
57. Subject file no. 335, third instalment, JPNP, 27.
58. Subject file no. 335, third instalment, JPNP, 32.
59. Subject file no. 340, third instalment, JPNP, 5.
60. Interview with N. M. Ghatate, Delhi, 14 November 2018.
61. Reel 6: DEPI, CRL.
62. Telephonic interview with Ravi Nair, 3 May 2022.
63. *Times of India*, 14 December 1976.
64. Bipin Chandra, *In the Name of Democracy: JP Movement and the Emergency* (Delhi: Penguin Books India, 2003) 213–14.

65. Advani, *A Prisoner's Scrap-Book*. Available at: https://play.google.com/books/reader?id=NcTfDAAAQBAJ&pg=GBS.PT184.w.5.0.48_182.
66. Interview with V. K. Malhotra, Delhi, 2 April 2018.
67. 'I will agree to contest the elections if the people want me to do so: Morarji Desai', *India Today*, 15 February 1977 issue. Available at: https://www.indiatoday.in/magazine/cover-story/story/19770215-i-will-agree-to-contest-the-elections-if-the-people-want-me-to-do-so-morarji-desai-818773-2015-03-09 (accessed on 23 July 2020).
68. *Times of India*, 24 January 1977.
69. *Times of India*, 29 January 1977.
70. Interview with N. M. Ghatate, Delhi, 14 November 2018.
71. *India Today*, 15 February 1977 issue. Available at: https://www.indiatoday.in/magazine/cover-story/story/19770215-pm-indira-gandhi-decides-to-dissolve-lok-sabha-relax-emergency-regulations-hold-general-elections-818754-2015-03-09 (accessed on 30 April 2020).
72. Tavleen Singh, *Durbar* (New Delhi: Hachette India, 2012) 59.
73. Tavleen Singh, 'Fifth column: A personal tribute to Atalji', *Indian Express*, 19 August 2018. Available at: https://indianexpress.com/article/opinion/columns/atal-bihari-vajpayee-a-personal-tribute-tavleen-singh-5313620/ (accessed on 30 April 2020).
74. *Los Angeles Times*, 31 January 1977.
75. *Times of India*, 31 January 1977.
76. Tavleen Singh, 'When Vajpayee rocked Ramlila Maidan', Hindu Vivek Kendra, 25 November 2012. Available at: http://www.hvk.org/2012/1112/85.html (accessed on 23 July 2020).
77. *Times of India*, 11 February 1977; *Times of India*, 23 March 1977.
78. Kapoor, *The Emergency: A Personal History*, 308–09.
79. *Times of India*, 7 February 1977.
80. *Times of India*, 28 February 1977; *Times of India*, 1 March 1977.
81. *Times of India*, 6 February 1977.
82. Roxna Swamy, *Evolving with Subramanian Swamy*, self-published in 2017.
83. *Times of India*, 17 February 1977.
84. Interview with N. M. Ghatate, Delhi, 14 November 2018.
85. Interview with V. K. Malhotra, Delhi, 2 April 2018.
86. *India Today*, 15 March 1977 issue. Available at: https://www.indiatoday.in/magazine/cover-story/story/19770315-general-elections-uttar-pradesh-

to-play-a-significant-role-in-determining-future-pm-818857-2015-04-21 (accessed on 30 April 2020).

87. Zindagi Ka Safar, 207.
88. Interview with N. M. Ghatate, Delhi, 14 November 2018.
89. *Times of India*, 26 February 1977.
90. *Times of India*, 4 March 1977.
91. *Times of India*, 15 March 1977.
92. *Times of India*, 18 March 1977.
93. Thapar, *All These Years*, 441.
94. Ibid, 442; *Times of India*, 2 March 1977.
95. *Times of India*, 2 March 1977.
96. *Guardian*, 2 March 1977.
97. *India Today*, 31 March 1977 issue. Available at: https://www.indiatoday.in/magazine/indiascope/story/19770331-a-day-in-the-life-of-a-candidate-atal-behari-vajpayee-823610-2014-07-31 (accessed on 23 July 2020).
98. *Times of India*, 13 March 1977.
99. *India Today*, 31 March, 1977 issue. Available at: https://www.indiatoday.in/magazine/indiascope/story/19770331-congress-stalwart-shashi-bhushan-tha-man-who-entered-the-election-arena-as-the-underdog-823631-2014-07-31 (accessed on 23 July 2020).
100. *Times of India*, 18 March 1977.
101. *Times of India*, 19 March 1977.
102. *Times of India*, 22 March 1977; *Boston Globe*, 21 March 1977.
103. 'March 25, 1977, Forty Years Ago', *Indian Express*, 25 March 2017. Available at: https://indianexpress.com/article/opinion/editorials/march-25-1977-forty-years-ago-4584268/.
104. Lloyd I. Rudolph and Susanne Hoeber Rudolph, *In Pursuit of Lakshmi: The Political Economy of the Indian State* (Chicago: University of Chicago Press, 1987), 167–68.
105. 'Ideals or opportunism?' (A Janata Party publication, August 1979), 9–17.
106. Ibid.
107. *Times of India*, 25 March 1977.
108. Vajpayee's speech at the Janata Party victory rally in Delhi. Available at: https://www.youtube.com/watch?v=YFOSkd9BxUo&t=1511s (accessed on 16 April 2020).
109. Ibid.

110. Ibid.
111. Interview with N. M. Ghatate, Delhi, 14 November 2018.
112. *Times of India*, 28 March 1977.
113. National Intelligence Daily Cable, 28 March 1977, 4–5. Available at: https://www.cia.gov/library/readingroom/docs/CIA-RDP79T00975A029900010048-8.pdf (accessed on 30 April 2020).
114. *New York Times*, 27 and 28 March 1977.
115. *Edmonton Journal*, 28 March 1977 issue, 78.
116. *Jerusalem Post*, 31 March 1977.
117. FCO 37/1923: Leading personalities in India, 1977, NAUK.
118. FCO 37/1929: Internal political situation in India (Folder 1), 1977, NAUK.
119. Maloy Krishna Dhar, *Open Secrets*: *India's Intelligence Unveiled* (Delhi: Manas Publication, 2005), 205.

Index

Note: ABV in the index stands for Atal Behari Vajpayee. Books, poems and articles are listed under the names of their authors.